Story thus far

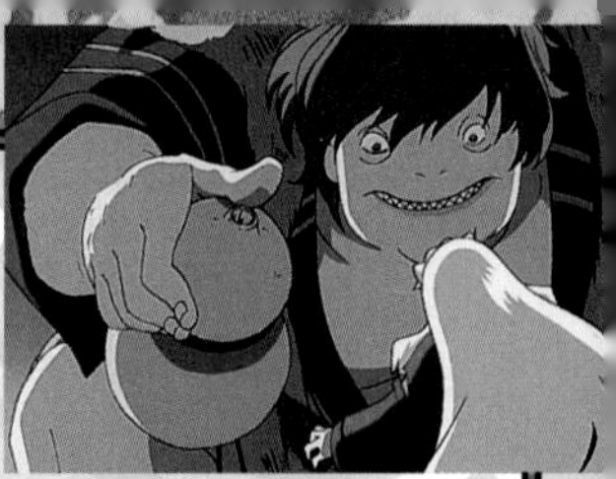

Kagome's mundane teenage existence was turned upside down when she was transported into a mythical version of Japan's medieval past! Kagome is the reincarnation of Lady Kikyo, a great warrior and the defender of the Shikon Jewel, or the Jewel of Four Souls. Kikyo was in love with Inuyasha, a dog-like half-demon who wishes to possess the jewel in order to transform himself into a full-fledged demon. But 50 years earlier, the evil shape-shifting Naraku tricked Kikyo and Inuyasha into betraying one another. The betrayal led to Kikyo's death and Inuyasha's imprisonment under a binding spell...and Inuyasha remained trapped by the spell until Kagome appeared in feudal Japan and unwittingly released him!

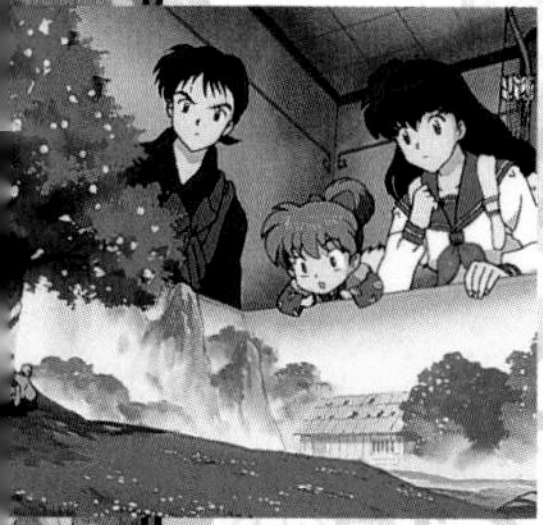

In a skirmish for possession of the Shikon Jewel, it accidentally shatters and is strewn across the land. Only Kagome has the power to find the jewel shards, and only Inuyasha has the strength to defeat the demons that now hold them, so the two unlikely partners are bound together in the quest to reclaim all the pieces of the sacred jewel. To prevent Inuyasha from stealing the jewel, Kikyo's sister, Lady Kaede, puts a magical necklace around Inuyasha's neck that allows Kagome to make him "sit" on command. Inuyasha's greatest tool in the fight to recover the sacred jewel shards is his father's sword, the Tetsusaiga, but Inuyasha's half-brother Sesshomaru covets the mighty blade and has tried to steal it more than once.

Kagome and Inuyasha are dealt a crushing blow when Kikyo, resurrected through witchcraft, steals all the shards of the sacred jewel that have been collected. Although Kikyo has grown to hate Naraku, she gives him all the jewel shards.

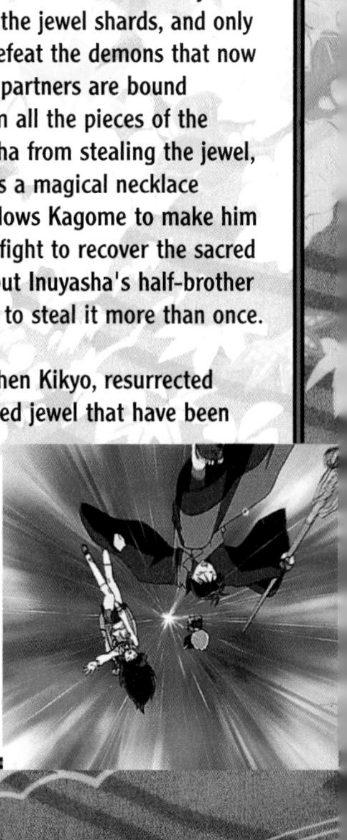

Inuyasha and the others come upon a temple inhabited by a false sage, who feeds upon others who want to become sage. Kagome is captured and the night of the new moon is upon Inuyasha. This causes him to temporarily lose his powers. Can he regain them in time to save her?

INUYASHA™
ANI-MANGA™ Vol. 20

Contents

58
Fateful Night in Togenkyo Part Two

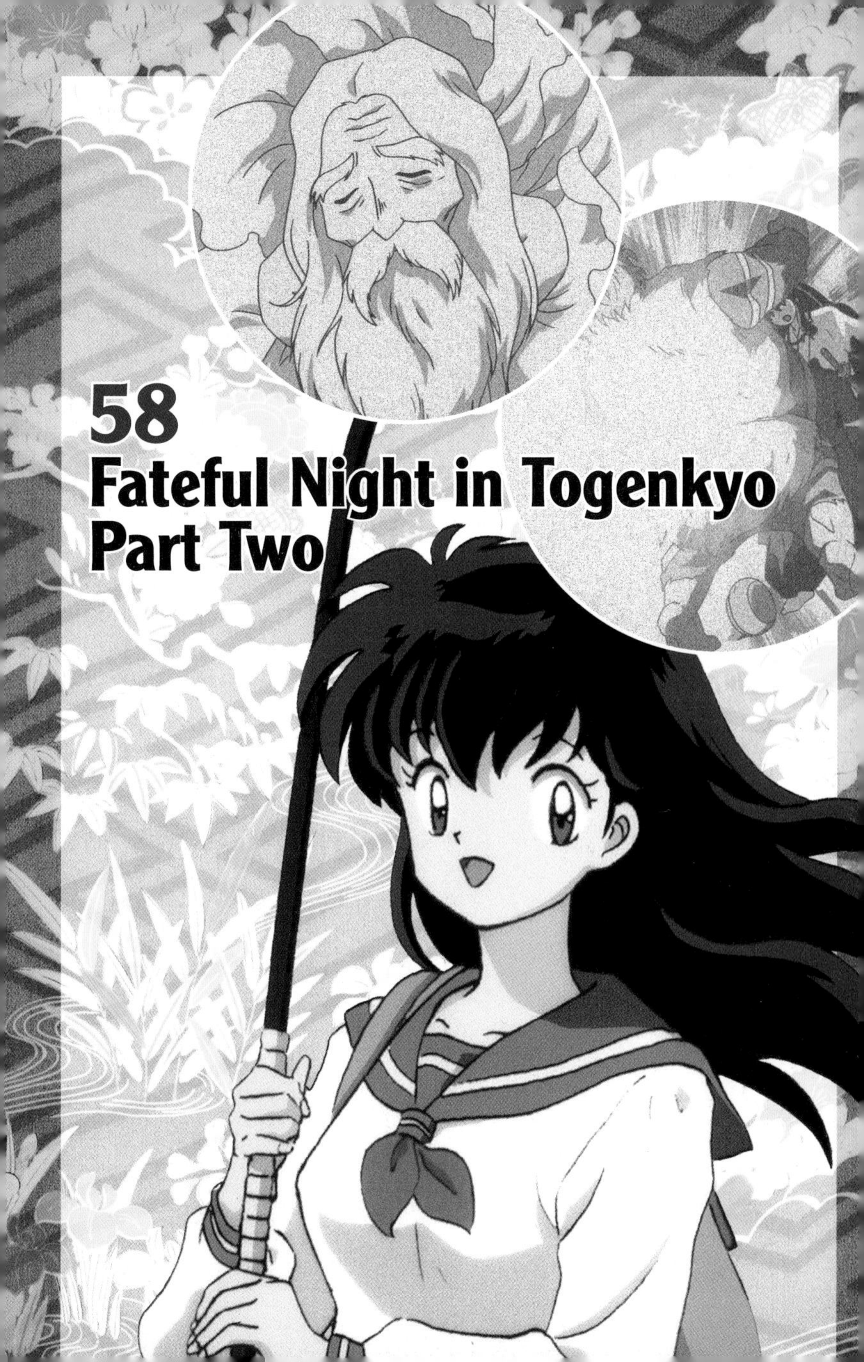

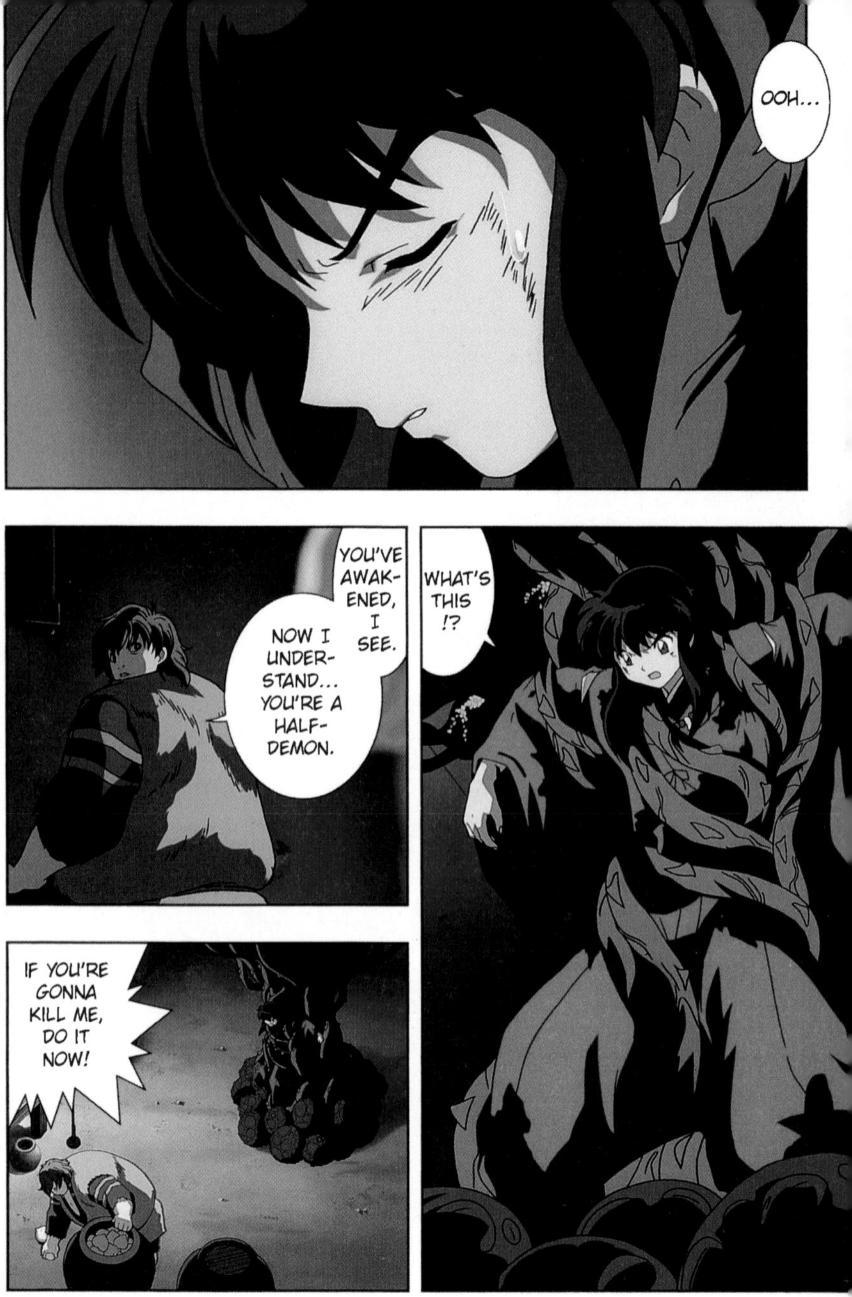
OOH...
WHAT'S THIS !?
YOU'VE AWAKENED, I SEE.
NOW I UNDERSTAND... YOU'RE A HALF-DEMON.
IF YOU'RE GONNA KILL ME, DO IT NOW!

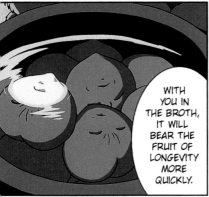

DEMON POWER IS GOOD NOURISHMENT FOR NINMENKA, THE TREE OF HUMAN-FACED FRUITS.

WITH YOU IN THE BROTH, IT WILL BEAR THE FRUIT OF LONGEVITY MORE QUICKLY.

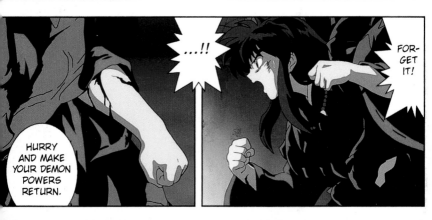

...!!

FOR-GET IT!

HURRY AND MAKE YOUR DEMON POWERS RETURN.

DAMN YOU ...!

!?

KEEP STRUG-GLING!

IF THE THORNS PIERCE YOUR SKIN, IT WILL JUST BE THAT MUCH EASIER TO EXTRACT YOUR JUICES.

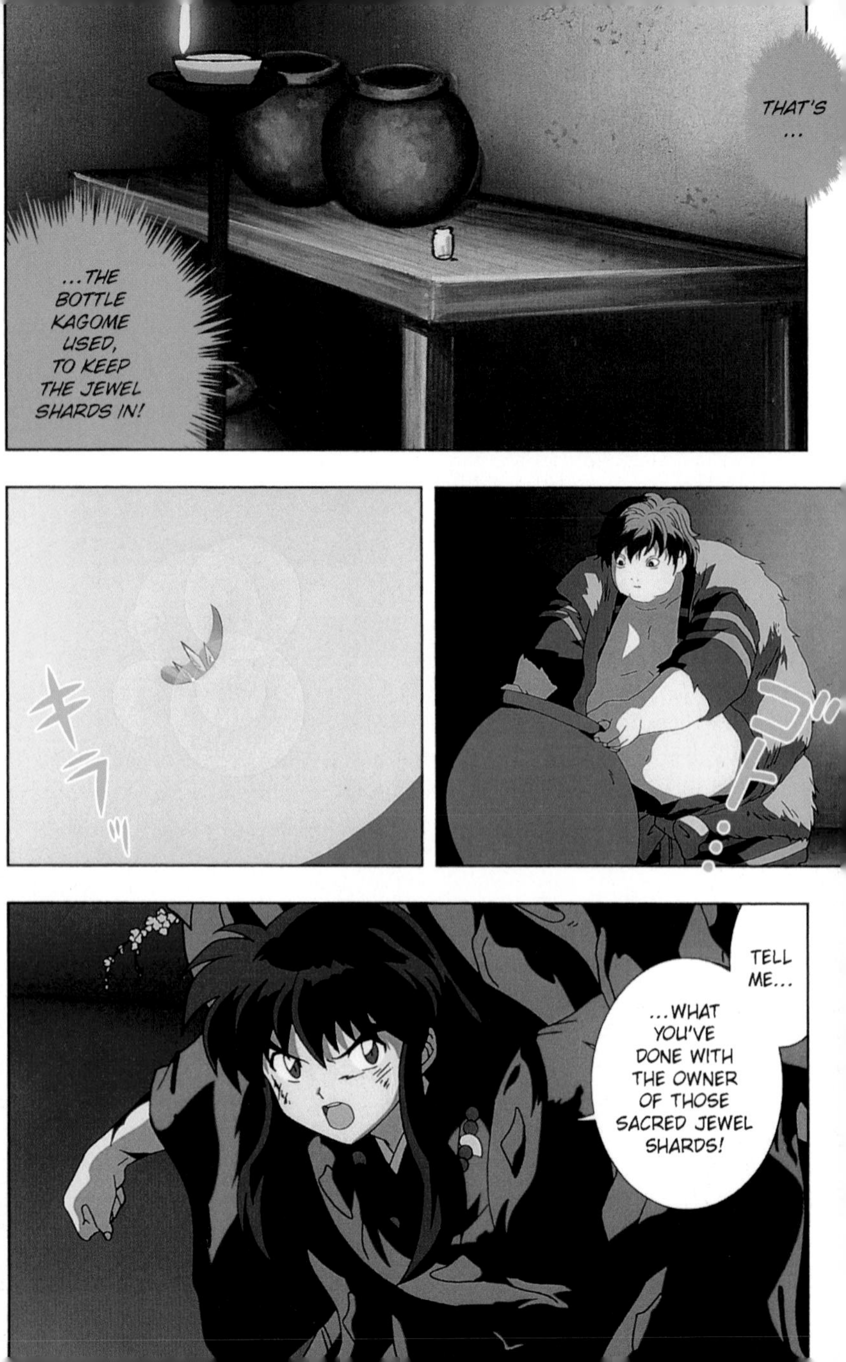
THAT'S ...
...THE BOTTLE KAGOME USED, TO KEEP THE JEWEL SHARDS IN!
ゴト...
キラッ
TELL ME...
...WHAT YOU'VE DONE WITH THE OWNER OF THOSE SACRED JEWEL SHARDS!

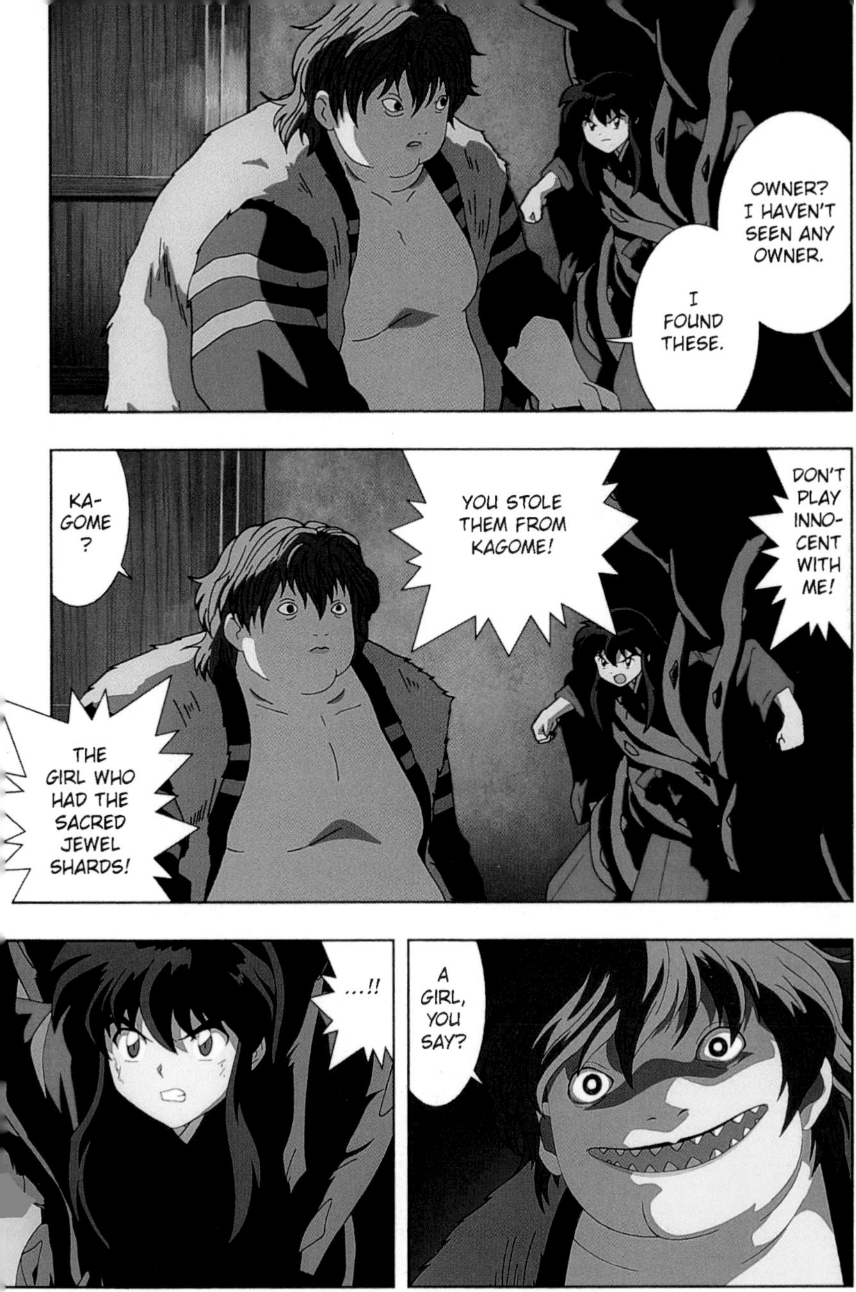
OWNER? I HAVEN'T SEEN ANY OWNER.
I FOUND THESE.
DON'T PLAY INNO-CENT WITH ME!
YOU STOLE THEM FROM KAGOME!
KA-GOME?
THE GIRL WHO HAD THE SACRED JEWEL SHARDS!
A GIRL, YOU SAY?
...!!

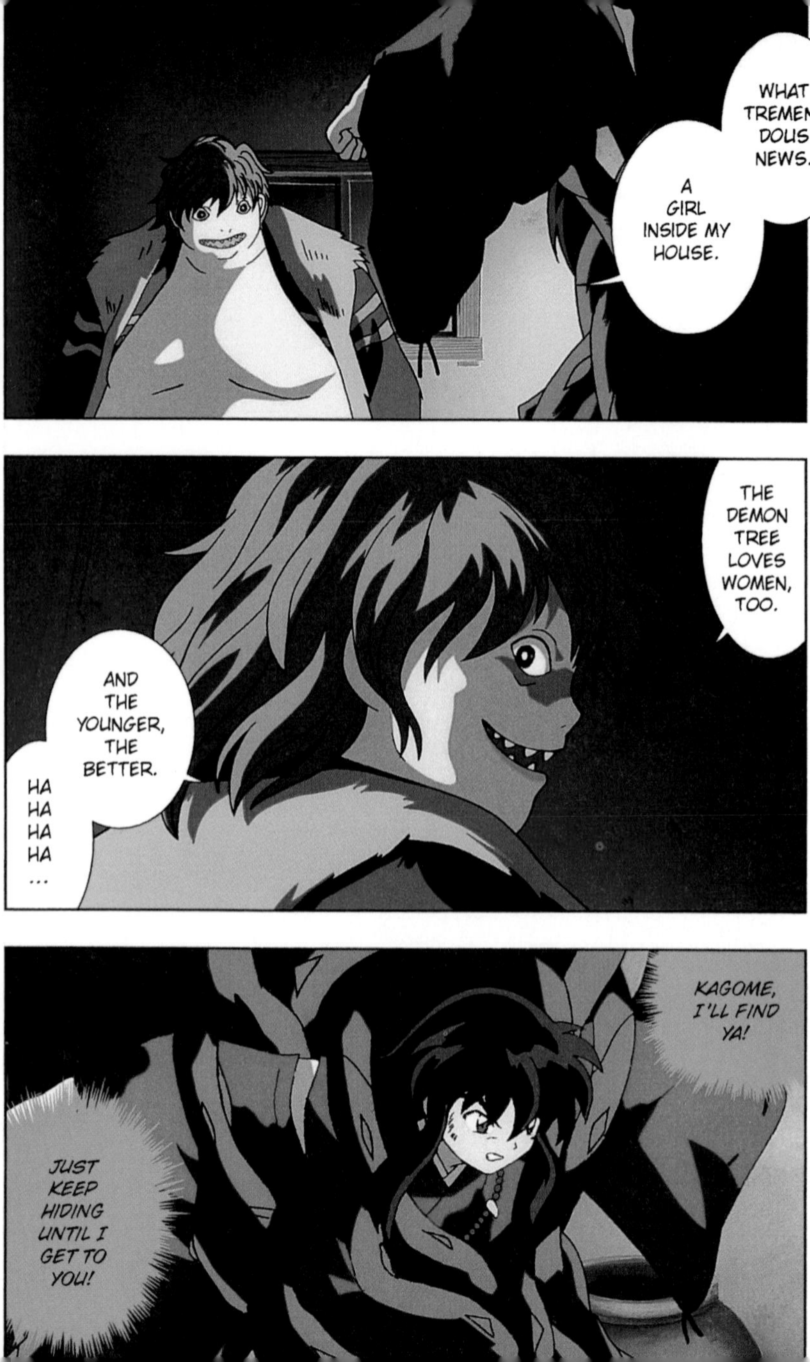
WHAT TREMENDOUS NEWS.
A GIRL INSIDE MY HOUSE.
THE DEMON TREE LOVES WOMEN, TOO.
AND THE YOUNGER, THE BETTER.
HA HA HA HA ...
KAGOME, I'LL FIND YA!
JUST KEEP HIDING UNTIL I GET TO YOU!

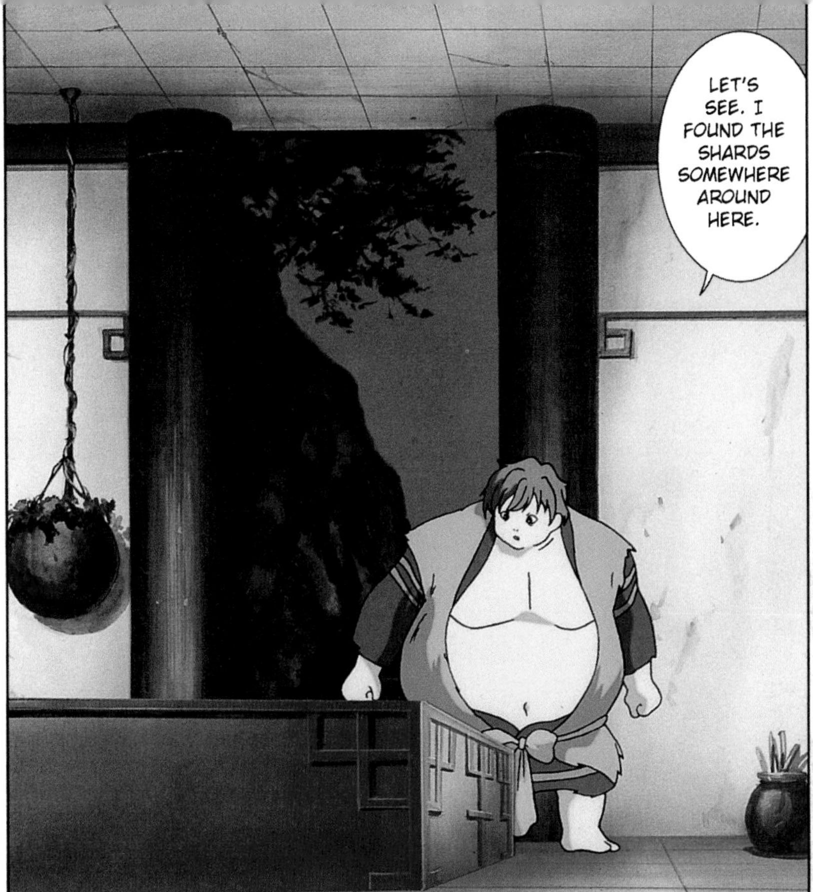
LET'S SEE. I FOUND THE SHARDS SOMEWHERE AROUND HERE.
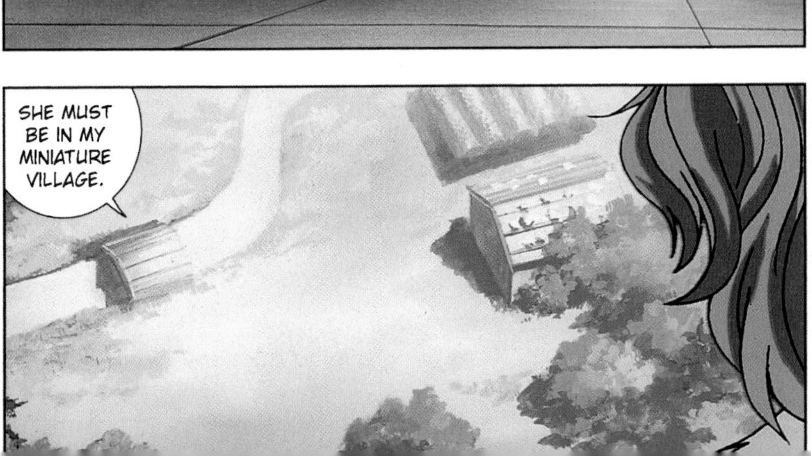
SHE MUST BE IN MY MINIATURE VILLAGE.

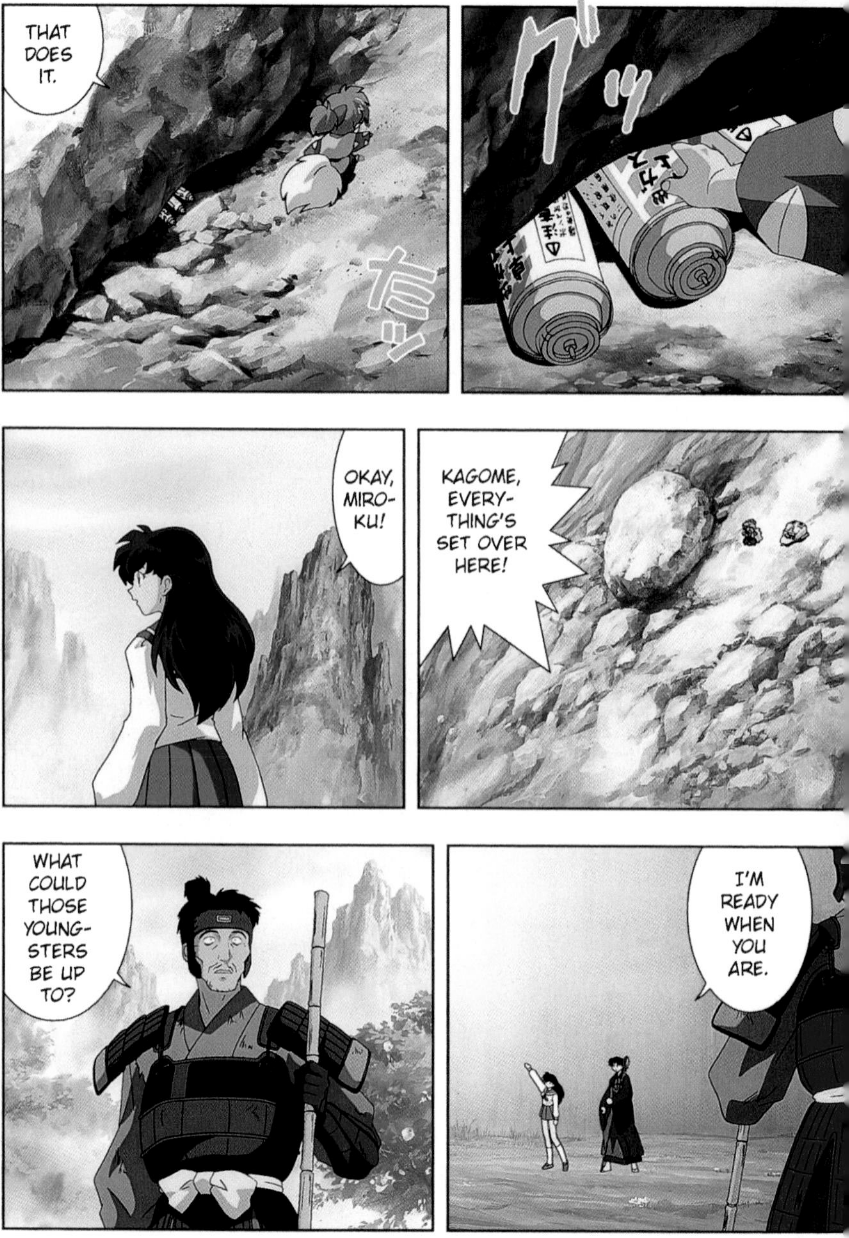
グッ
THAT DOES IT.
たッ
KAGOME, EVERYTHING'S SET OVER HERE!
OKAY, MIROKU!
I'M READY WHEN YOU ARE.
WHAT COULD THOSE YOUNGSTERS BE UP TO?

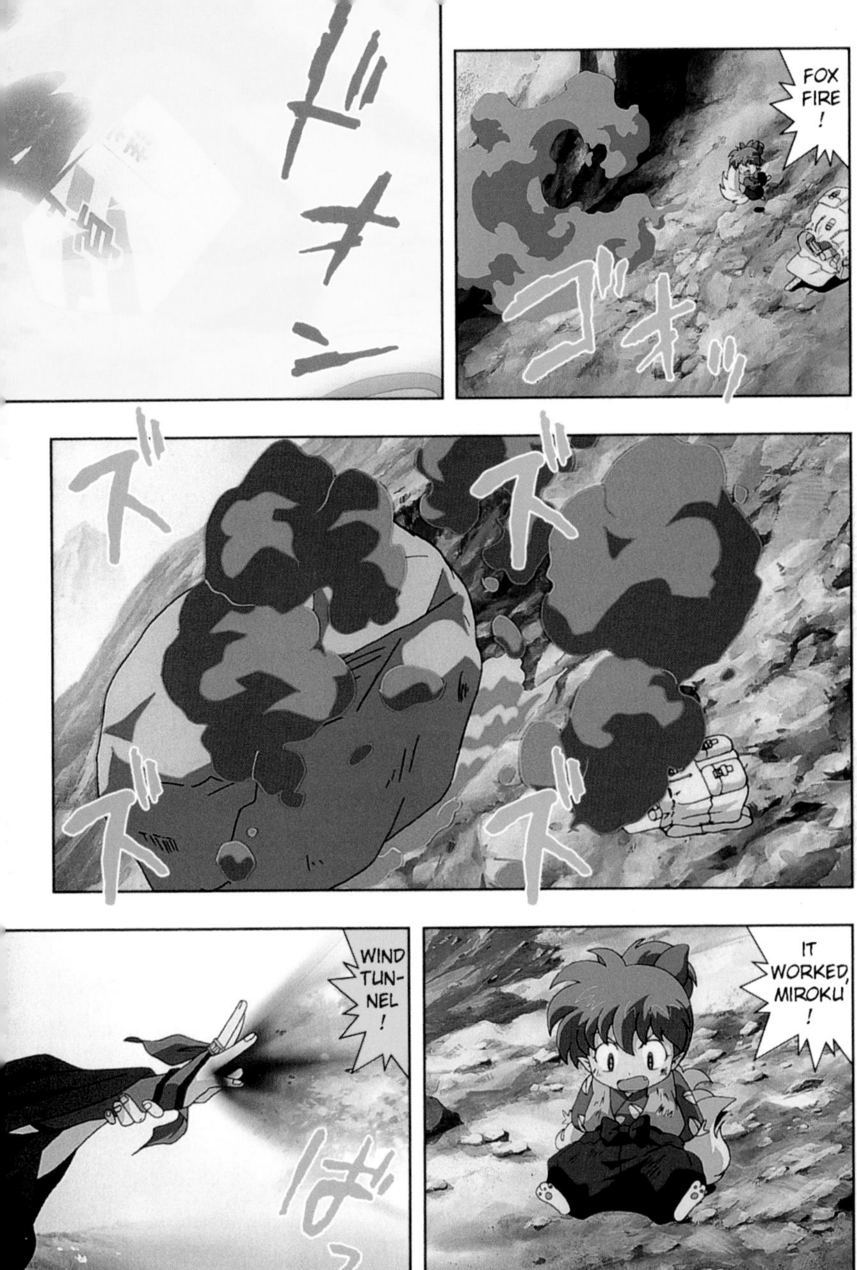
FOX FIRE!
ゴオッ
ドオン
ズズ
ズズ
IT WORKED, MIROKU!
WIND TUN-NEL!
ばっ

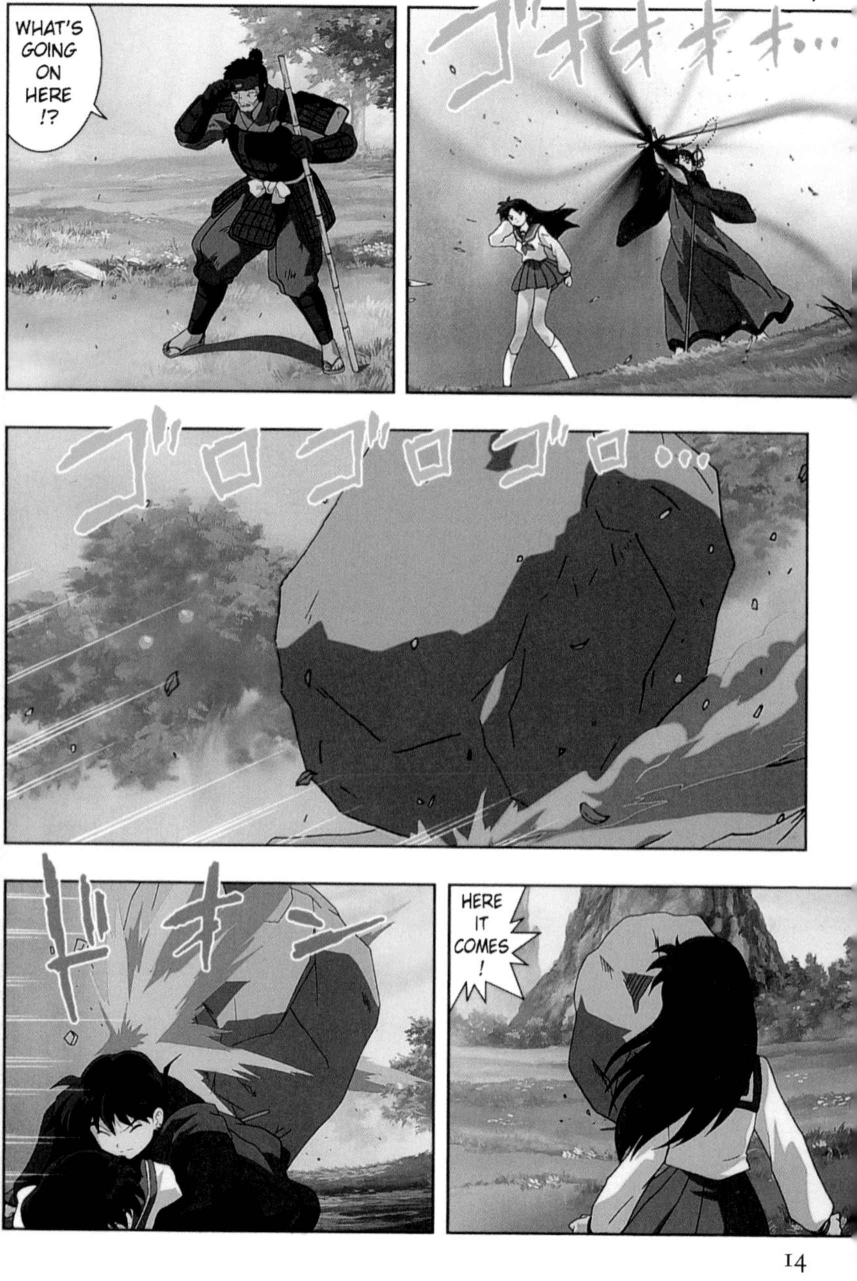
ゴオオオオ…
WHAT'S GOING ON HERE !?
ゴロゴロゴロ…
HERE IT COMES!
ドオン

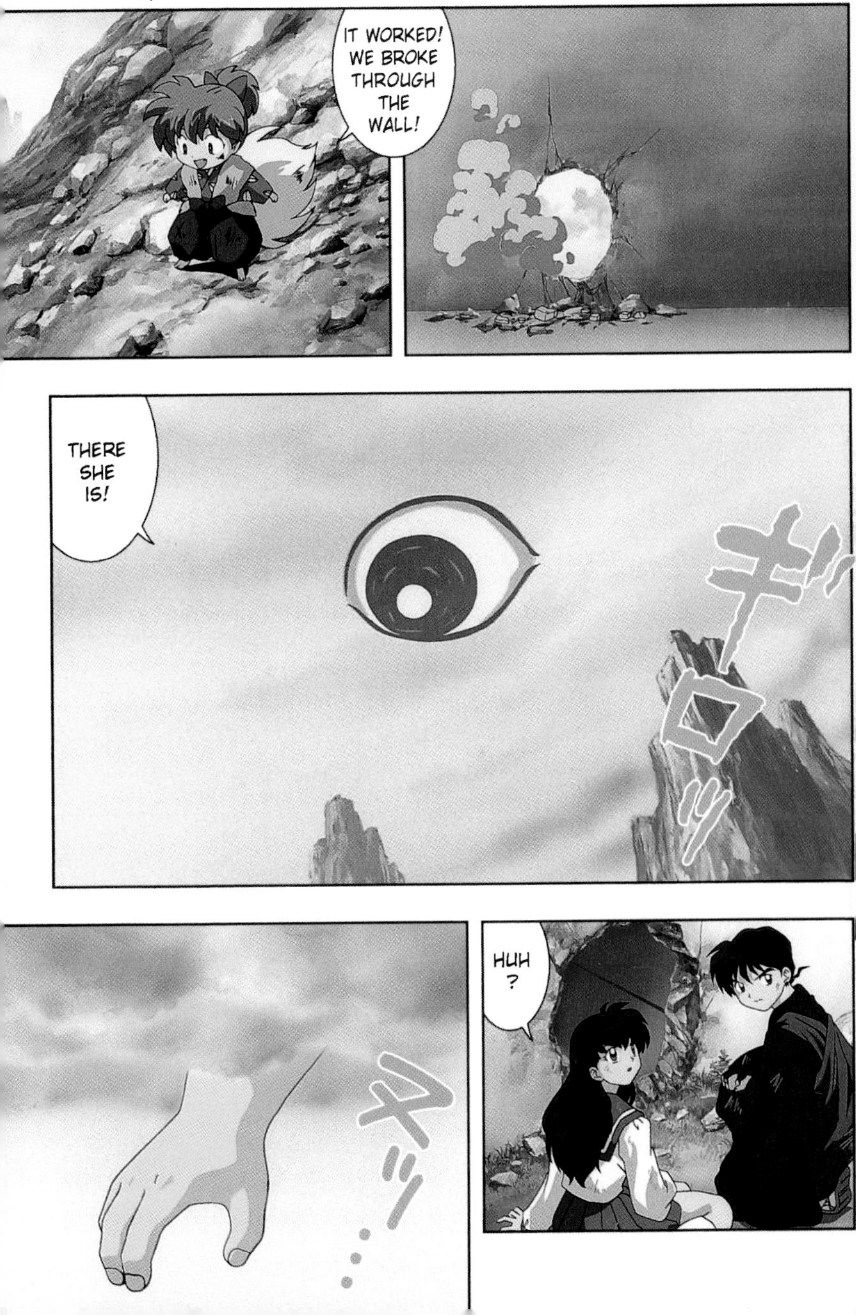
IT WORKED! WE BROKE THROUGH THE WALL!
THERE SHE IS!
ギロッ
HUH?
スッ…

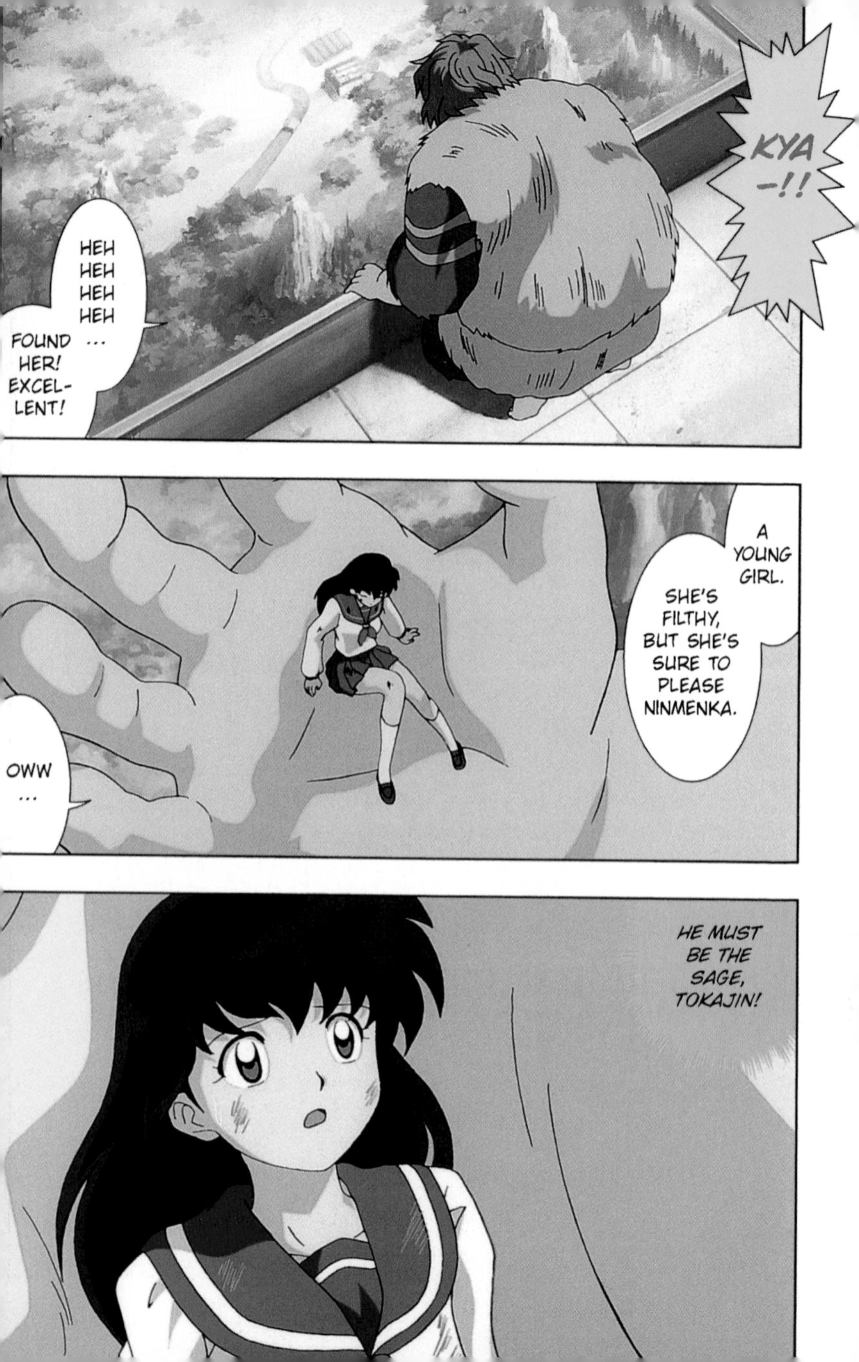
KYA-!!
HEH HEH HEH HEH ... FOUND HER! EXCEL-LENT!
A YOUNG GIRL.
SHE'S FILTHY, BUT SHE'S SURE TO PLEASE NINMENKA.
OWW ...
HE MUST BE THE SAGE, TOKAJIN!

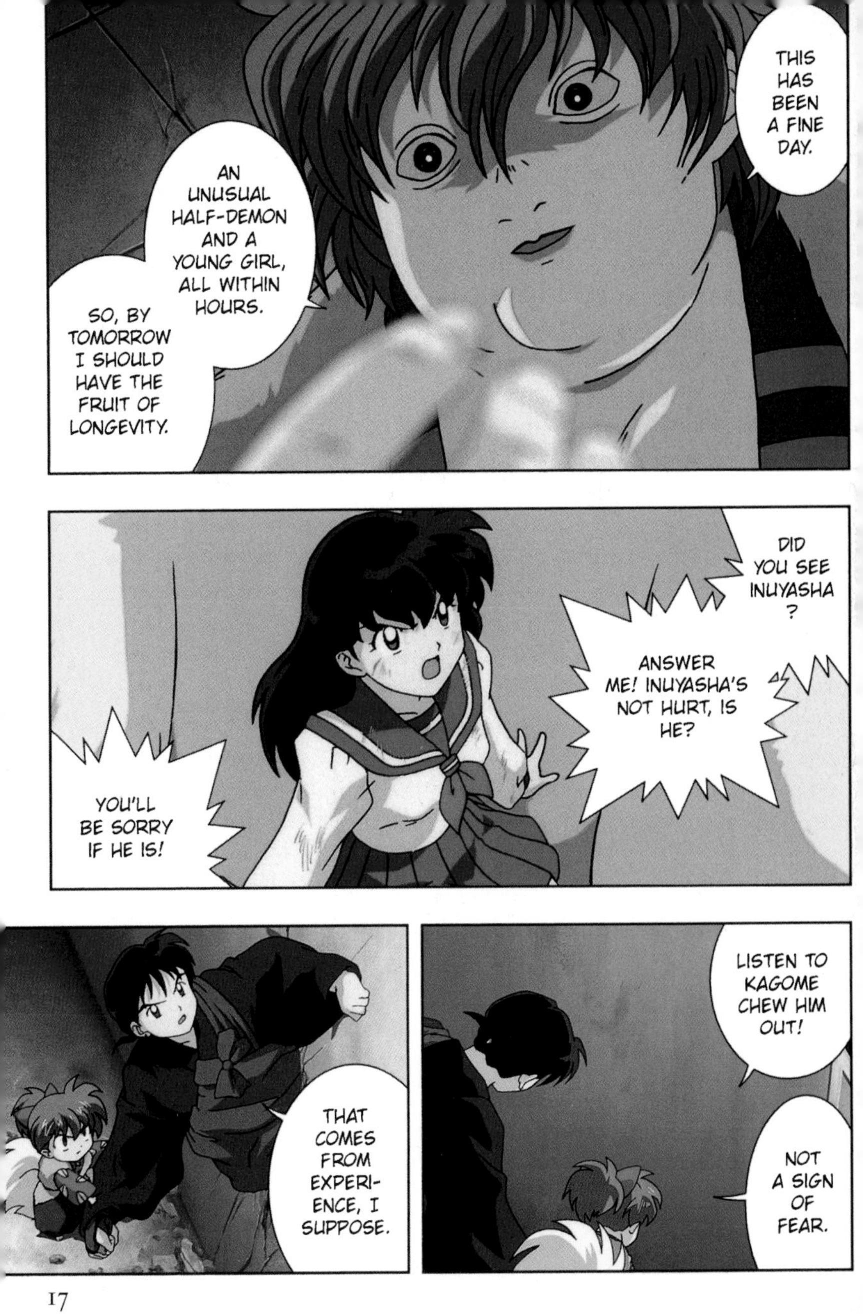
THIS HAS BEEN A FINE DAY.
AN UNUSUAL HALF-DEMON AND A YOUNG GIRL, ALL WITHIN HOURS.
SO, BY TOMORROW I SHOULD HAVE THE FRUIT OF LONGEVITY.
DID YOU SEE INUYASHA ?
ANSWER ME! INUYASHA'S NOT HURT, IS HE?
YOU'LL BE SORRY IF HE IS!
LISTEN TO KAGOME CHEW HIM OUT!
NOT A SIGN OF FEAR.
THAT COMES FROM EXPERIENCE, I SUPPOSE.

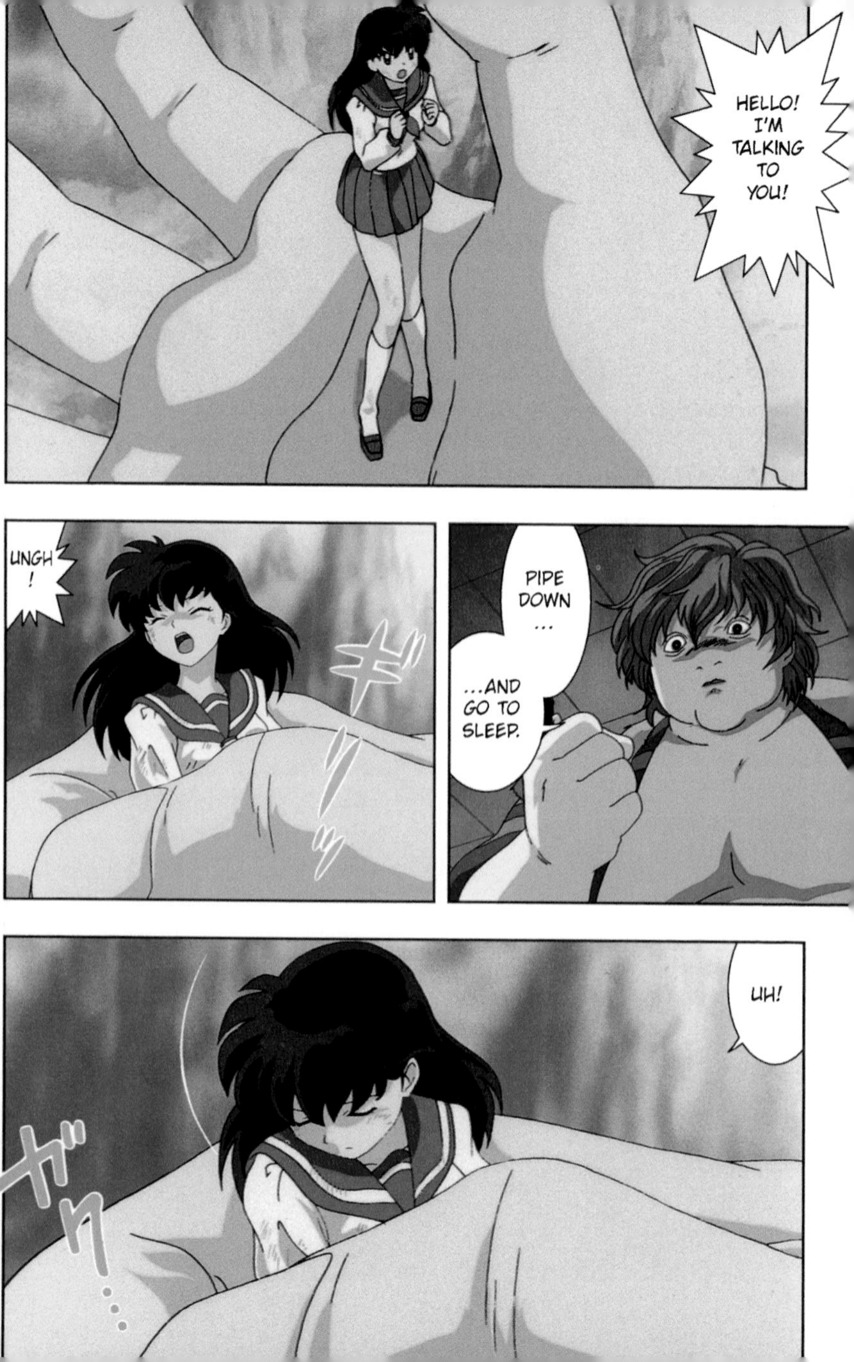
HELLO! I'M TALKING TO YOU!
PIPE DOWN...
...AND GO TO SLEEP.
UNGH!
UH!

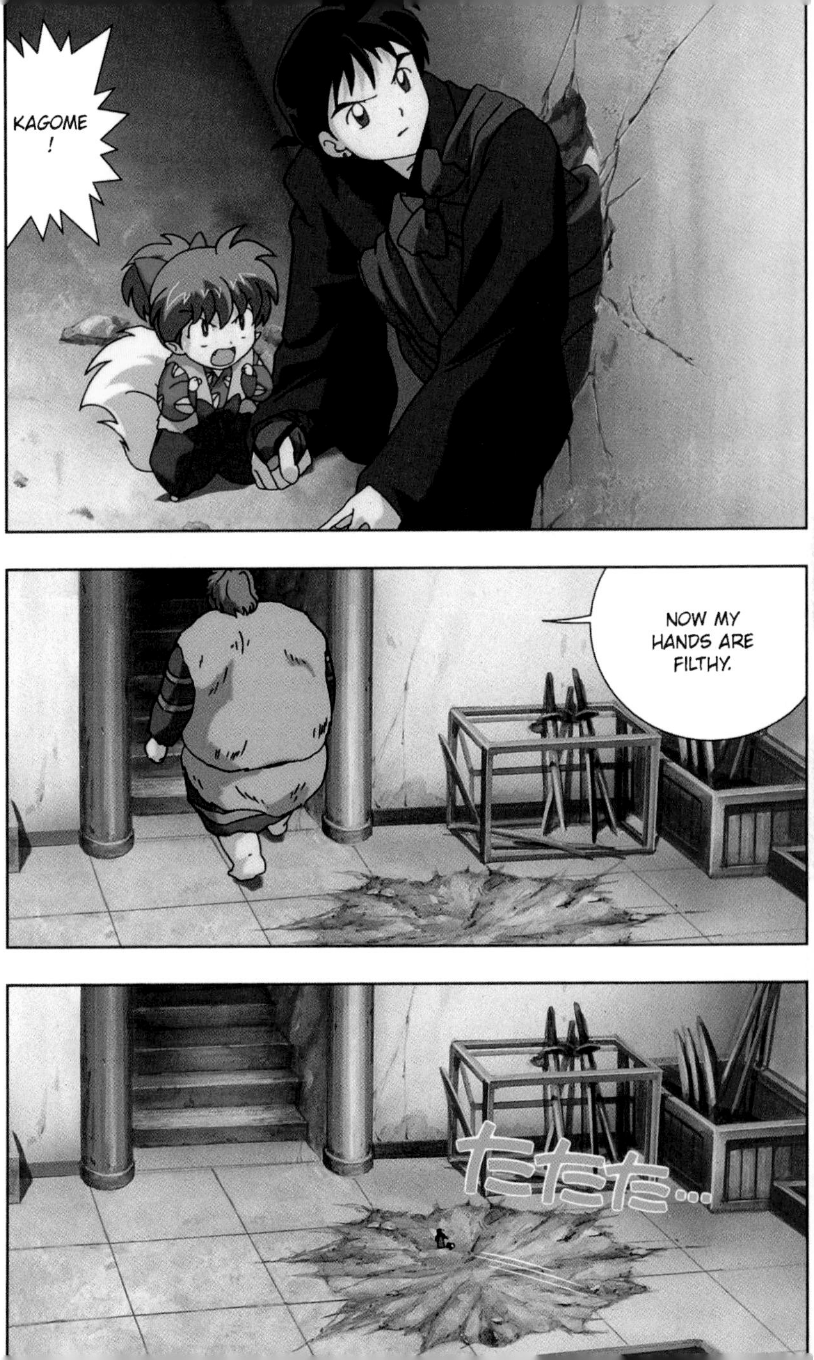
KAGOME!
NOW MY HANDS ARE FILTHY.
たたた…

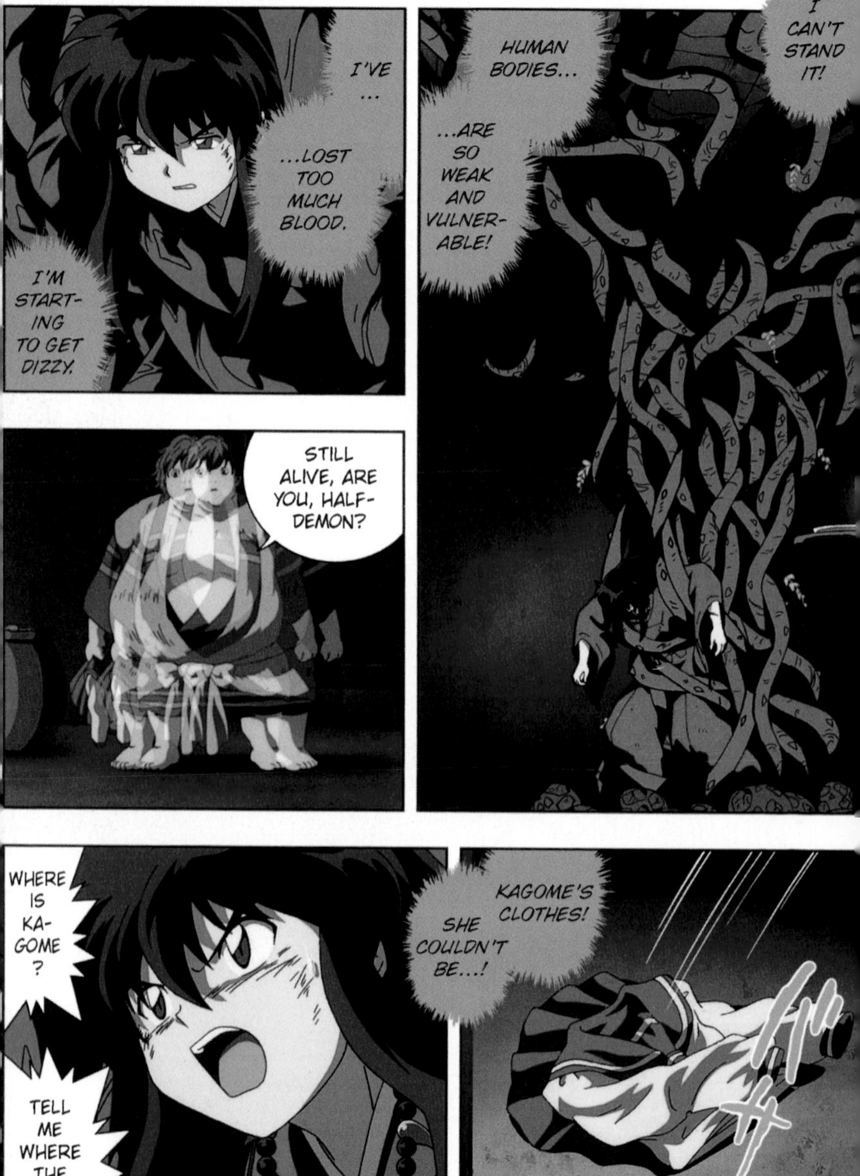
I CAN'T STAND IT!
HUMAN BODIES...
...ARE SO WEAK AND VULNER-ABLE!
I'VE ...
...LOST TOO MUCH BLOOD.
I'M START-ING TO GET DIZZY.
STILL ALIVE, ARE YOU, HALF-DEMON?
KAGOME'S CLOTHES!
SHE COULDN'T BE...!
WHERE IS KA-GOME?
TELL ME WHERE THE GIRL IS!

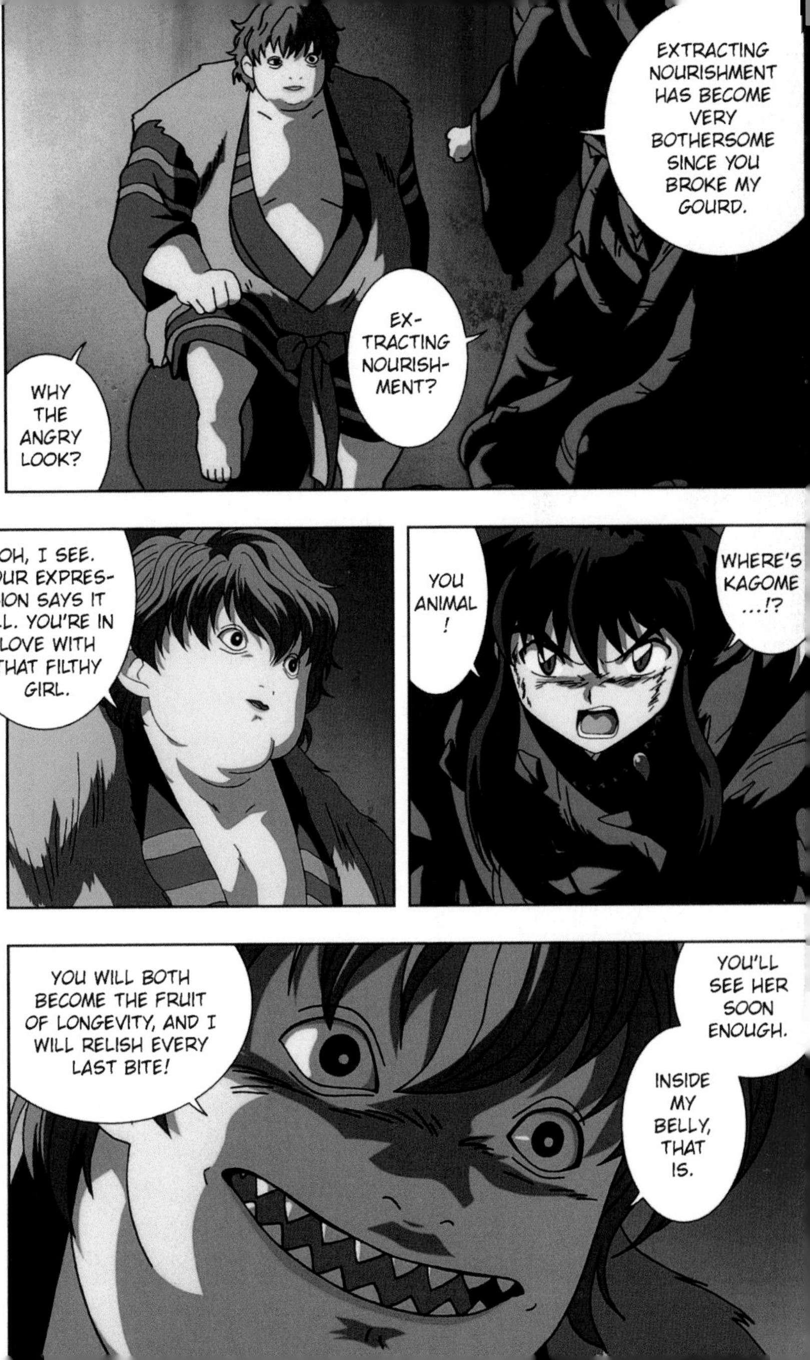
EXTRACTING NOURISHMENT HAS BECOME VERY BOTHERSOME SINCE YOU BROKE MY GOURD.
EX-TRACTING NOURISH-MENT?
WHY THE ANGRY LOOK?
WHERE'S KAGOME ...!?
YOU ANIMAL!
OH, I SEE. YOUR EXPRES-SION SAYS IT ALL. YOU'RE IN LOVE WITH THAT FILTHY GIRL.
YOU'LL SEE HER SOON ENOUGH.
INSIDE MY BELLY, THAT IS.
YOU WILL BOTH BECOME THE FRUIT OF LONGEVITY, AND I WILL RELISH EVERY LAST BITE!

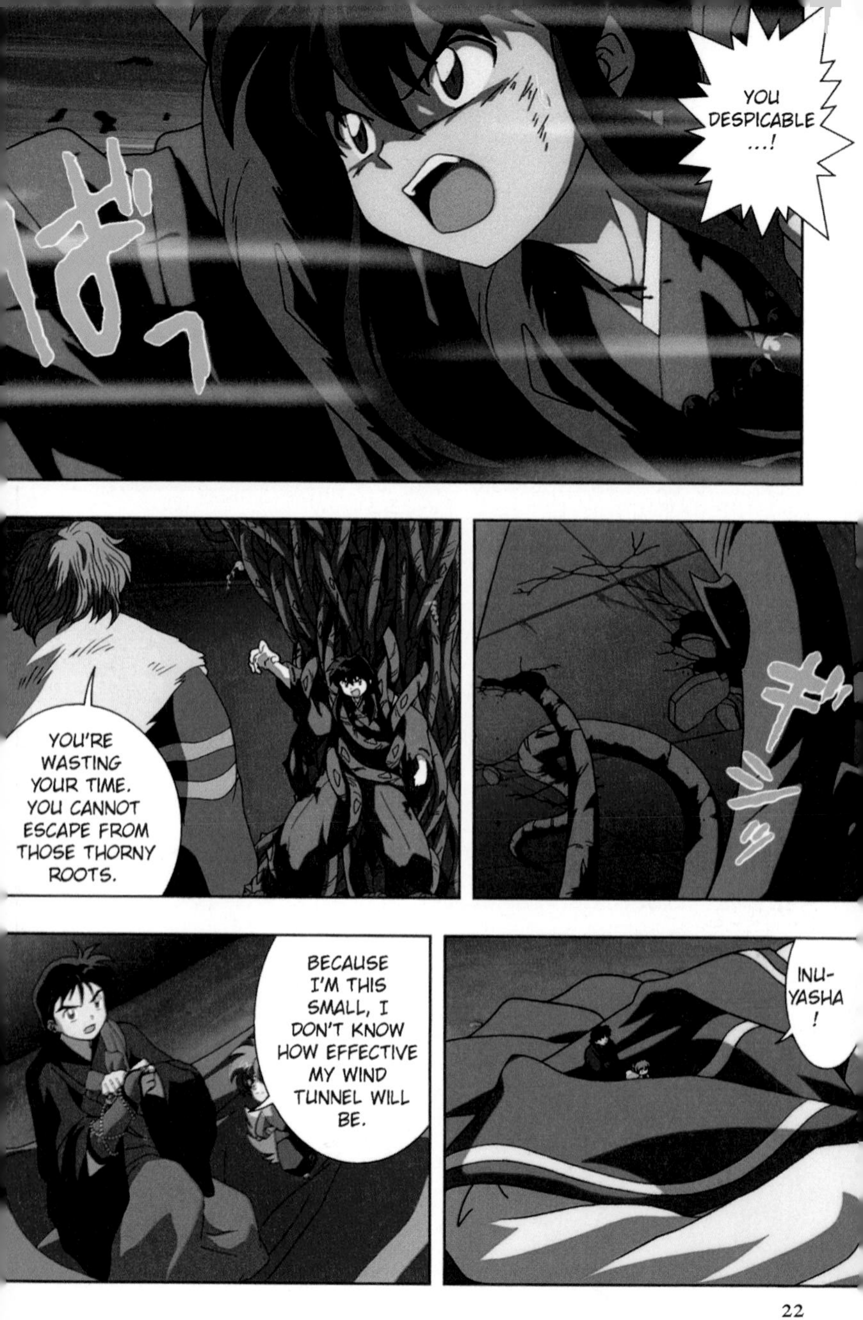
YOU DESPICABLE ...!
ぱっ
ギシッ
YOU'RE WASTING YOUR TIME. YOU CANNOT ESCAPE FROM THOSE THORNY ROOTS.
INU-YASHA!
BECAUSE I'M THIS SMALL, I DON'T KNOW HOW EFFECTIVE MY WIND TUNNEL WILL BE.

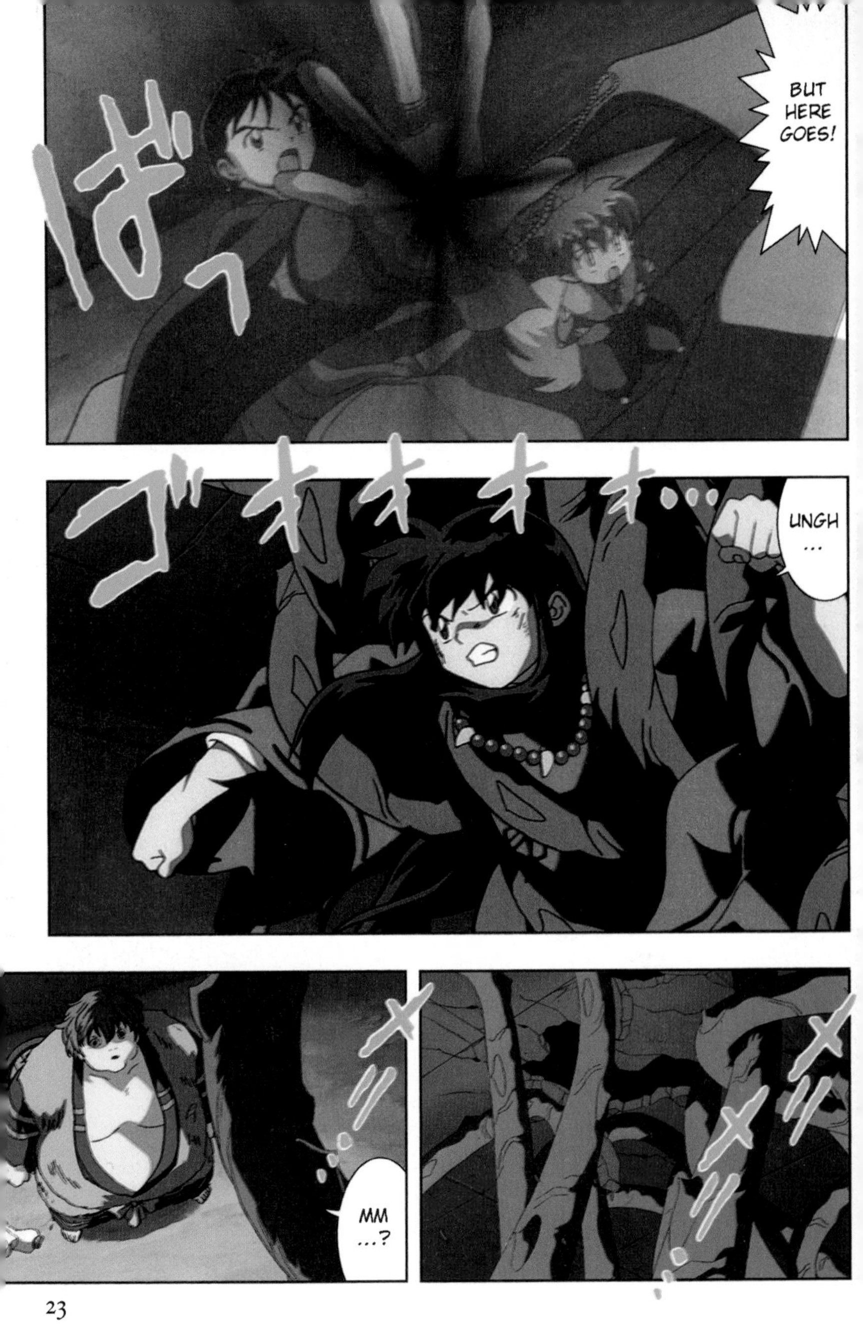
BUT HERE GOES!
ぼっ
ゴォォォォ…
UNGH ...
MM ...?

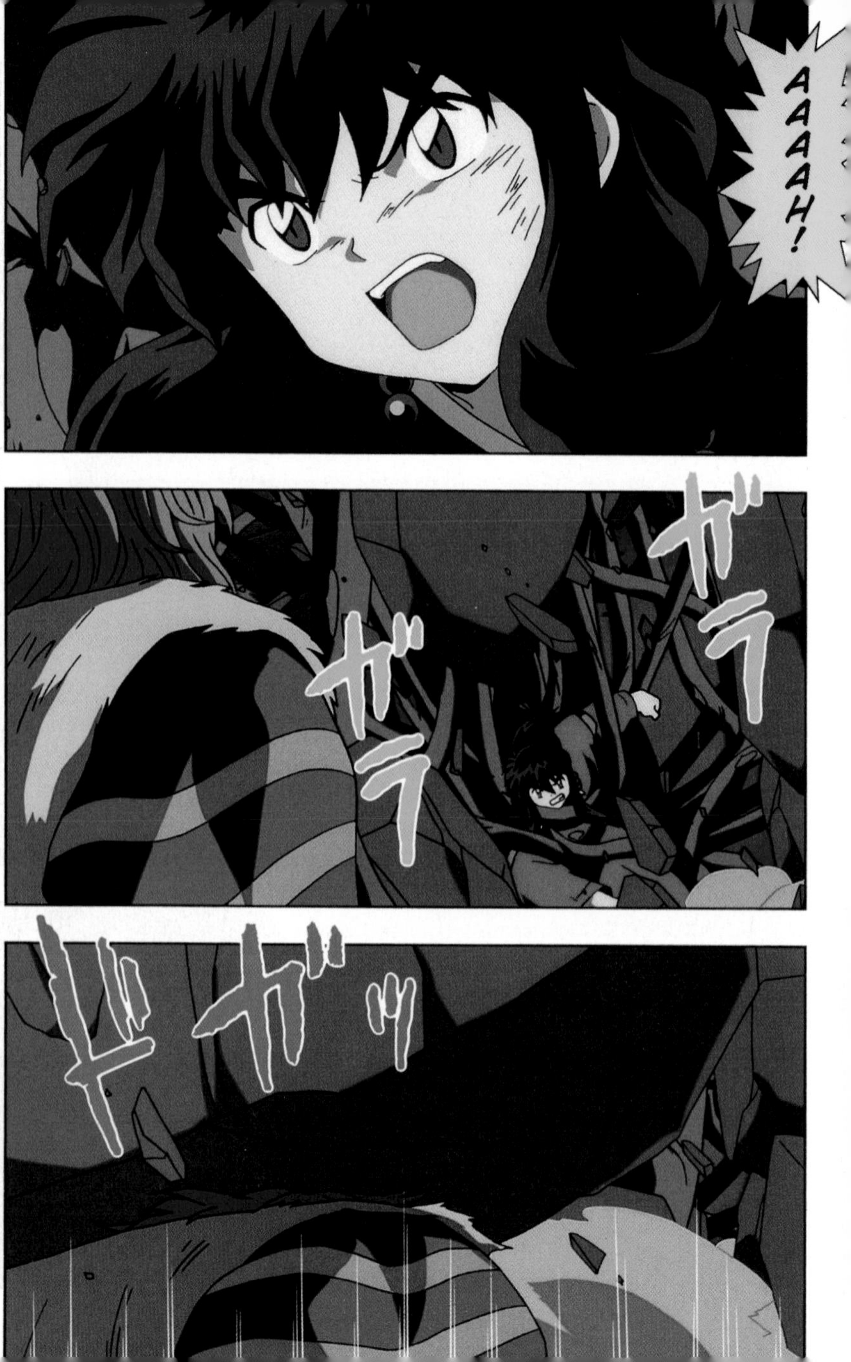
AAAAAH!
ガラ
ガラ
ドガッ

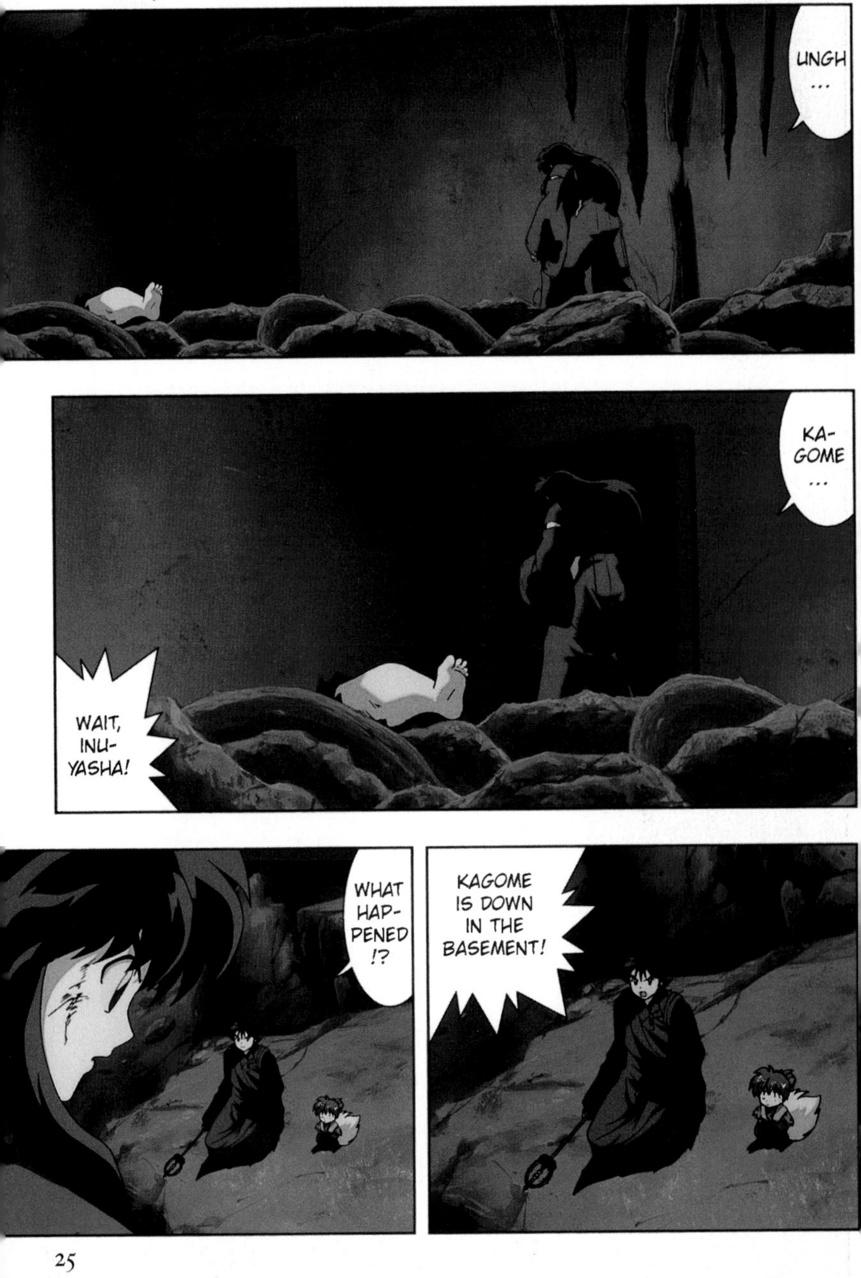
UNGH ...
KA-GOME ...
WAIT, INU-YASHA!
KAGOME IS DOWN IN THE BASEMENT!
WHAT HAP-PENED !?

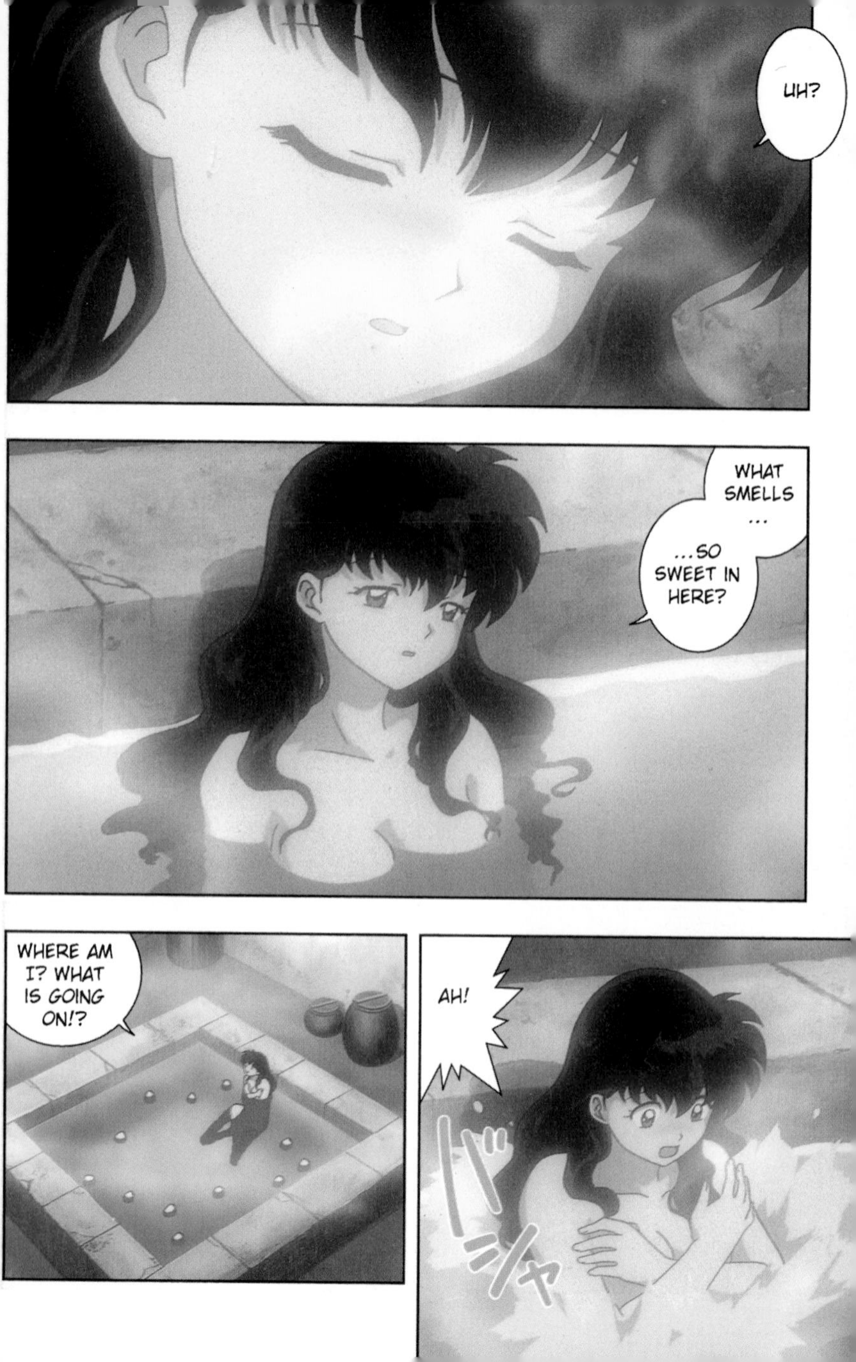
UH?
WHAT SMELLS ...
...SO SWEET IN HERE?
AH!
バシャ
WHERE AM I? WHAT IS GOING ON!?

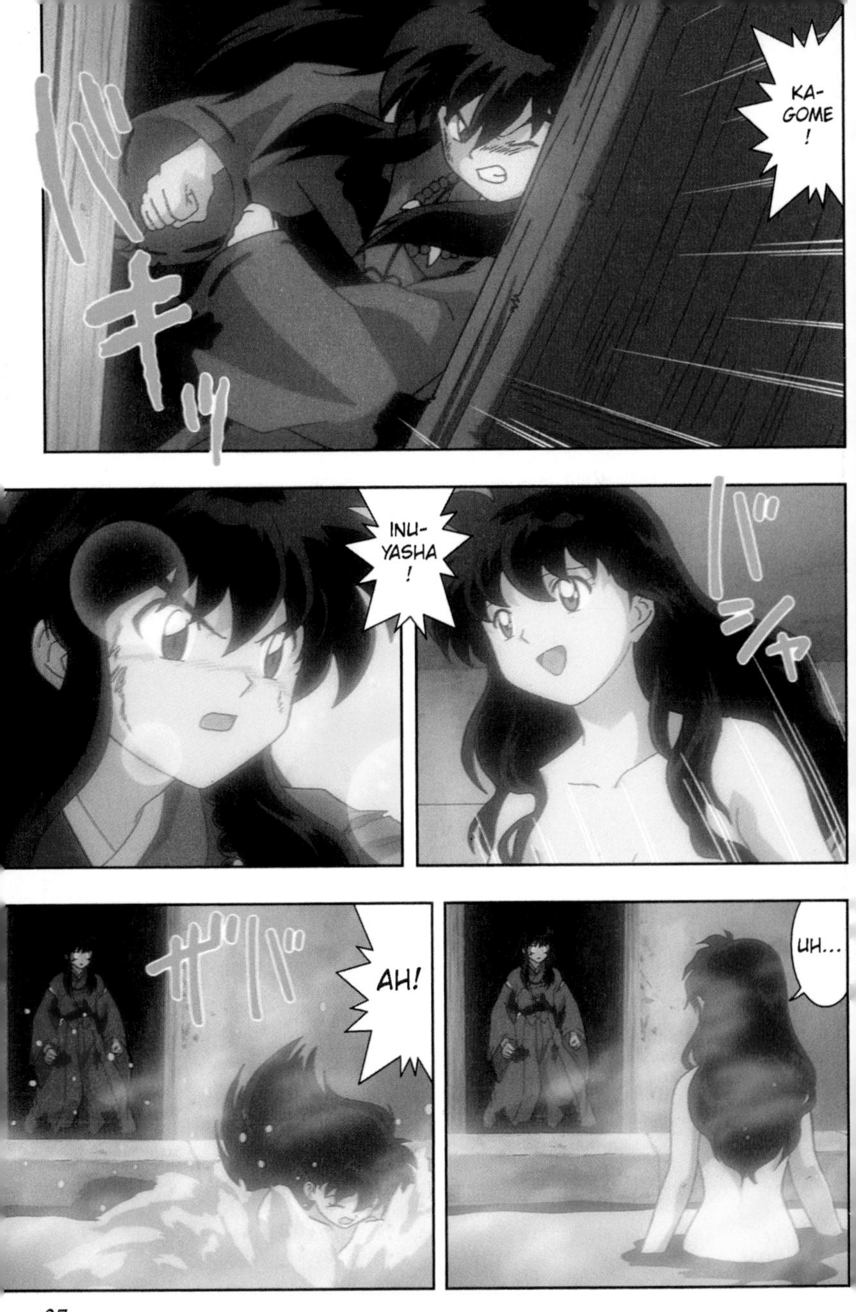
KA-GOME!
バキッ
INU-YASHA!
バシャ
UH...
AH!
ザバ

SHE'S ALIVE!

ARE YOU ALL RIGHT?

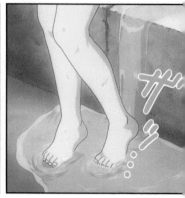

THESE ARE JUST SCRATCHES.

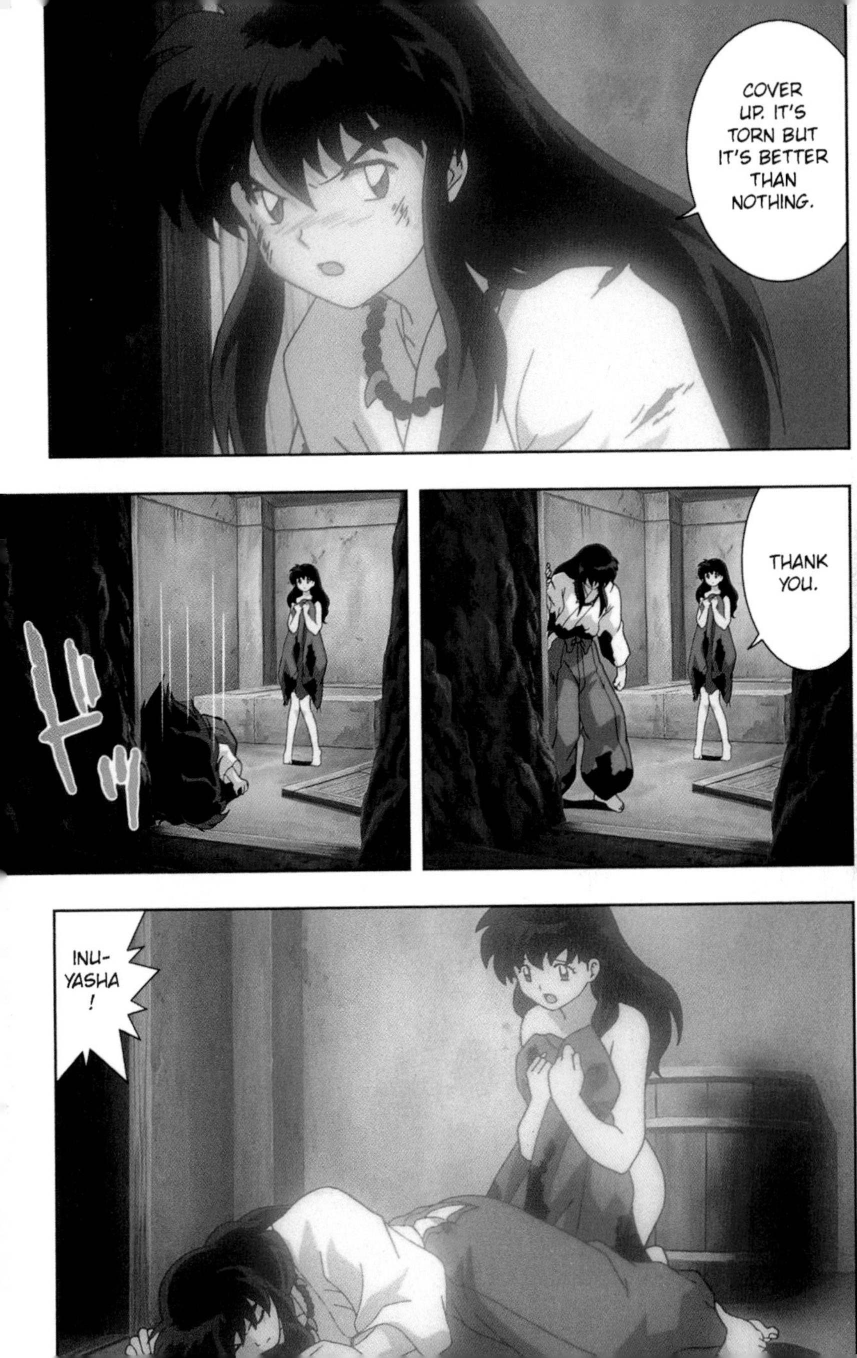
COVER UP. IT'S TORN BUT IT'S BETTER THAN NOTHING.
THANK YOU.
ドッ
INU-YASHA!

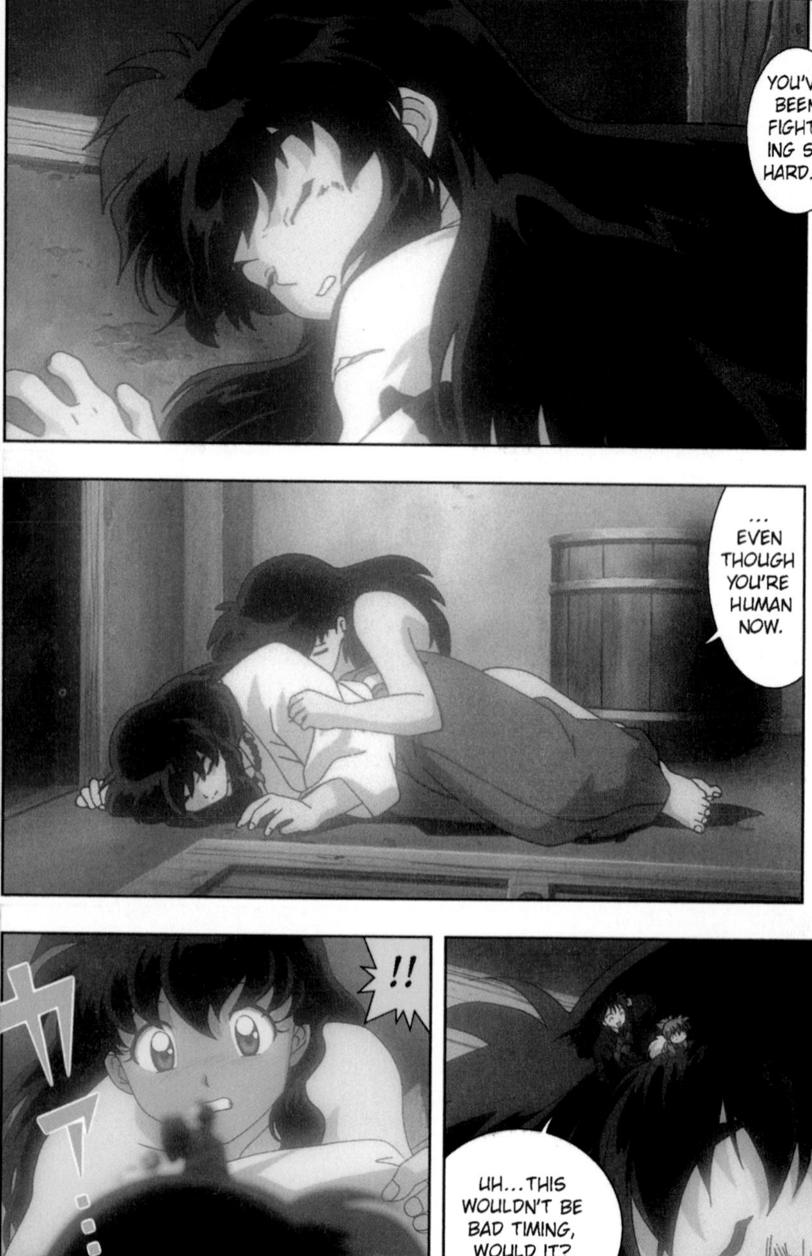
YOU'VE BEEN FIGHT-ING SO HARD...
...EVEN THOUGH YOU'RE HUMAN NOW.
UH...THIS WOULDN'T BE BAD TIMING, WOULD IT?
!!

KYA
-!!
HEH HEH HEH...THEY WON'T GET AWAY.

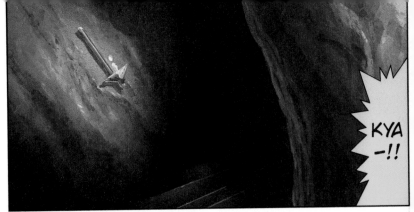

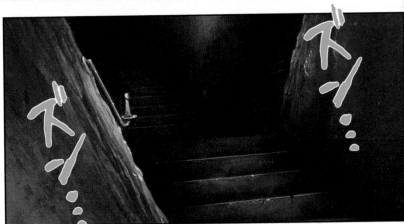

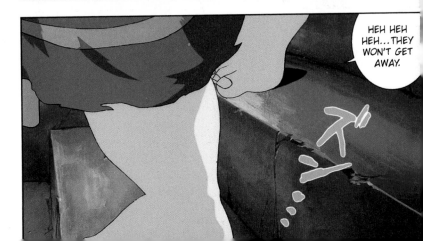

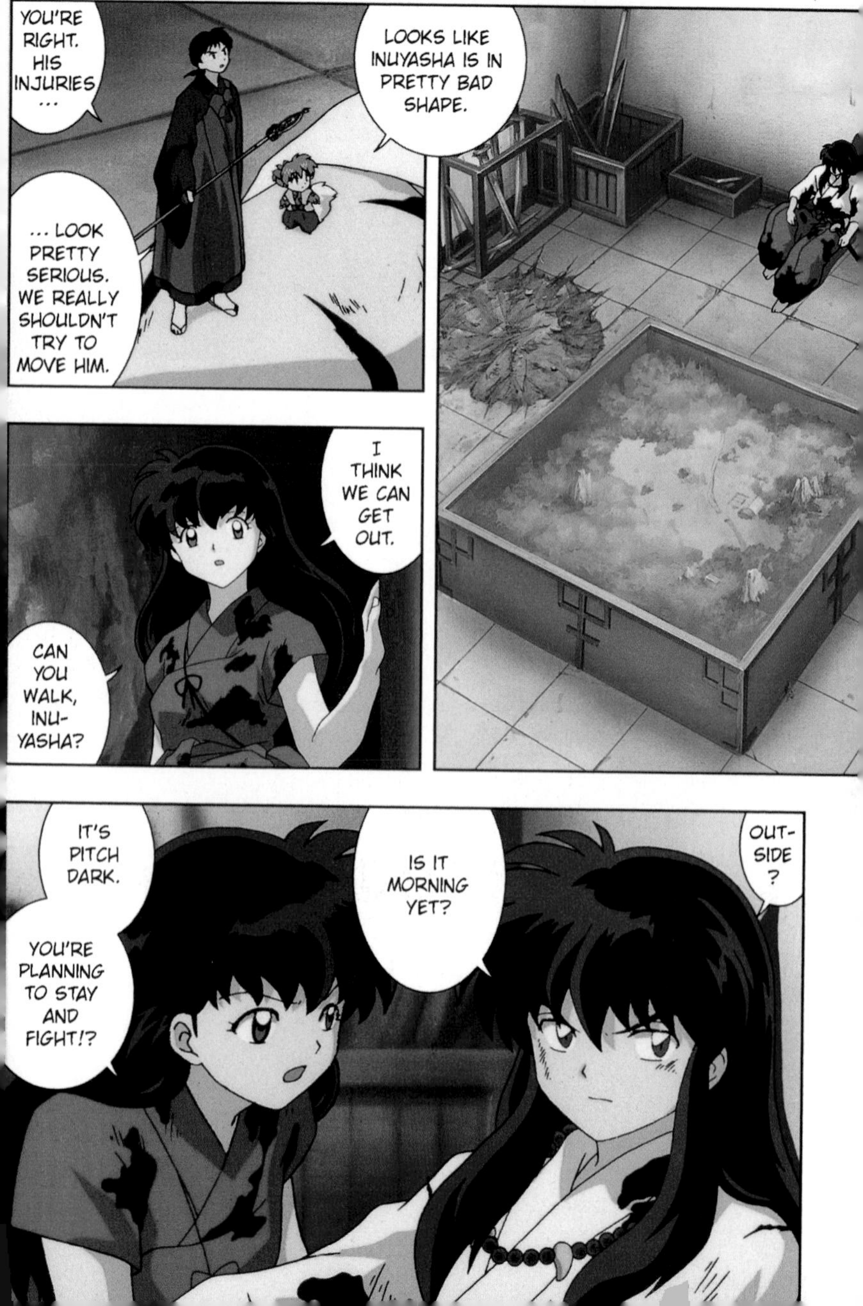
LOOKS LIKE INUYASHA IS IN PRETTY BAD SHAPE.
YOU'RE RIGHT. HIS INJURIES ...
... LOOK PRETTY SERIOUS. WE REALLY SHOULDN'T TRY TO MOVE HIM.
I THINK WE CAN GET OUT.
CAN YOU WALK, INU-YASHA?
OUT-SIDE?
IS IT MORNING YET?
IT'S PITCH DARK.
YOU'RE PLANNING TO STAY AND FIGHT!?

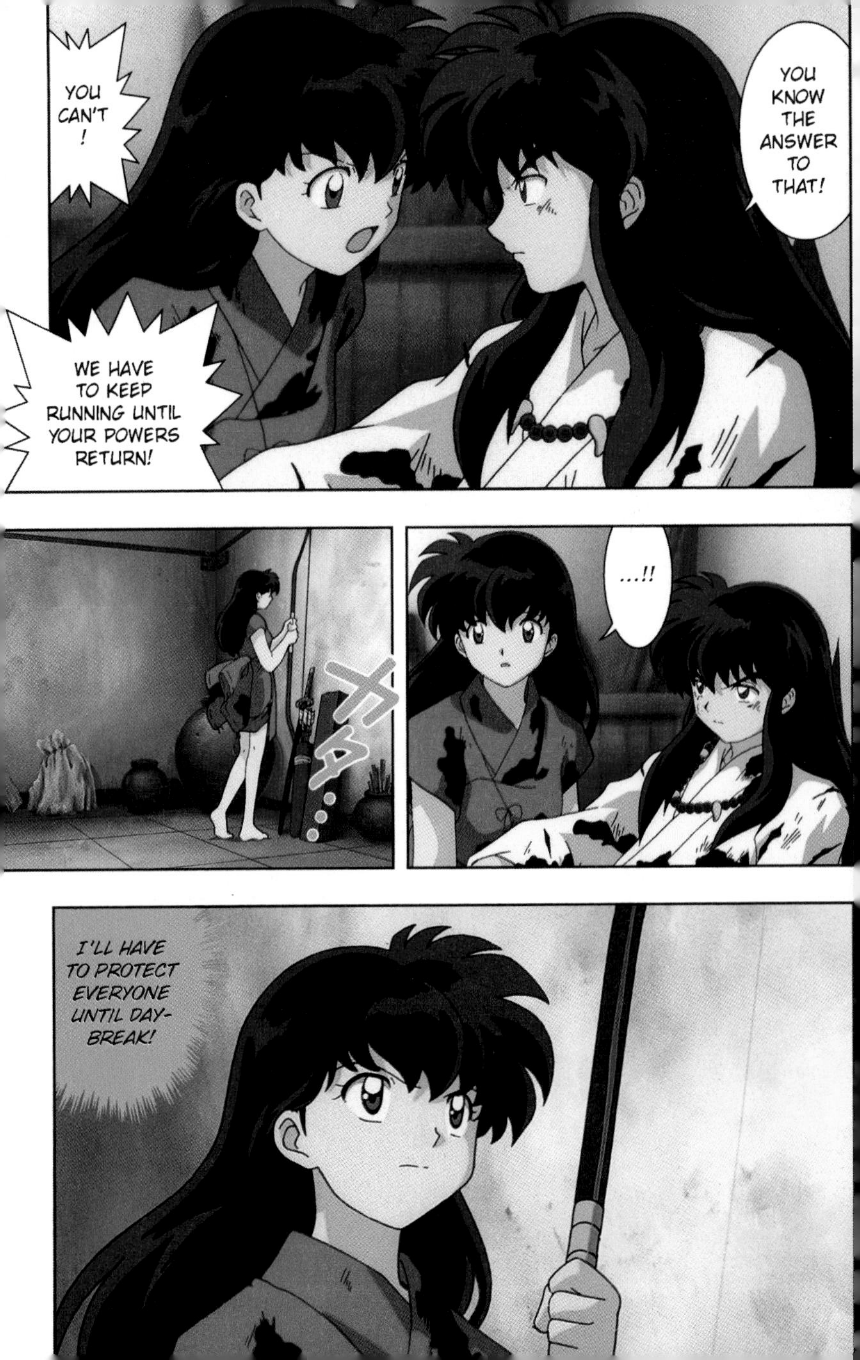
YOU KNOW THE ANSWER TO THAT!
YOU CAN'T!
WE HAVE TO KEEP RUNNING UNTIL YOUR POWERS RETURN!
...!!
カタ…
I'LL HAVE TO PROTECT EVERYONE UNTIL DAY-BREAK!

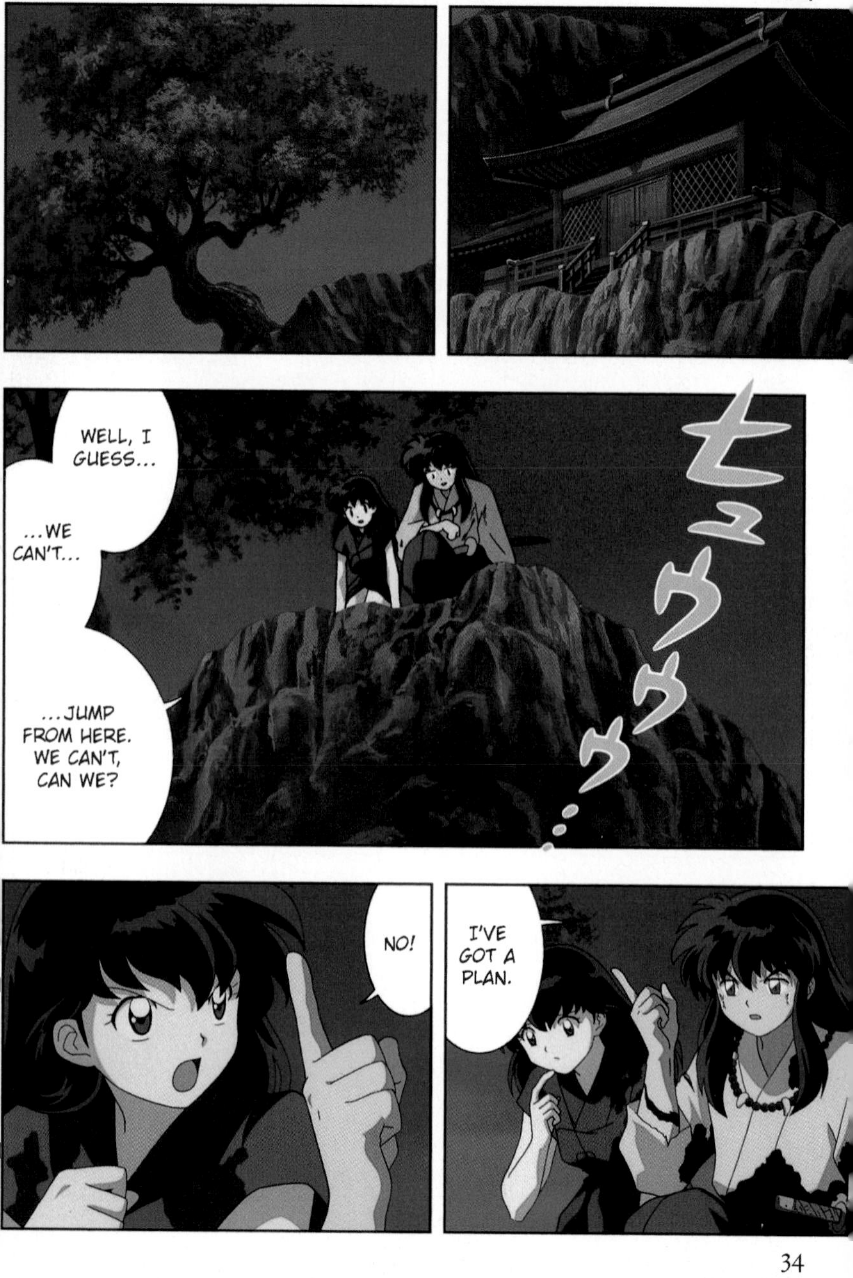
ヒュウウウ…
WELL, I GUESS...
...WE CAN'T...
...JUMP FROM HERE. WE CAN'T, CAN WE?
I'VE GOT A PLAN.
NO!

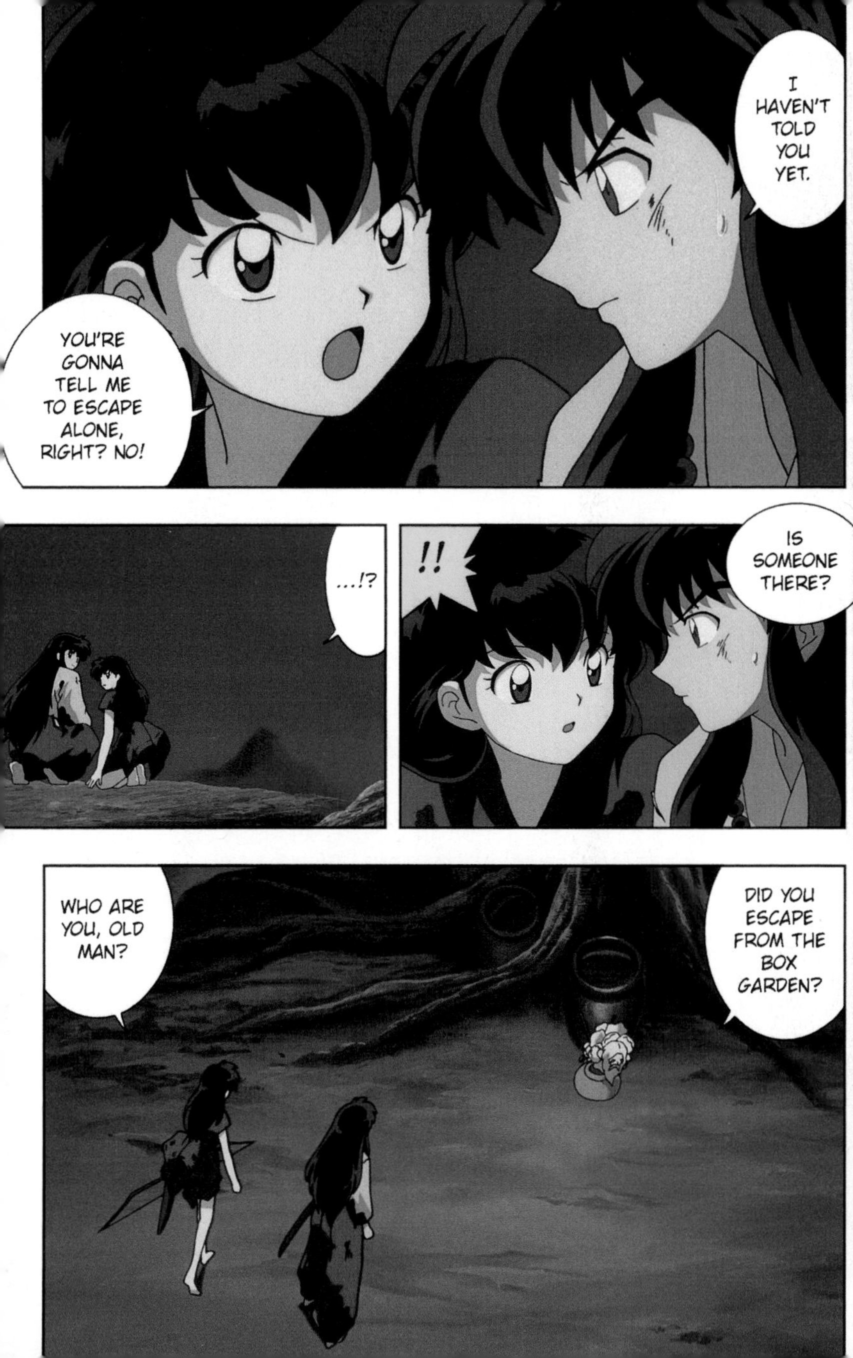
I HAVEN'T TOLD YOU YET.
YOU'RE GONNA TELL ME TO ESCAPE ALONE, RIGHT? NO!
IS SOMEONE THERE?
!!
...!?
DID YOU ESCAPE FROM THE BOX GARDEN?
WHO ARE YOU, OLD MAN?

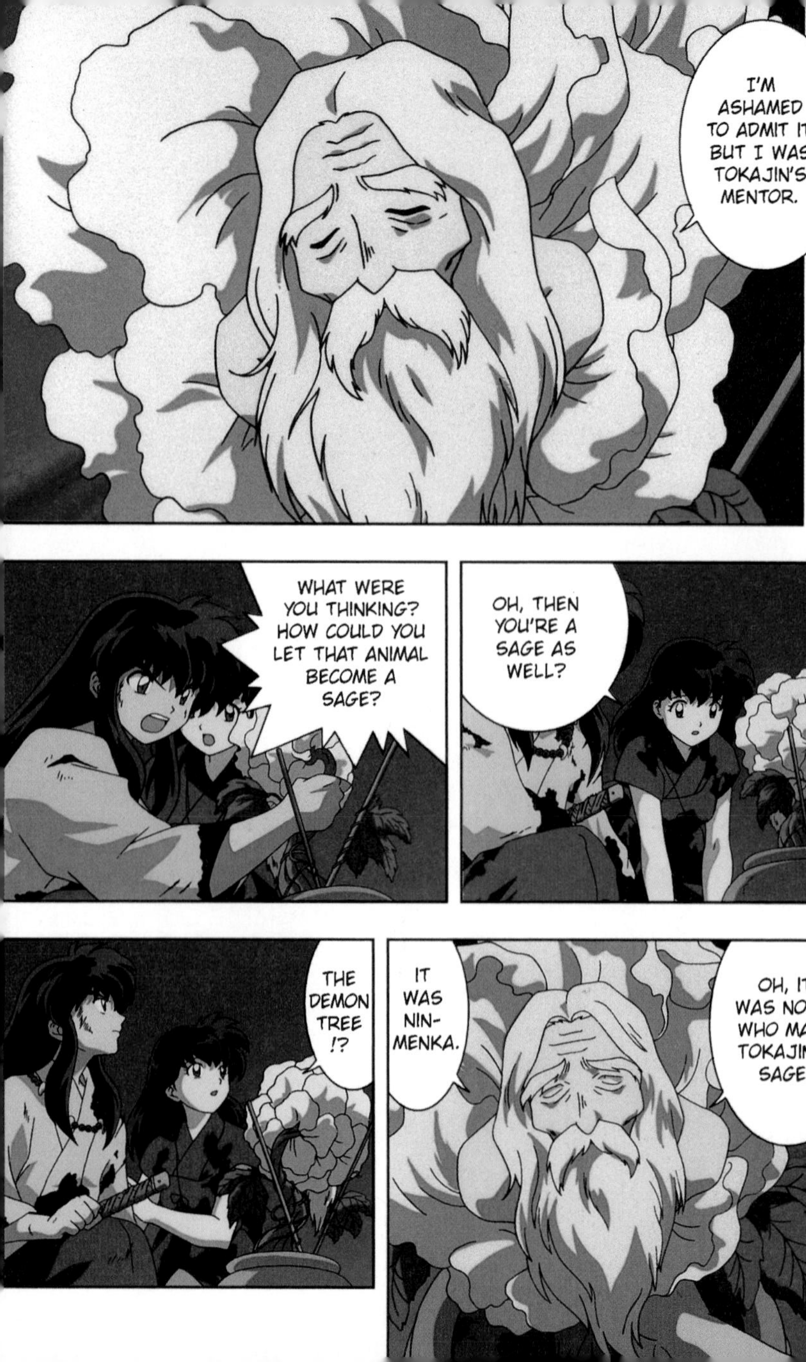
I'M ASHAMED TO ADMIT IT, BUT I WAS TOKAJIN'S MENTOR.
OH, THEN YOU'RE A SAGE AS WELL?
WHAT WERE YOU THINKING? HOW COULD YOU LET THAT ANIMAL BECOME A SAGE?
OH, IT WAS NOT I WHO MADE TOKAJIN A SAGE.
IT WAS NIN-MENKA.
THE DEMON TREE !?

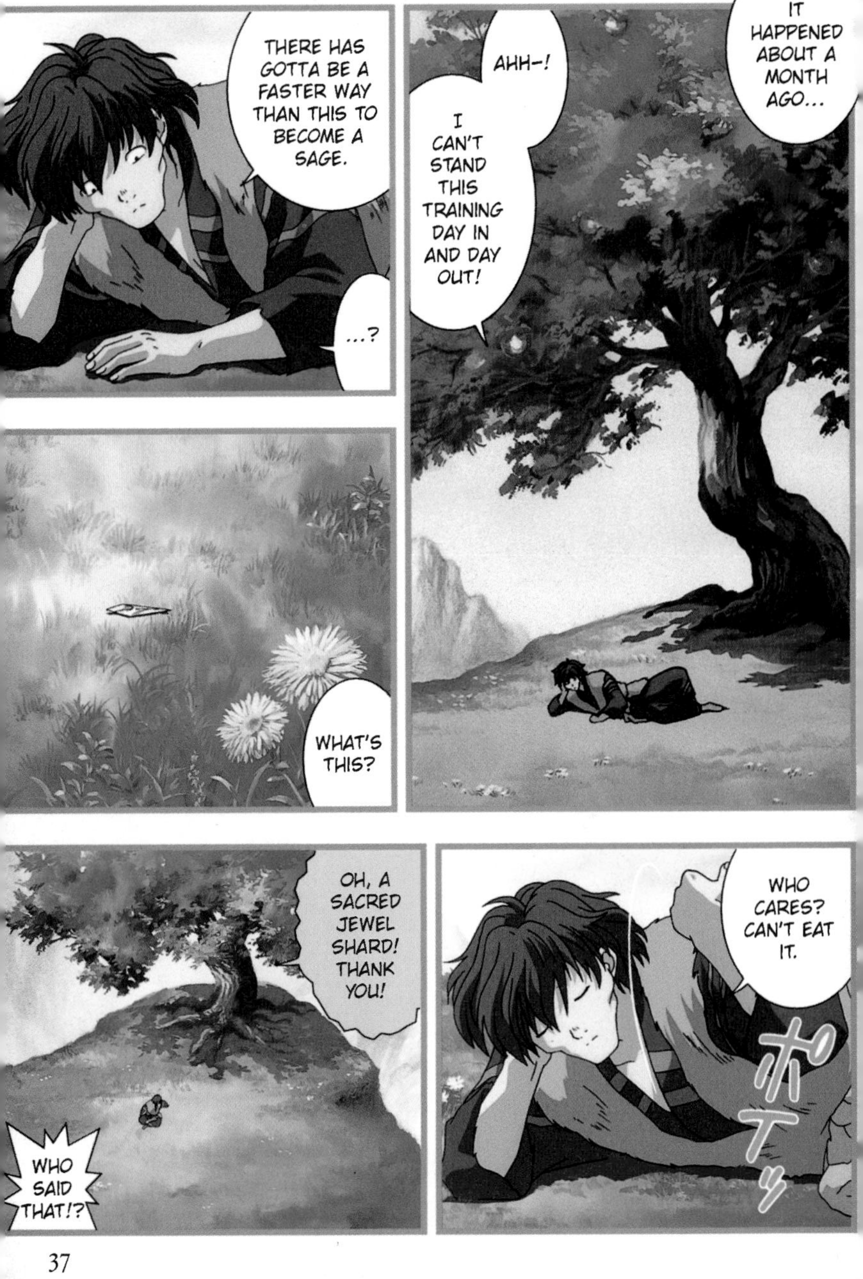
YES. IT HAPPENED ABOUT A MONTH AGO...
AHH-!
I CAN'T STAND THIS TRAINING DAY IN AND DAY OUT!
THERE HAS GOTTA BE A FASTER WAY THAN THIS TO BECOME A SAGE.
...?
WHAT'S THIS?
WHO CARES? CAN'T EAT IT.
ポイッ
OH, A SACRED JEWEL SHARD! THANK YOU!
WHO SAID THAT!?

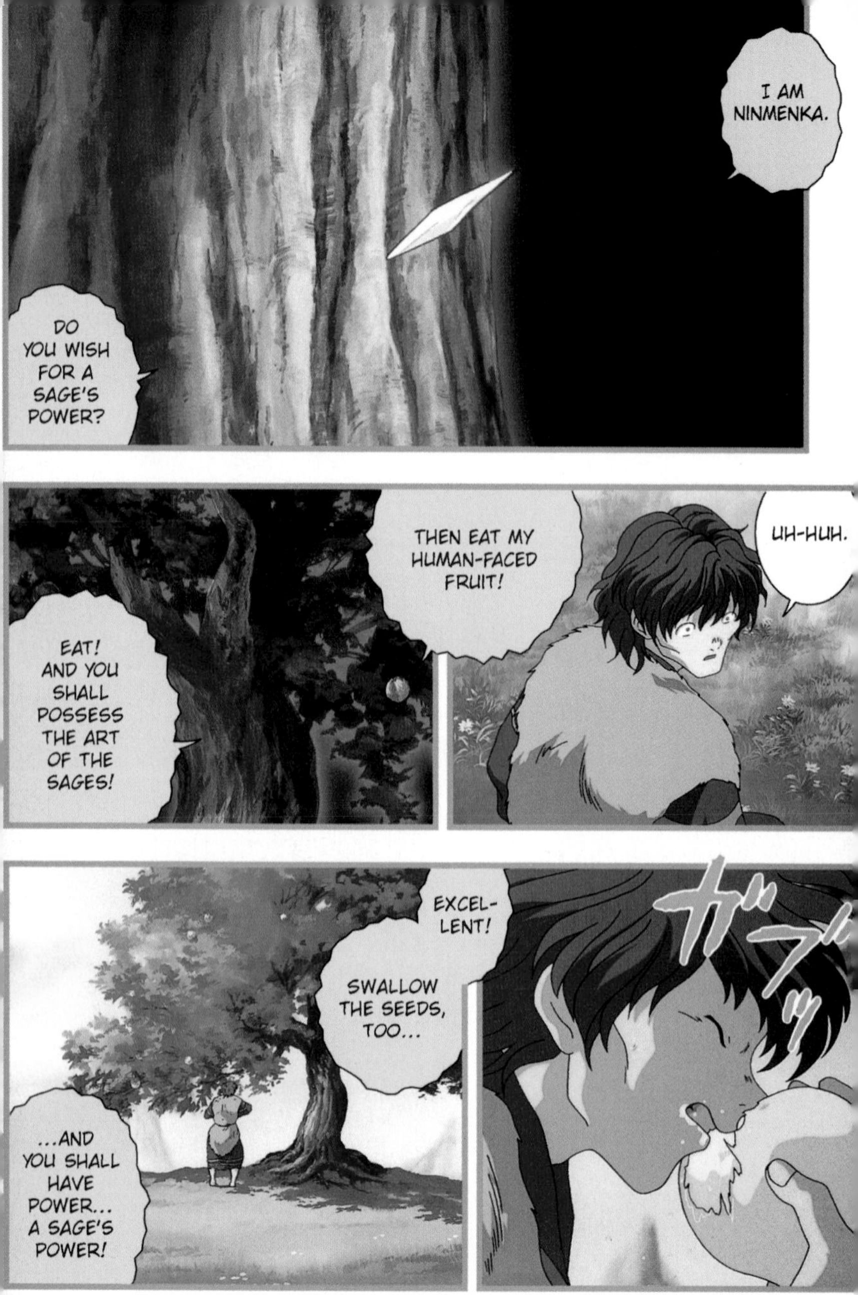
I AM NINMENKA.
DO YOU WISH FOR A SAGE'S POWER?
UH-HUH.
THEN EAT MY HUMAN-FACED FRUIT!
EAT! AND YOU SHALL POSSESS THE ART OF THE SAGES!
ガブッ
EXCEL-LENT!
SWALLOW THE SEEDS, TOO…
…AND YOU SHALL HAVE POWER… A SAGE'S POWER!

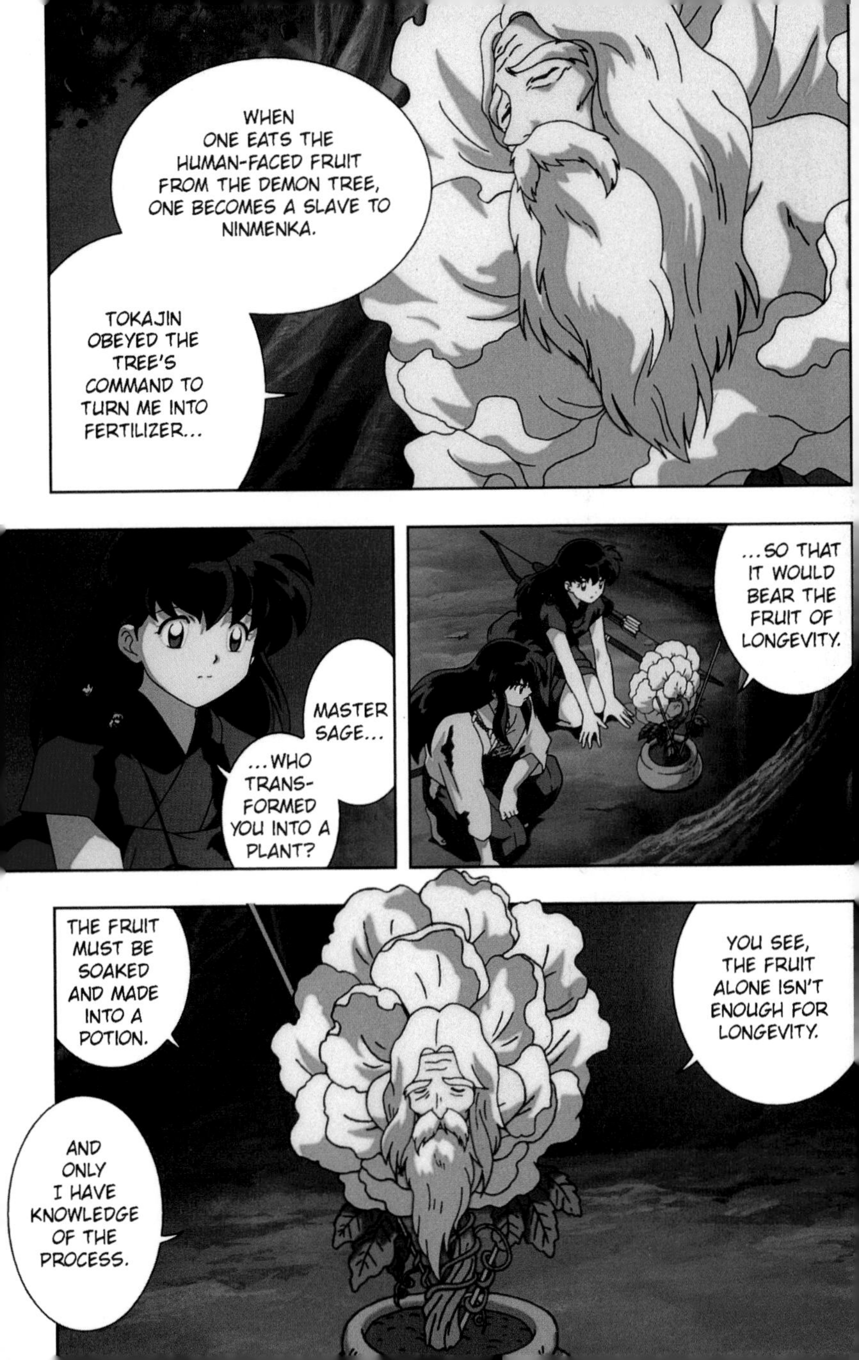
WHEN ONE EATS THE HUMAN-FACED FRUIT FROM THE DEMON TREE, ONE BECOMES A SLAVE TO NINMENKA.
TOKAJIN OBEYED THE TREE'S COMMAND TO TURN ME INTO FERTILIZER...
...SO THAT IT WOULD BEAR THE FRUIT OF LONGEVITY.
MASTER SAGE...
...WHO TRANS-FORMED YOU INTO A PLANT?
YOU SEE, THE FRUIT ALONE ISN'T ENOUGH FOR LONGEVITY.
THE FRUIT MUST BE SOAKED AND MADE INTO A POTION.
AND ONLY I HAVE KNOWLEDGE OF THE PROCESS.

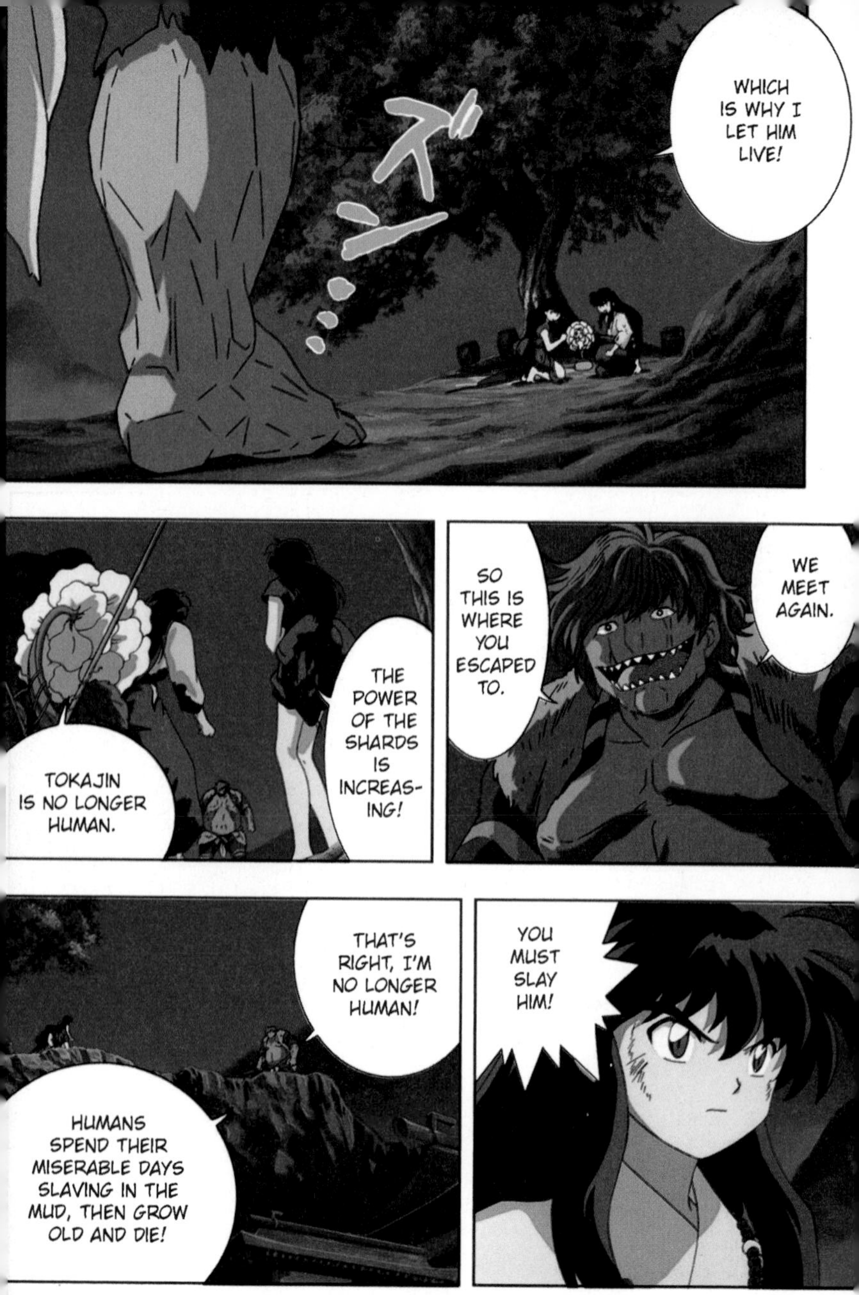
WHICH IS WHY I LET HIM LIVE!
WE MEET AGAIN.
SO THIS IS WHERE YOU ESCAPED TO.
THE POWER OF THE SHARDS IS INCREAS-ING!
TOKAJIN IS NO LONGER HUMAN.
YOU MUST SLAY HIM!
THAT'S RIGHT, I'M NO LONGER HUMAN!
HUMANS SPEND THEIR MISERABLE DAYS SLAVING IN THE MUD, THEN GROW OLD AND DIE!

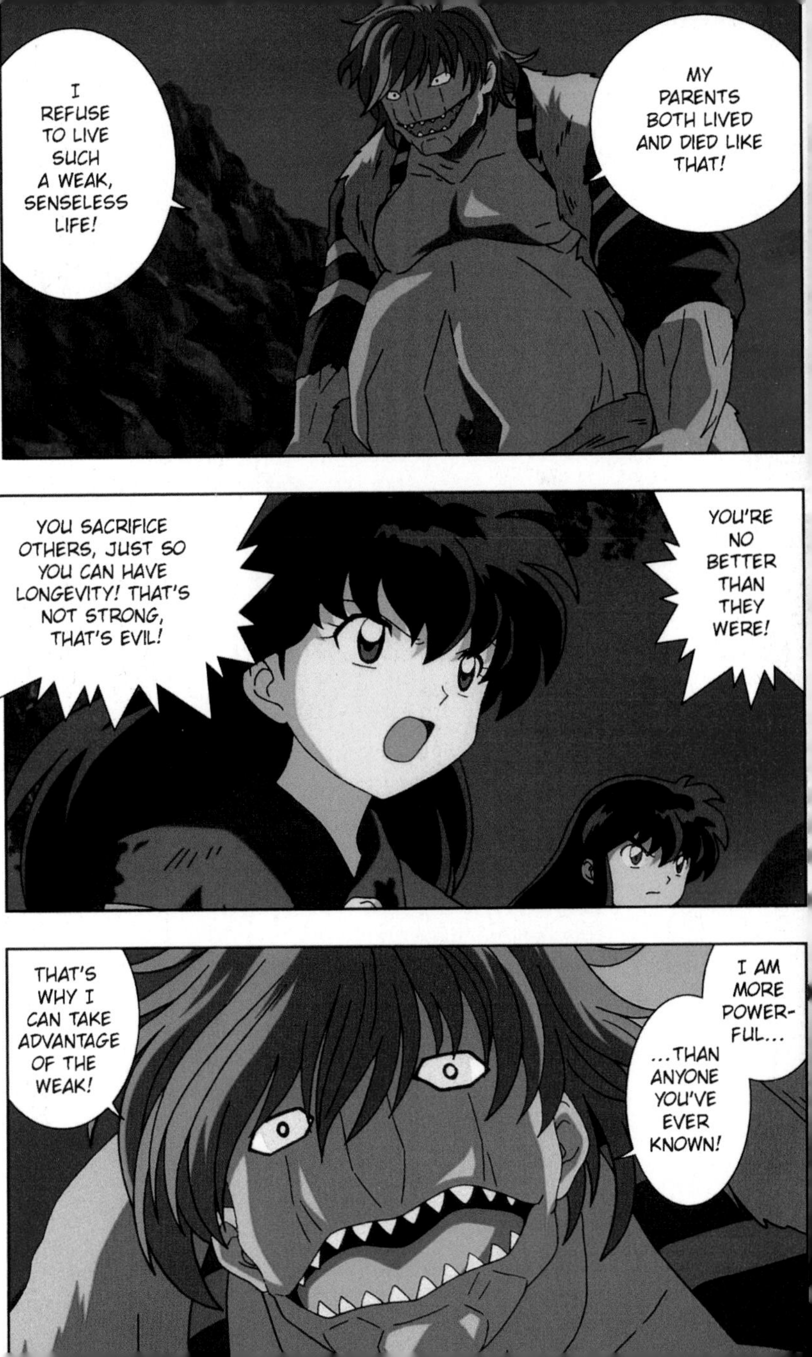
MY PARENTS BOTH LIVED AND DIED LIKE THAT!
I REFUSE TO LIVE SUCH A WEAK, SENSELESS LIFE!
YOU'RE NO BETTER THAN THEY WERE!
YOU SACRIFICE OTHERS, JUST SO YOU CAN HAVE LONGEVITY! THAT'S NOT STRONG, THAT'S EVIL!
I AM MORE POWER-FUL...
...THAN ANYONE YOU'VE EVER KNOWN!
THAT'S WHY I CAN TAKE ADVANTAGE OF THE WEAK!

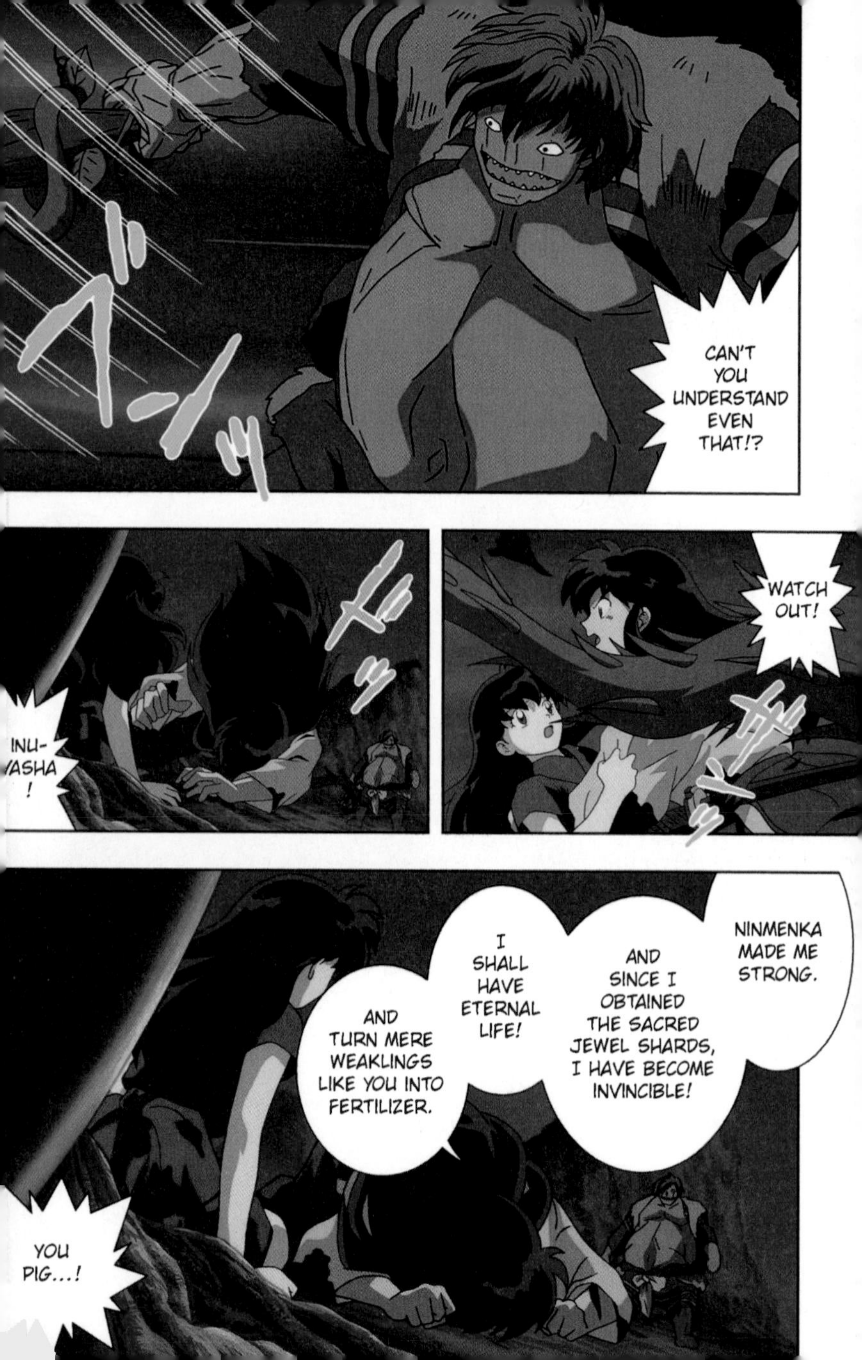
CAN'T YOU UNDERSTAND EVEN THAT!?
WATCH OUT!
INU-YASHA!
NINMENKA MADE ME STRONG.
AND SINCE I OBTAINED THE SACRED JEWEL SHARDS, I HAVE BECOME INVINCIBLE!
I SHALL HAVE ETERNAL LIFE!
AND TURN MERE WEAKLINGS LIKE YOU INTO FERTILIZER.
YOU PIG...!

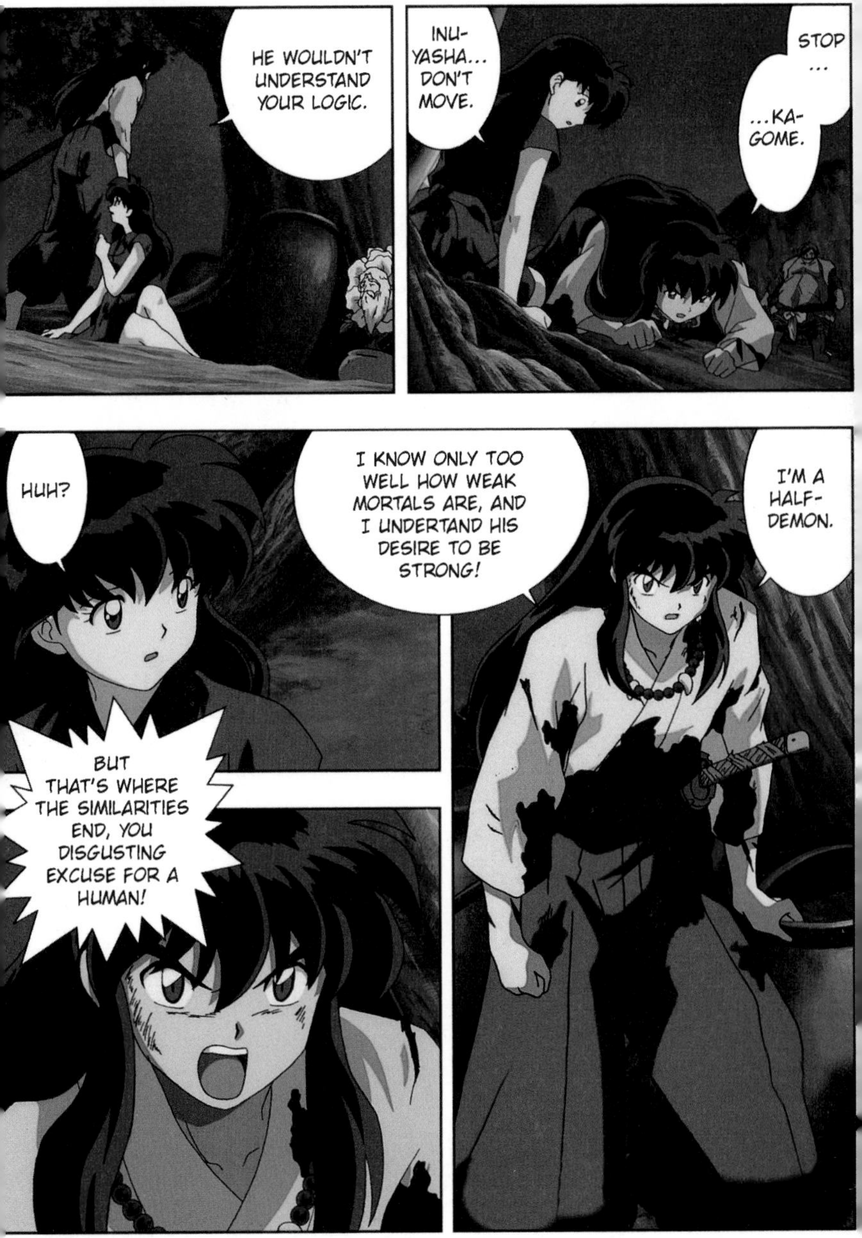
STOP ...
...KA-GOME.
INU-YASHA... DON'T MOVE.
HE WOULDN'T UNDERSTAND YOUR LOGIC.
I'M A HALF-DEMON.
I KNOW ONLY TOO WELL HOW WEAK MORTALS ARE, AND I UNDERTAND HIS DESIRE TO BE STRONG!
HUH?
BUT THAT'S WHERE THE SIMILARITIES END, YOU DISGUSTING EXCUSE FOR A HUMAN!

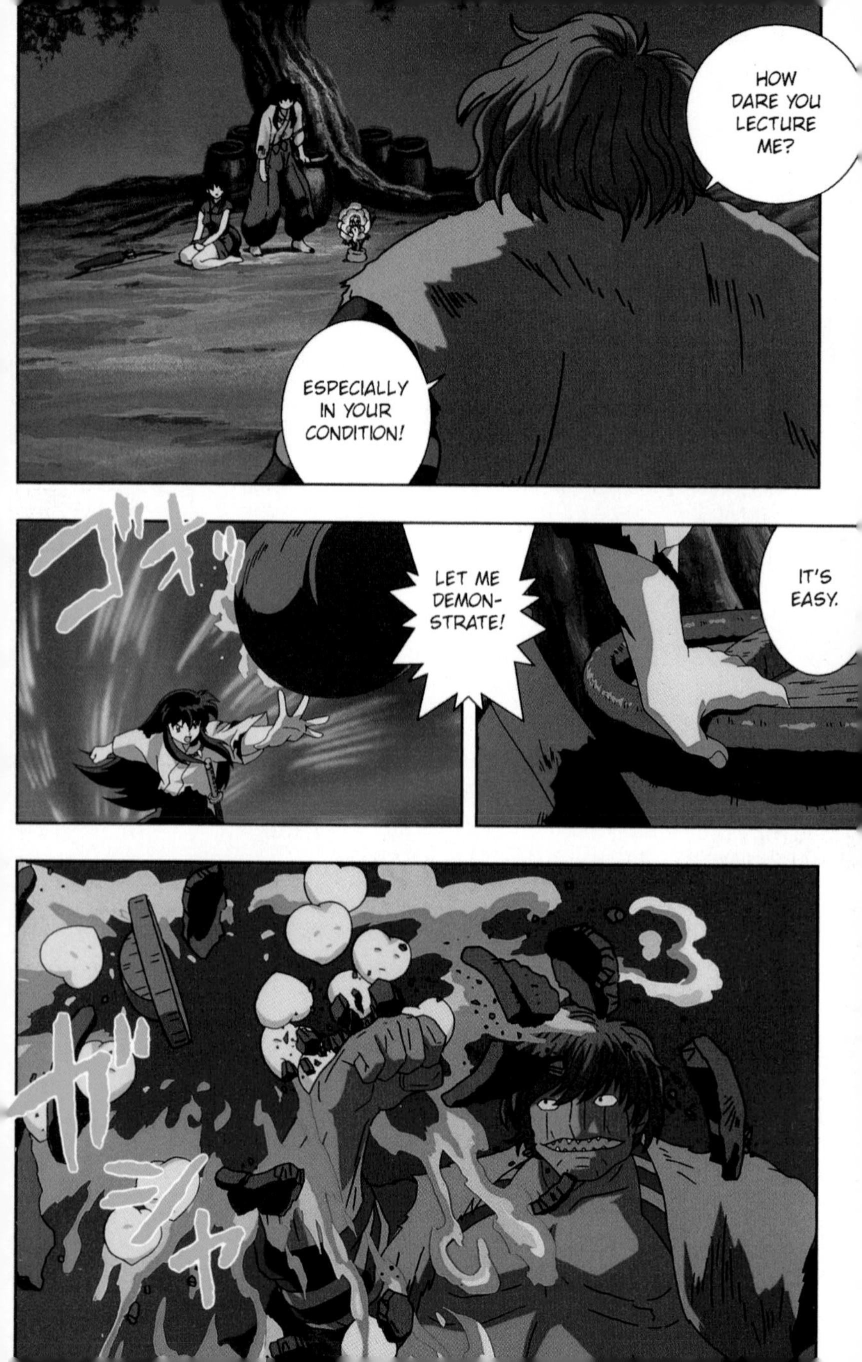
HOW DARE YOU LECTURE ME?
ESPECIALLY IN YOUR CONDITION!
IT'S EASY.
LET ME DEMON-STRATE!
ゴオッ
ガシャ

I'VE GOT TO GET THE JEWEL SHARDS BEFORE THEY MELT INTO HIS BODY!

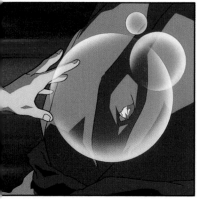

UNGH !!

INU-YASHA !

45

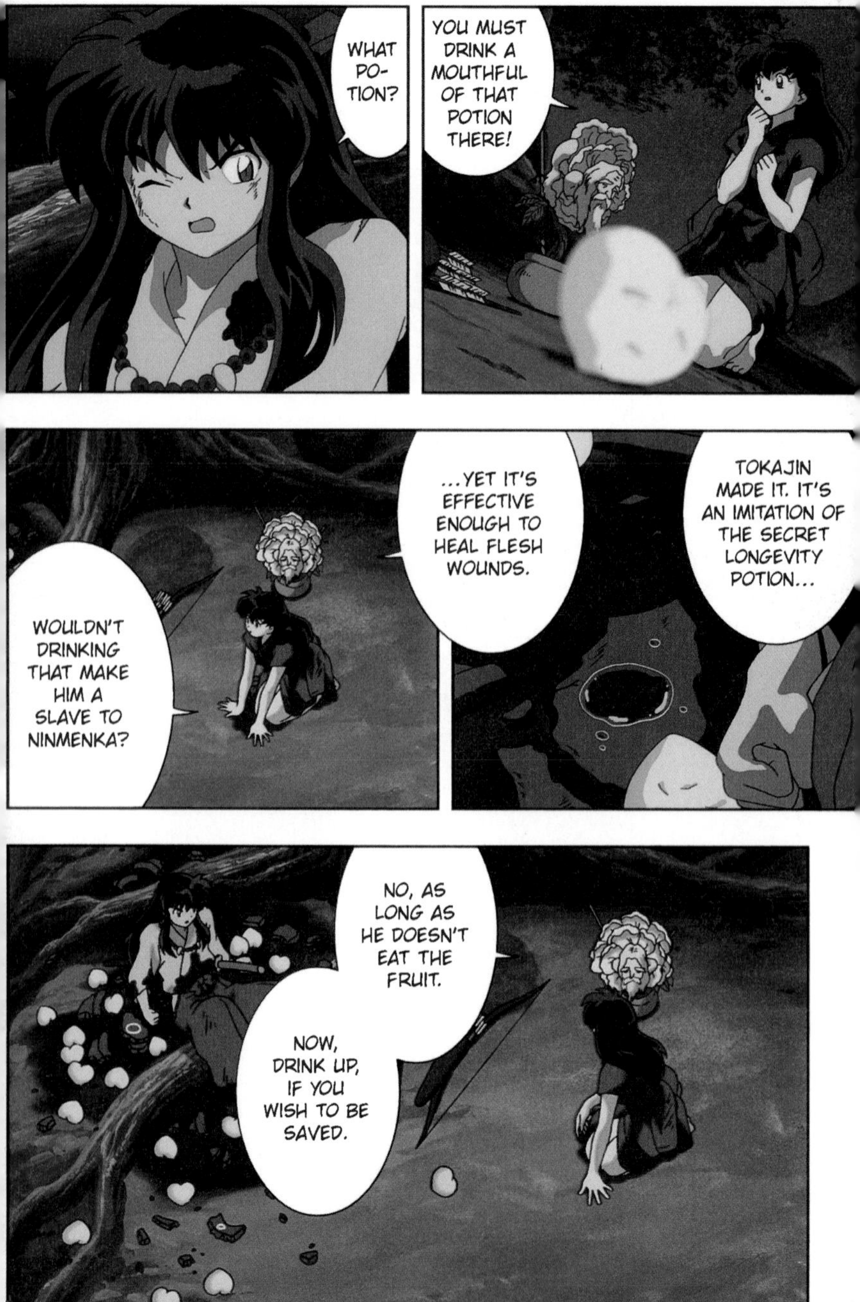
YOU MUST DRINK A MOUTHFUL OF THAT POTION THERE!
WHAT PO-TION?
TOKAJIN MADE IT. IT'S AN IMITATION OF THE SECRET LONGEVITY POTION...
...YET IT'S EFFECTIVE ENOUGH TO HEAL FLESH WOUNDS.
WOULDN'T DRINKING THAT MAKE HIM A SLAVE TO NINMENKA?
NO, AS LONG AS HE DOESN'T EAT THE FRUIT.
NOW, DRINK UP, IF YOU WISH TO BE SAVED.

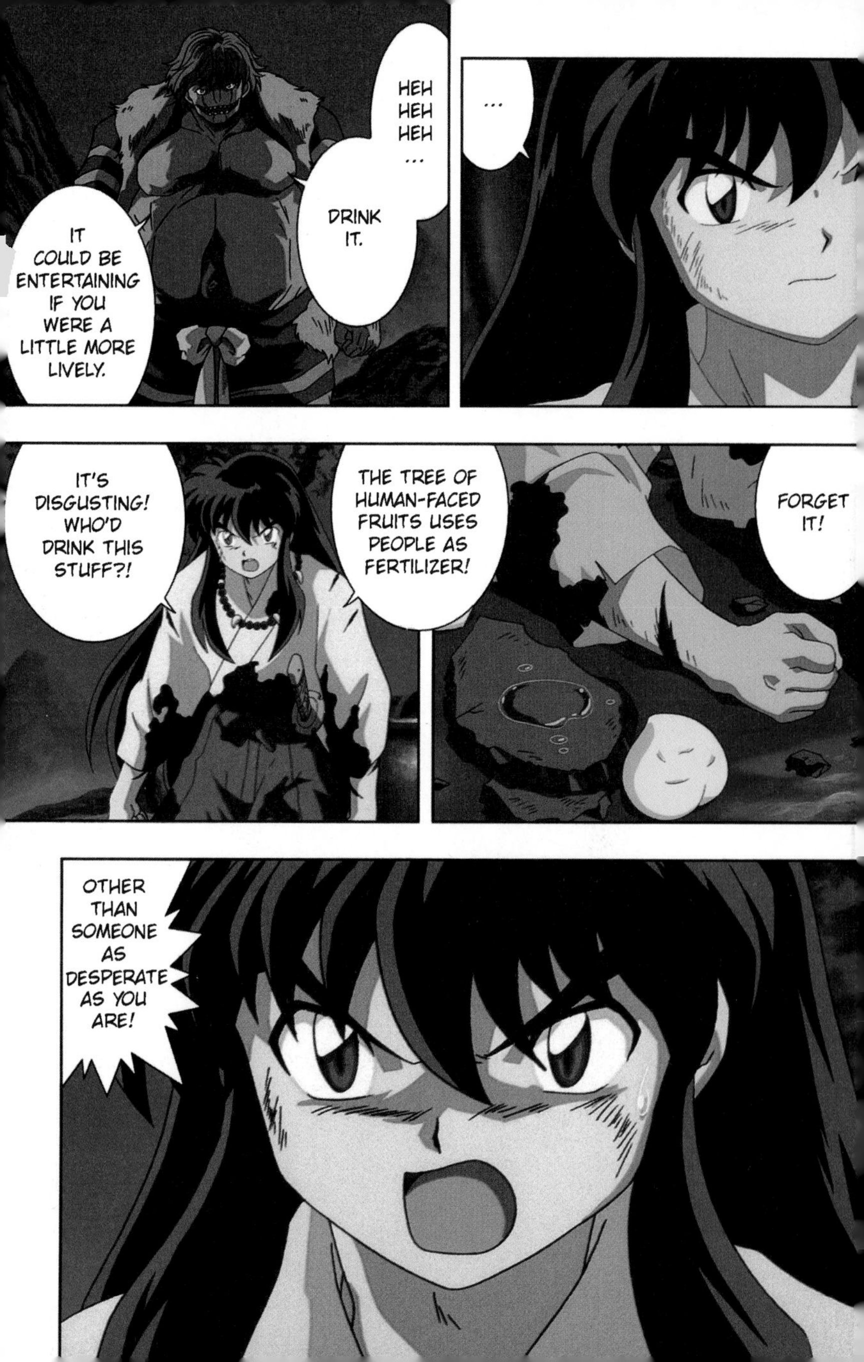
...
HEH HEH HEH ...
DRINK IT.
IT COULD BE ENTERTAINING IF YOU WERE A LITTLE MORE LIVELY.
FORGET IT!
THE TREE OF HUMAN-FACED FRUITS USES PEOPLE AS FERTILIZER!
IT'S DISGUSTING! WHO'D DRINK THIS STUFF?!
OTHER THAN SOMEONE AS DESPERATE AS YOU ARE!

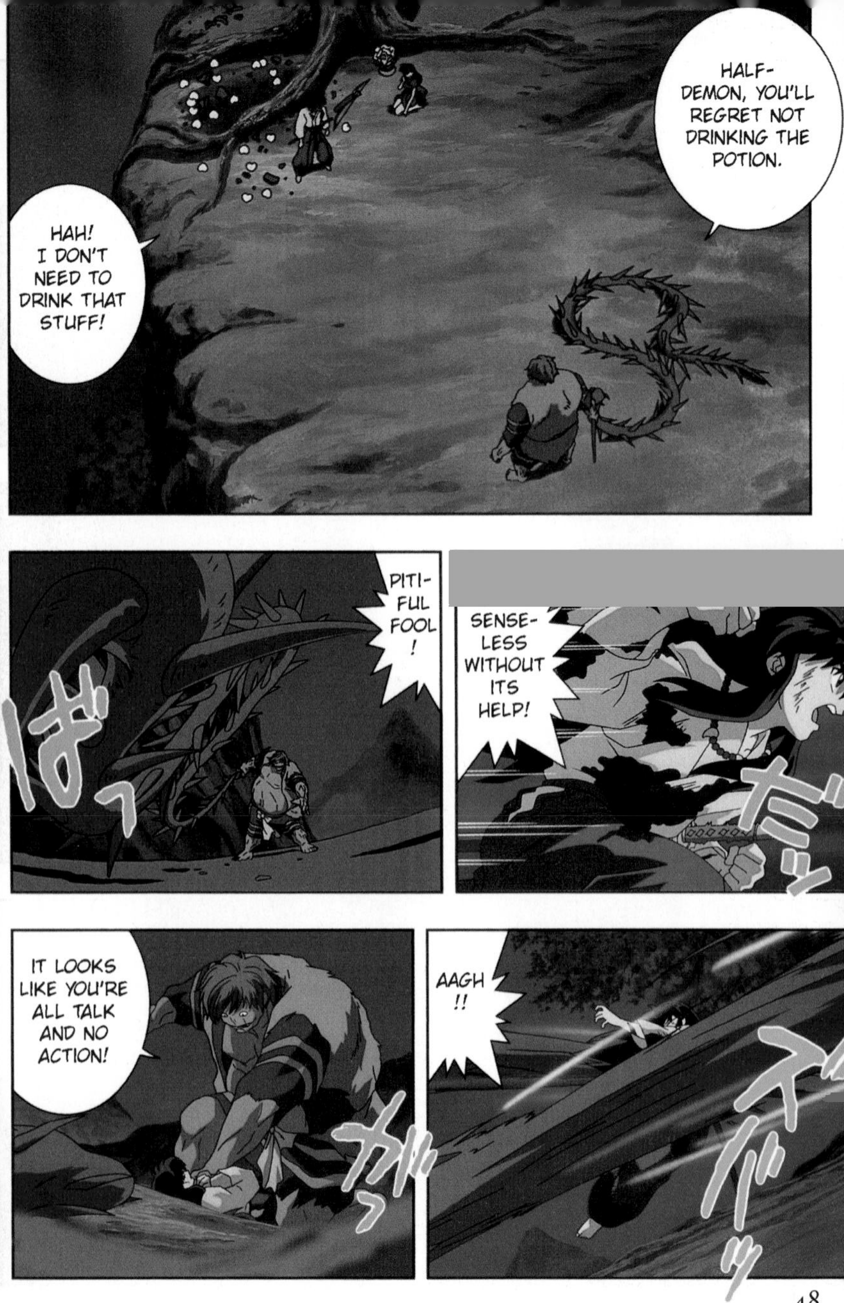
HALF-DEMON, YOU'LL REGRET NOT DRINKING THE POTION.
HAH! I DON'T NEED TO DRINK THAT STUFF!
SENSELESS WITHOUT ITS HELP!
PITIFUL FOOL!
AAGH!!
IT LOOKS LIKE YOU'RE ALL TALK AND NO ACTION!

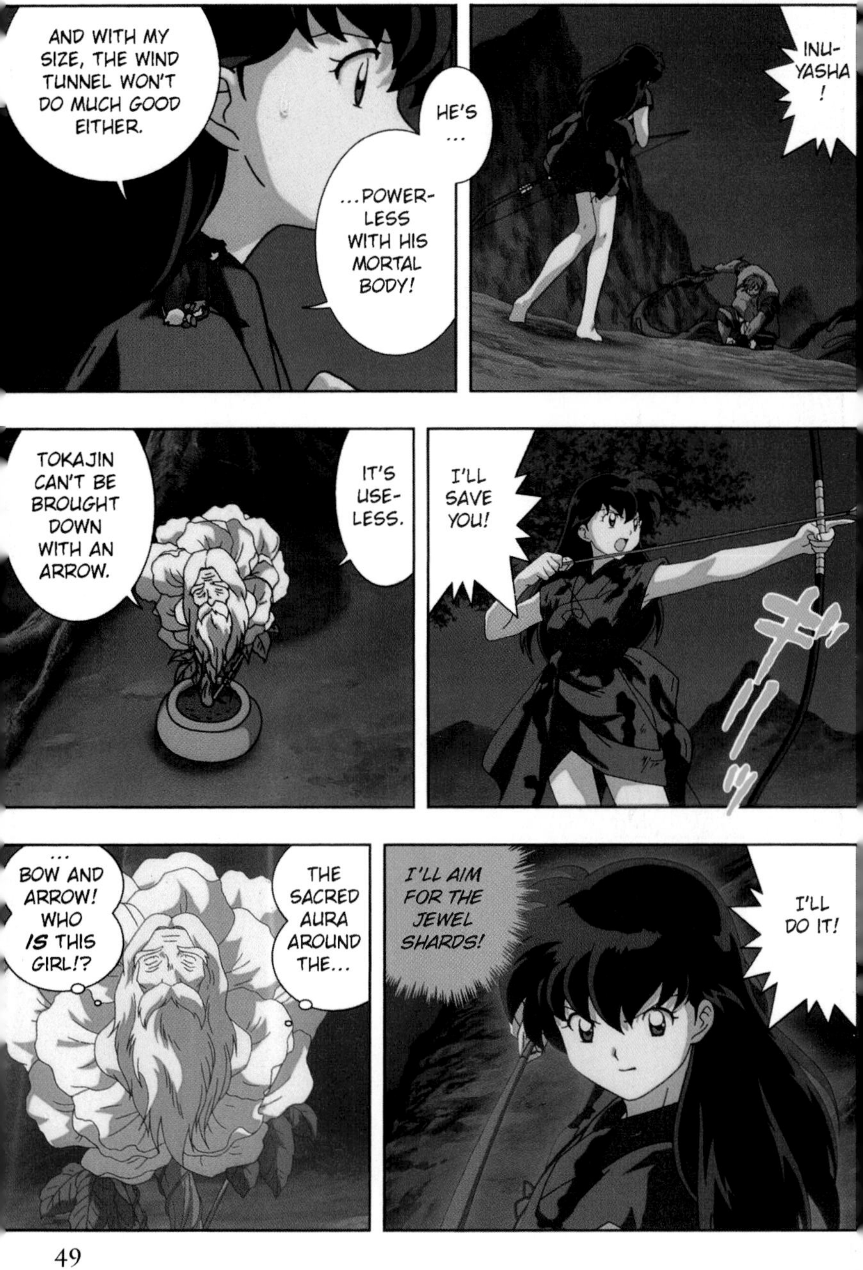
INU-YASHA!
HE'S ...
...POWER-LESS WITH HIS MORTAL BODY!
AND WITH MY SIZE, THE WIND TUNNEL WON'T DO MUCH GOOD EITHER.
I'LL SAVE YOU!
IT'S USE-LESS.
TOKAJIN CAN'T BE BROUGHT DOWN WITH AN ARROW.
I'LL DO IT!
I'LL AIM FOR THE JEWEL SHARDS!
THE SACRED AURA AROUND THE...
... BOW AND ARROW! WHO *IS* THIS GIRL!?

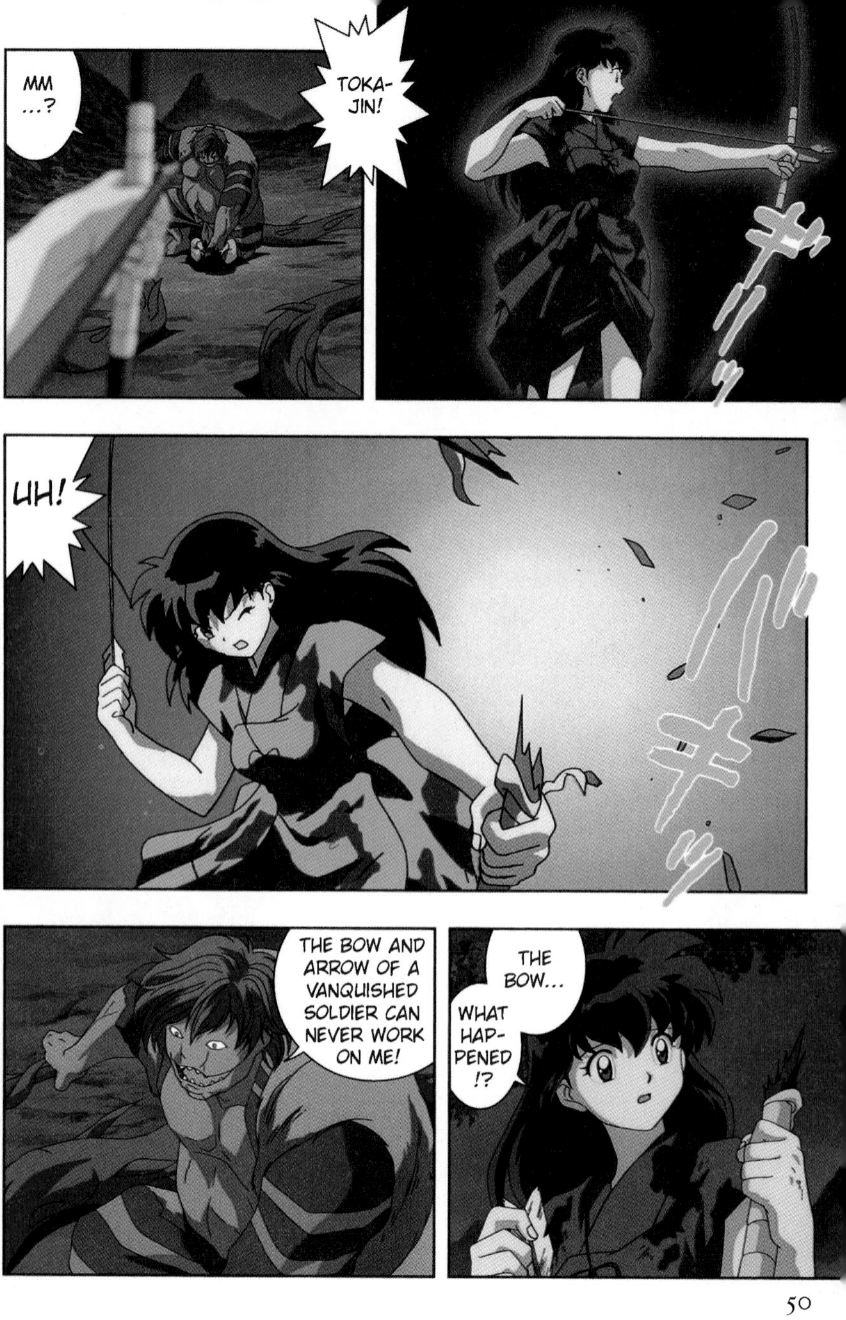
TOKA-JIN!
ギリッ
MM ...?
UH!
バキッ
THE BOW...
WHAT HAP-PENED !?
THE BOW AND ARROW OF A VANQUISHED SOLDIER CAN NEVER WORK ON ME!

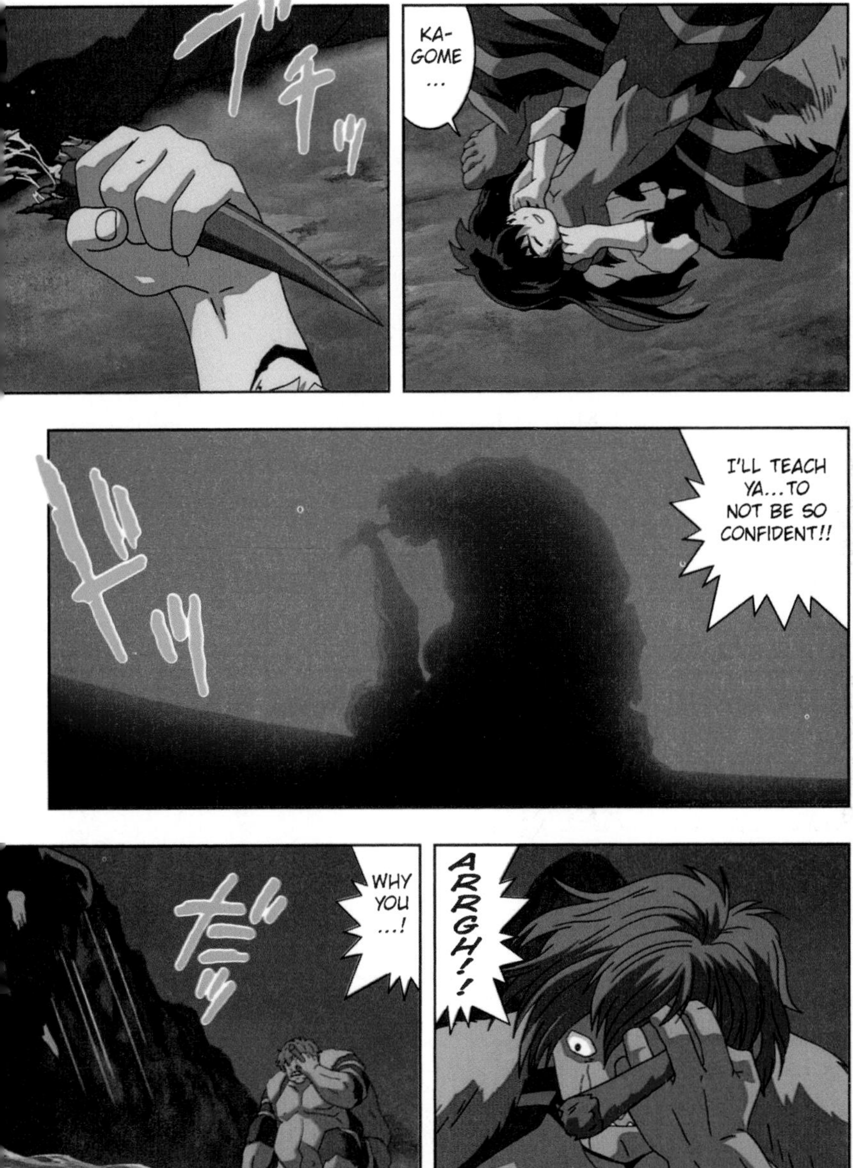

KA-
GOME
...
ブチッ
I'LL TEACH YA...TO NOT BE SO CONFIDENT!!
ARRGH!!
WHY YOU ...!

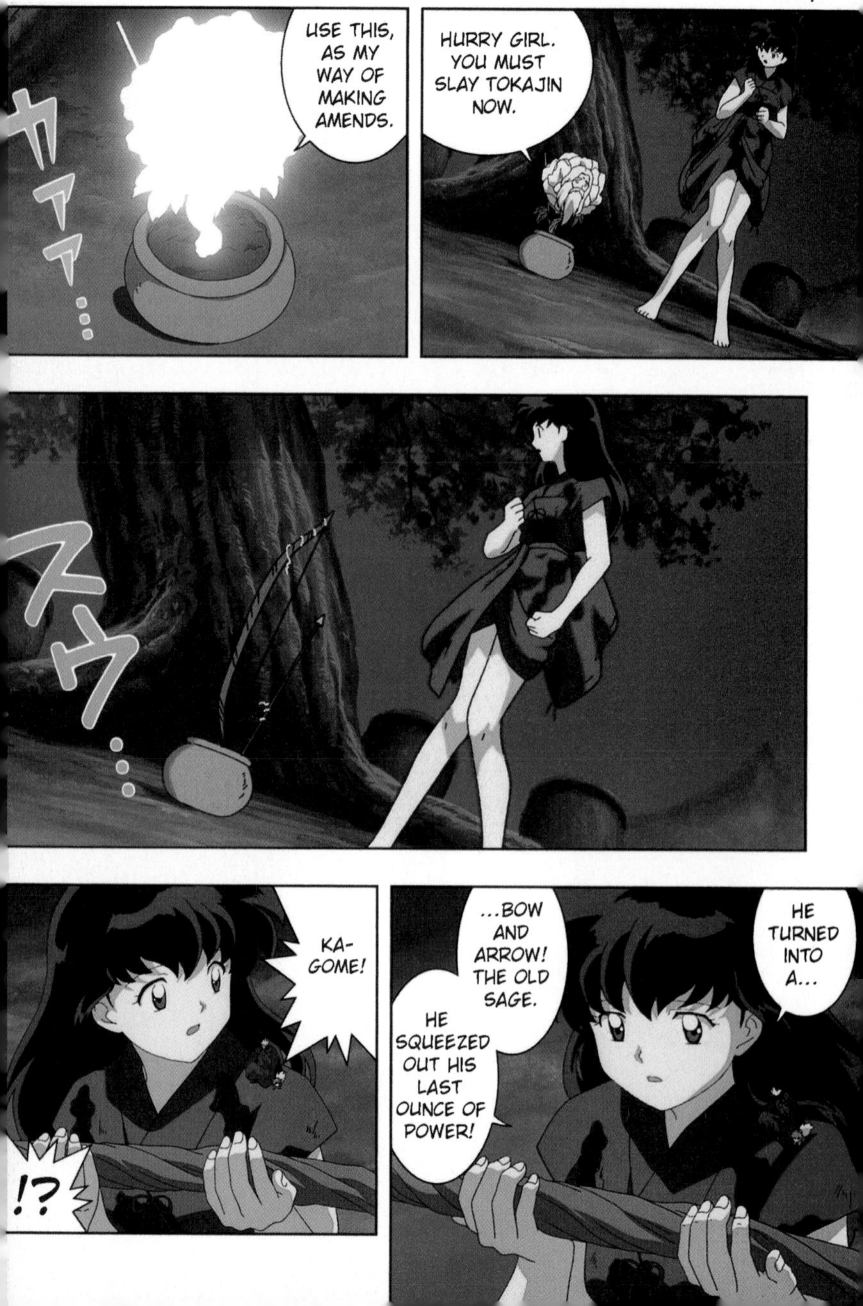
HURRY GIRL. YOU MUST SLAY TOKAJIN NOW.
USE THIS, AS MY WAY OF MAKING AMENDS.
ヤァァ…
スゥ…
HE TURNED INTO A...
...BOW AND ARROW! THE OLD SAGE.
HE SQUEEZED OUT HIS LAST OUNCE OF POWER!
KA-GOME!
!?

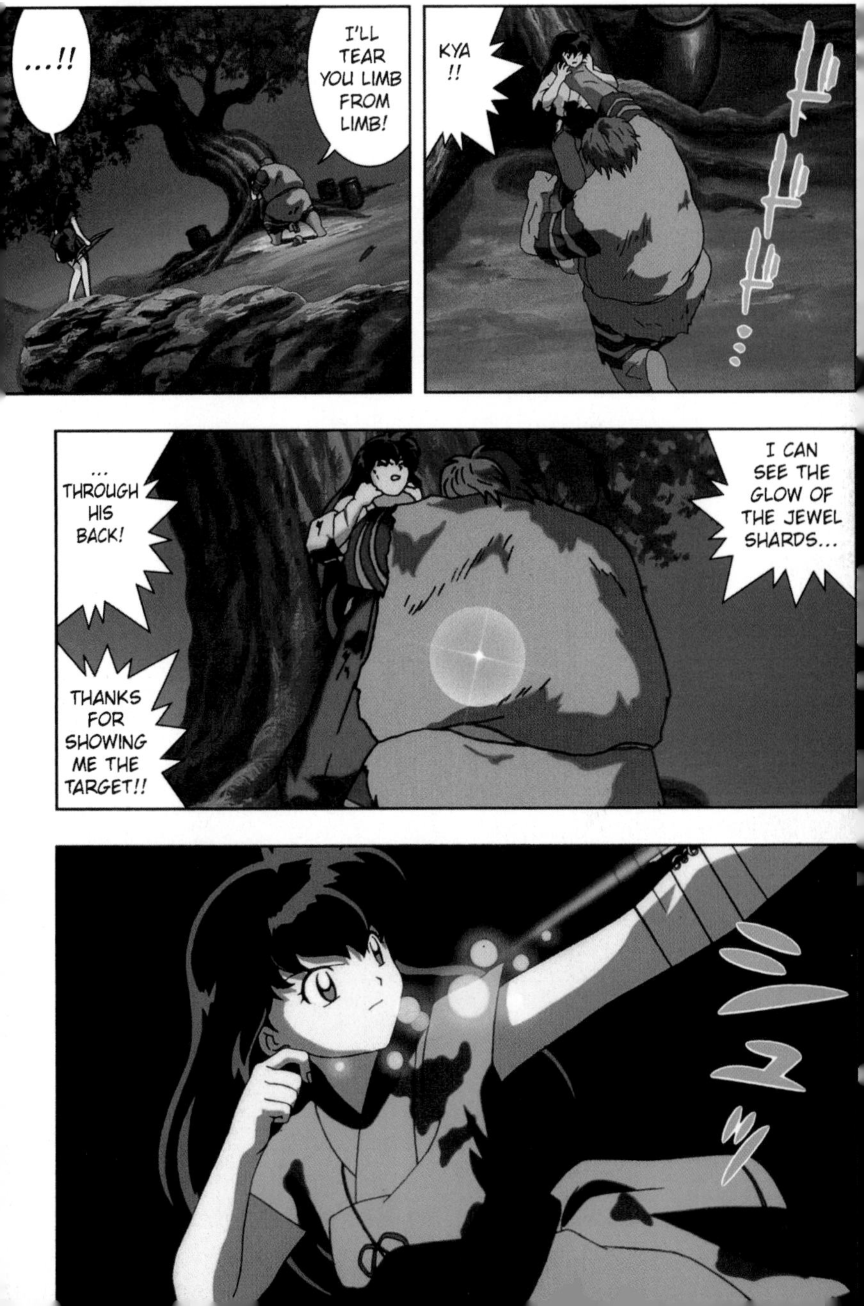
KYA !!
I'LL TEAR YOU LIMB FROM LIMB!
...!!
I CAN SEE THE GLOW OF THE JEWEL SHARDS...
... THROUGH HIS BACK!
THANKS FOR SHOWING ME THE TARGET!!

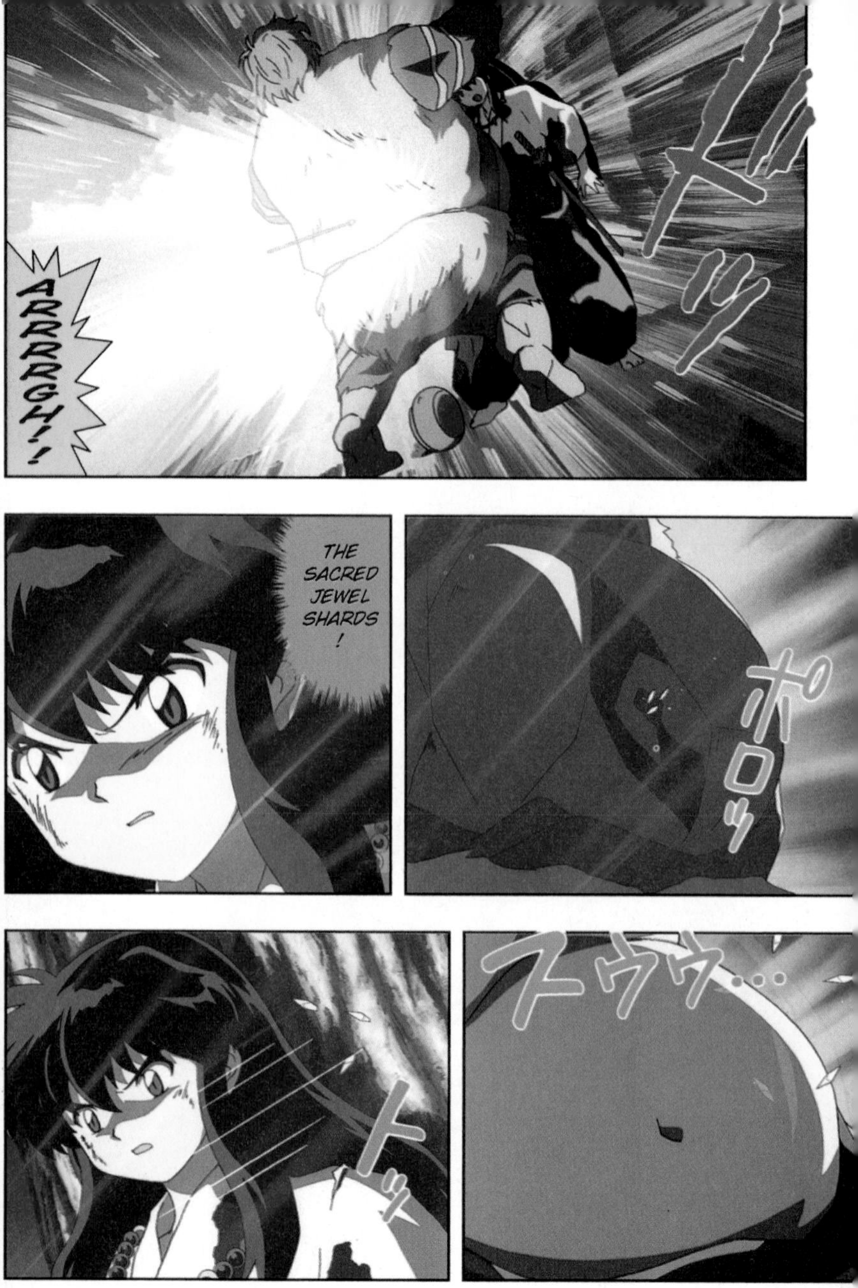
ARRRRGH!!
ポロッ
THE SACRED JEWEL SHARDS!
スゥゥ…
トッ

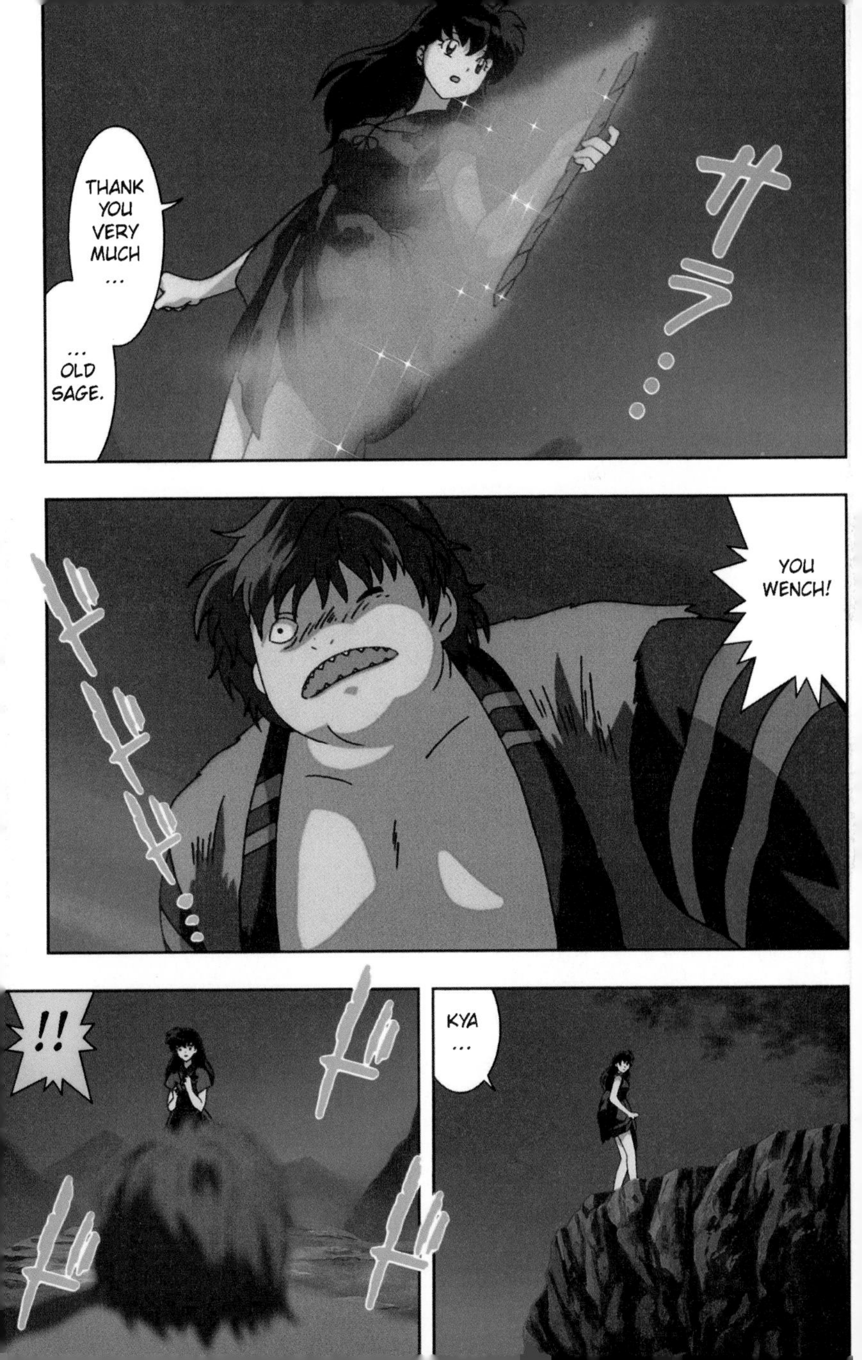
サラ…
THANK YOU VERY MUCH ...
... OLD SAGE.
YOU WENCH!
KYA ...
!!

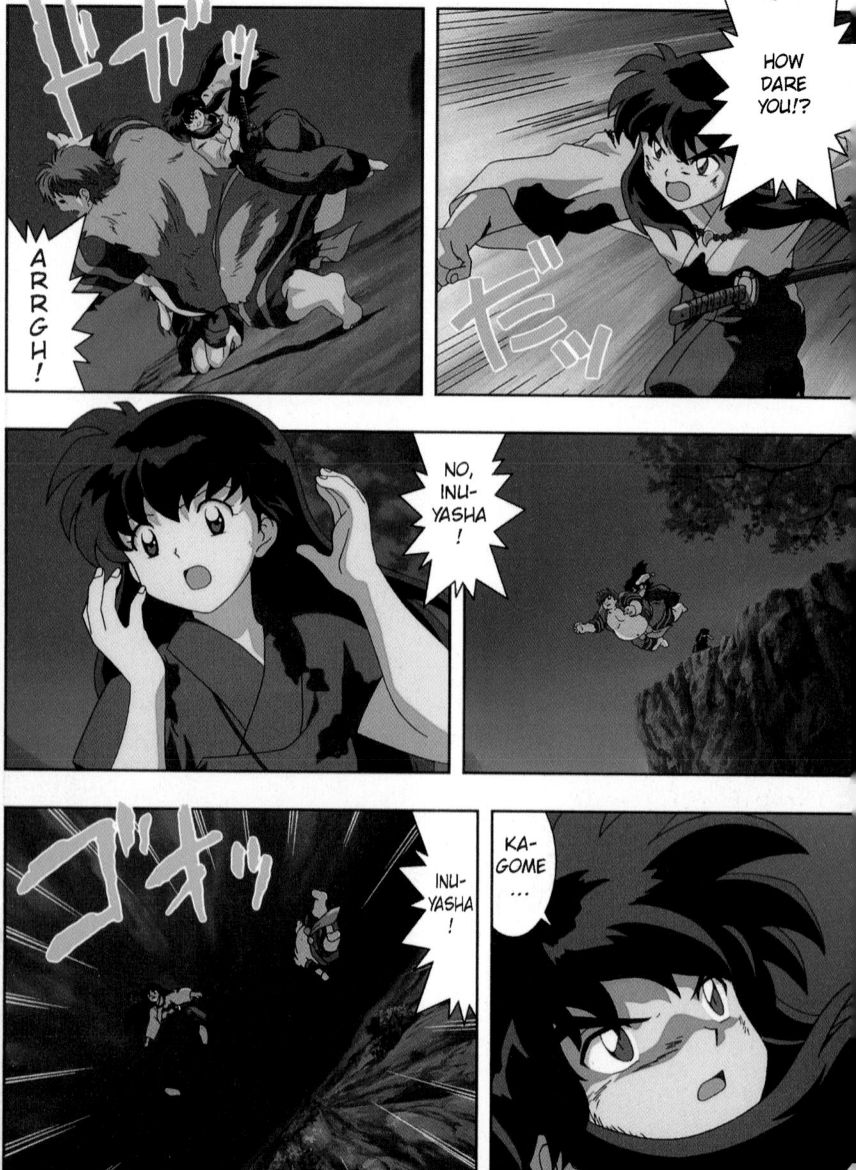
HOW DARE YOU!?
ARRGH!
ドガッ
NO, INU-YASHA!
KA-GOME...
INU-YASHA!
ゴオッ

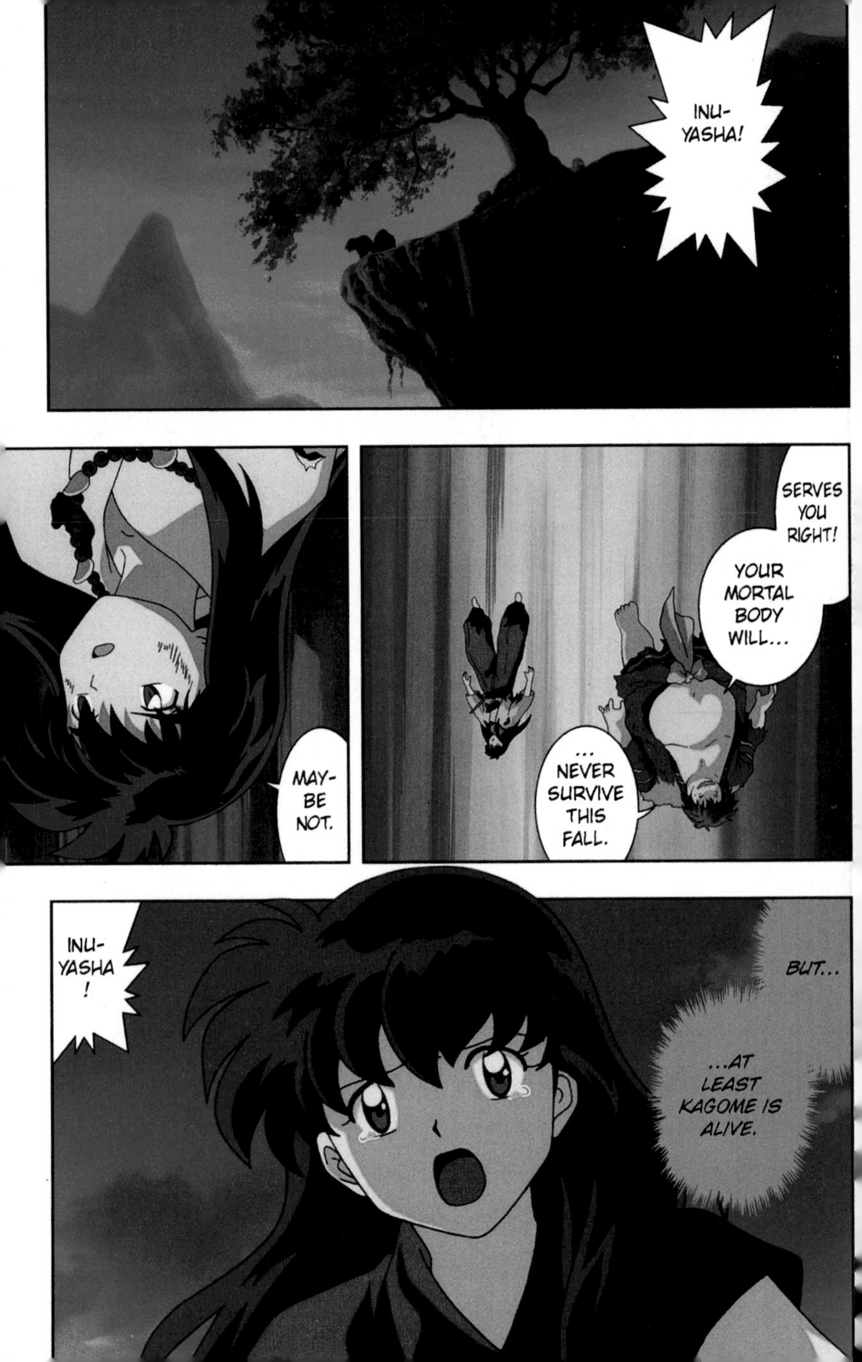
INU-YASHA!
SERVES YOU RIGHT!
YOUR MORTAL BODY WILL...
...NEVER SURVIVE THIS FALL.
MAY-BE NOT.
BUT...
...AT LEAST KAGOME IS ALIVE.
INU-YASHA!

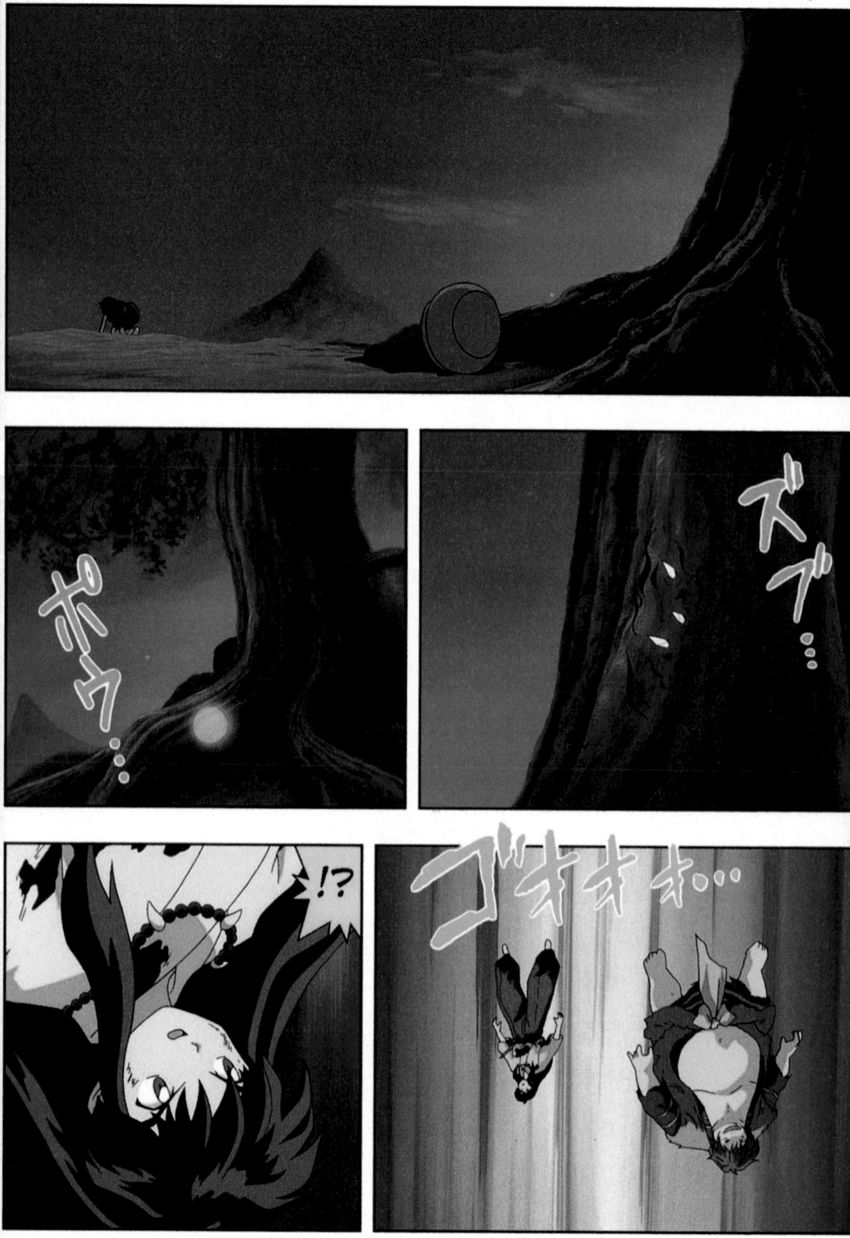
ズブ…
ポウ…
ゴオオオ…
!?

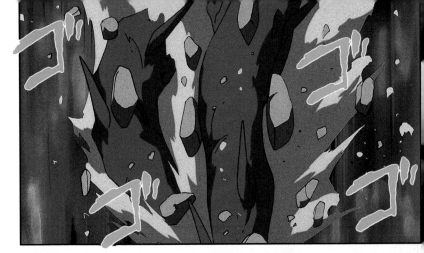

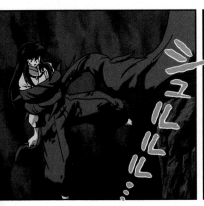

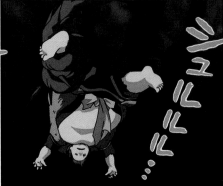

ゴゴゴゴ
シュルルル…
シュルルル…
NIN-MENKA!
YOU'RE RESCUING ME!
NO SUCH THING. I SIMPLY DON'T WANT TO LOSE PRECIOUS NOURISHMENT!

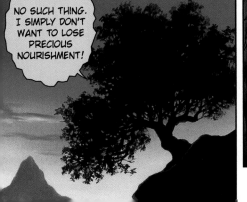

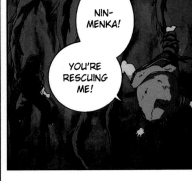

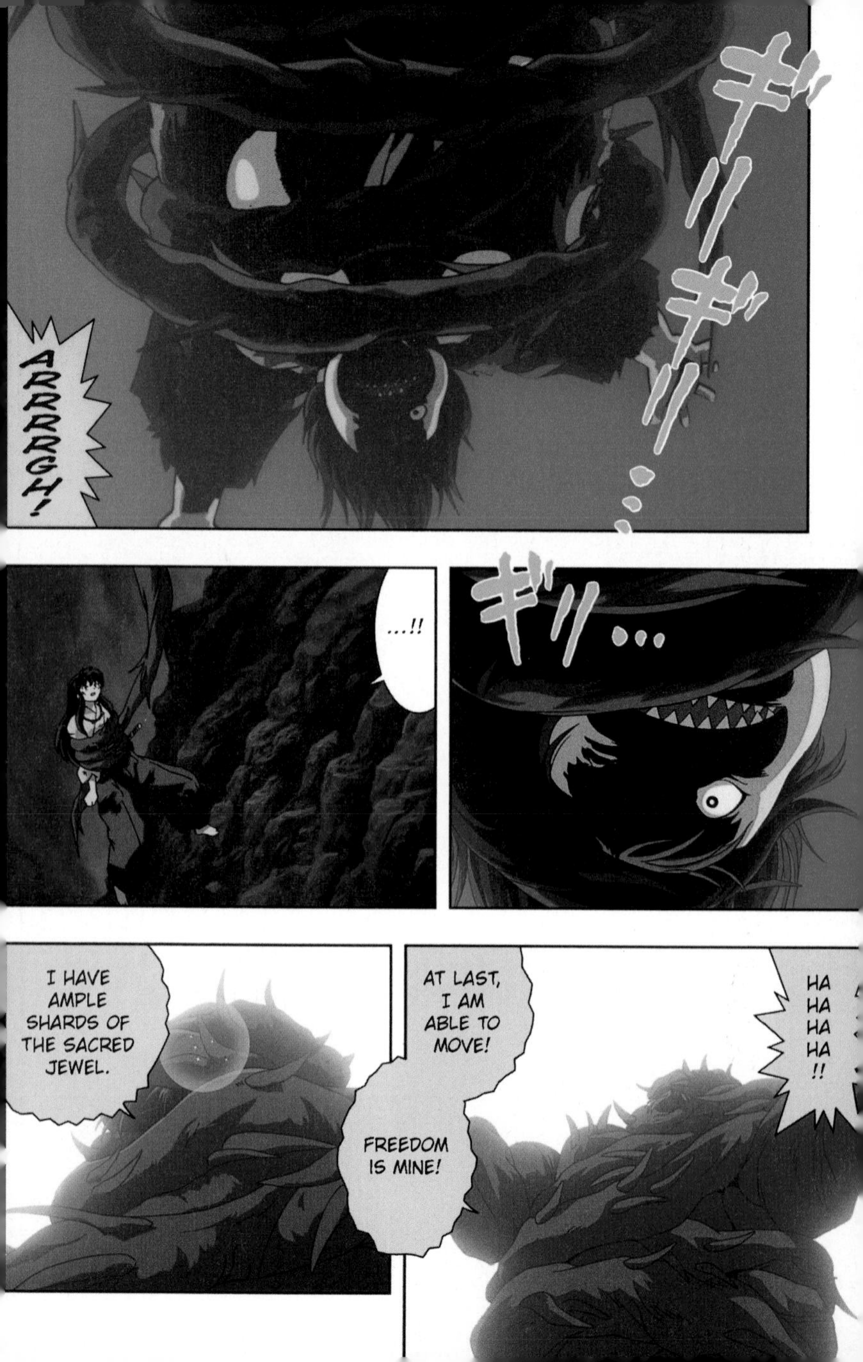
ギリギリ…
ARRRRGH!
ギリ…
...!!
HA HA HA HA!!
AT LAST, I AM ABLE TO MOVE!
FREEDOM IS MINE!
I HAVE AMPLE SHARDS OF THE SACRED JEWEL.

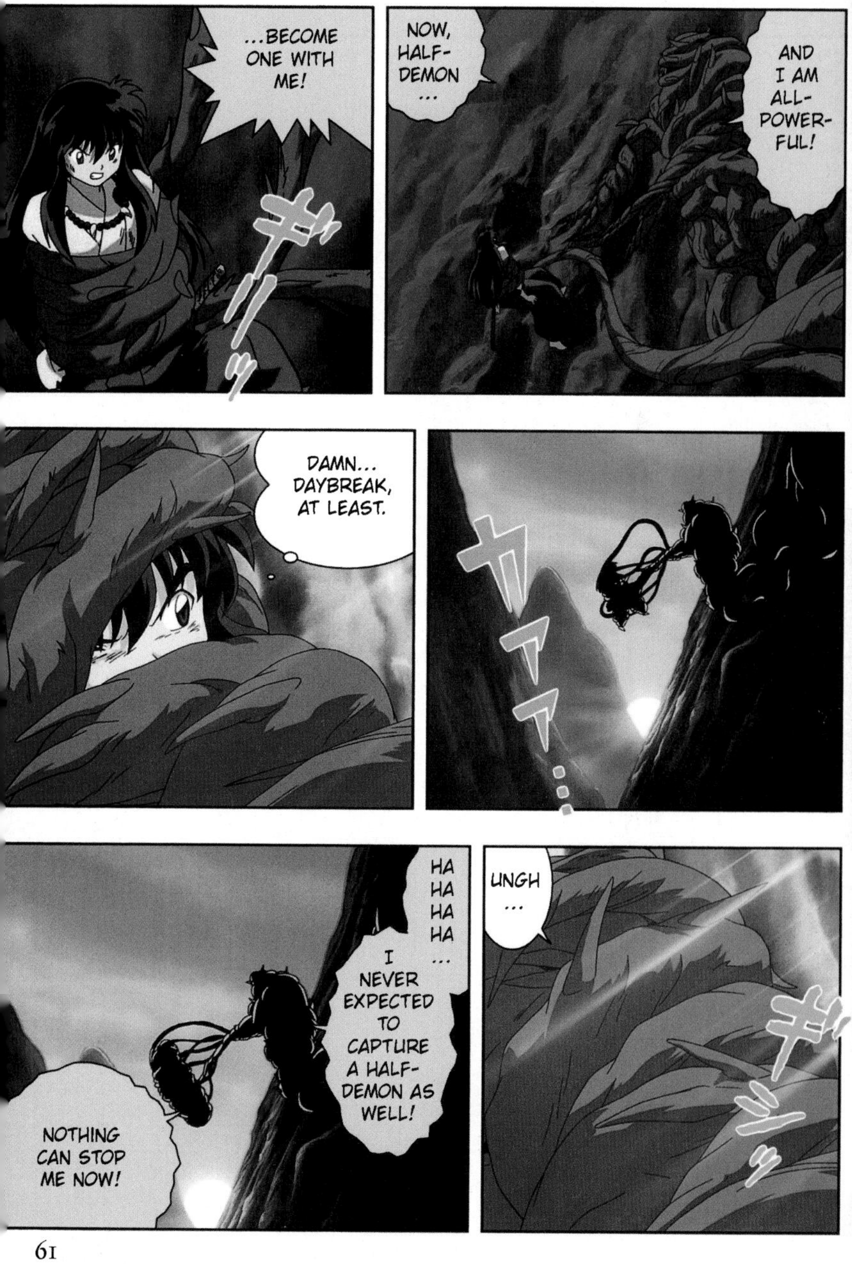
AND I AM ALL-POWERFUL!
NOW, HALF-DEMON...
...BECOME ONE WITH ME!
ギリッ
カァァ…
DAMN... DAYBREAK, AT LEAST.
ギシッ
UNGH...
HA HA HA HA...
I NEVER EXPECTED TO CAPTURE A HALF-DEMON AS WELL!
NOTHING CAN STOP ME NOW!

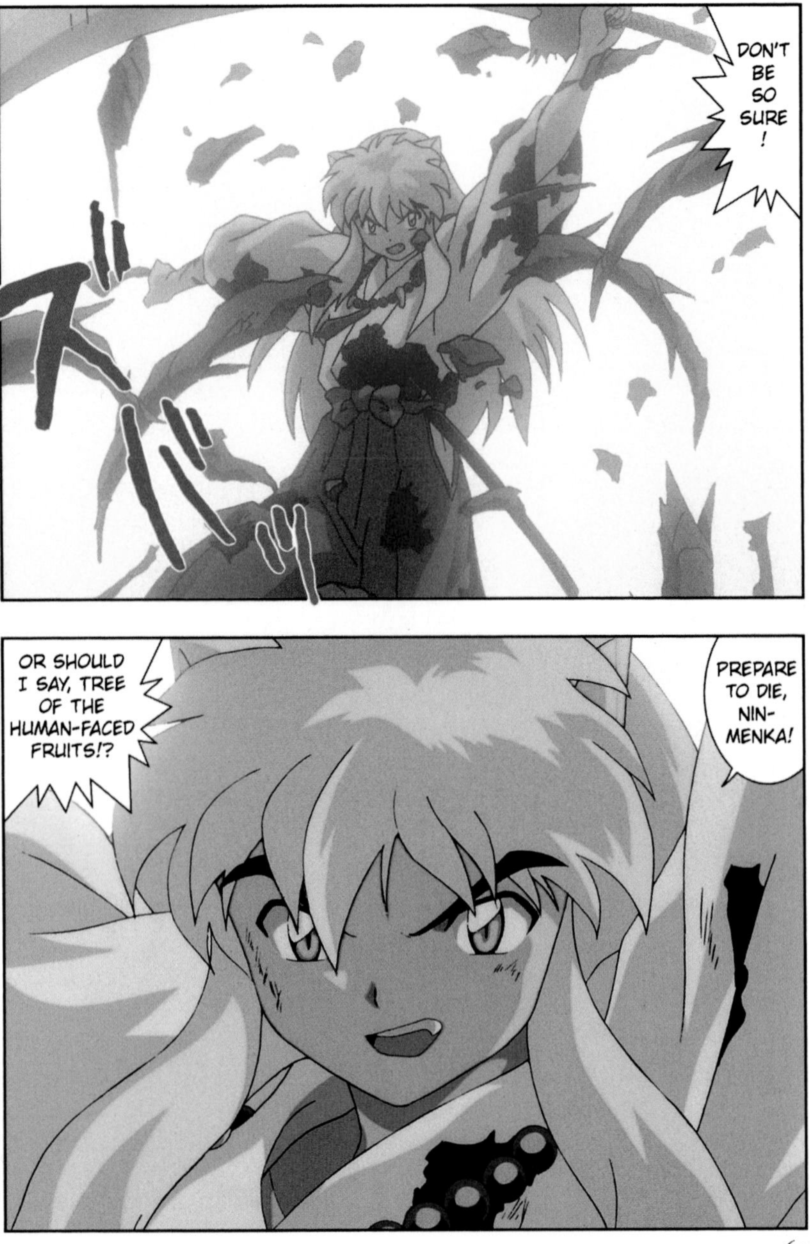
DON'T BE SO SURE!
ズバッ
PREPARE TO DIE, NIN-MENKA!
OR SHOULD I SAY, TREE OF THE HUMAN-FACED FRUITS!?

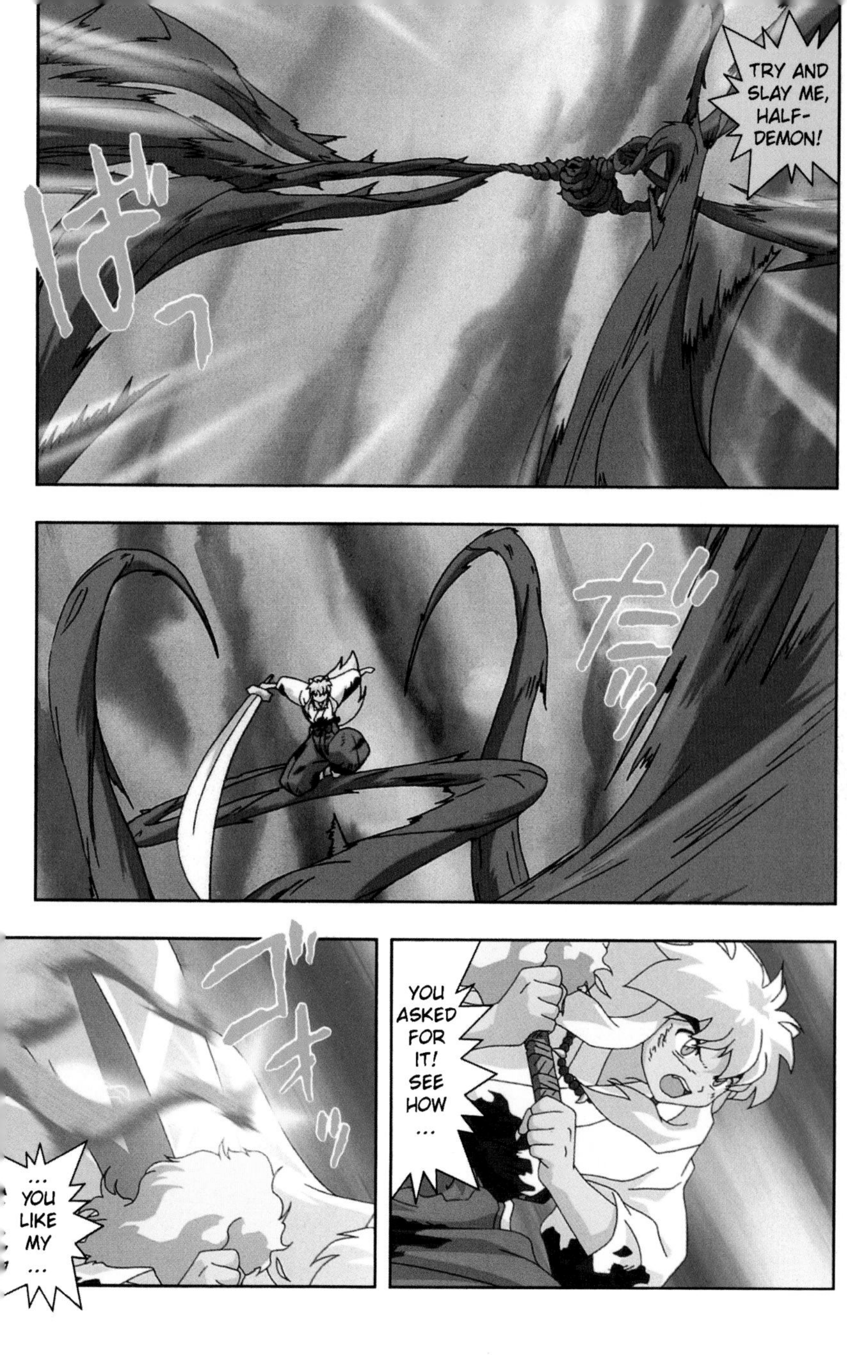
TRY AND SLAY ME, HALF-DEMON!
ばっ
だッ
YOU ASKED FOR IT! SEE HOW ...
ゴォッ
... YOU LIKE MY ...

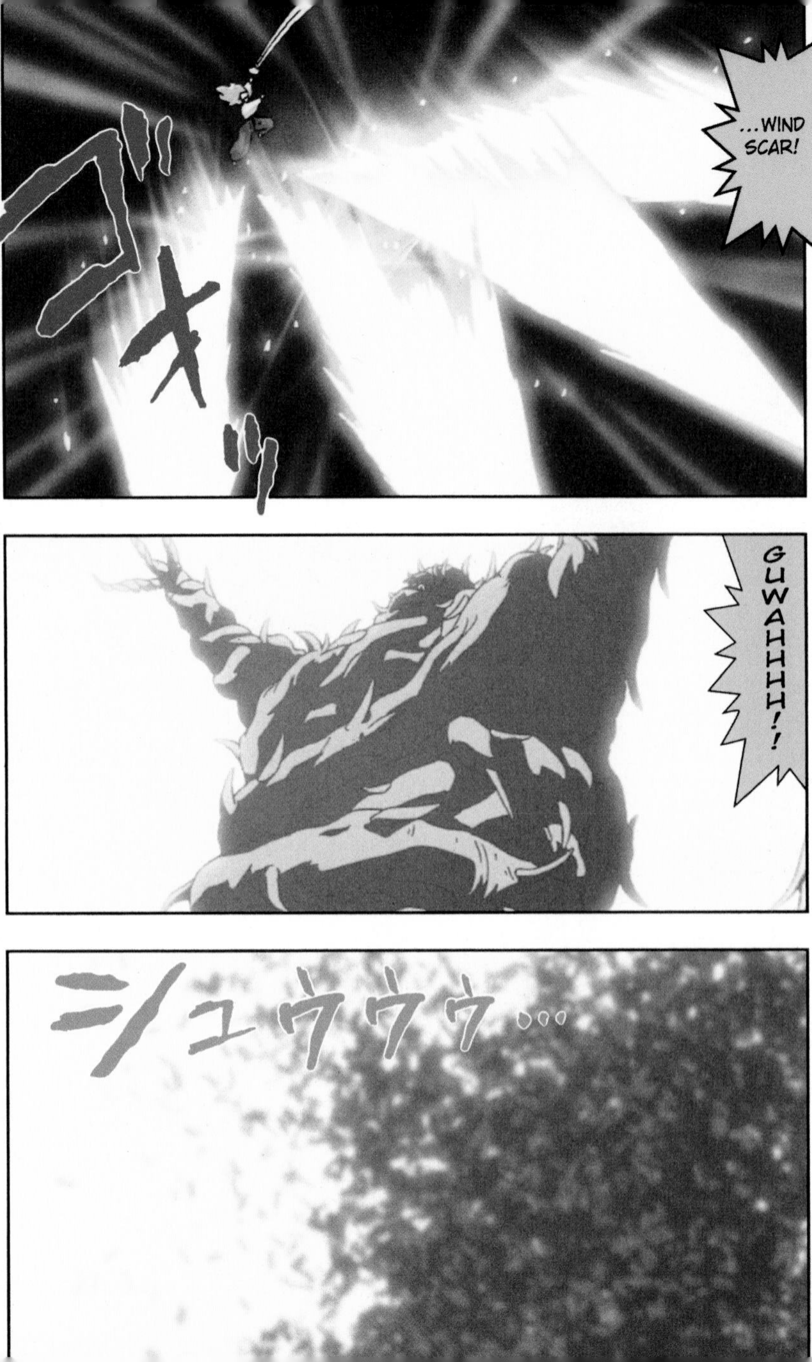
...WIND SCAR!
ゴオッ
GUWAHHHH!!
シュウウウ...

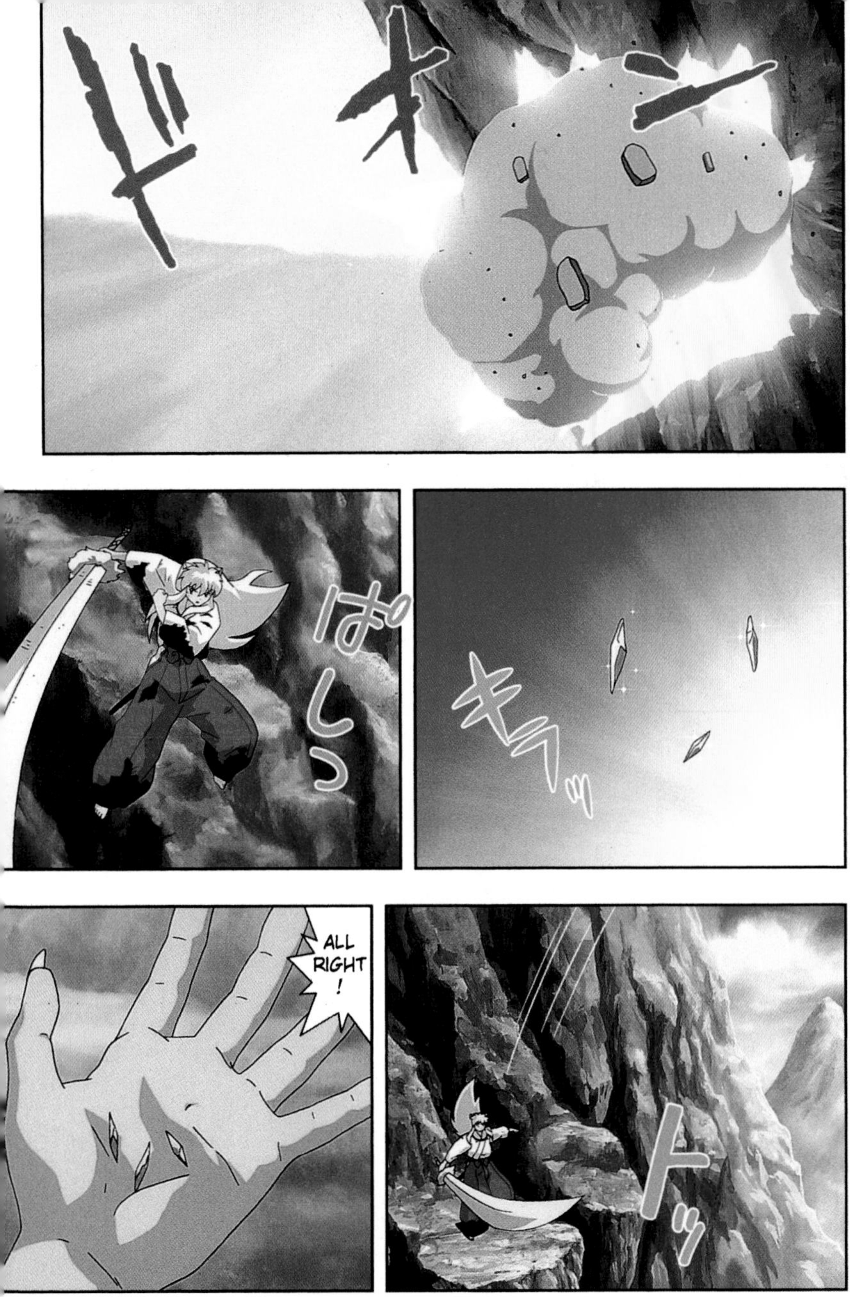
ドオー
キラッ
ぱしっ
トッ
ALL RIGHT!

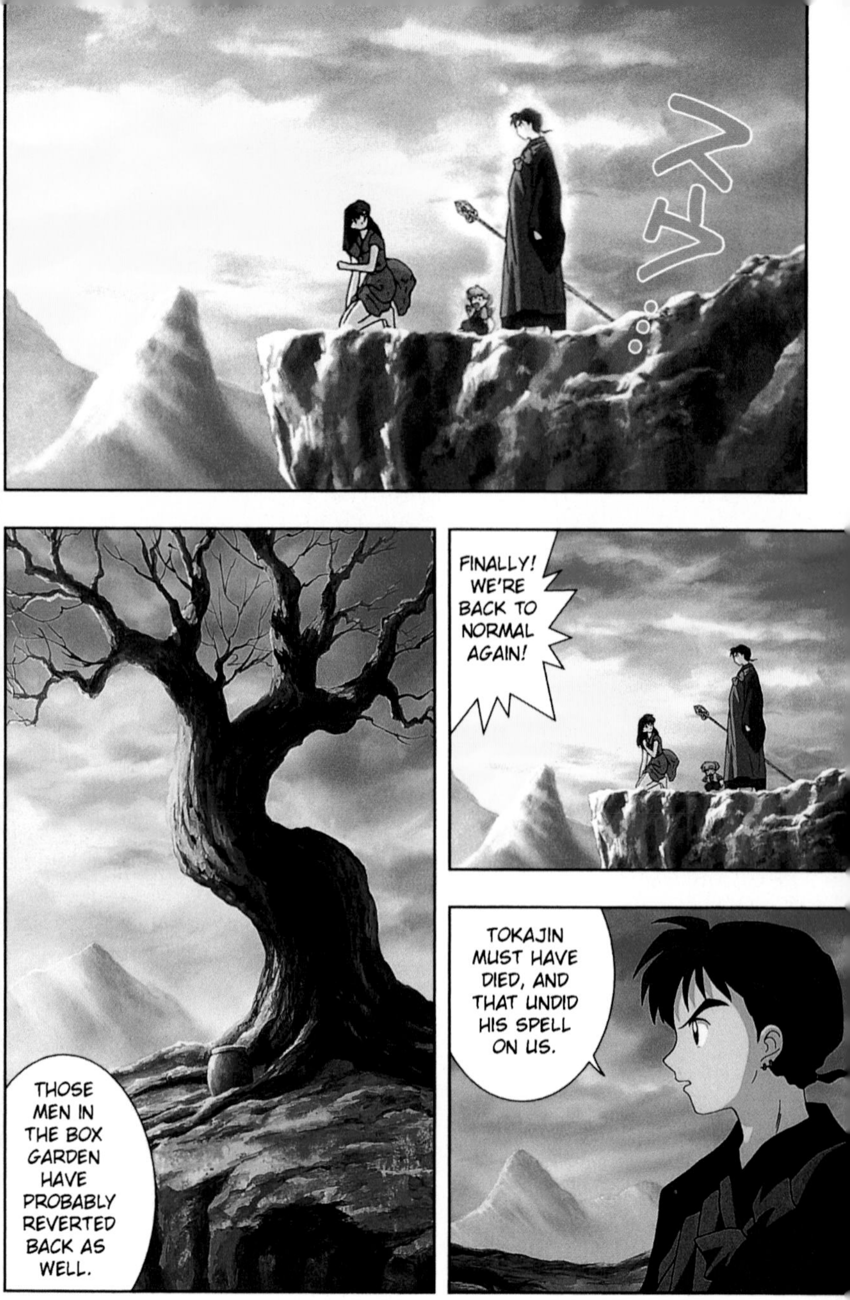
FINALLY! WE'RE BACK TO NORMAL AGAIN!
TOKAJIN MUST HAVE DIED, AND THAT UNDID HIS SPELL ON US.
THOSE MEN IN THE BOX GARDEN HAVE PROBABLY REVERTED BACK AS WELL.

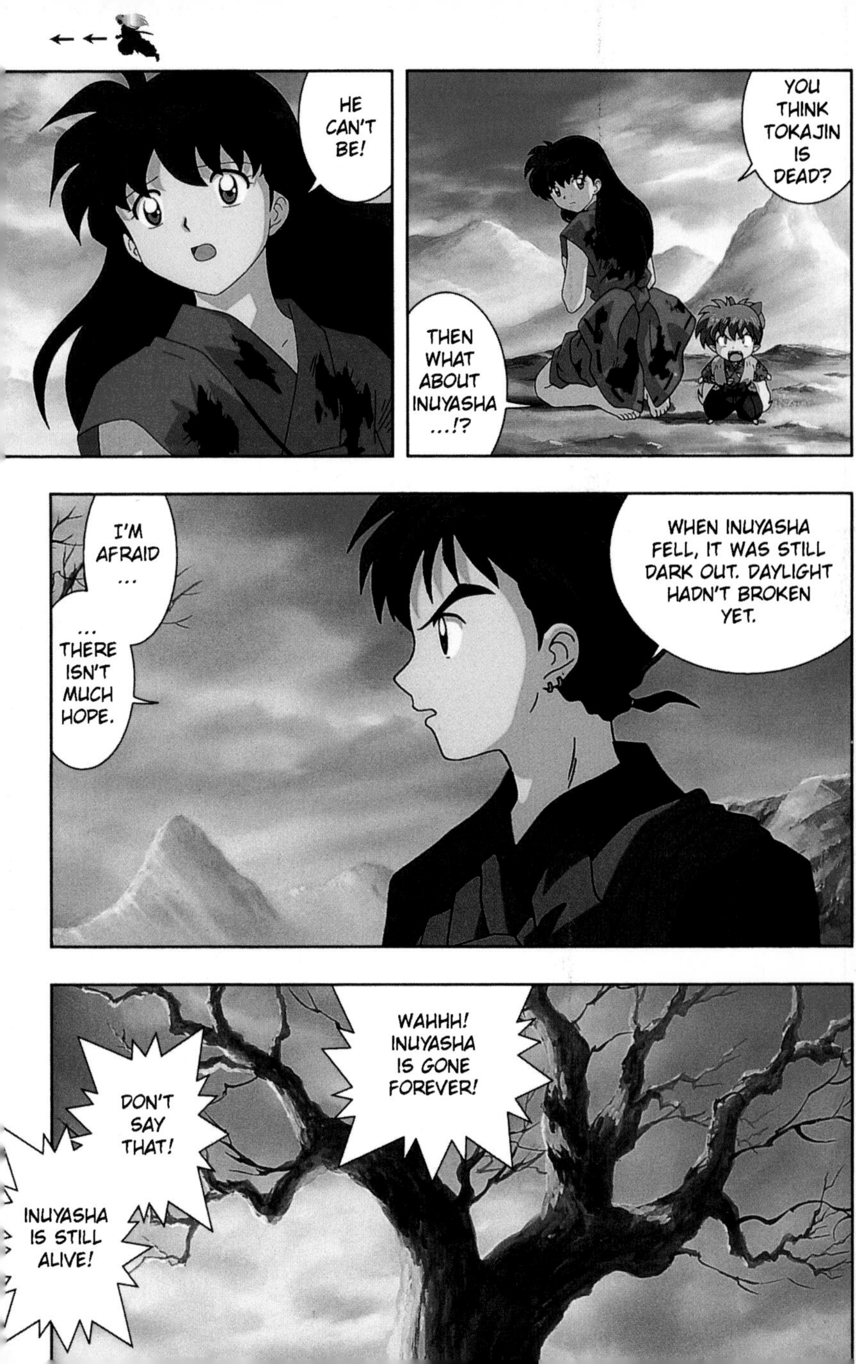
YOU THINK TOKAJIN IS DEAD?
THEN WHAT ABOUT INUYASHA ...!?
HE CAN'T BE!
WHEN INUYASHA FELL, IT WAS STILL DARK OUT. DAYLIGHT HADN'T BROKEN YET.
I'M AFRAID ...
... THERE ISN'T MUCH HOPE.
WAHHH! INUYASHA IS GONE FOREVER!
DON'T SAY THAT!
INUYASHA IS STILL ALIVE!

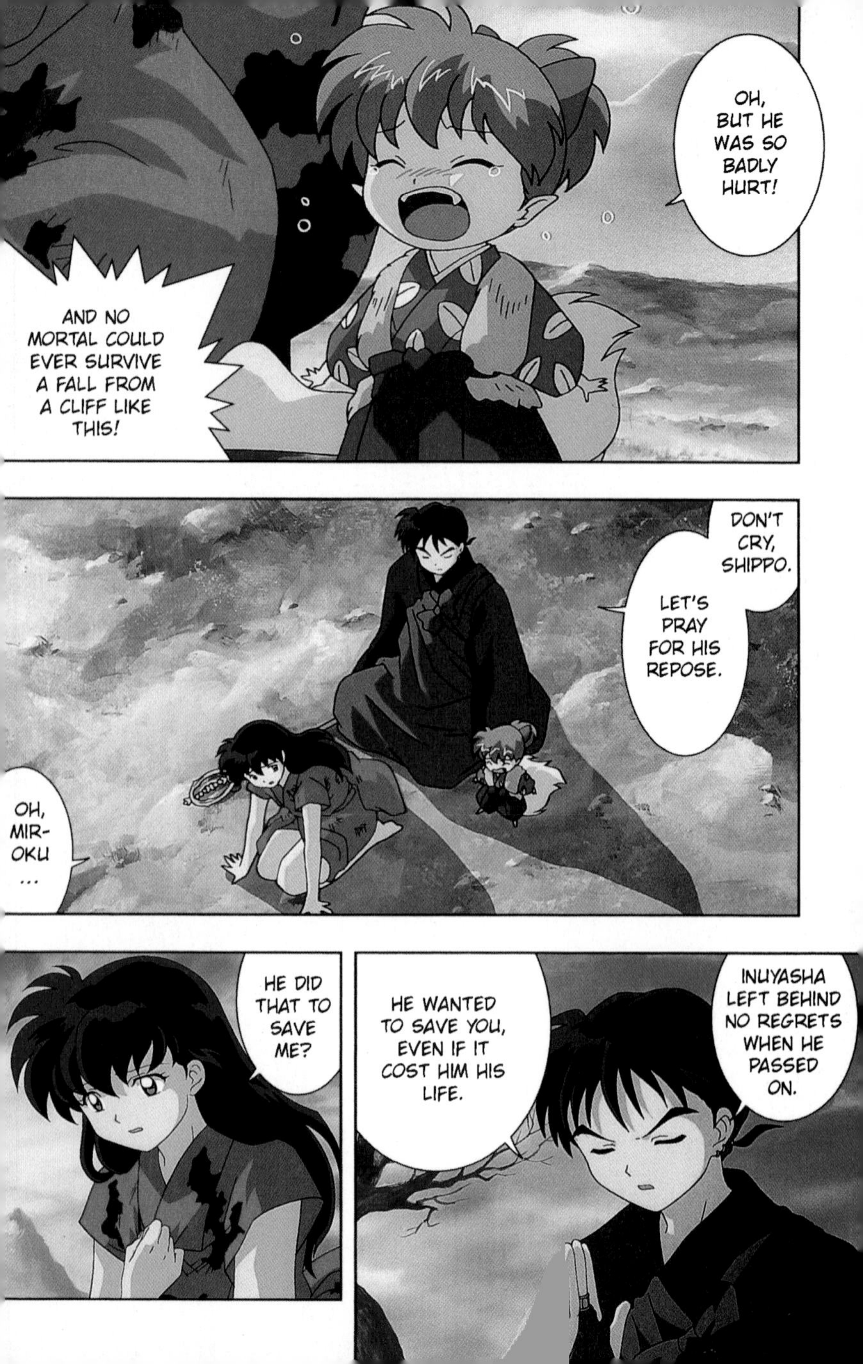
OH, BUT HE WAS SO BADLY HURT!
AND NO MORTAL COULD EVER SURVIVE A FALL FROM A CLIFF LIKE THIS!
DON'T CRY, SHIPPO.
LET'S PRAY FOR HIS REPOSE.
OH, MIR-OKU ...
INUYASHA LEFT BEHIND NO REGRETS WHEN HE PASSED ON.
HE WANTED TO SAVE YOU, EVEN IF IT COST HIM HIS LIFE.
HE DID THAT TO SAVE ME?

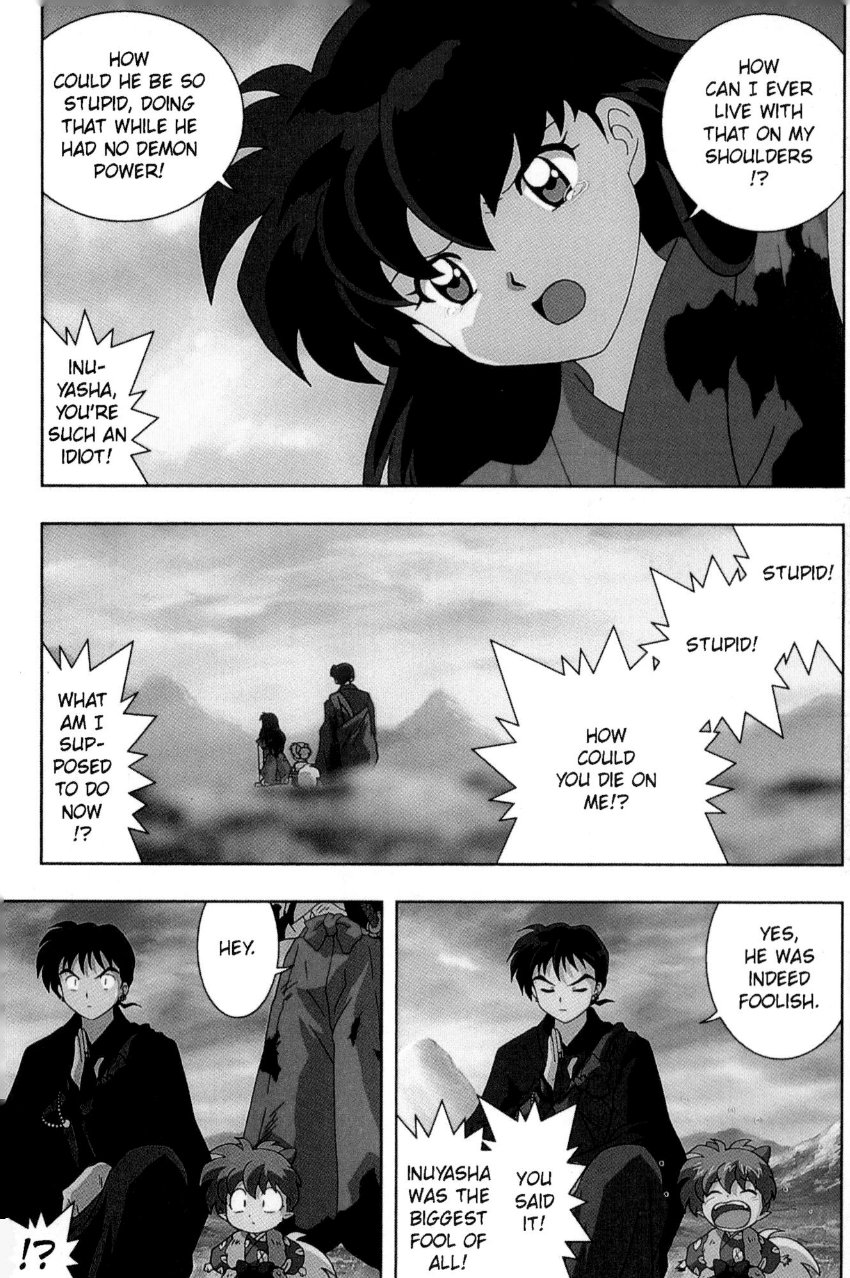
HOW CAN I EVER LIVE WITH THAT ON MY SHOULDERS!?
HOW COULD HE BE SO STUPID, DOING THAT WHILE HE HAD NO DEMON POWER!
INU-YASHA, YOU'RE SUCH AN IDIOT!
STUPID!
STUPID!
HOW COULD YOU DIE ON ME!?
WHAT AM I SUP-POSED TO DO NOW!?
YES, HE WAS INDEED FOOLISH.
YOU SAID IT!
INUYASHA WAS THE BIGGEST FOOL OF ALL!
HEY.
!?

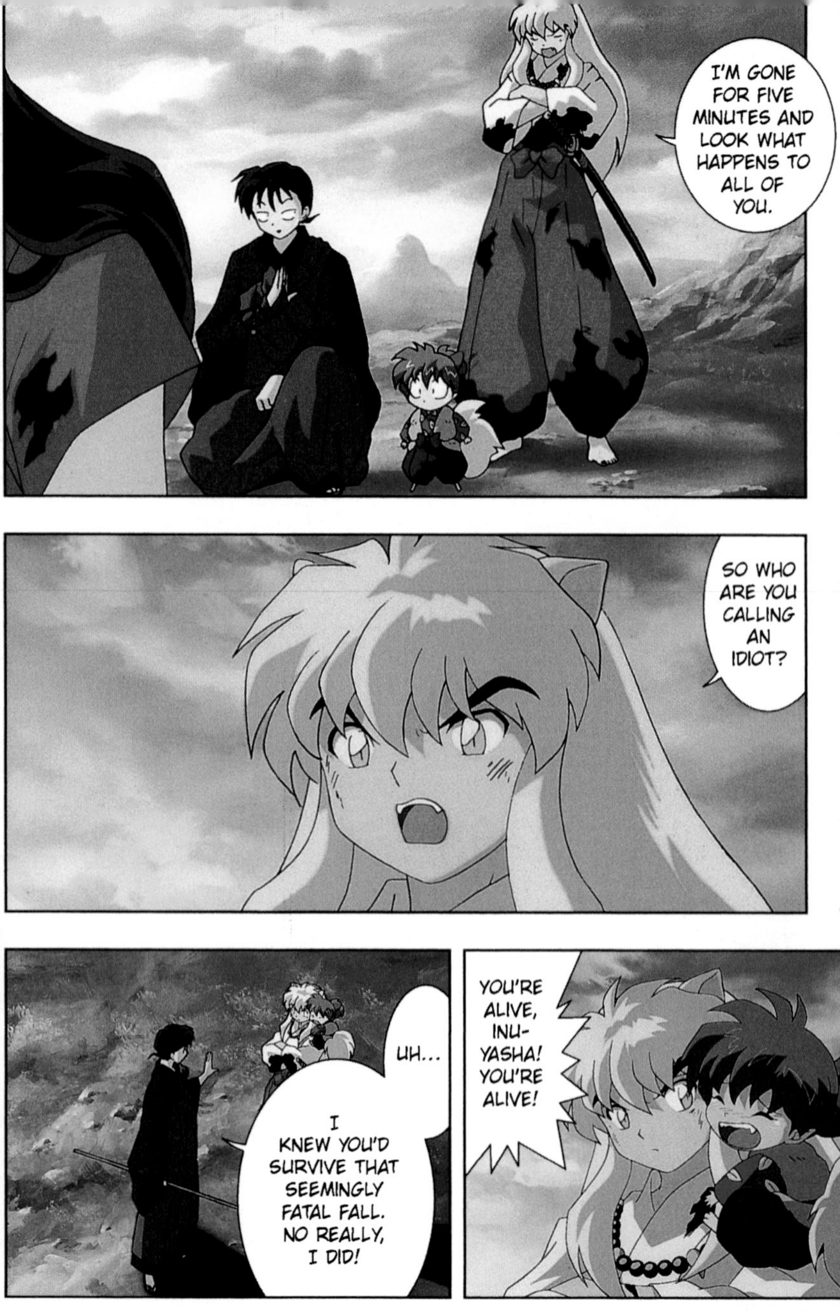
I'M GONE FOR FIVE MINUTES AND LOOK WHAT HAPPENS TO ALL OF YOU.
SO WHO ARE YOU CALLING AN IDIOT?
YOU'RE ALIVE, INU-YASHA! YOU'RE ALIVE!
UH...
I KNEW YOU'D SURVIVE THAT SEEMINGLY FATAL FALL. NO REALLY, I DID!

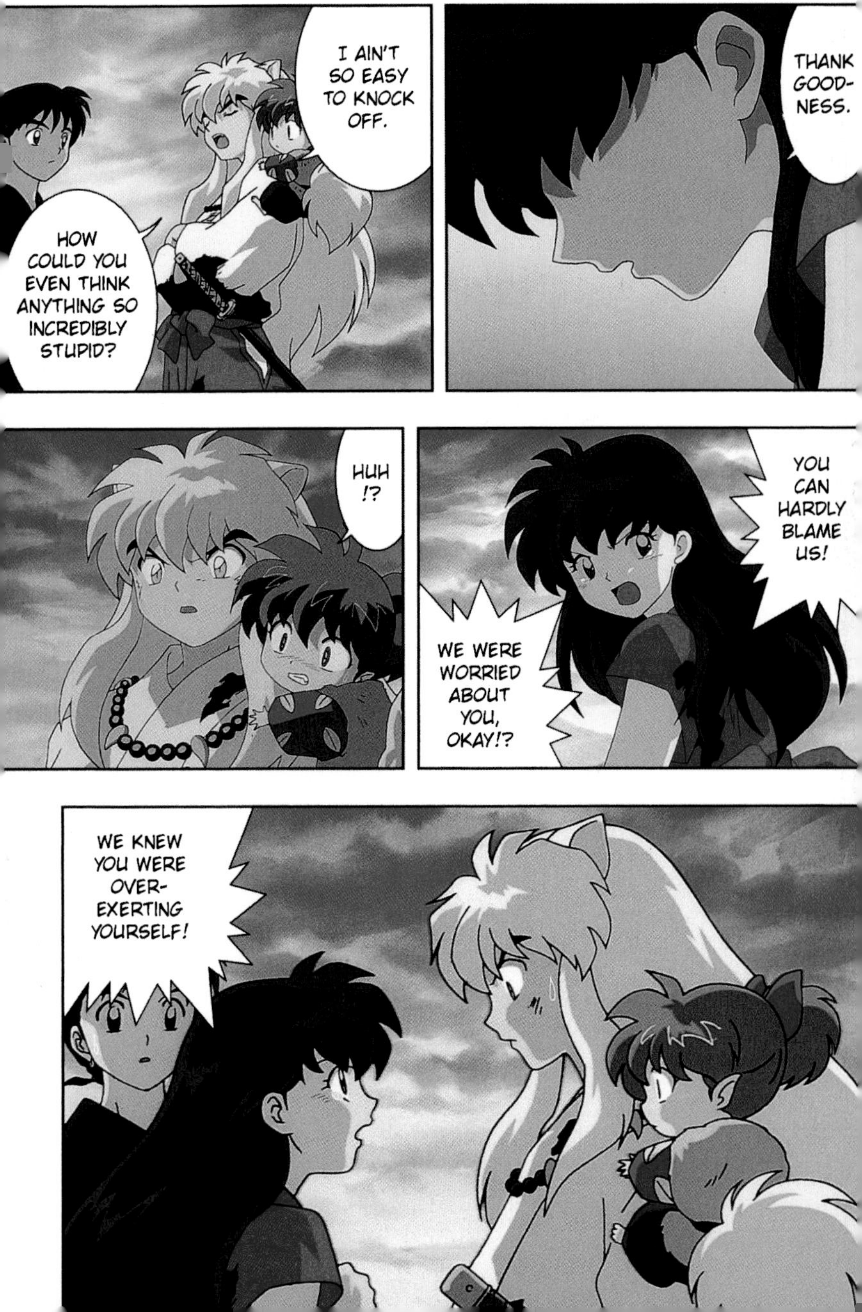
THANK GOOD-NESS.
I AIN'T SO EASY TO KNOCK OFF.
HOW COULD YOU EVEN THINK ANYTHING SO INCREDIBLY STUPID?
YOU CAN HARDLY BLAME US!
WE WERE WORRIED ABOUT YOU, OKAY!?
HUH!?
WE KNEW YOU WERE OVER-EXERTING YOURSELF!

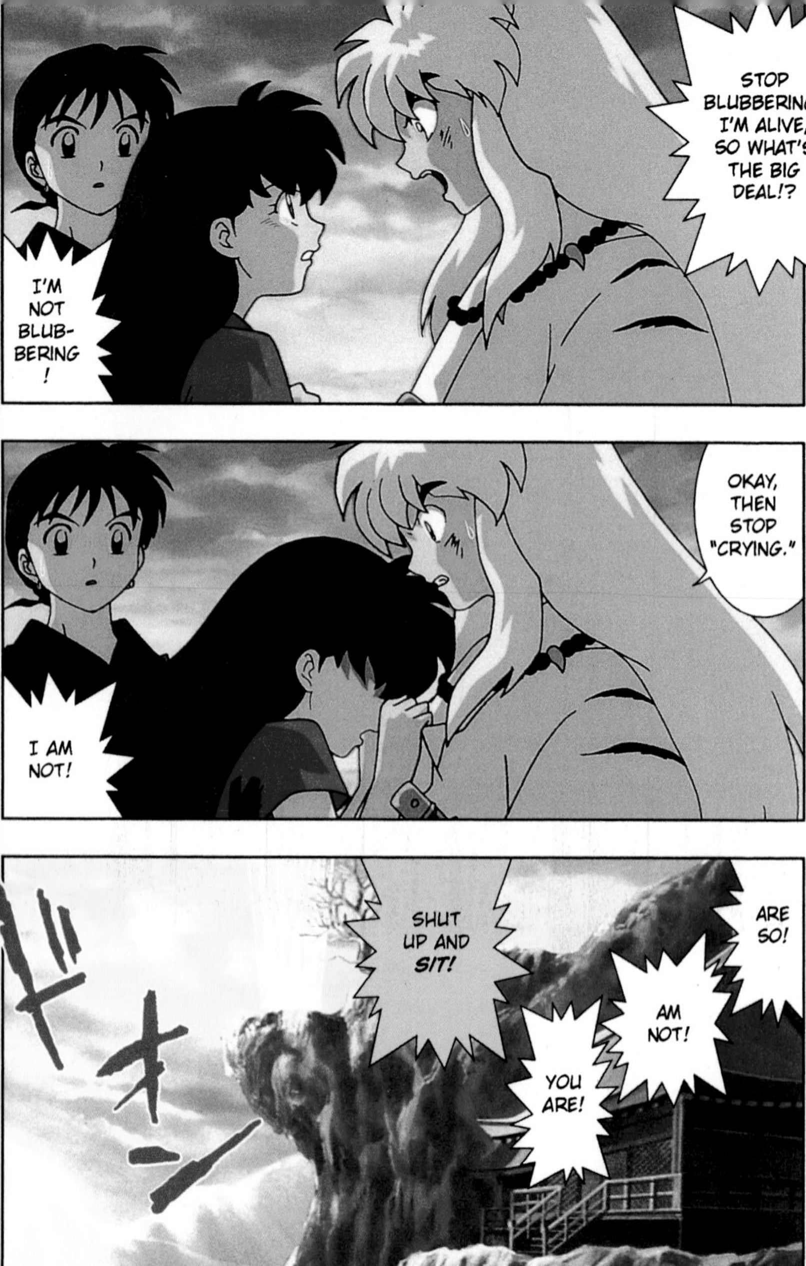
STOP BLUBBERING! I'M ALIVE, SO WHAT'S THE BIG DEAL!?
I'M NOT BLUB-BERING!
OKAY, THEN STOP "CRYING."
I AM NOT!
ARE SO!
AM NOT!
SHUT UP AND *SIT!*
YOU ARE!

59
The Beautiful Sister Apprentices

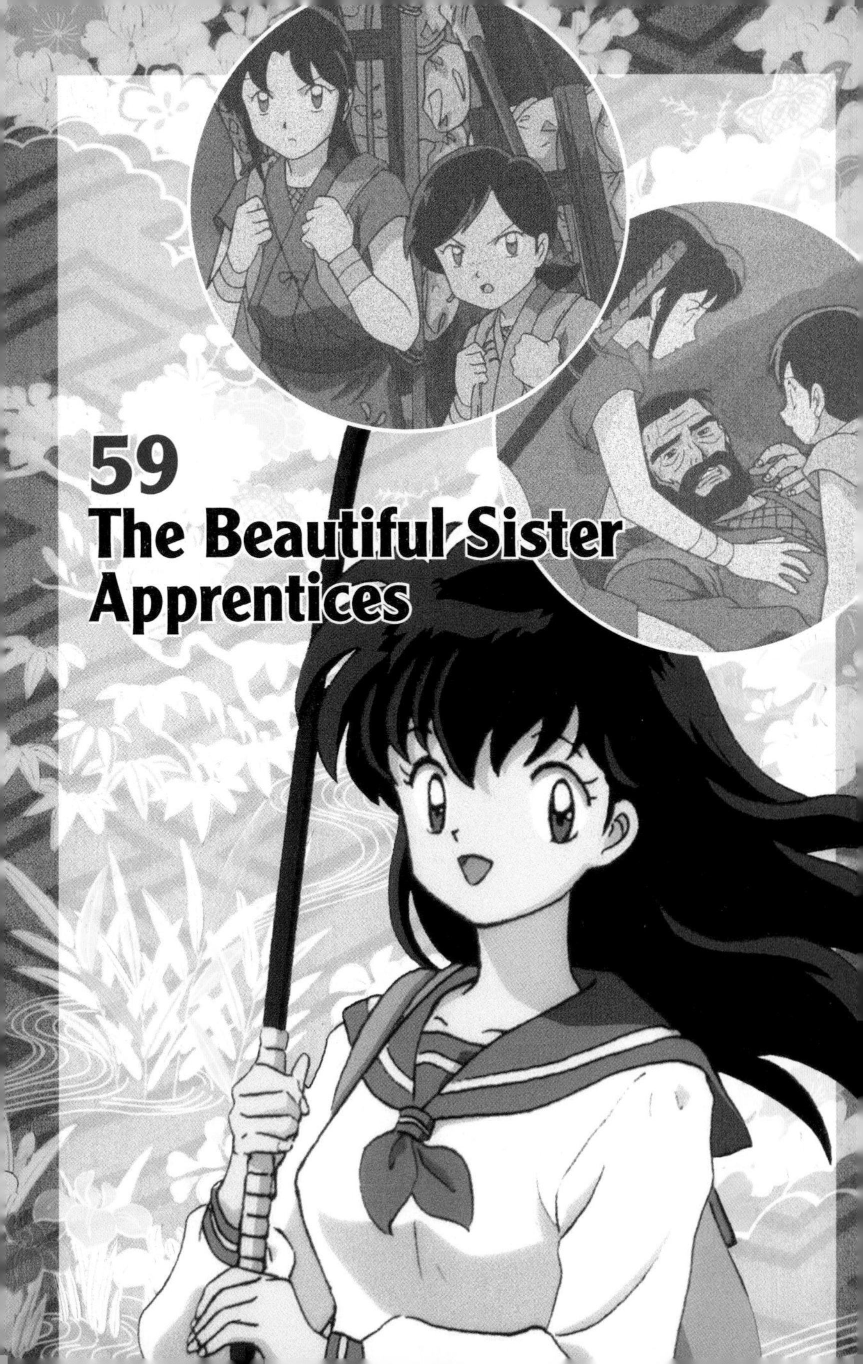

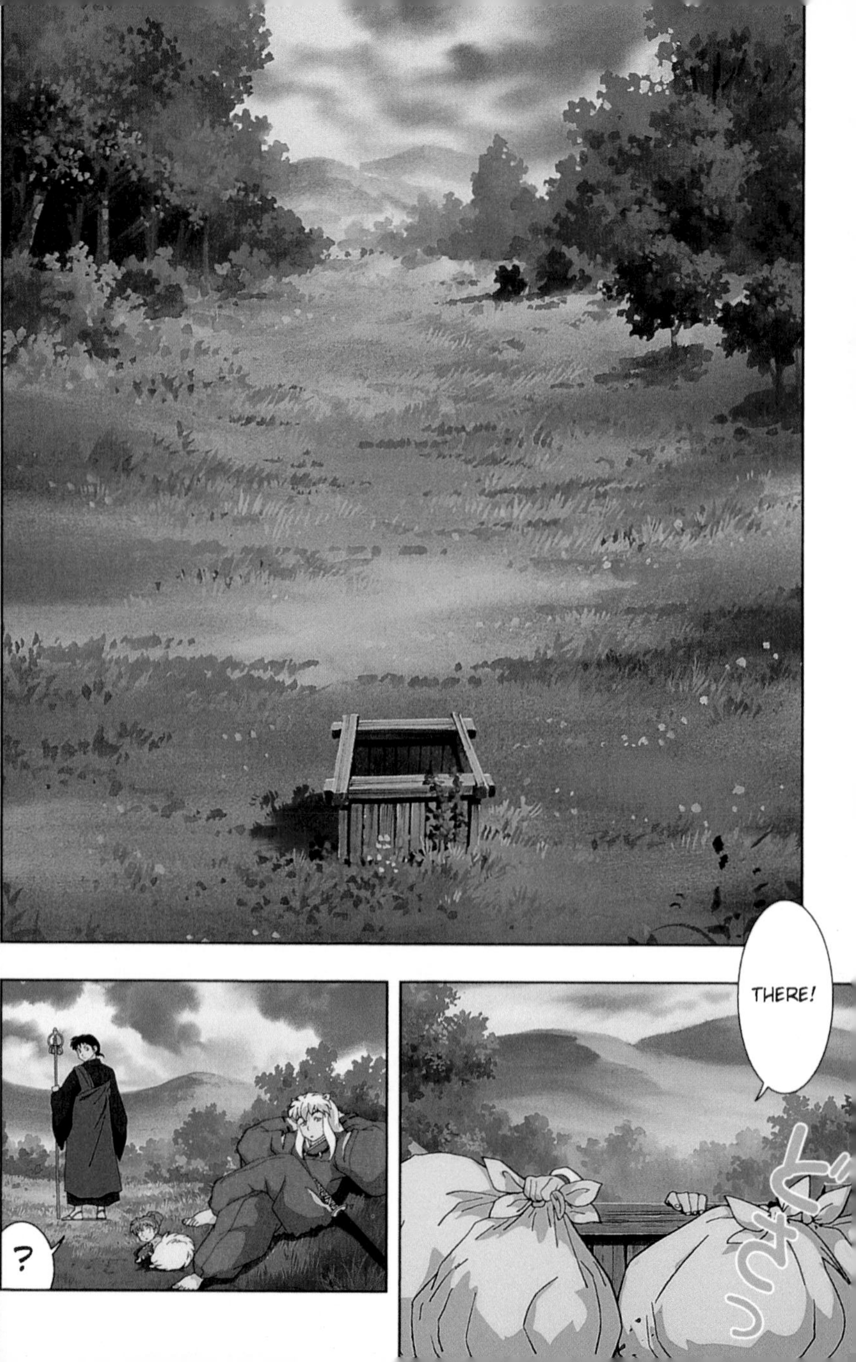
THERE!
?

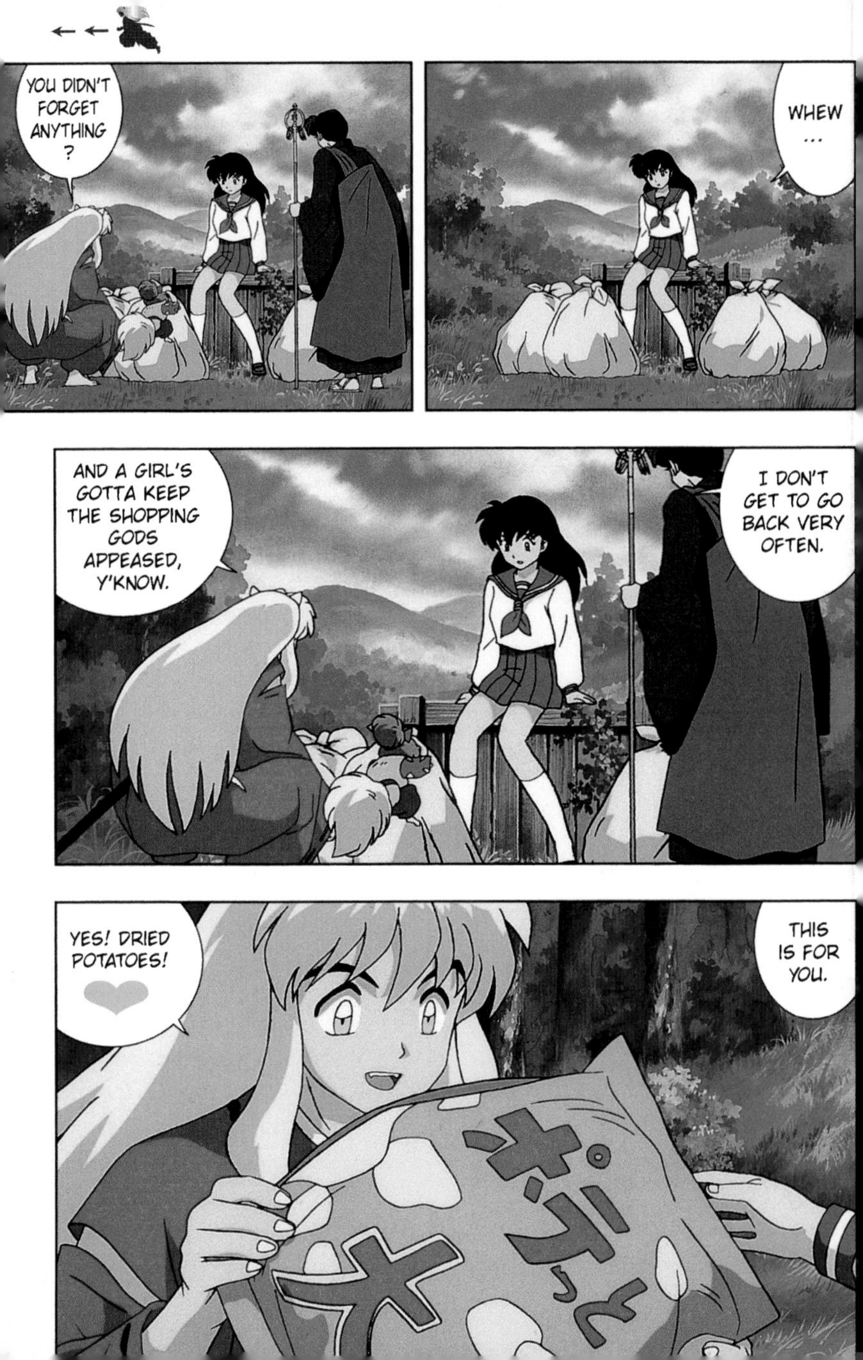
WHEW ...
YOU DIDN'T FORGET ANYTHING ?
I DON'T GET TO GO BACK VERY OFTEN.
AND A GIRL'S GOTTA KEEP THE SHOPPING GODS APPEASED, Y'KNOW.
THIS IS FOR YOU.
YES! DRIED POTATOES!

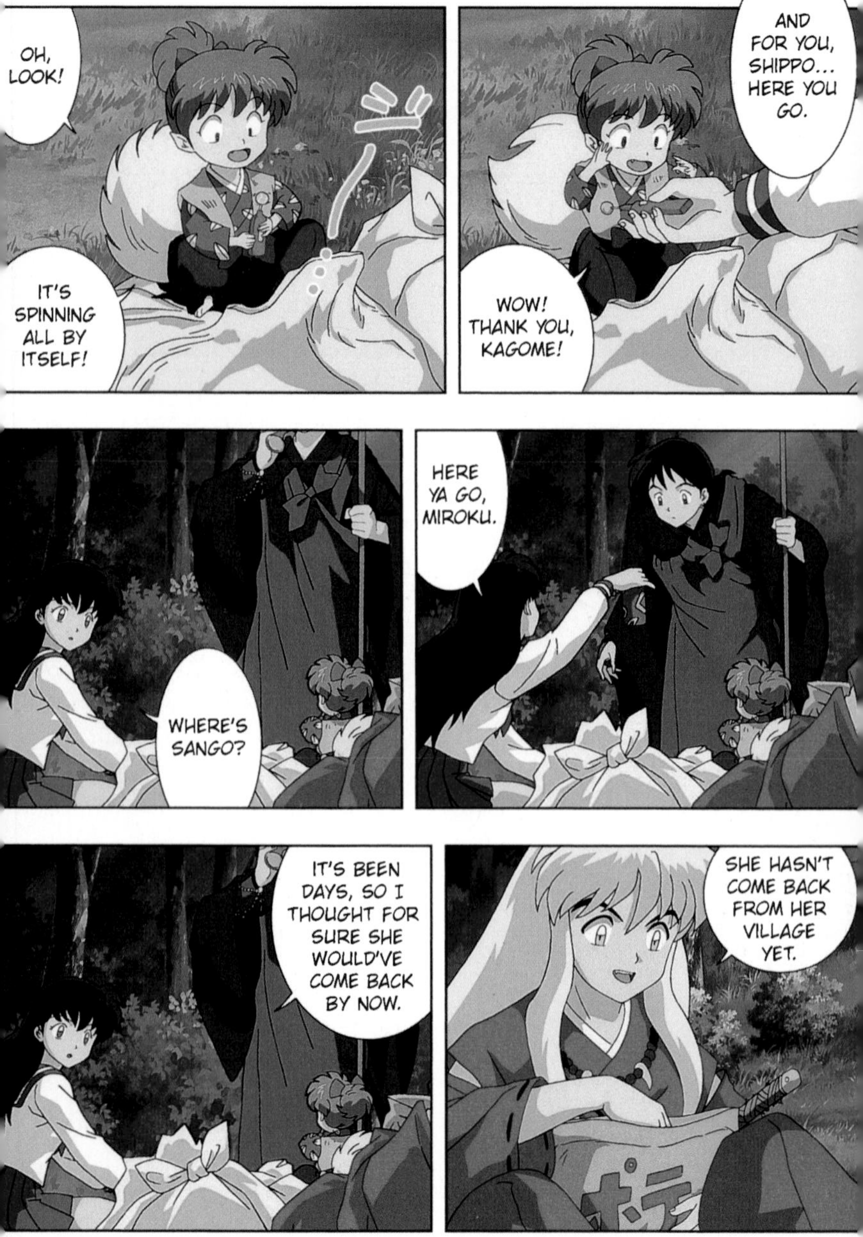
AND FOR YOU, SHIPPO... HERE YOU GO.
WOW! THANK YOU, KAGOME!
OH, LOOK!
IT'S SPINNING ALL BY ITSELF!
HERE YA GO, MIROKU.
WHERE'S SANGO?
SHE HASN'T COME BACK FROM HER VILLAGE YET.
IT'S BEEN DAYS, SO I THOUGHT FOR SURE SHE WOULD'VE COME BACK BY NOW.

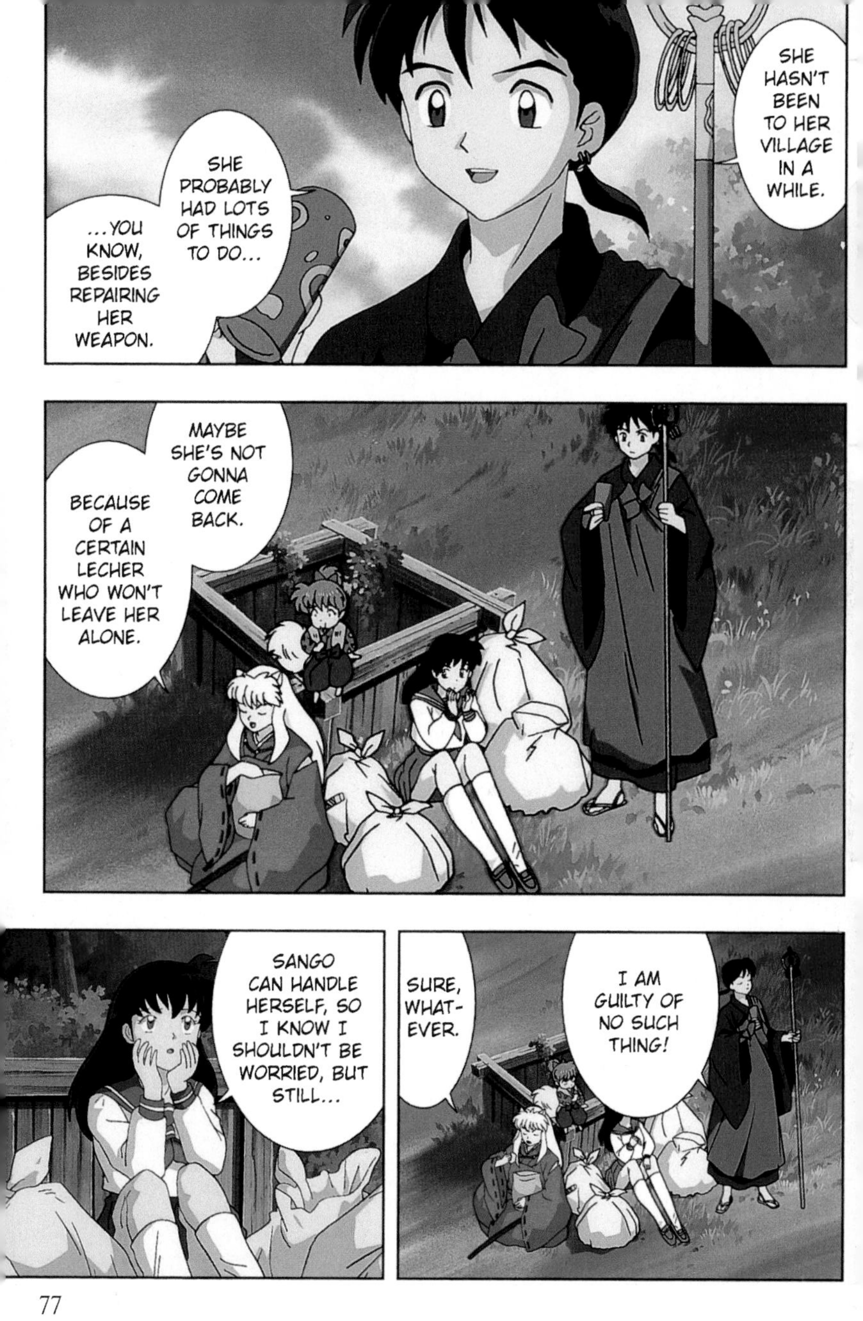
SHE HASN'T BEEN TO HER VILLAGE IN A WHILE.
SHE PROBABLY HAD LOTS OF THINGS TO DO...
...YOU KNOW, BESIDES REPAIRING HER WEAPON.
MAYBE SHE'S NOT GONNA COME BACK.
BECAUSE OF A CERTAIN LECHER WHO WON'T LEAVE HER ALONE.
I AM GUILTY OF NO SUCH THING!
SURE, WHAT-EVER.
SANGO CAN HANDLE HERSELF, SO I KNOW I SHOULDN'T BE WORRIED, BUT STILL...

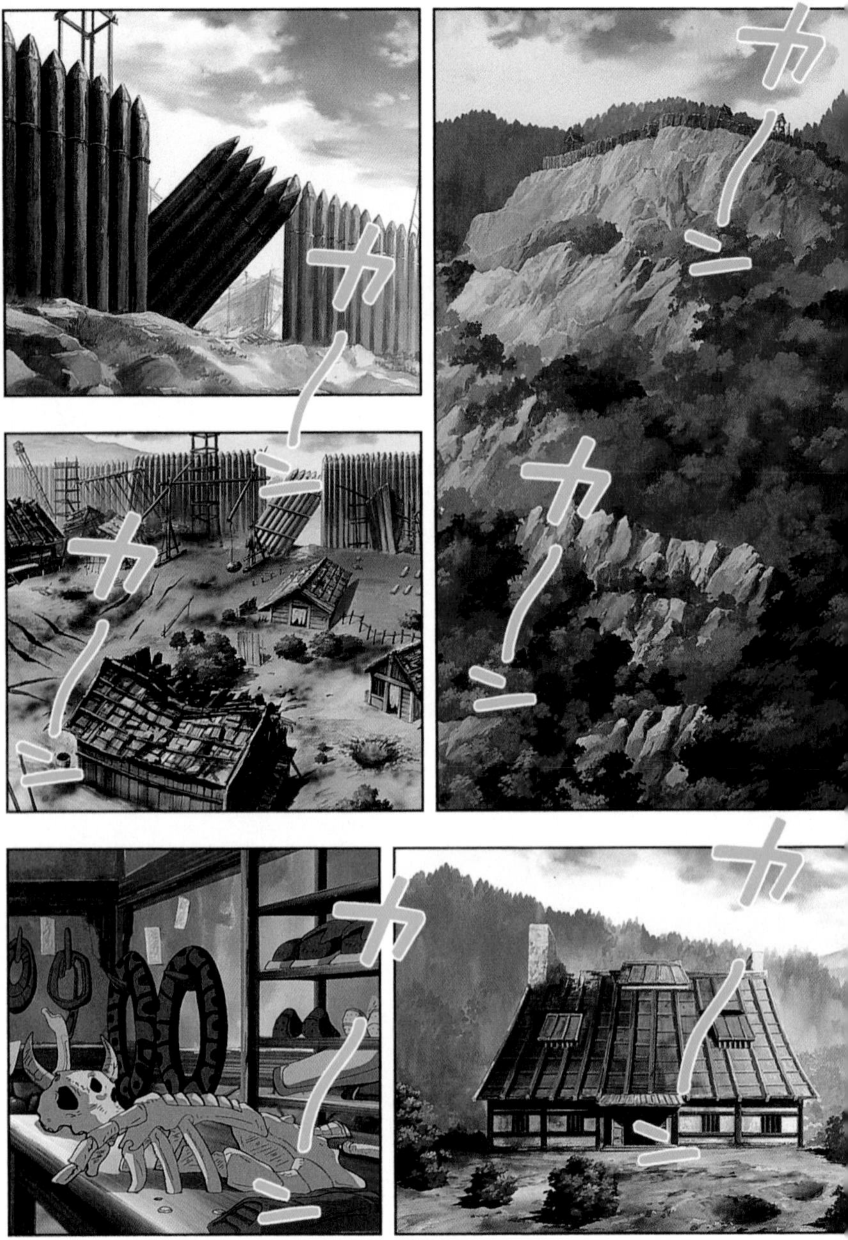
カーン
カーン
カーン
カーン
カーン
カーン

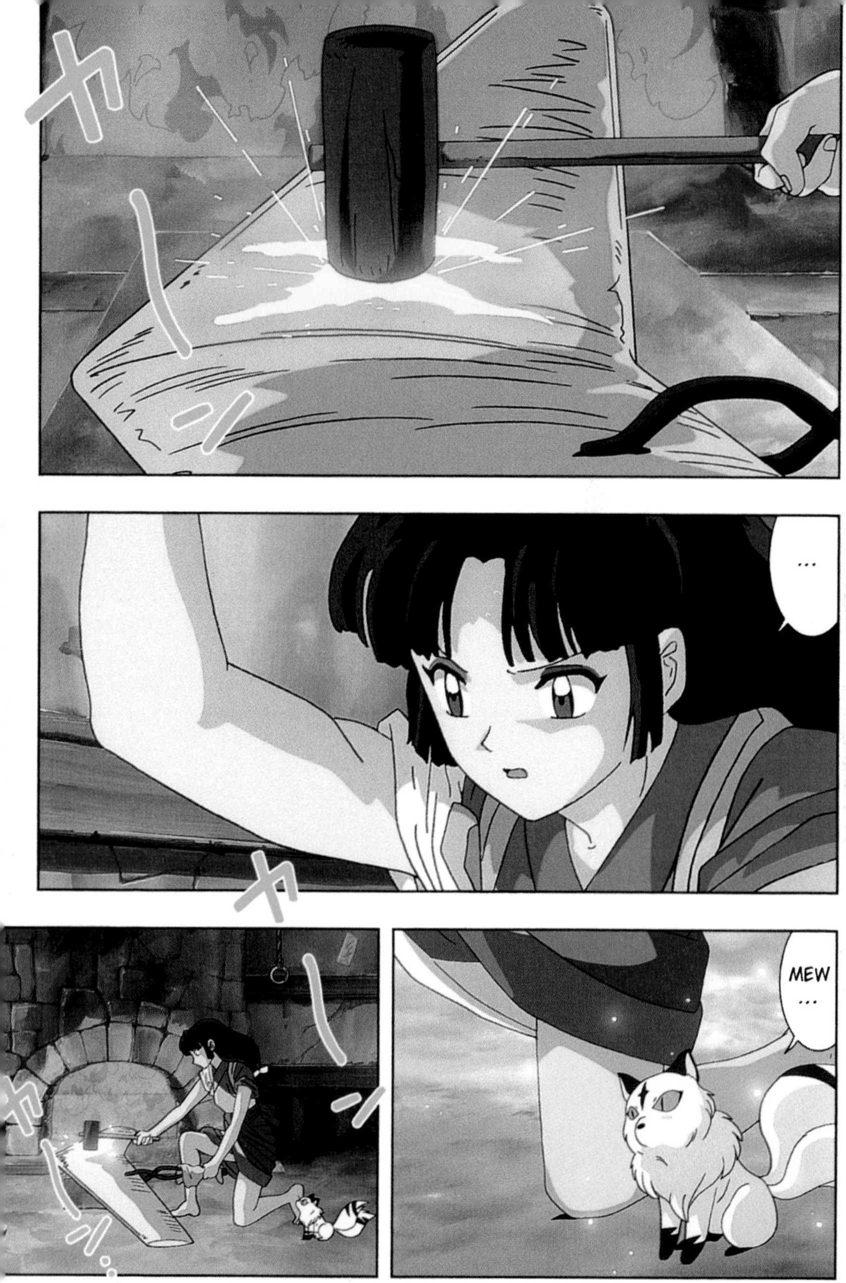
...
MEW ...

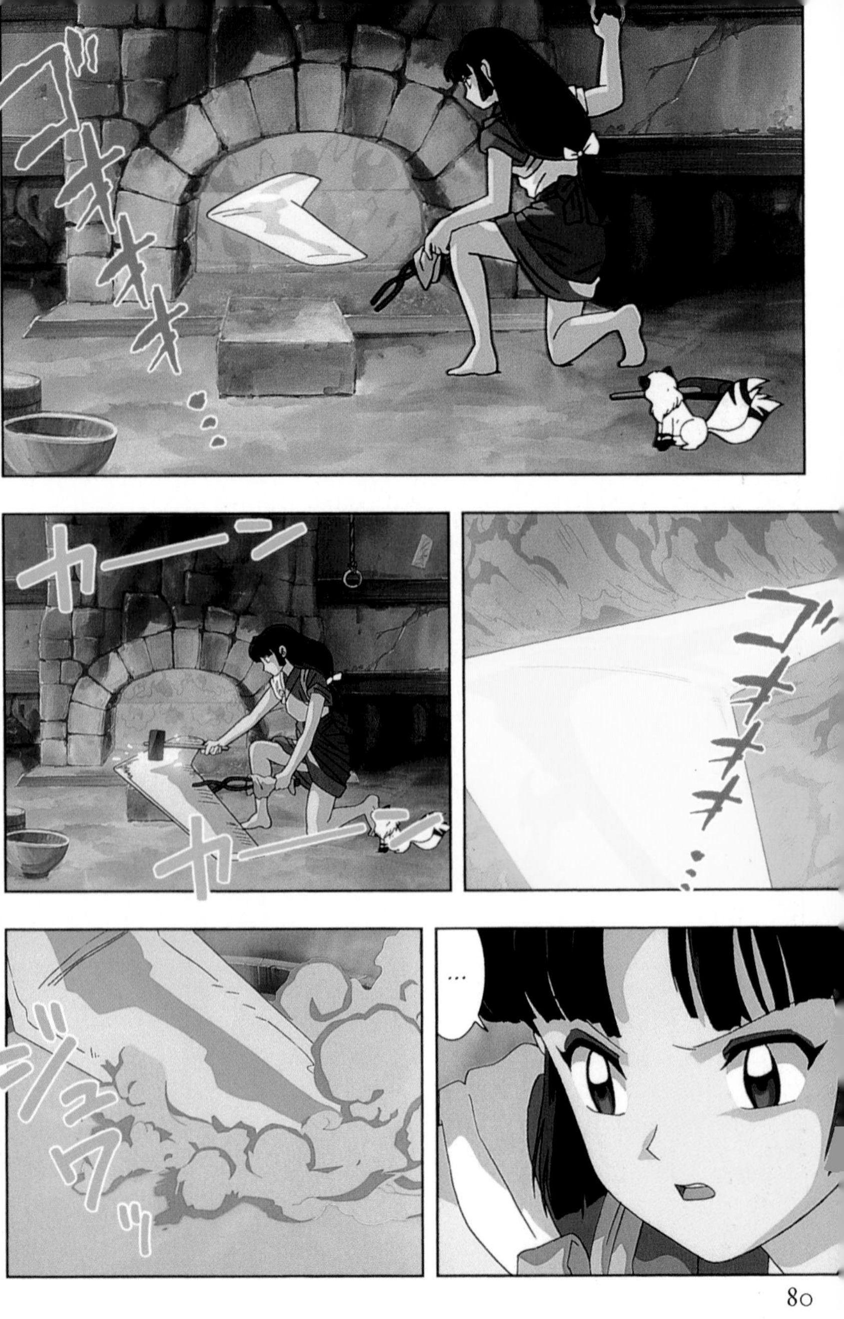
ゴオォォォ
ゴオォォォ…
ヤーーン
ヤーー
…
ジュワッ

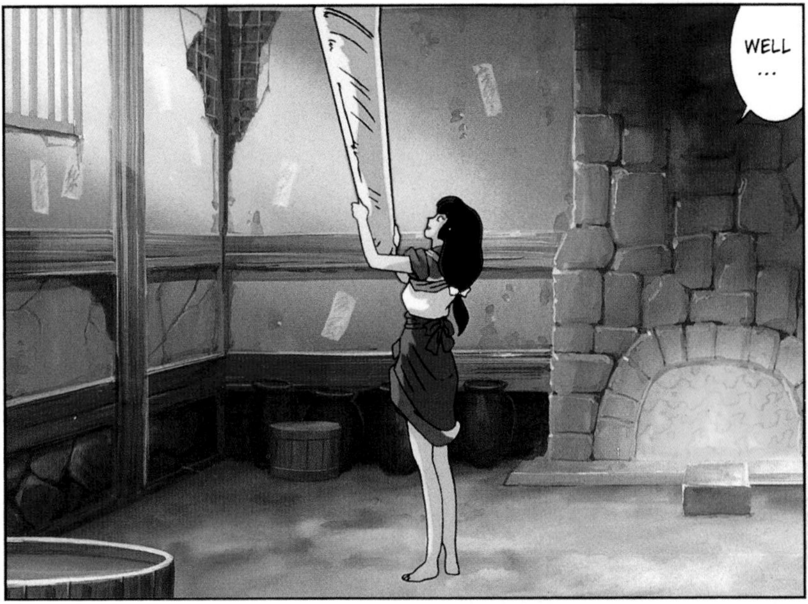
WELL ...

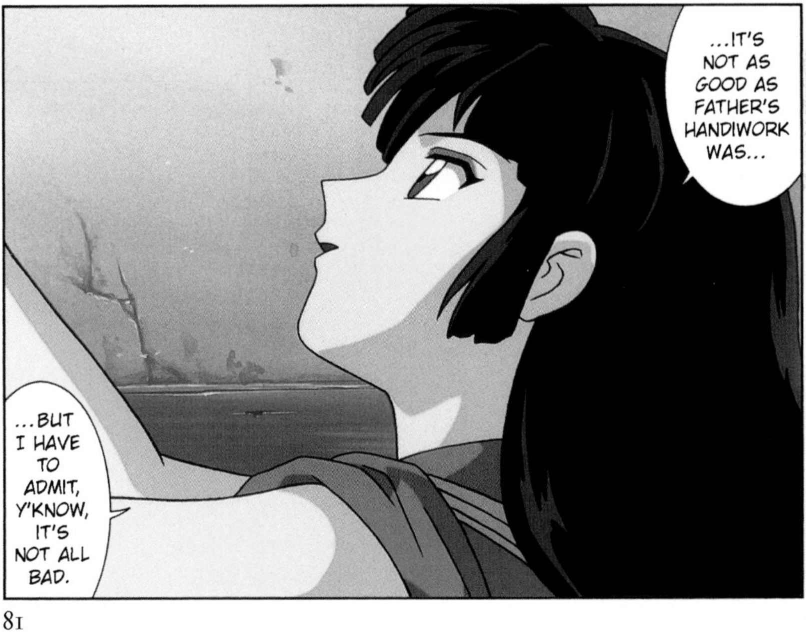
...IT'S NOT AS GOOD AS FATHER'S HANDIWORK WAS...
...BUT I HAVE TO ADMIT, Y'KNOW, IT'S NOT ALL BAD.

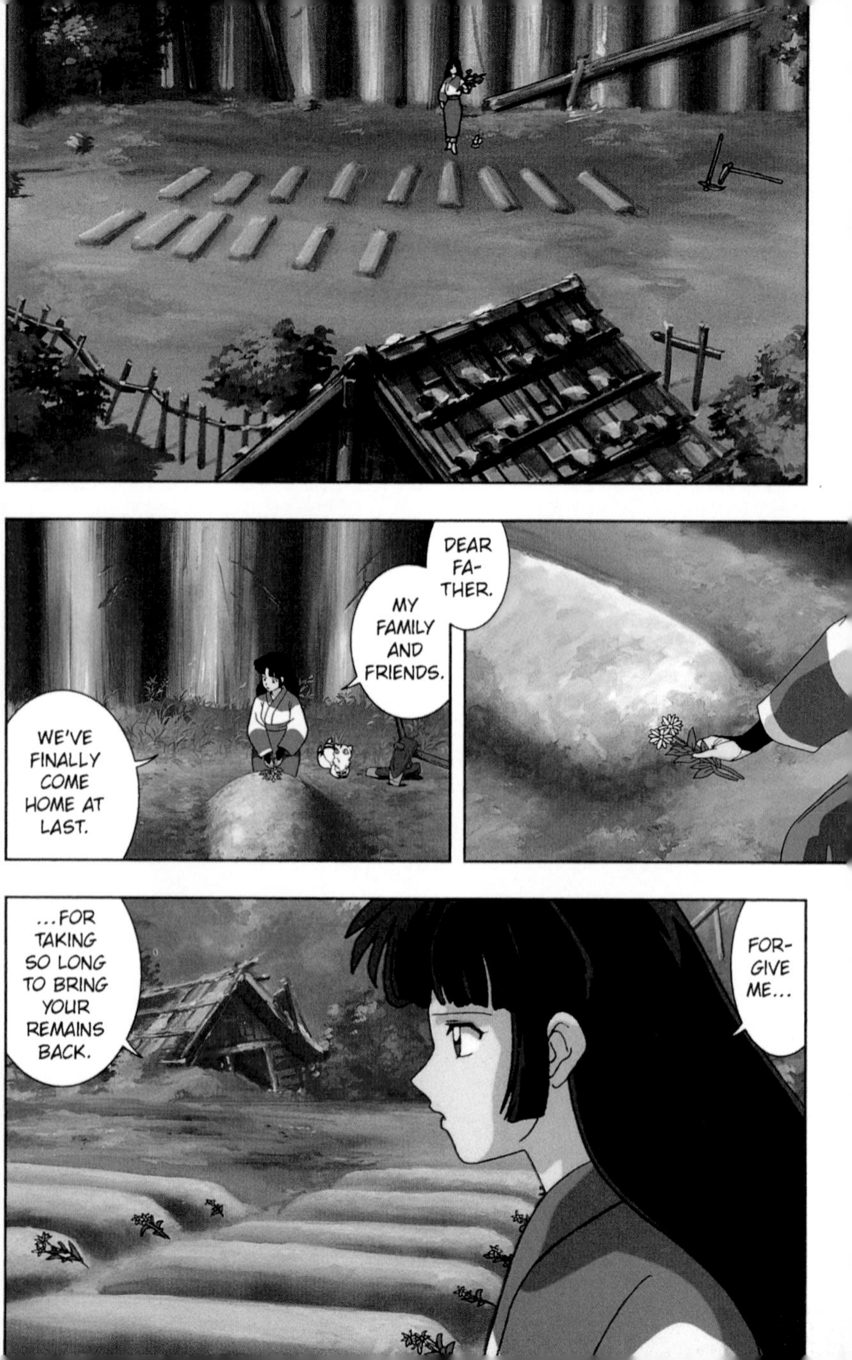
DEAR FA-THER.
MY FAMILY AND FRIENDS.
WE'VE FINALLY COME HOME AT LAST.
FOR-GIVE ME...
...FOR TAKING SO LONG TO BRING YOUR REMAINS BACK.

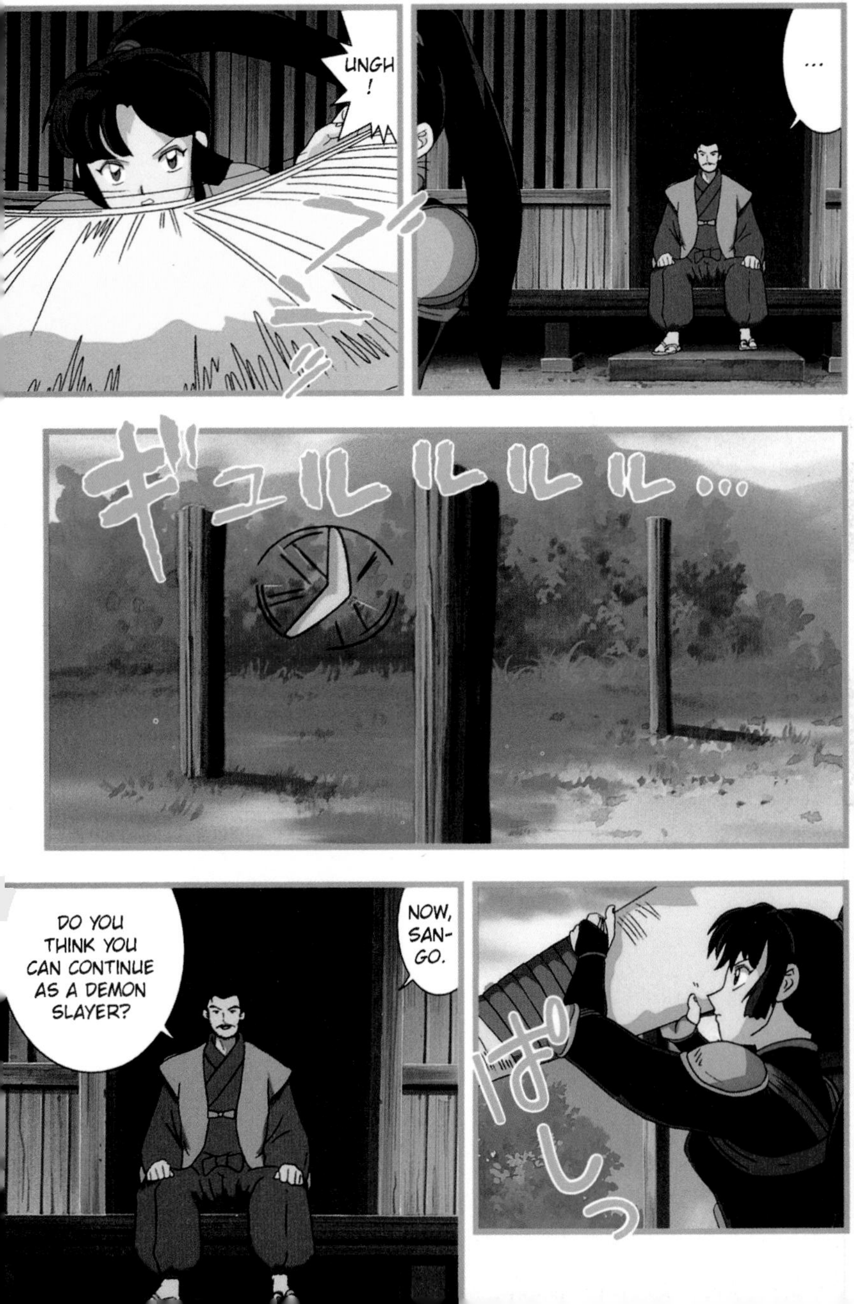
...
UNGH!
ギュルルル...
ぱしっ
NOW, SAN-GO.
DO YOU THINK YOU CAN CONTINUE AS A DEMON SLAYER?

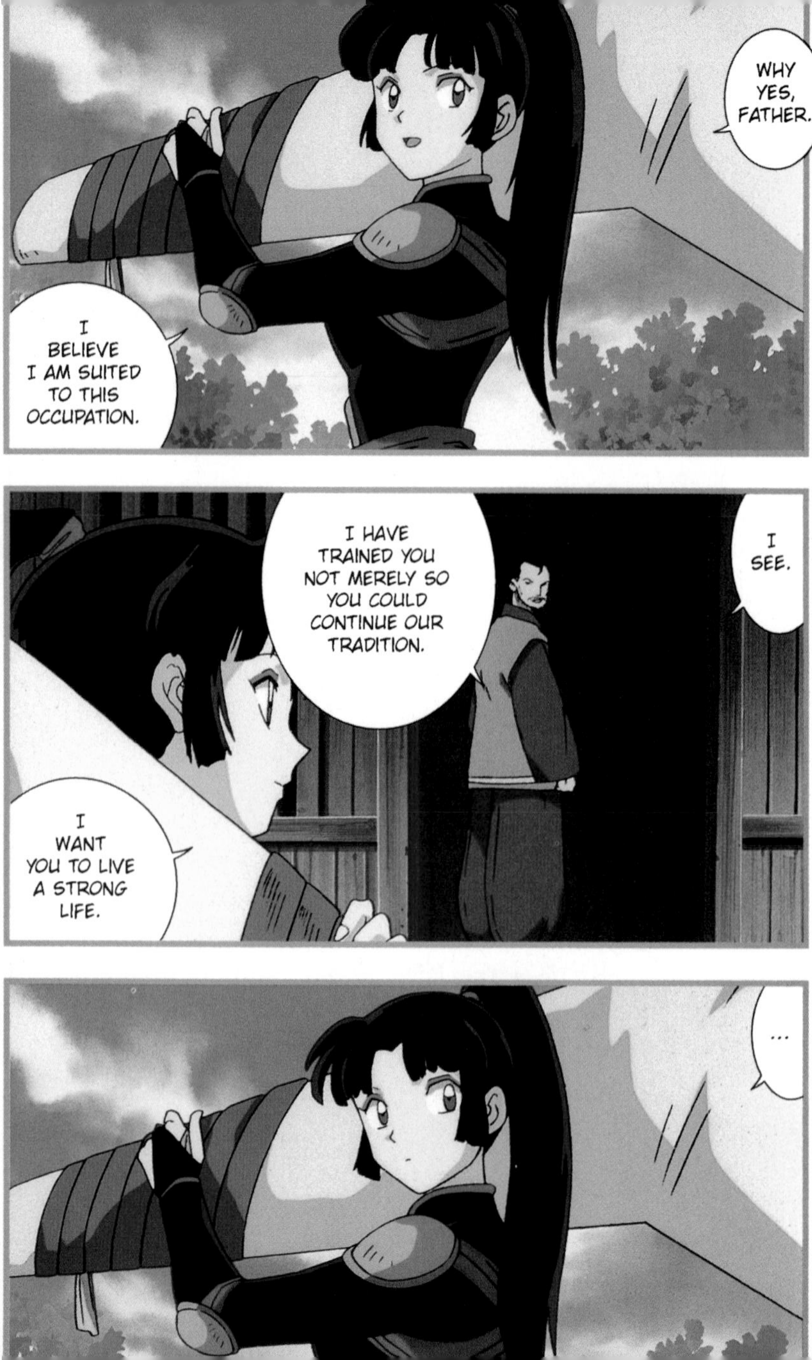
WHY YES, FATHER.
I BELIEVE I AM SUITED TO THIS OCCUPATION.
I SEE.
I HAVE TRAINED YOU NOT MERELY SO YOU COULD CONTINUE OUR TRADITION.
I WANT YOU TO LIVE A STRONG LIFE.
...

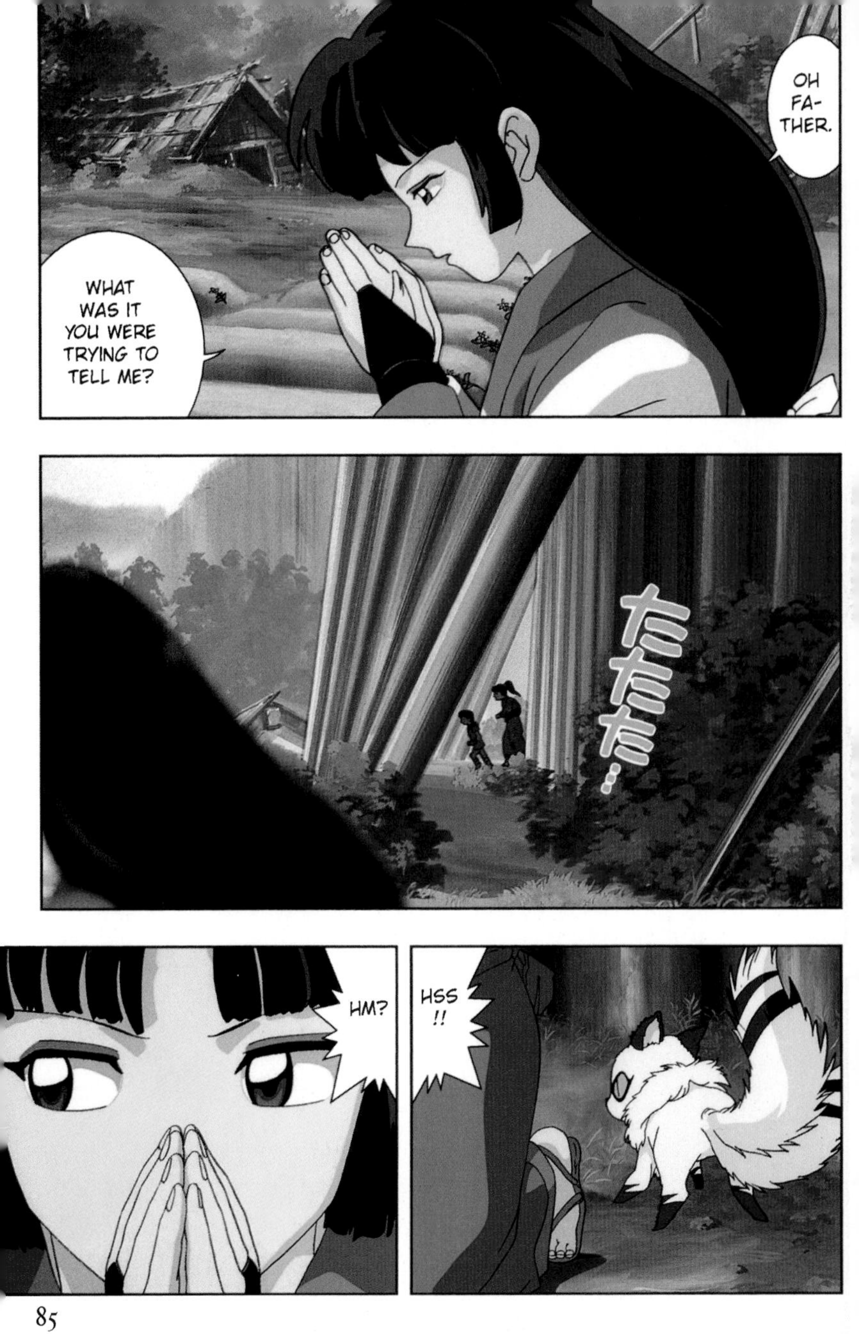
OH FA-THER.
WHAT WAS IT YOU WERE TRYING TO TELL ME?
たたた…
HSS !!
HM?

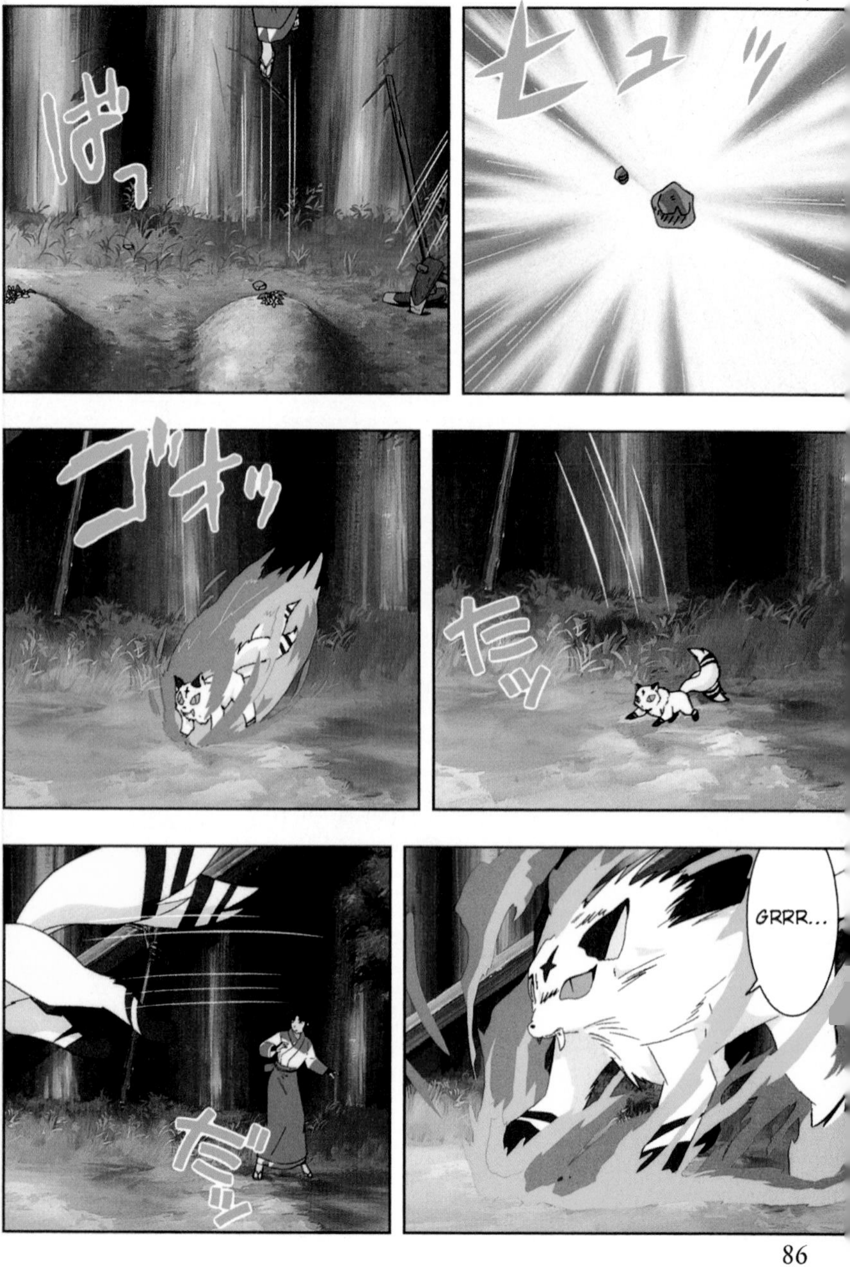
ヒュッ
ぱっ
たッ
ゴオッ
GRRR...
だッ

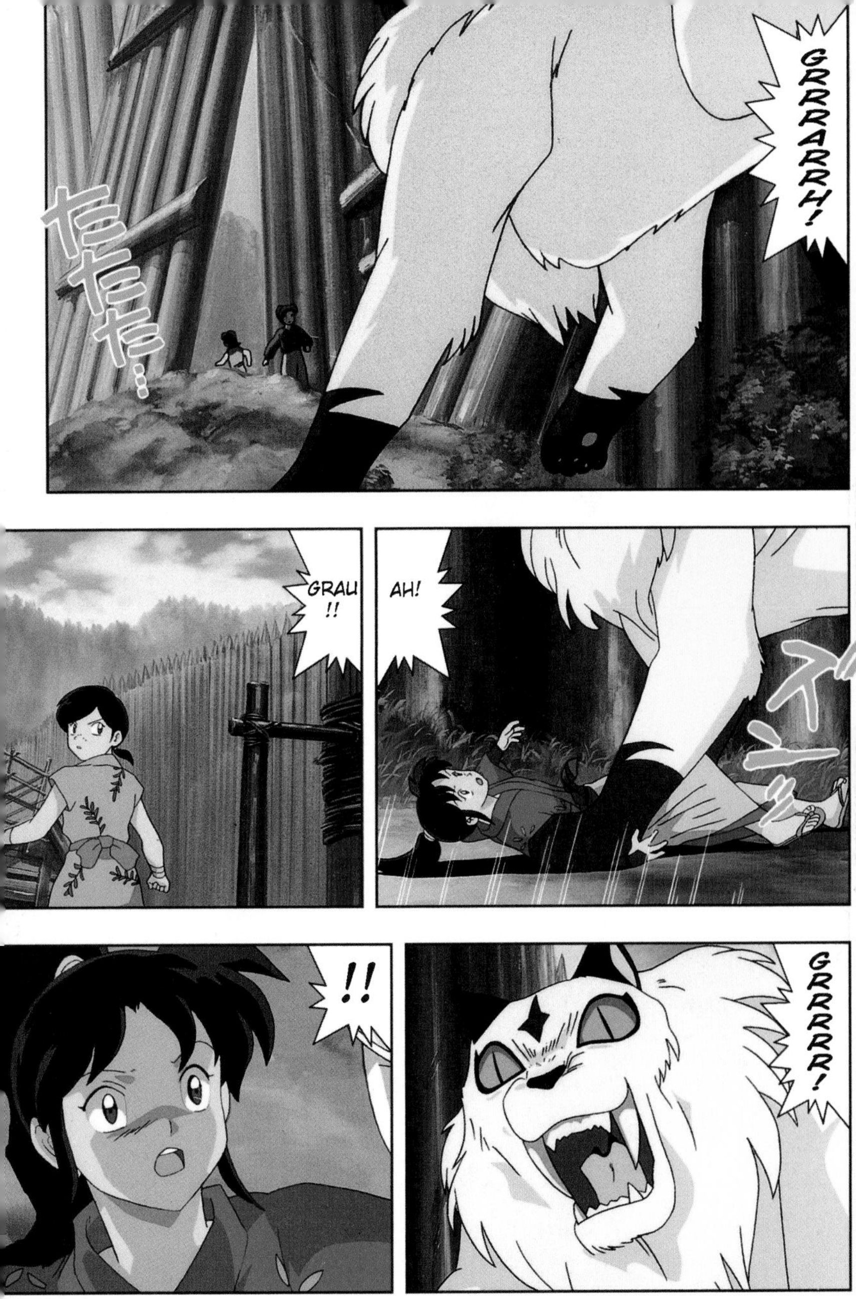
GRRRARRH!
たたた…
AH!
GRAU !!
GRRRRR!
!!

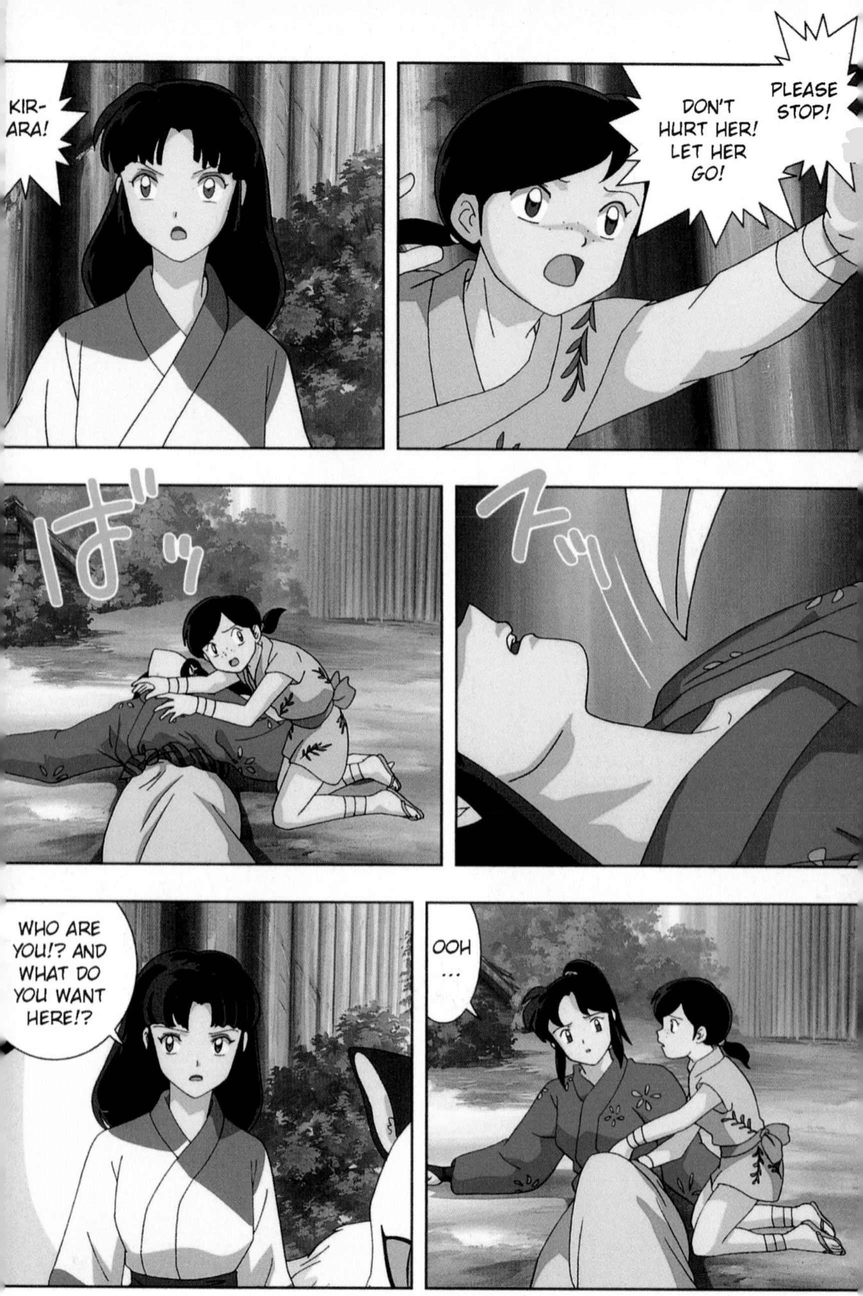
PLEASE STOP!
DON'T HURT HER! LET HER GO!
KIR-ARA!
ズッ
ばッ
OOH ...
WHO ARE YOU!? AND WHAT DO YOU WANT HERE!?

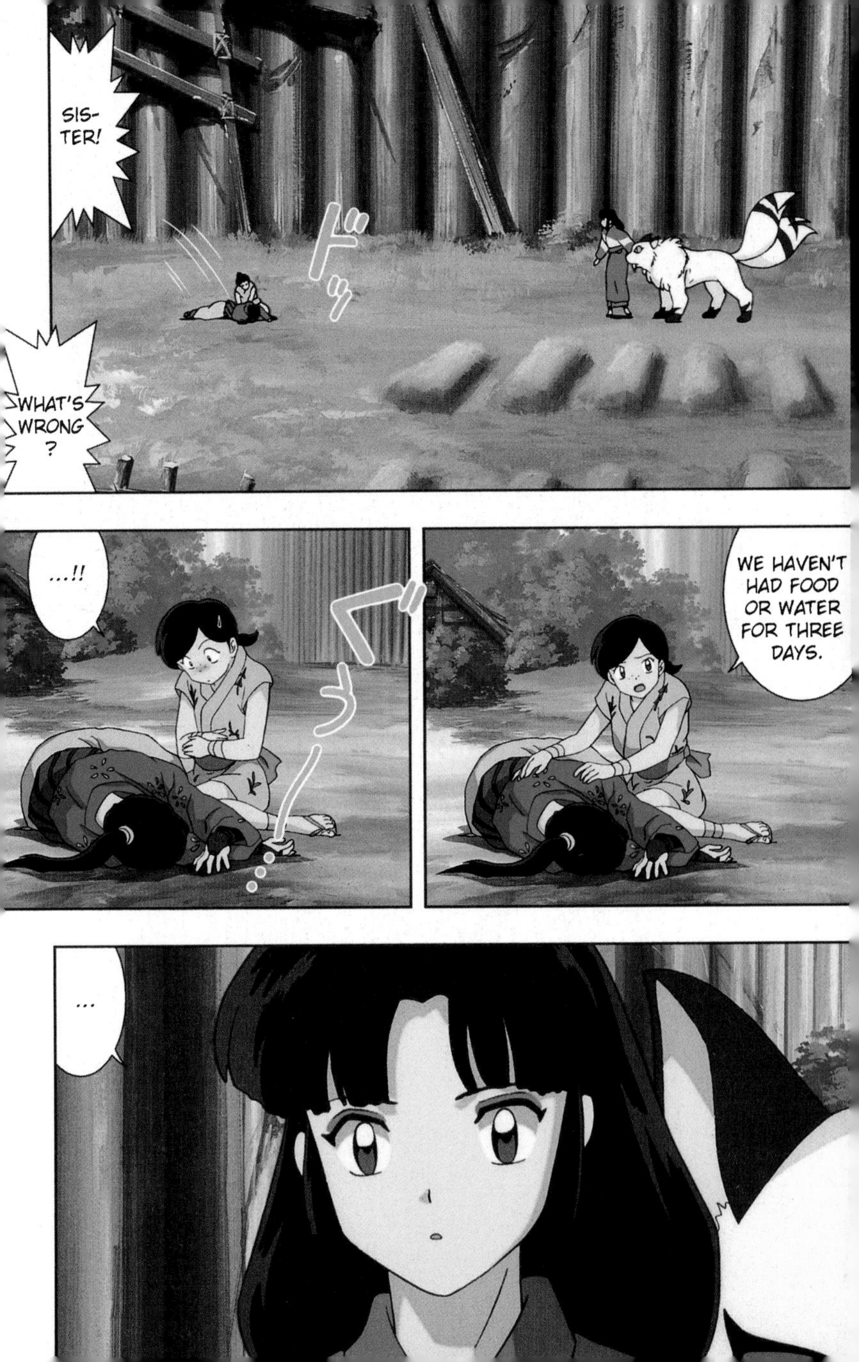
SIS-TER!
ドッ
WHAT'S WRONG?
WE HAVEN'T HAD FOOD OR WATER FOR THREE DAYS.
...!!
...

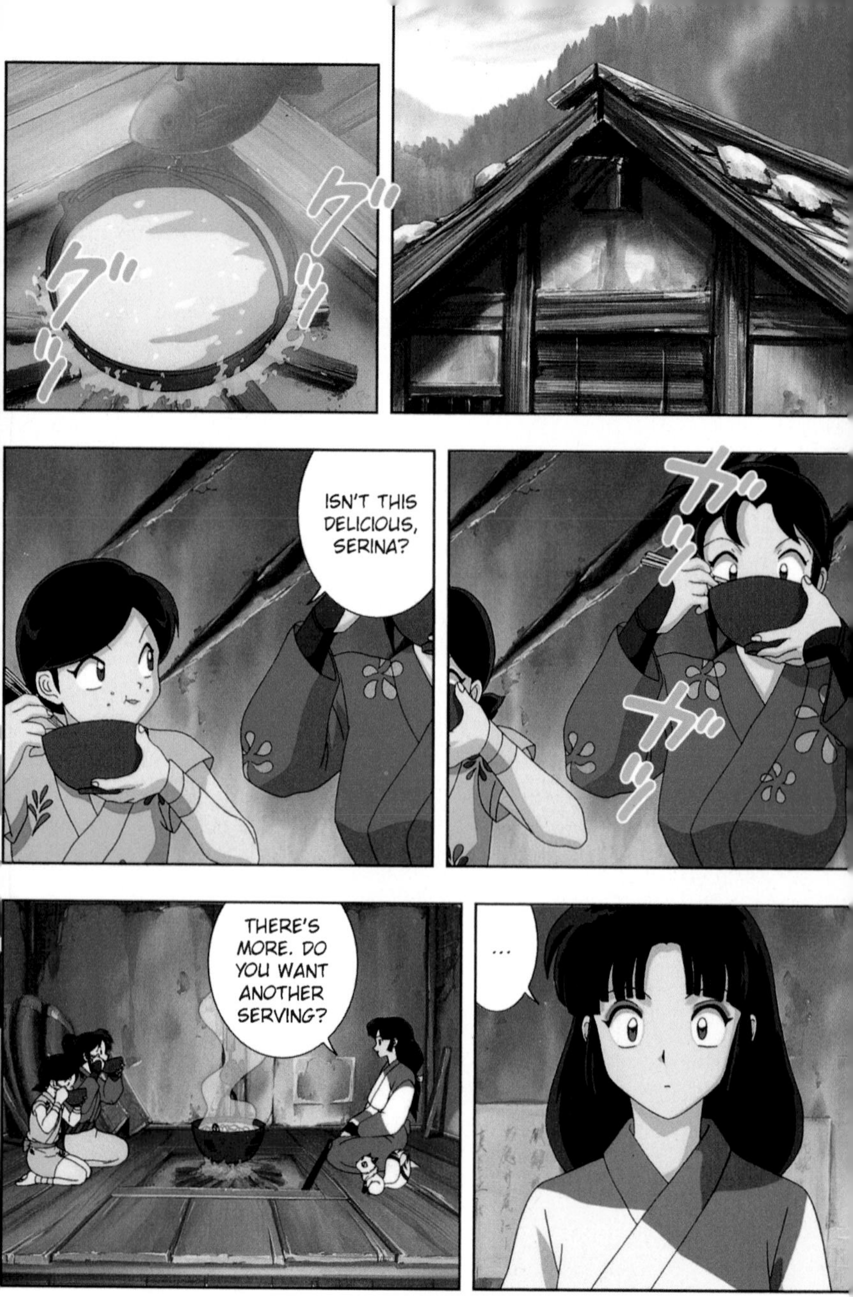
ISN'T THIS DELICIOUS, SERINA?
...
THERE'S MORE. DO YOU WANT ANOTHER SERVING?

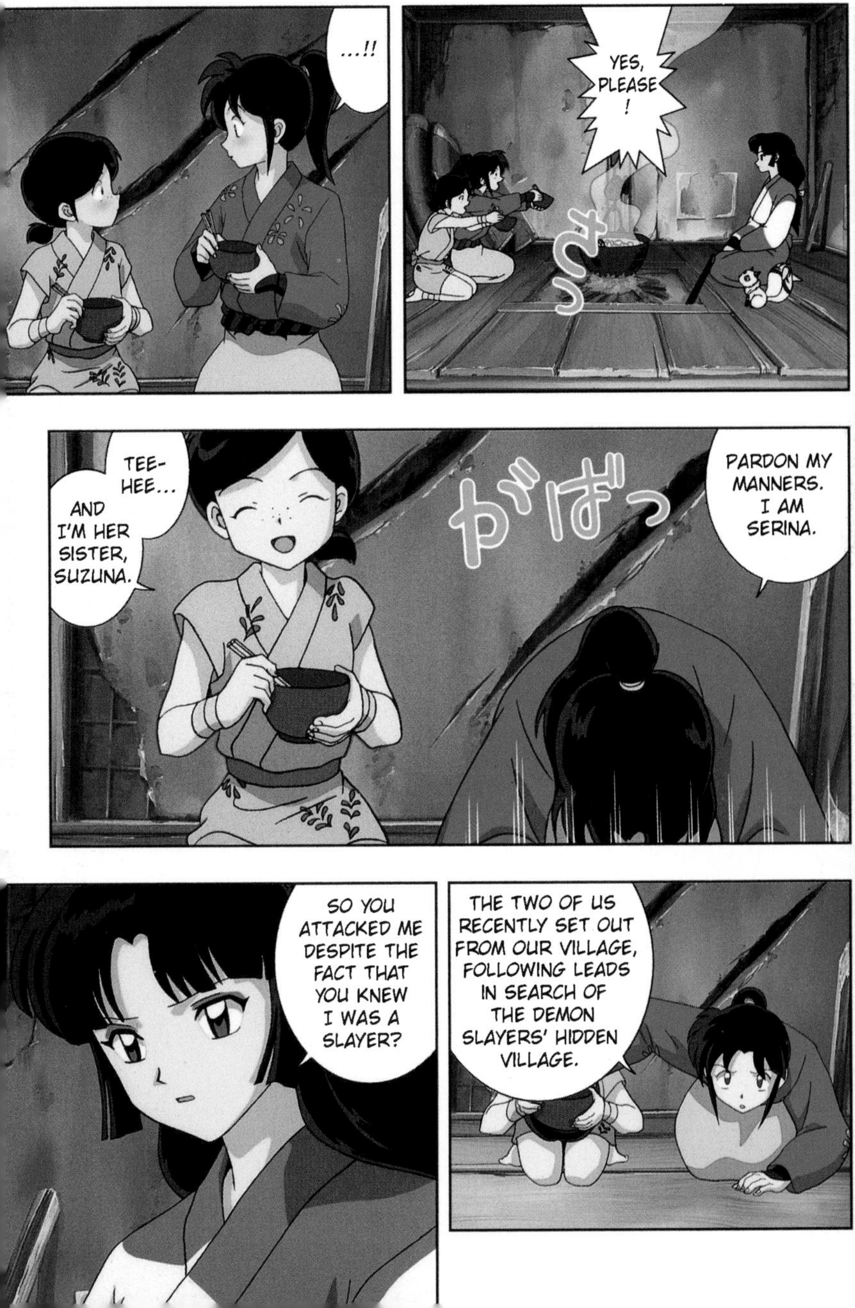
YES, PLEASE!
さっ
...!!
PARDON MY MANNERS. I AM SERINA.
がばっ
TEE-HEE... AND I'M HER SISTER, SUZUNA.
THE TWO OF US RECENTLY SET OUT FROM OUR VILLAGE, FOLLOWING LEADS IN SEARCH OF THE DEMON SLAYERS' HIDDEN VILLAGE.
SO YOU ATTACKED ME DESPITE THE FACT THAT YOU KNEW I WAS A SLAYER?

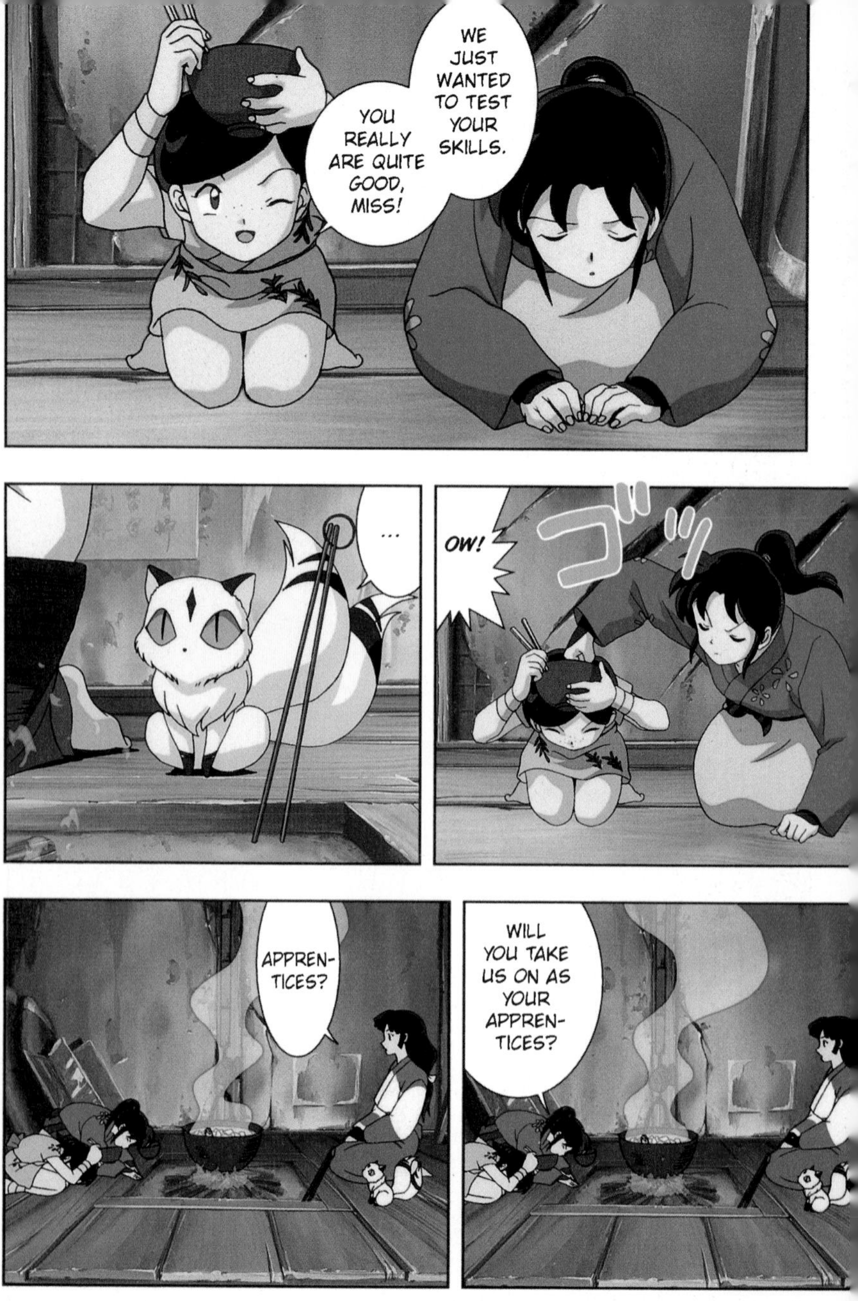
WE JUST WANTED TO TEST YOUR SKILLS.
YOU REALLY ARE QUITE GOOD, MISS!
ゴッ
OW!
...
WILL YOU TAKE US ON AS YOUR APPREN-TICES?
APPREN-TICES?

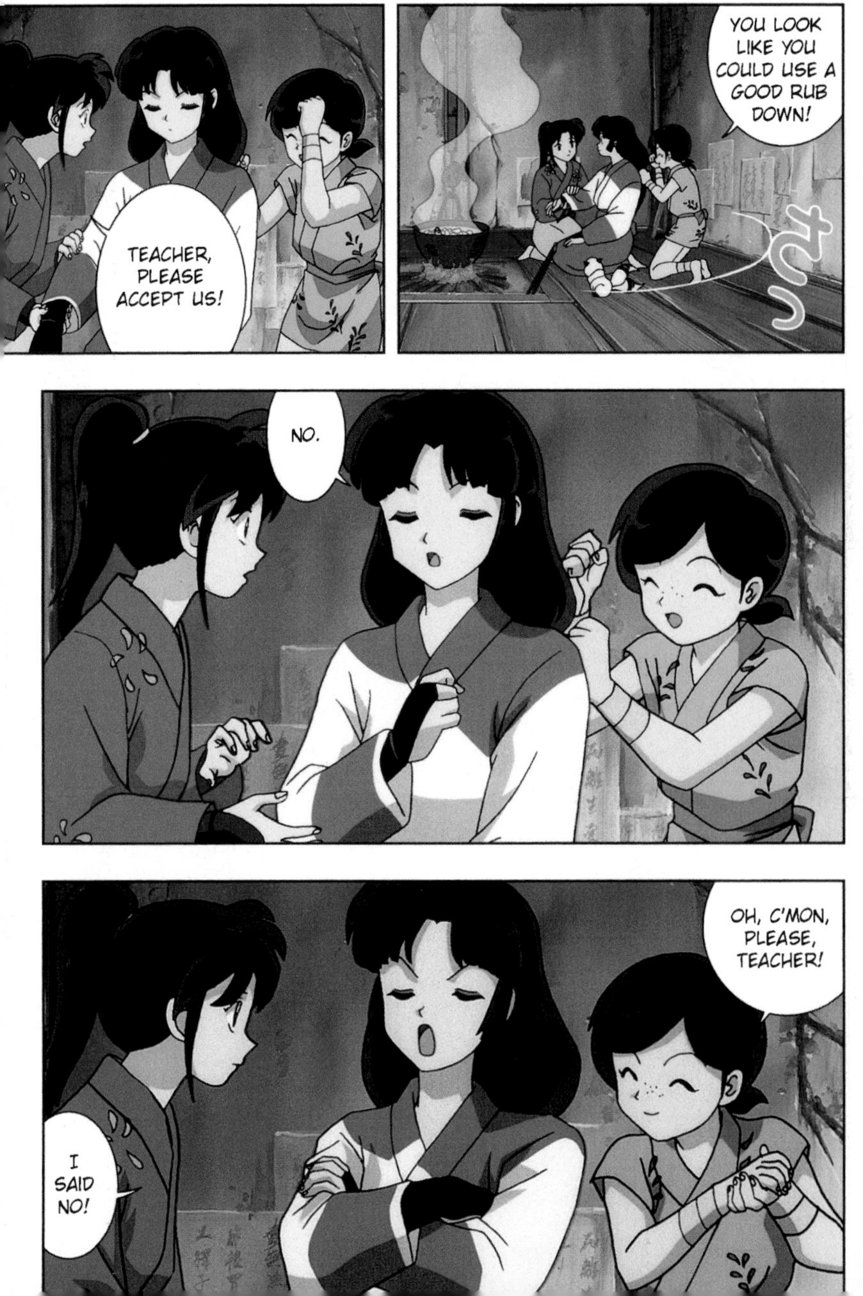
YOU LOOK LIKE YOU COULD USE A GOOD RUB DOWN!
さっ
TEACHER, PLEASE ACCEPT US!
NO.
OH, C'MON, PLEASE, TEACHER!
I SAID NO!

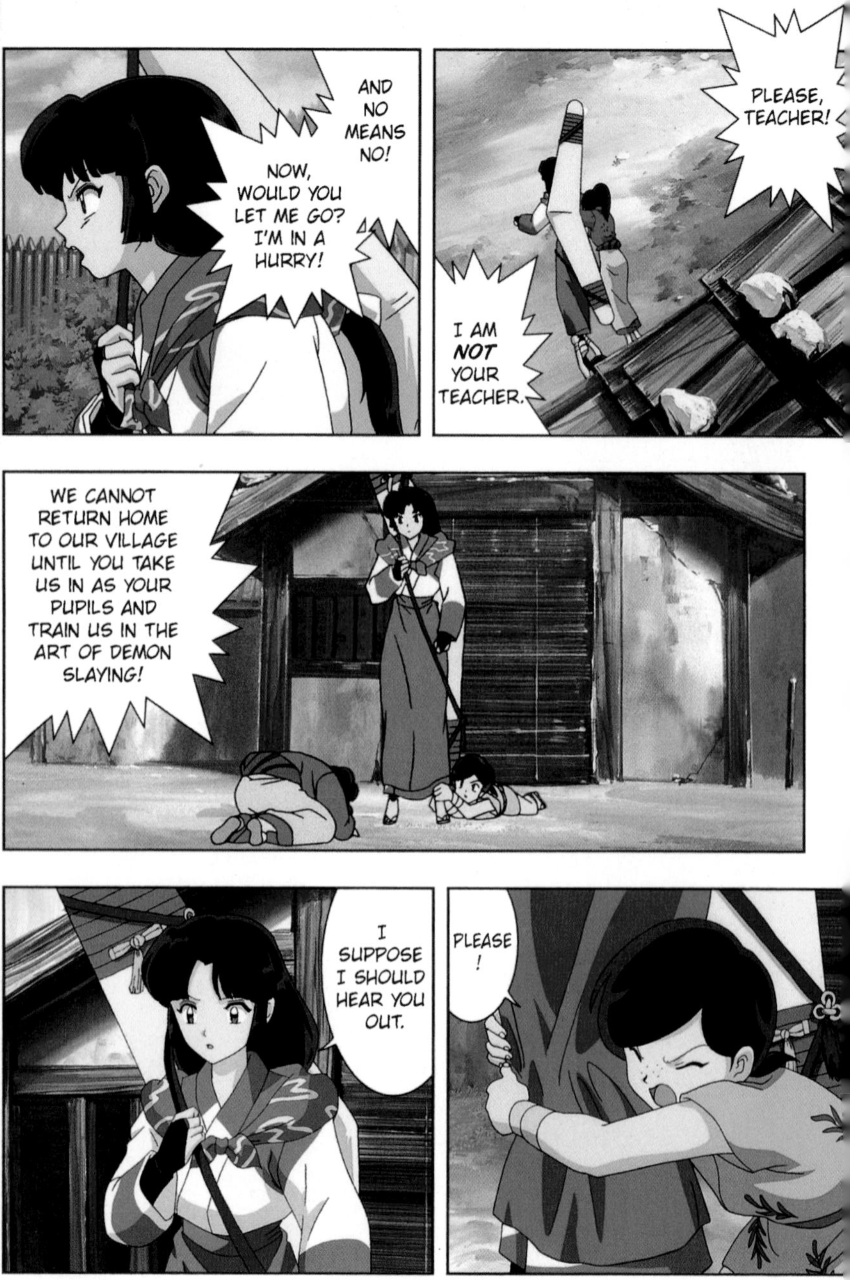
PLEASE, TEACHER!
I AM NOT YOUR TEACHER.
AND NO MEANS NO!
NOW, WOULD YOU LET ME GO? I'M IN A HURRY!
WE CANNOT RETURN HOME TO OUR VILLAGE UNTIL YOU TAKE US IN AS YOUR PUPILS AND TRAIN US IN THE ART OF DEMON SLAYING!
PLEASE!
I SUPPOSE I SHOULD HEAR YOU OUT.

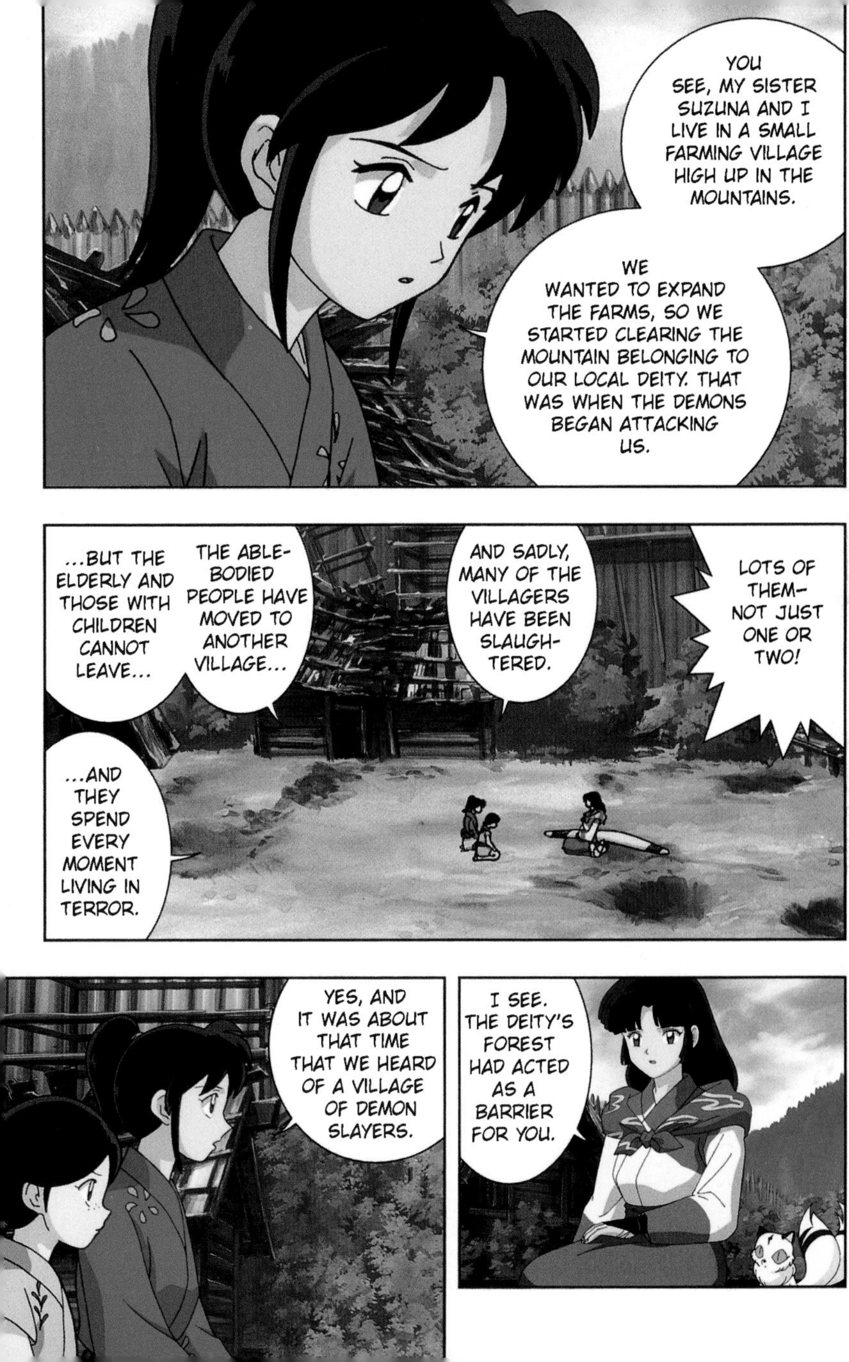
YOU SEE, MY SISTER SUZUNA AND I LIVE IN A SMALL FARMING VILLAGE HIGH UP IN THE MOUNTAINS.
WE WANTED TO EXPAND THE FARMS, SO WE STARTED CLEARING THE MOUNTAIN BELONGING TO OUR LOCAL DEITY. THAT WAS WHEN THE DEMONS BEGAN ATTACKING US.
LOTS OF THEM—NOT JUST ONE OR TWO!
AND SADLY, MANY OF THE VILLAGERS HAVE BEEN SLAUGH-TERED.
THE ABLE-BODIED PEOPLE HAVE MOVED TO ANOTHER VILLAGE...
...BUT THE ELDERLY AND THOSE WITH CHILDREN CANNOT LEAVE...
...AND THEY SPEND EVERY MOMENT LIVING IN TERROR.
I SEE. THE DEITY'S FOREST HAD ACTED AS A BARRIER FOR YOU.
YES, AND IT WAS ABOUT THAT TIME THAT WE HEARD OF A VILLAGE OF DEMON SLAYERS.

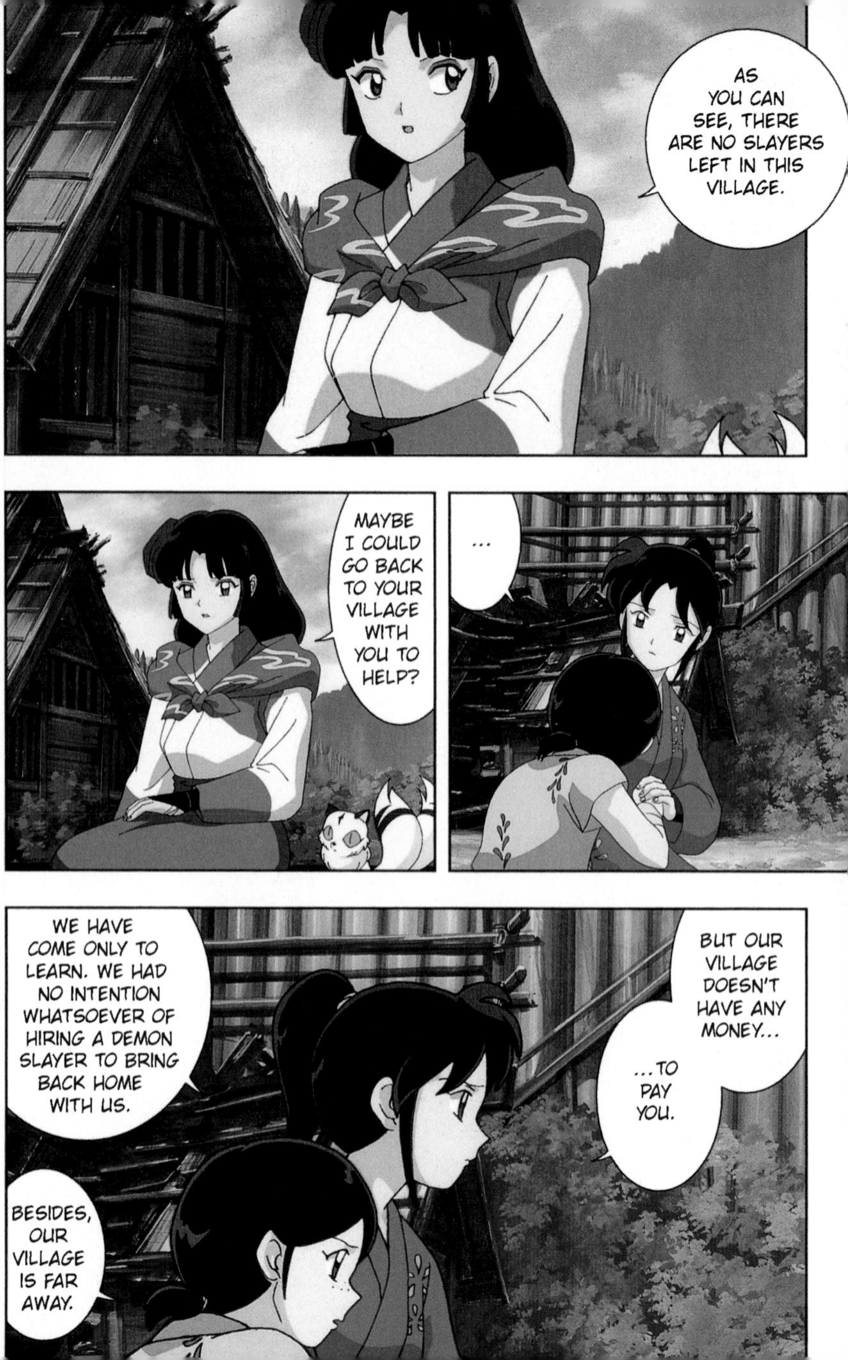
AS YOU CAN SEE, THERE ARE NO SLAYERS LEFT IN THIS VILLAGE.
...
MAYBE I COULD GO BACK TO YOUR VILLAGE WITH YOU TO HELP?
BUT OUR VILLAGE DOESN'T HAVE ANY MONEY...
...TO PAY YOU.
WE HAVE COME ONLY TO LEARN. WE HAD NO INTENTION WHATSOEVER OF HIRING A DEMON SLAYER TO BRING BACK HOME WITH US.
BESIDES, OUR VILLAGE IS FAR AWAY.

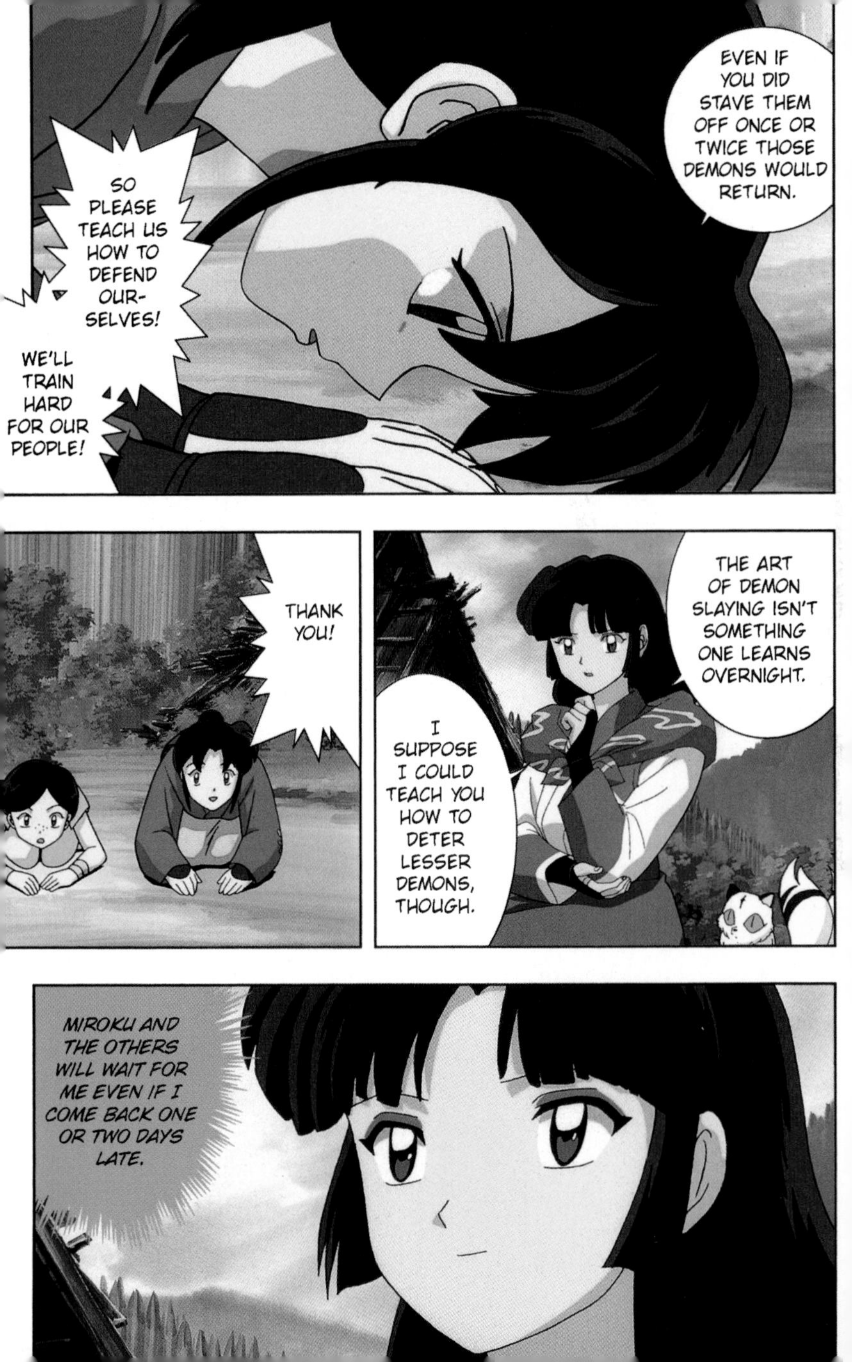
EVEN IF YOU DID STAVE THEM OFF ONCE OR TWICE THOSE DEMONS WOULD RETURN.
SO PLEASE TEACH US HOW TO DEFEND OUR-SELVES!
WE'LL TRAIN HARD FOR OUR PEOPLE!
THE ART OF DEMON SLAYING ISN'T SOMETHING ONE LEARNS OVERNIGHT.
I SUPPOSE I COULD TEACH YOU HOW TO DETER LESSER DEMONS, THOUGH.
THANK YOU!
MIROKU AND THE OTHERS WILL WAIT FOR ME EVEN IF I COME BACK ONE OR TWO DAYS LATE.

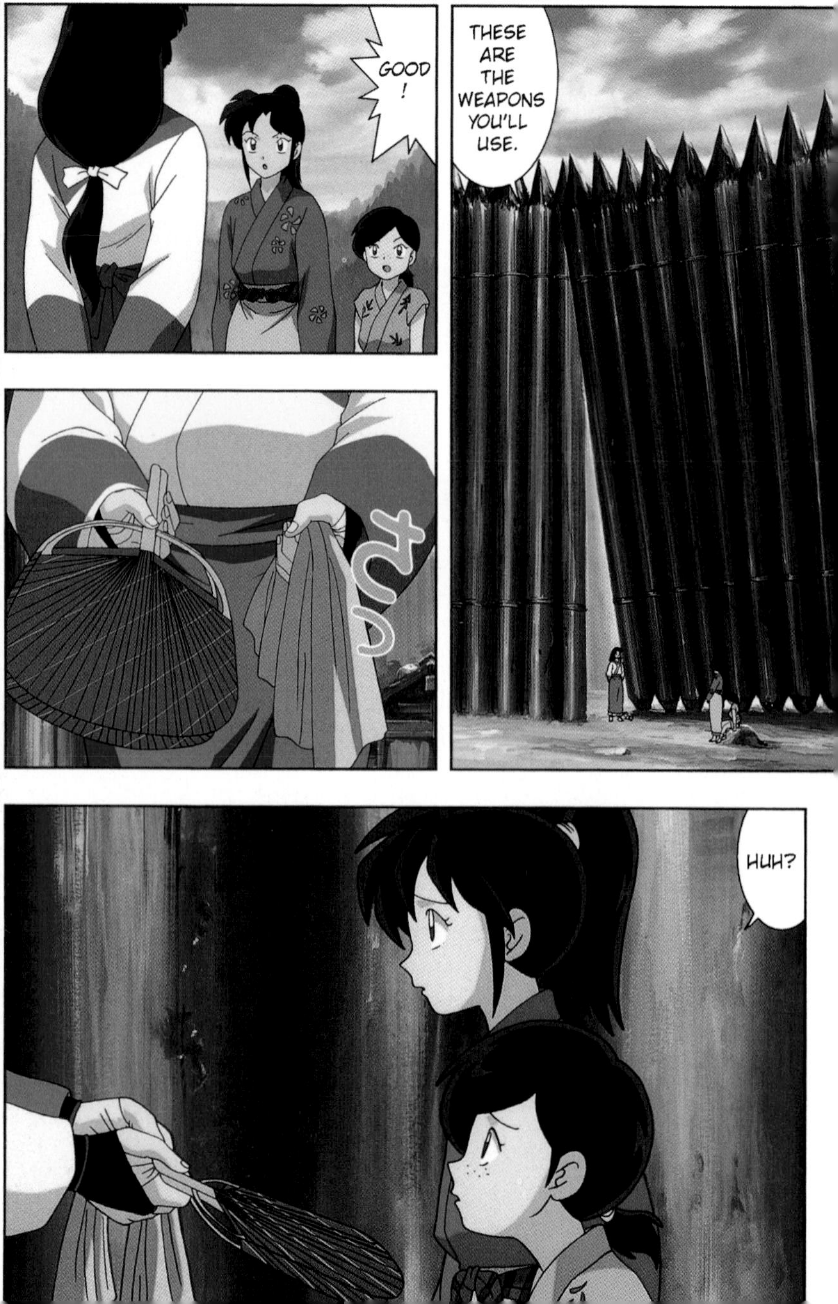
THESE ARE THE WEAPONS YOU'LL USE.
GOOD!
さっ
HUH?

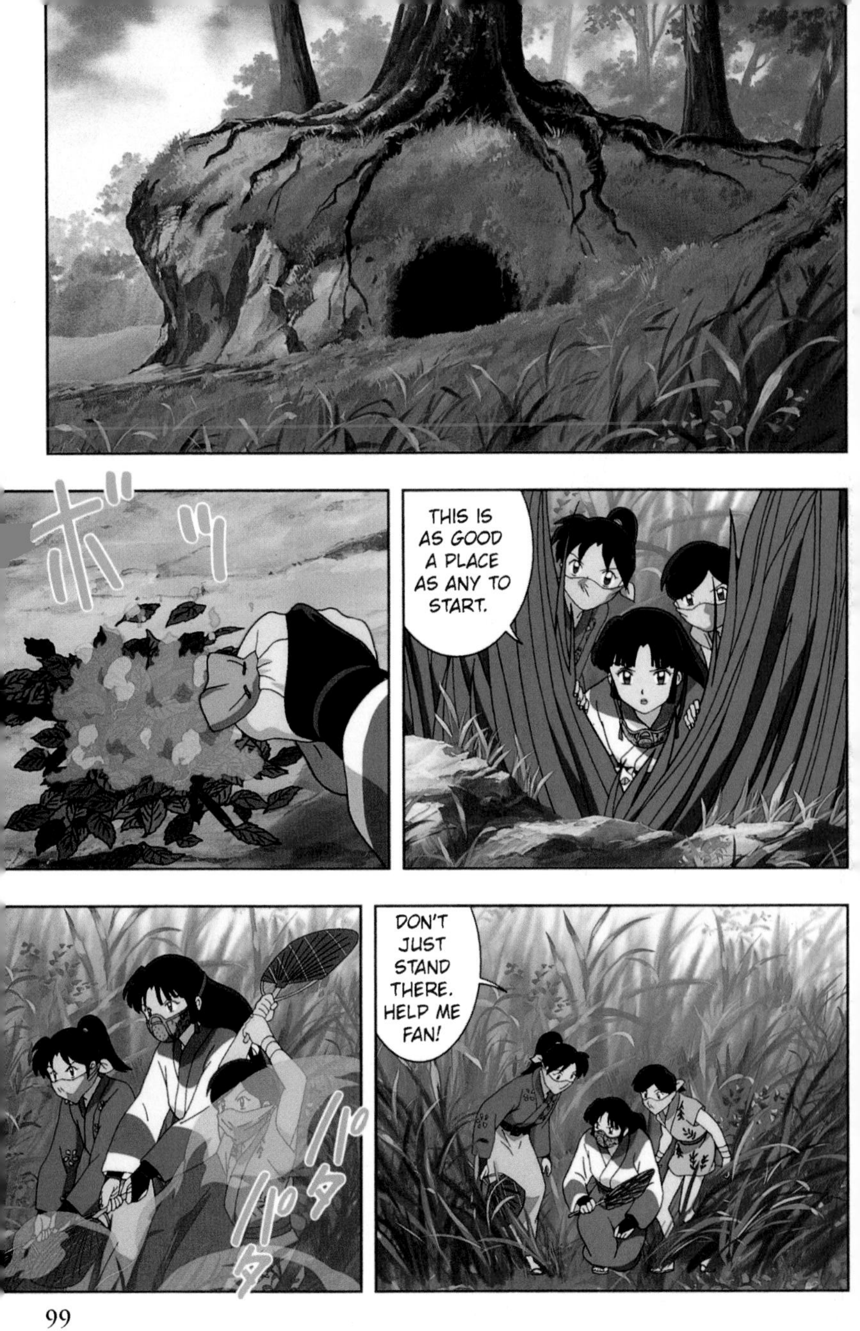
THIS IS AS GOOD A PLACE AS ANY TO START.
ボッ
DON'T JUST STAND THERE. HELP ME FAN!
パタパタ

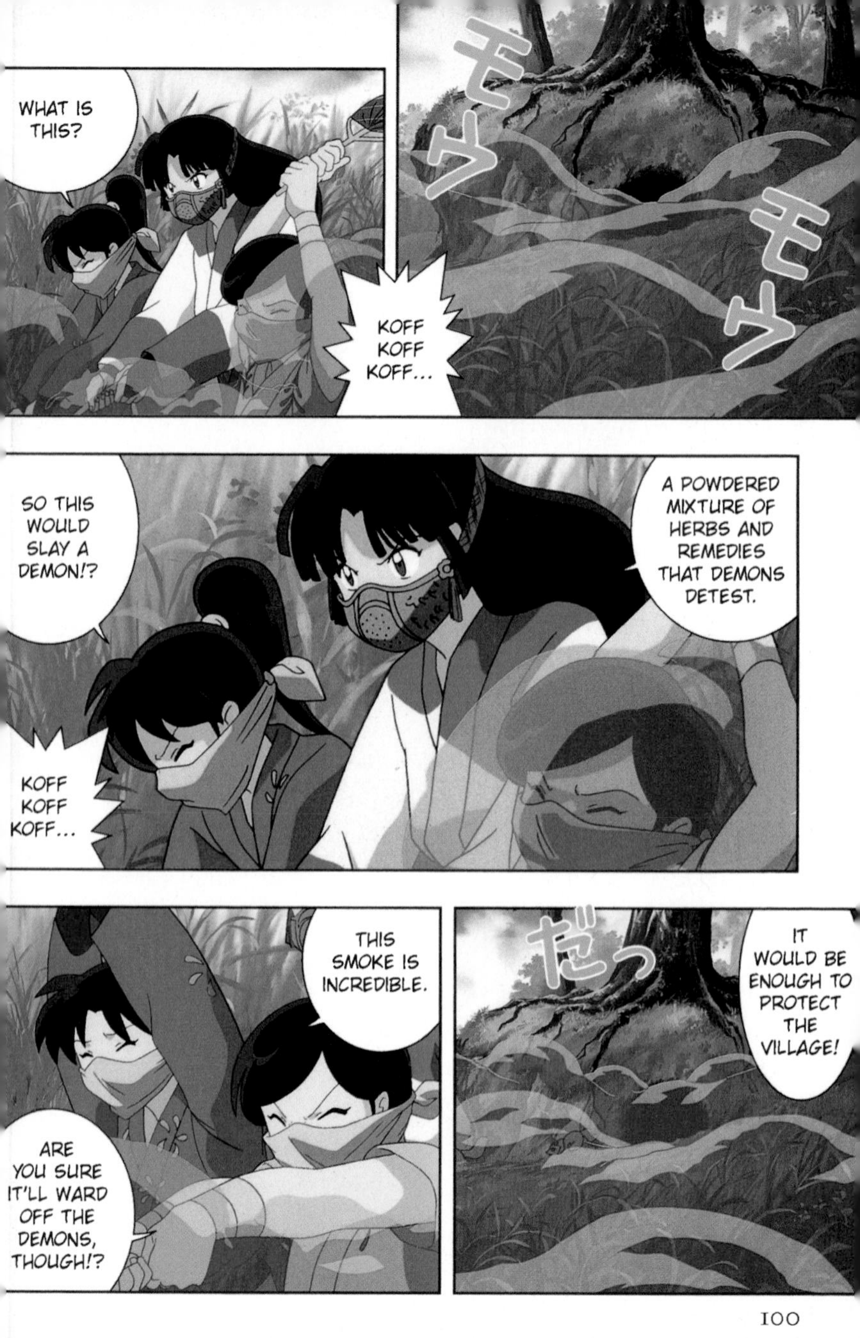
モヤ
モヤ
WHAT IS THIS?
KOFF KOFF KOFF...
A POWDERED MIXTURE OF HERBS AND REMEDIES THAT DEMONS DETEST.
SO THIS WOULD SLAY A DEMON!?
KOFF KOFF KOFF...
だっ
IT WOULD BE ENOUGH TO PROTECT THE VILLAGE!
THIS SMOKE IS INCREDIBLE.
ARE YOU SURE IT'LL WARD OFF THE DEMONS, THOUGH!?

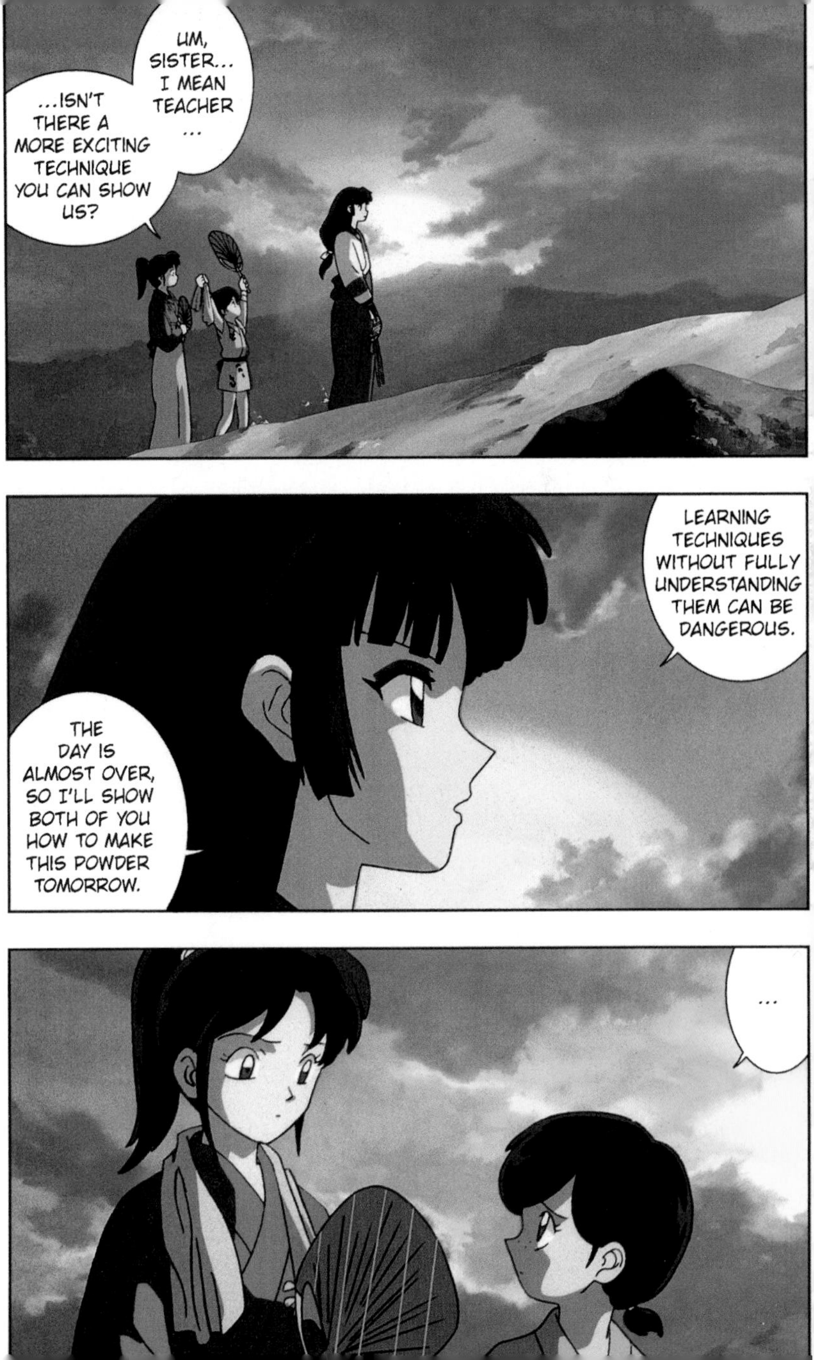
UM, SISTER... I MEAN TEACHER...
...ISN'T THERE A MORE EXCITING TECHNIQUE YOU CAN SHOW US?
LEARNING TECHNIQUES WITHOUT FULLY UNDERSTANDING THEM CAN BE DANGEROUS.
THE DAY IS ALMOST OVER, SO I'LL SHOW BOTH OF YOU HOW TO MAKE THIS POWDER TOMORROW.
...

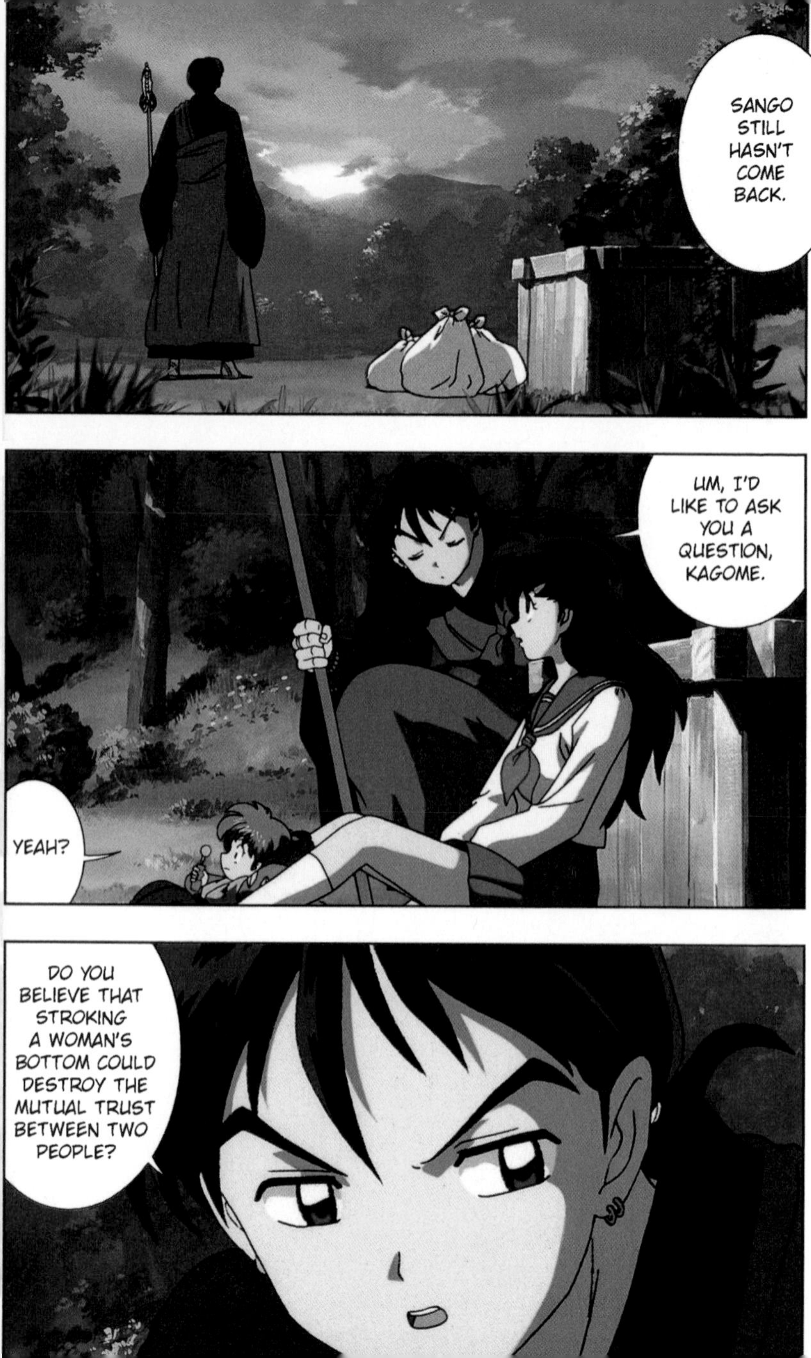
SANGO STILL HASN'T COME BACK.
UM, I'D LIKE TO ASK YOU A QUESTION, KAGOME.
YEAH?
DO YOU BELIEVE THAT STROKING A WOMAN'S BOTTOM COULD DESTROY THE MUTUAL TRUST BETWEEN TWO PEOPLE?

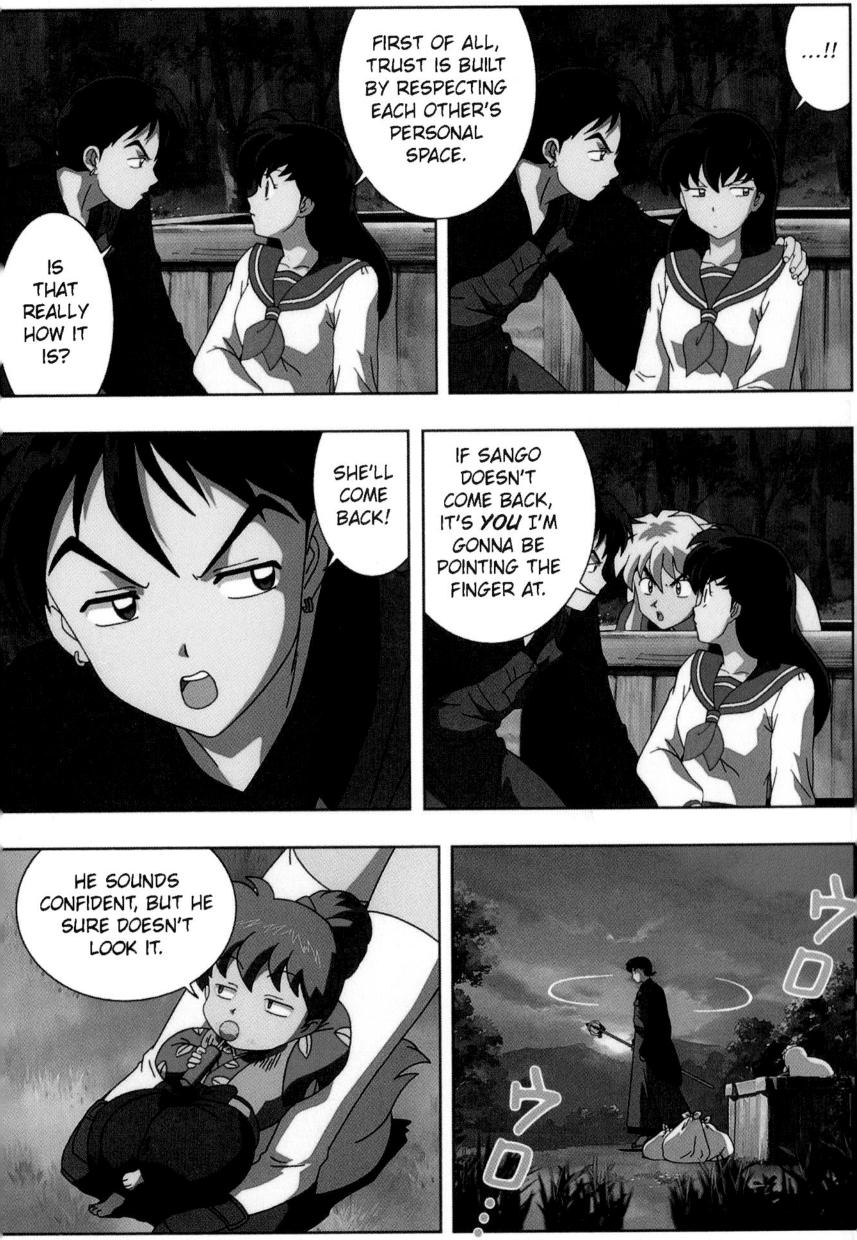
...!!
FIRST OF ALL, TRUST IS BUILT BY RESPECTING EACH OTHER'S PERSONAL SPACE.
IS THAT REALLY HOW IT IS?
IF SANGO DOESN'T COME BACK, IT'S ***YOU*** I'M GONNA BE POINTING THE FINGER AT.
SHE'LL COME BACK!
ウロ
ウロ...
HE SOUNDS CONFIDENT, BUT HE SURE DOESN'T LOOK IT.

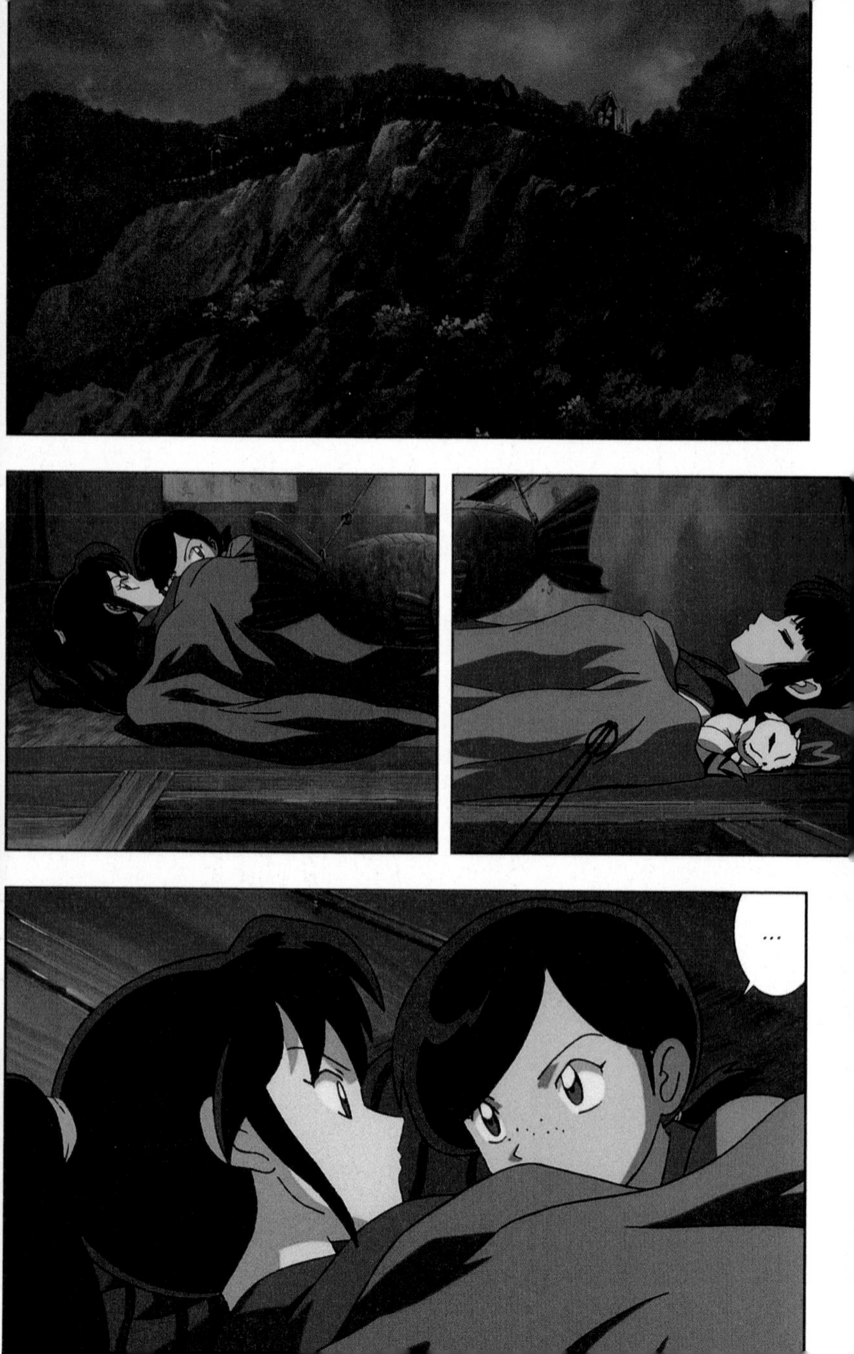
...

SERINA, LET ME DO IT!

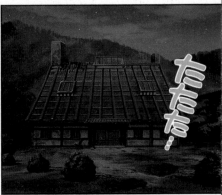

THAT WAS EASY ENOUGH TO BREAK OFF!

CAN'T BEAT A NINJA'S SKILLS.

THANKS. I COULDN'T HAVE DONE IT WITHOUT YOU.

HAH!

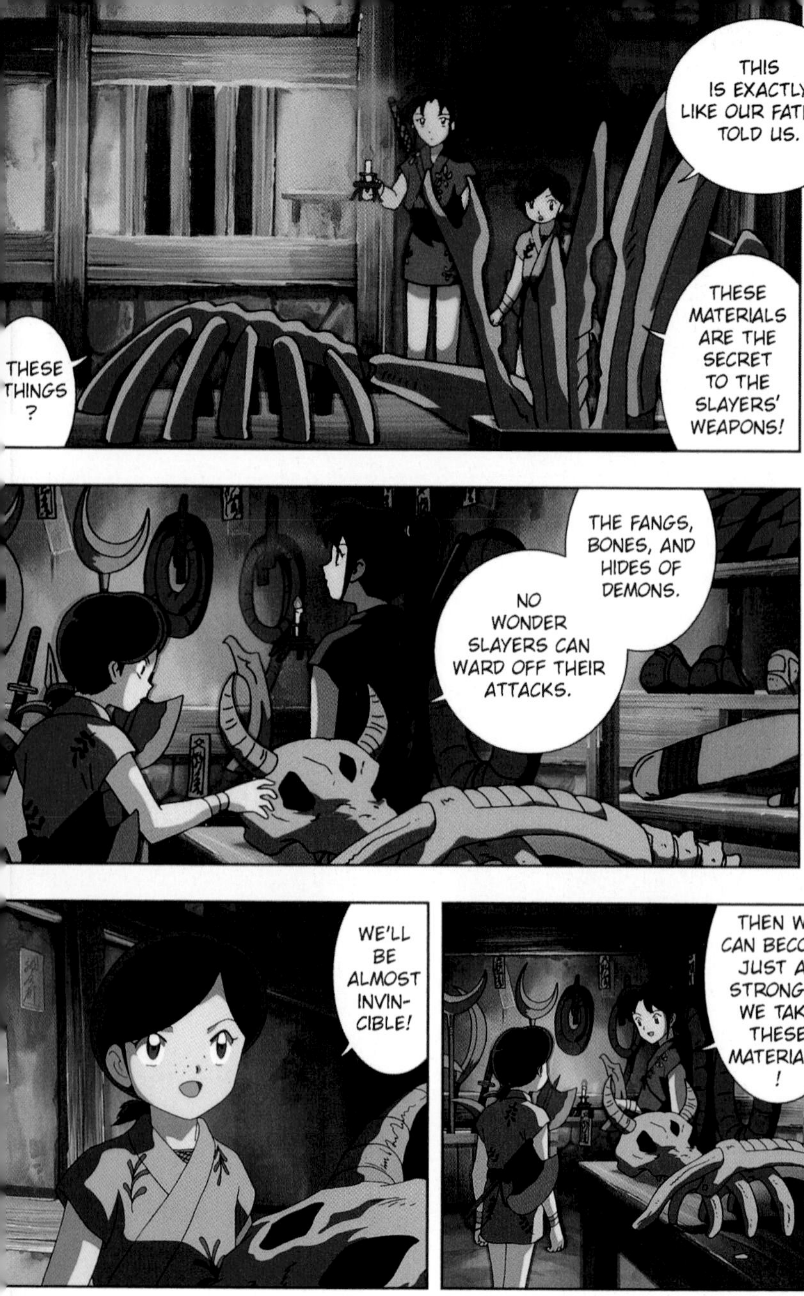
THIS IS EXACTLY LIKE OUR FATHER TOLD US.
THESE MATERIALS ARE THE SECRET TO THE SLAYERS' WEAPONS!
THESE THINGS?
THE FANGS, BONES, AND HIDES OF DEMONS.
NO WONDER SLAYERS CAN WARD OFF THEIR ATTACKS.
THEN WE CAN BECOME JUST AS STRONG IF WE TAKE THESE MATERIALS!
WE'LL BE ALMOST INVINCIBLE!

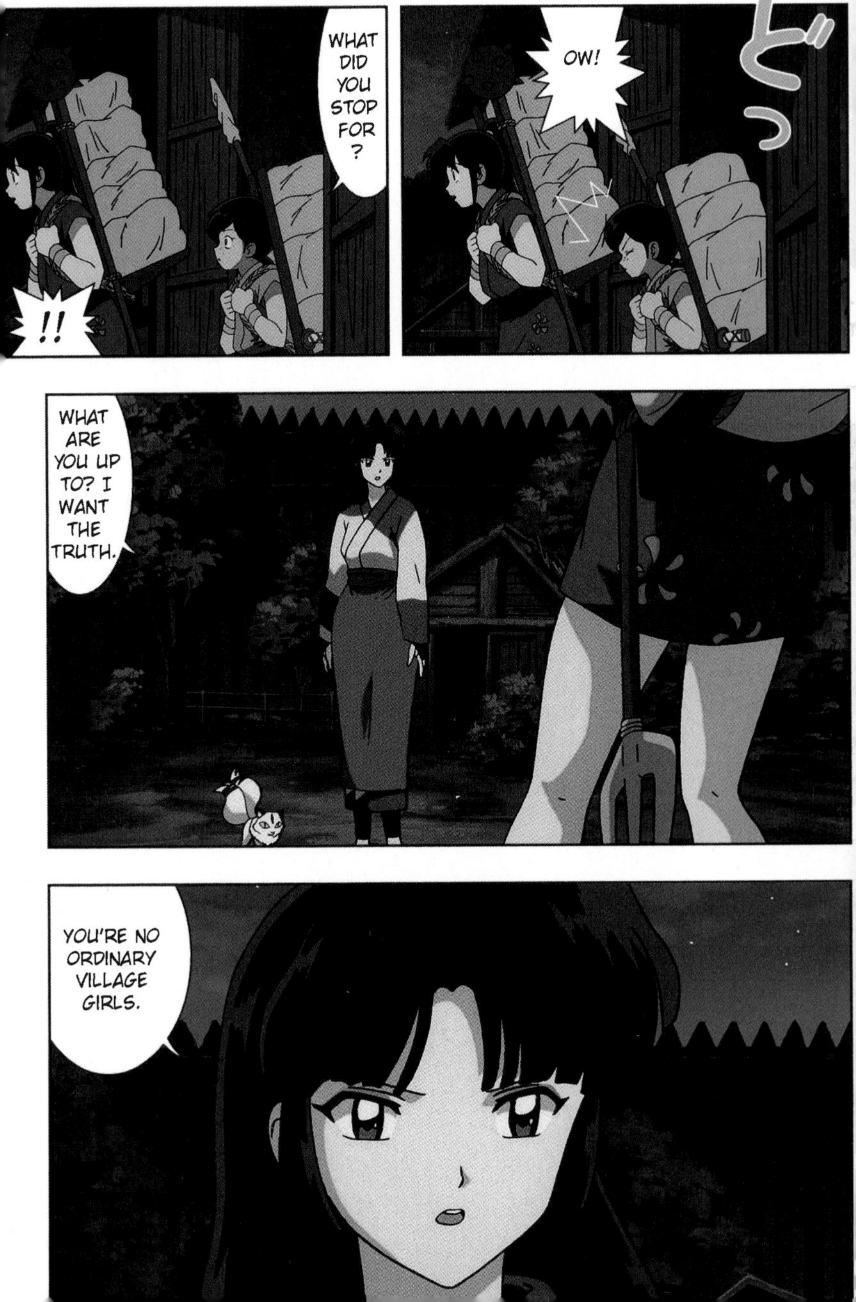
どっ
OW!
WHAT DID YOU STOP FOR?
!!
WHAT ARE YOU UP TO? I WANT THE TRUTH.
YOU'RE NO ORDINARY VILLAGE GIRLS.

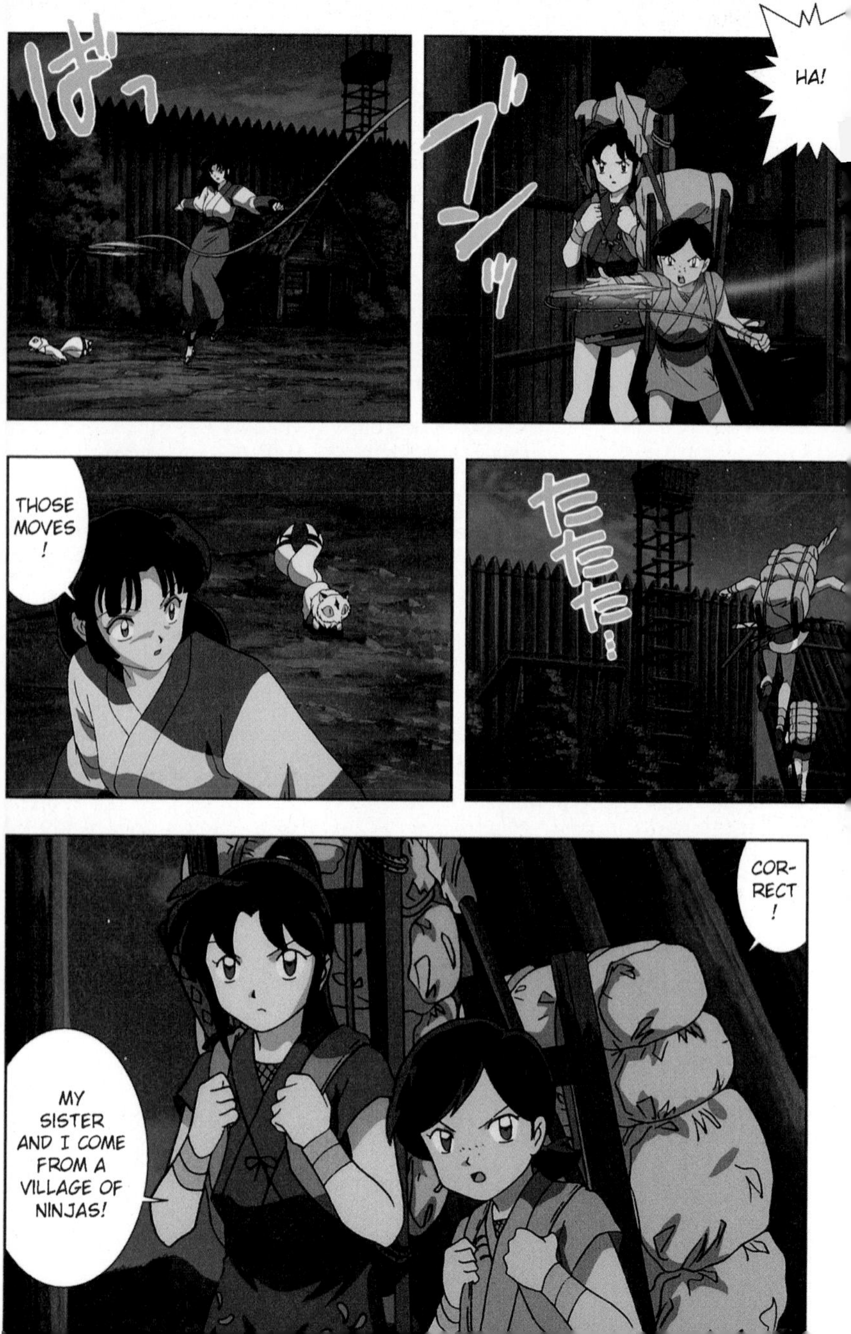
HA!
ブンッ
ぱっ
たたた..
THOSE MOVES!
CORRECT!
MY SISTER AND I COME FROM A VILLAGE OF NINJAS!

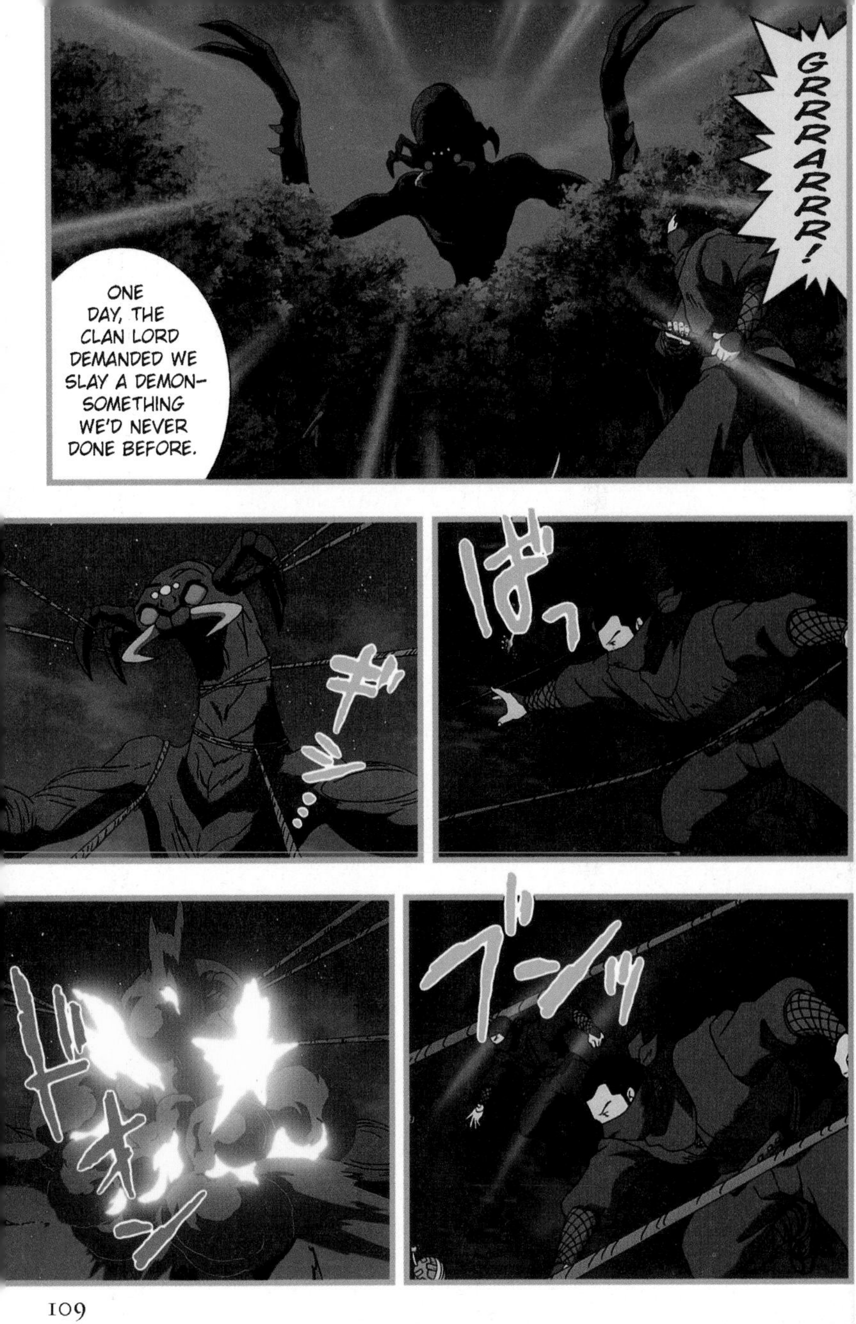
GRRRARRR!
ONE DAY, THE CLAN LORD DEMANDED WE SLAY A DEMON-SOMETHING WE'D NEVER DONE BEFORE.
ばっ
ギシ...
ブンッ
ドォン

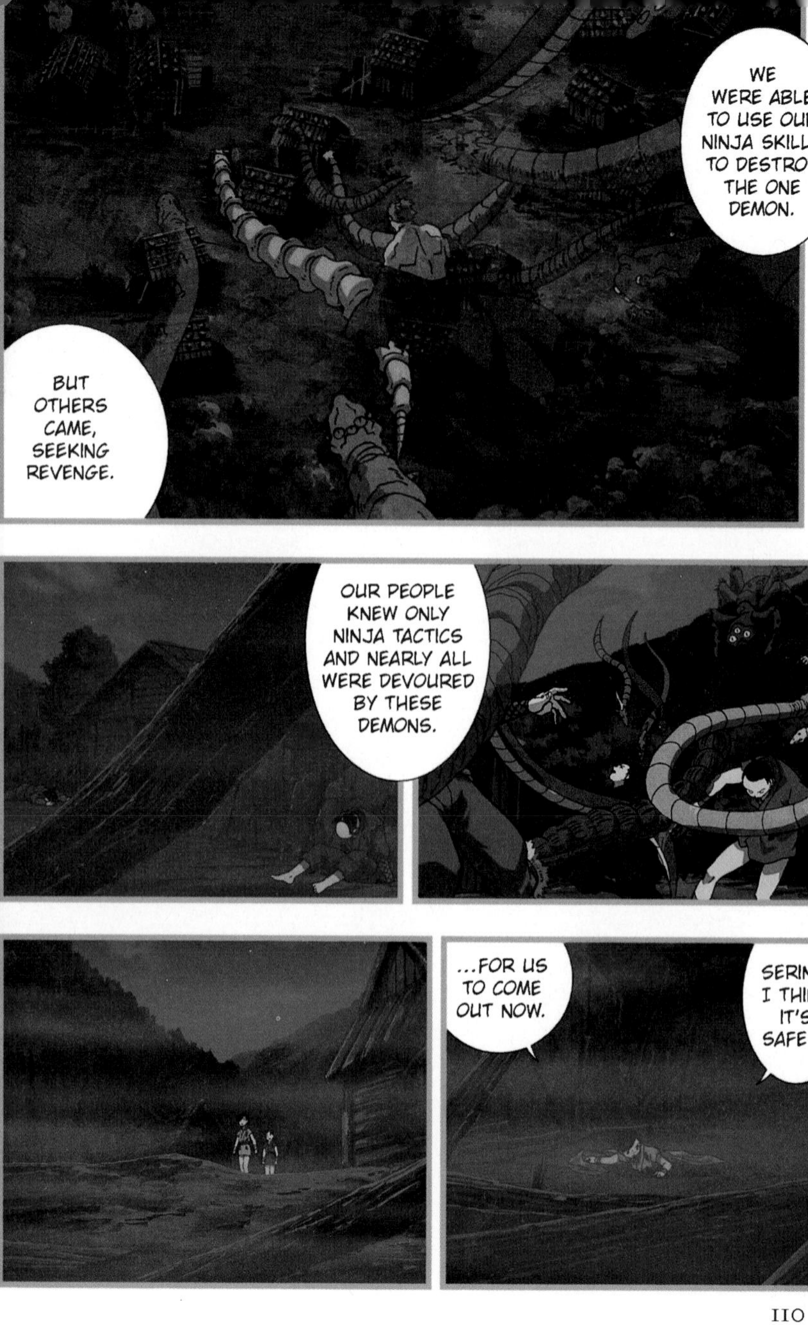
WE WERE ABLE TO USE OUR NINJA SKILLS TO DESTROY THE ONE DEMON.
BUT OTHERS CAME, SEEKING REVENGE.
OUR PEOPLE KNEW ONLY NINJA TACTICS AND NEARLY ALL WERE DEVOURED BY THESE DEMONS.
SERINA, I THINK IT'S SAFE...
...FOR US TO COME OUT NOW.

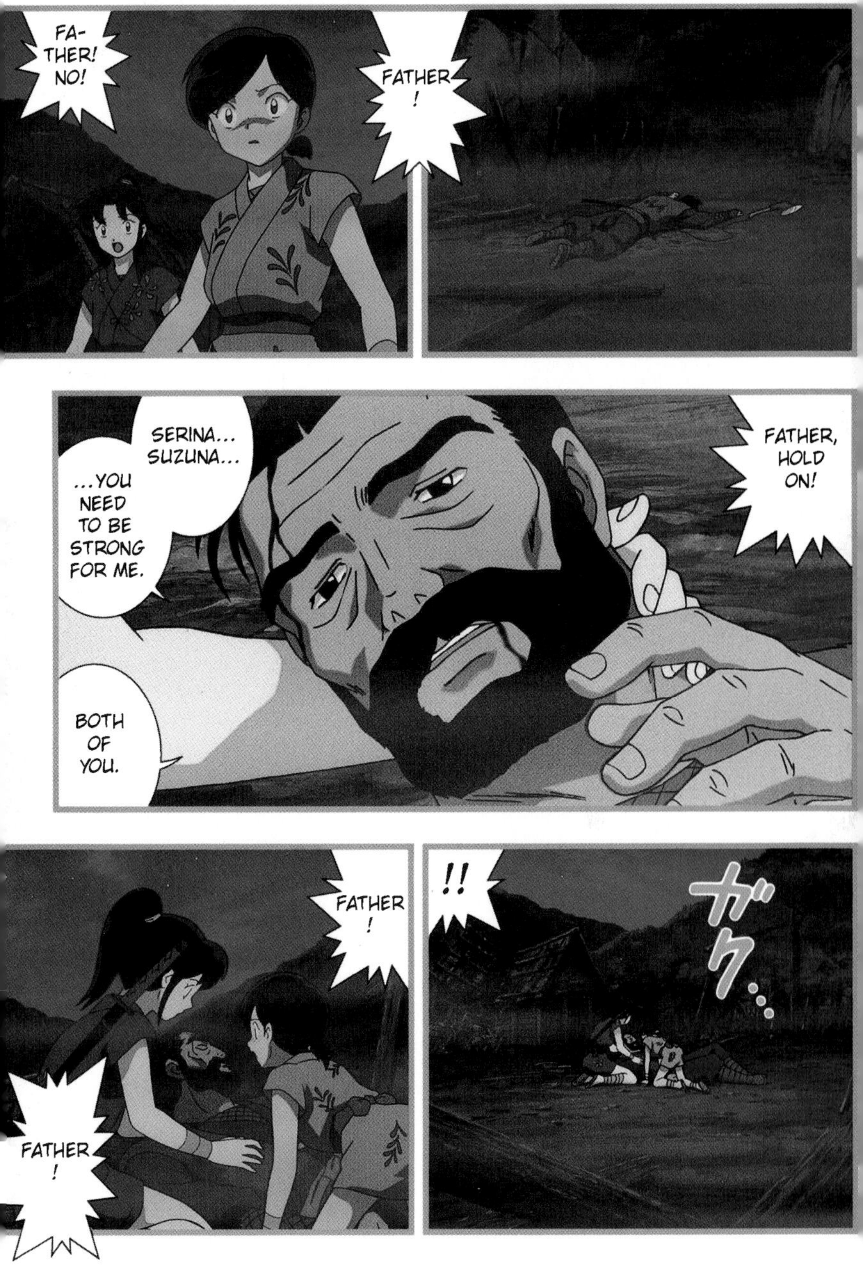
FATHER!
FA-THER! NO!
FATHER, HOLD ON!
SERINA... SUZUNA...
...YOU NEED TO BE STRONG FOR ME.
BOTH OF YOU.
!!
ガク...
FATHER!
FATHER!

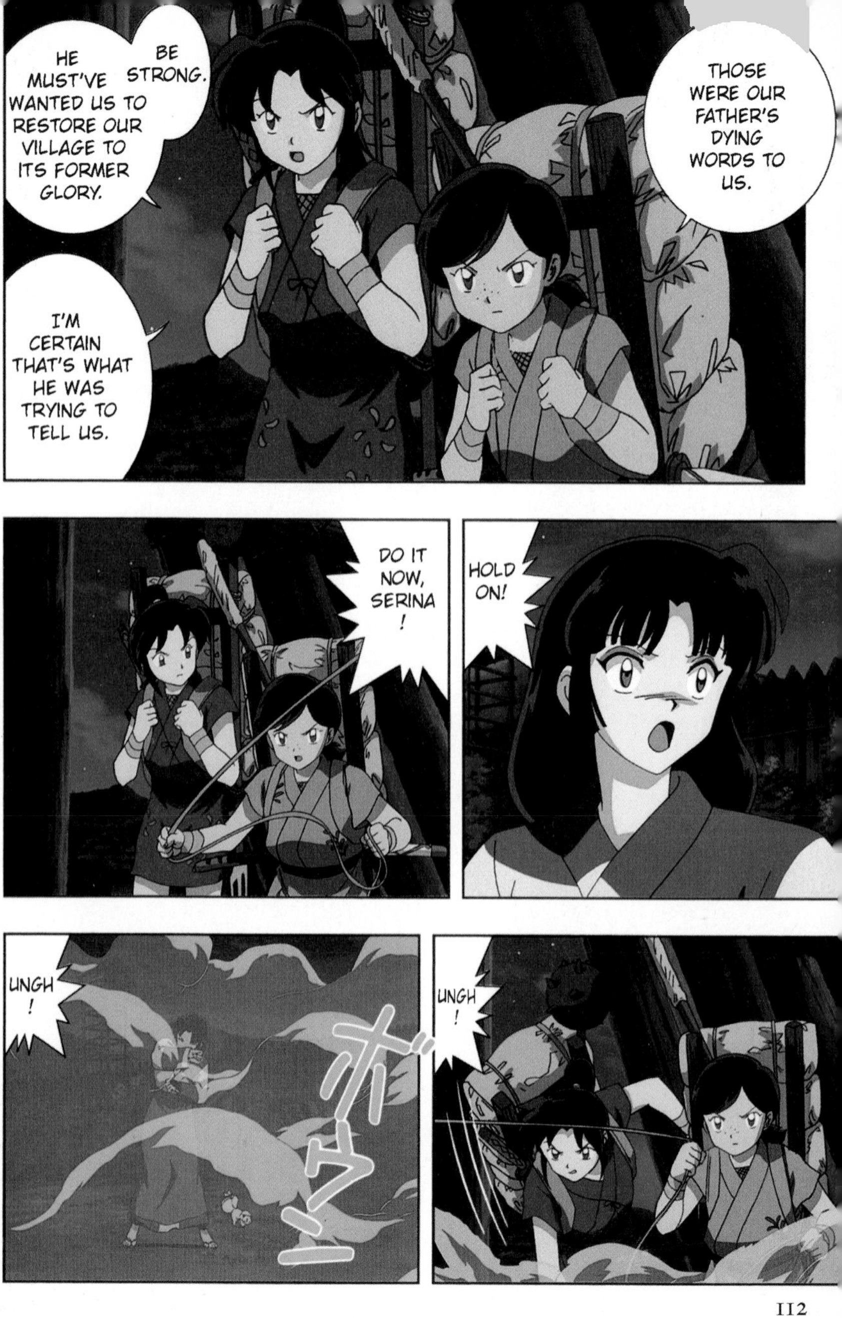
THOSE WERE OUR FATHER'S DYING WORDS TO US.
BE STRONG.
HE MUST'VE WANTED US TO RESTORE OUR VILLAGE TO ITS FORMER GLORY.
I'M CERTAIN THAT'S WHAT HE WAS TRYING TO TELL US.
HOLD ON!
DO IT NOW, SERINA!
UNGH!
UNGH!

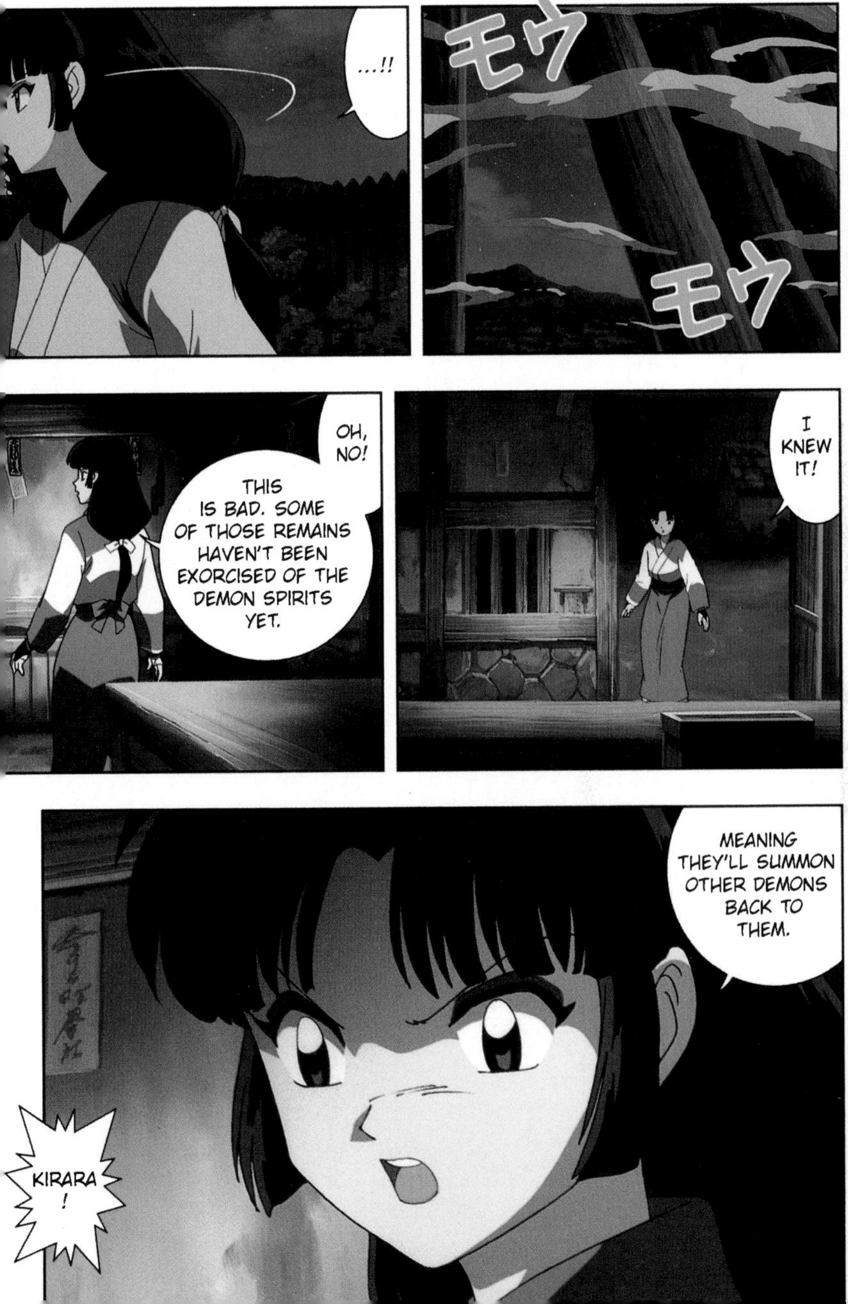
モウ
モウ
...!!
I KNEW IT!
OH, NO!
THIS IS BAD. SOME OF THOSE REMAINS HAVEN'T BEEN EXORCISED OF THE DEMON SPIRITS YET.
MEANING THEY'LL SUMMON OTHER DEMONS BACK TO THEM.
KIRARA!

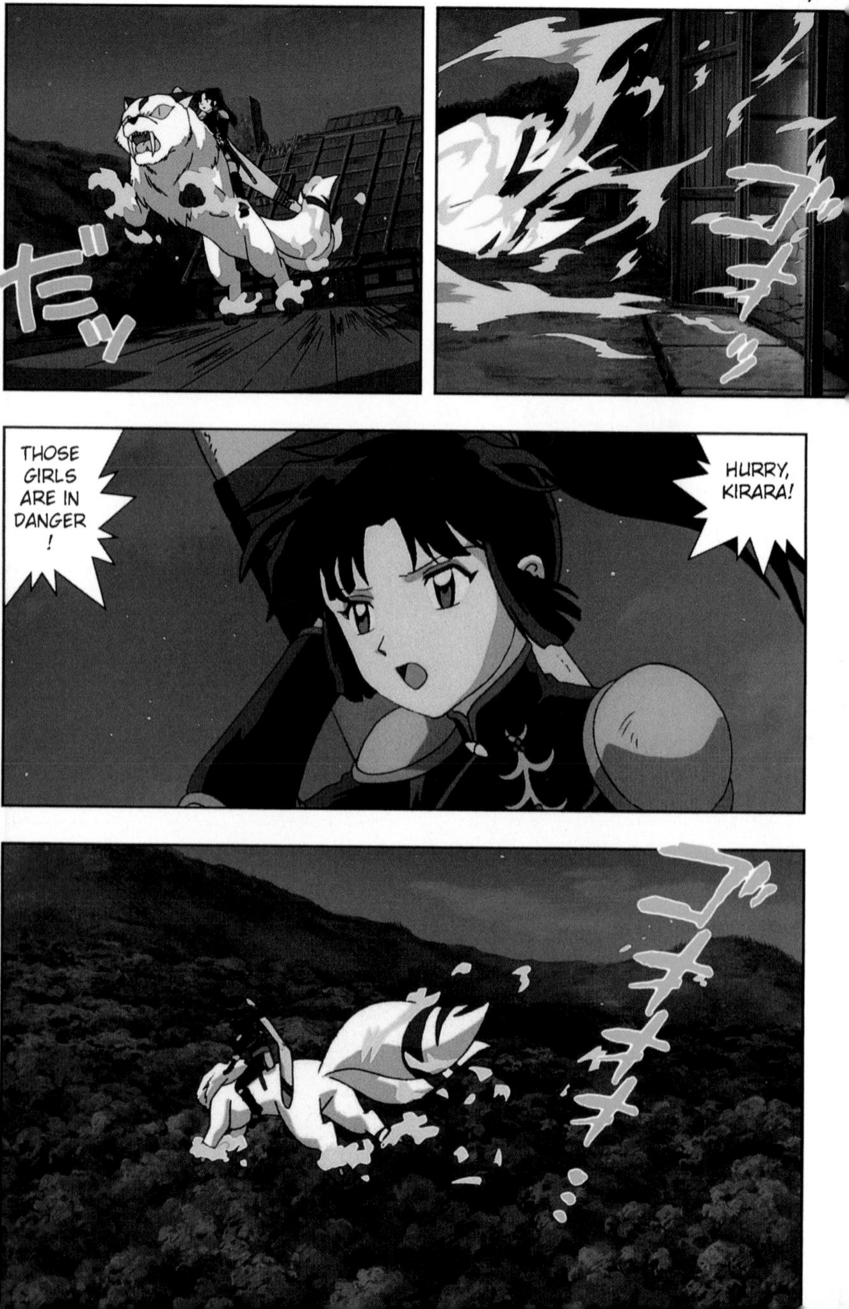
ゴオッ
ダッ
HURRY, KIRARA!
THOSE GIRLS ARE IN DANGER!
ゴオオオ…

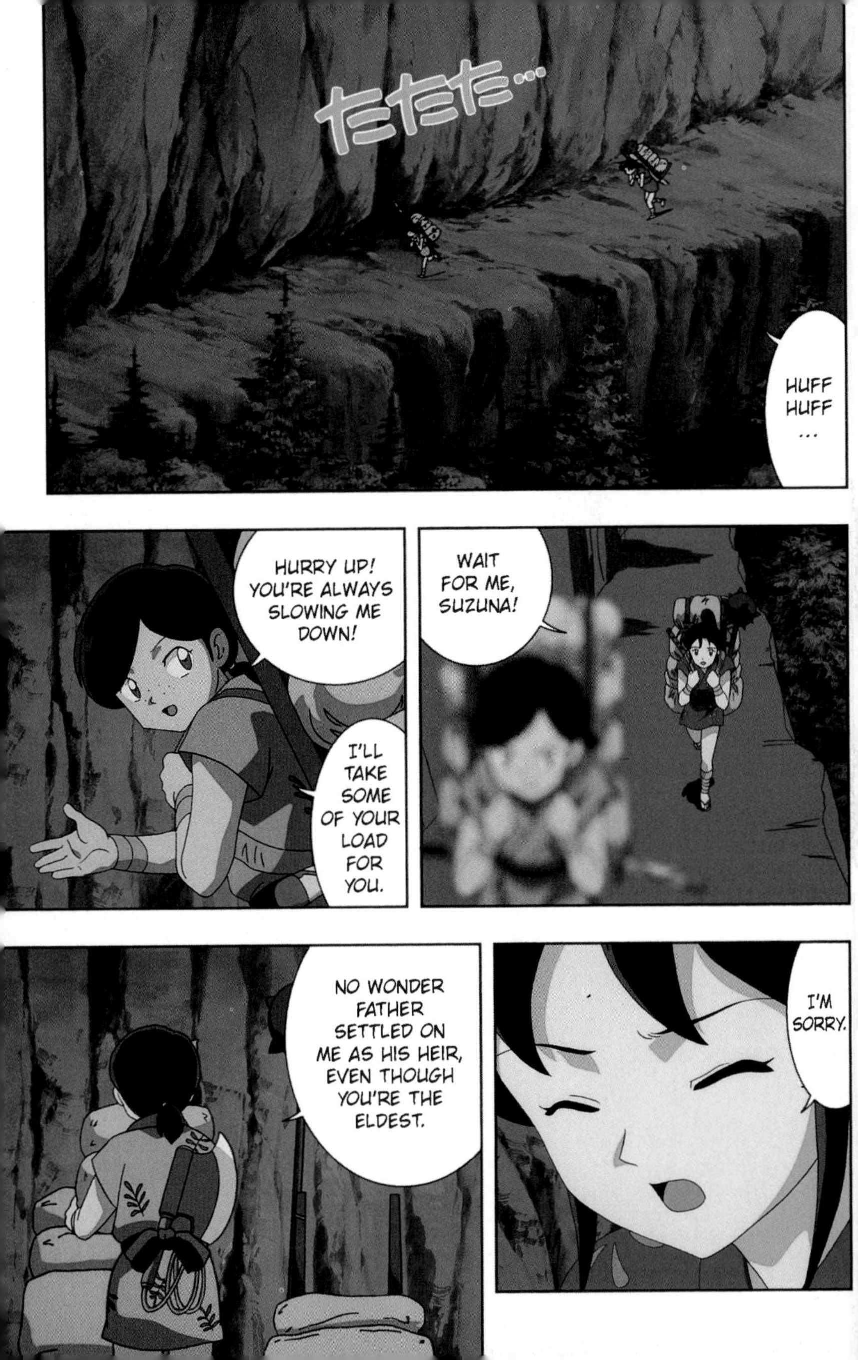
たたた…
HUFF HUFF ...
WAIT FOR ME, SUZUNA!
HURRY UP! YOU'RE ALWAYS SLOWING ME DOWN!
I'LL TAKE SOME OF YOUR LOAD FOR YOU.
I'M SORRY.
NO WONDER FATHER SETTLED ON ME AS HIS HEIR, EVEN THOUGH YOU'RE THE ELDEST.

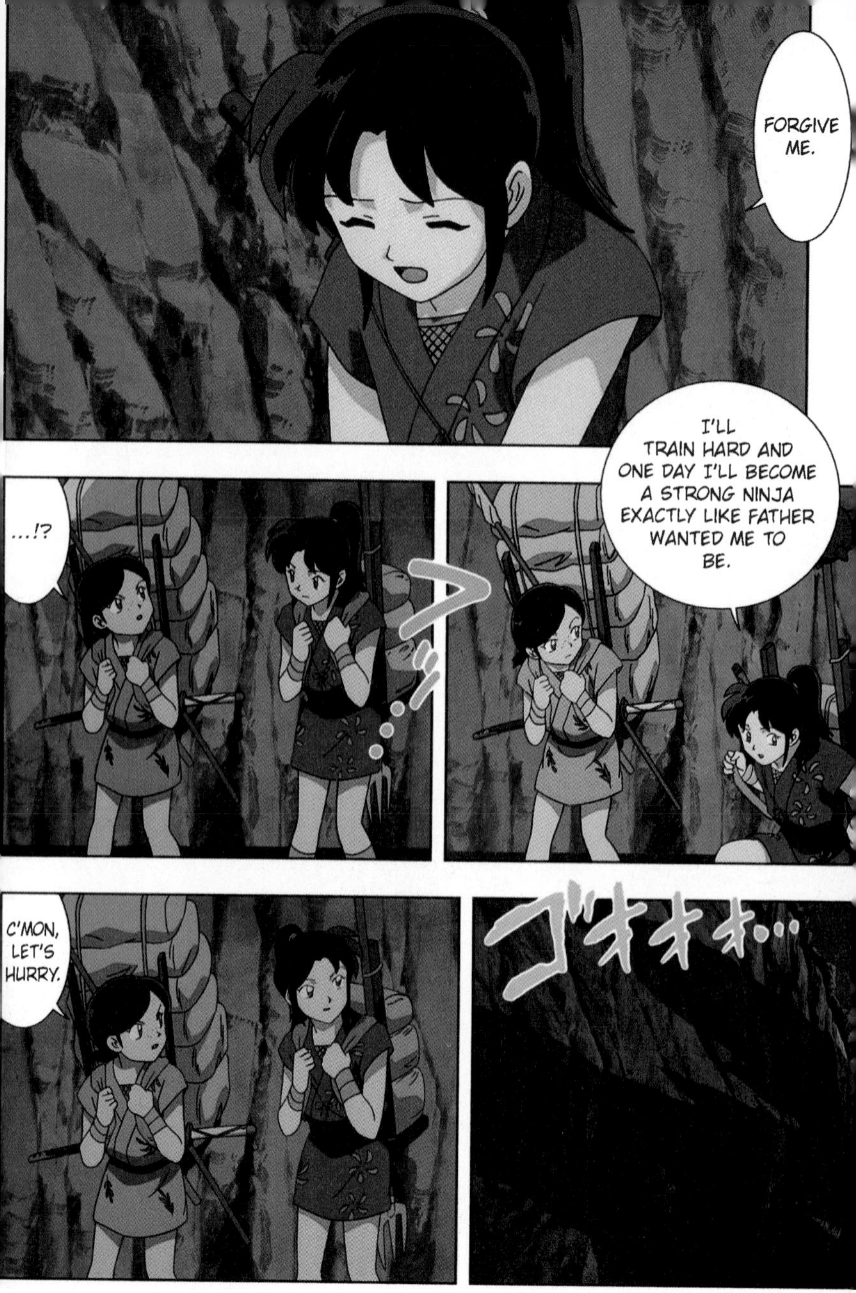
FORGIVE ME.
I'LL TRAIN HARD AND ONE DAY I'LL BECOME A STRONG NINJA EXACTLY LIKE FATHER WANTED ME TO BE.
...!?
ゴオオオ…
C'MON, LET'S HURRY.

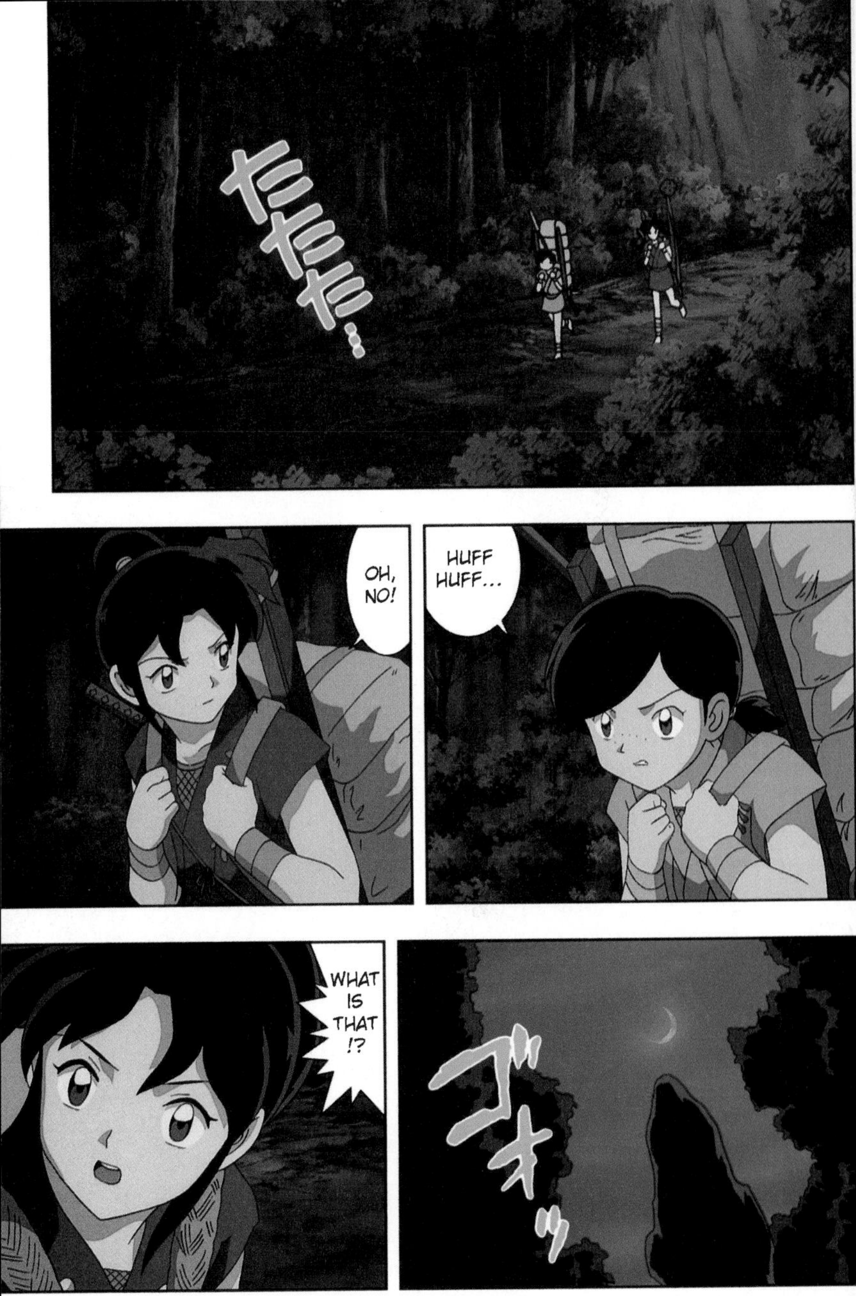
たたた…
HUFF HUFF…
OH, NO!
ゴォッ
WHAT IS THAT !?

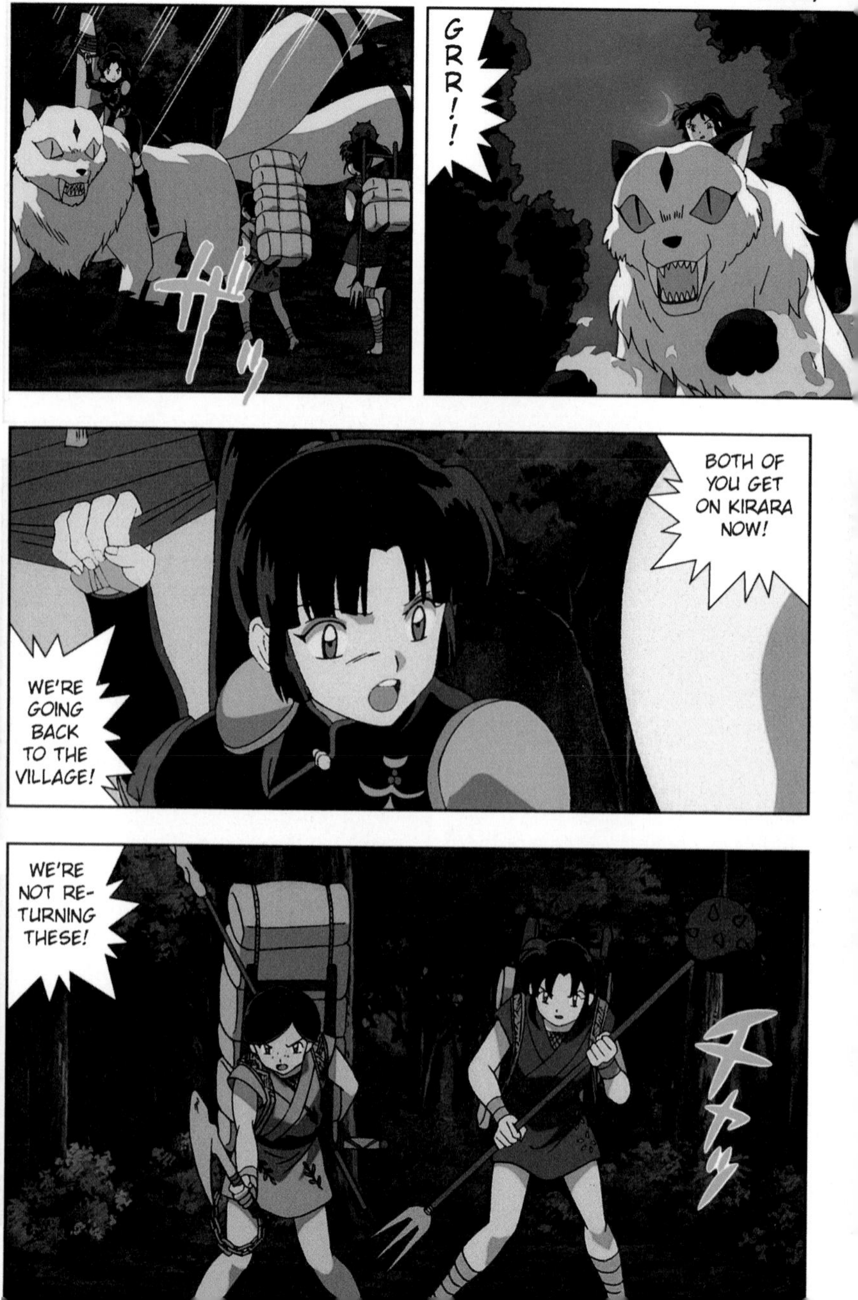
GRR!!
BOTH OF YOU GET ON KIRARA NOW!
WE'RE GOING BACK TO THE VILLAGE!
WE'RE NOT RE-TURNING THESE!

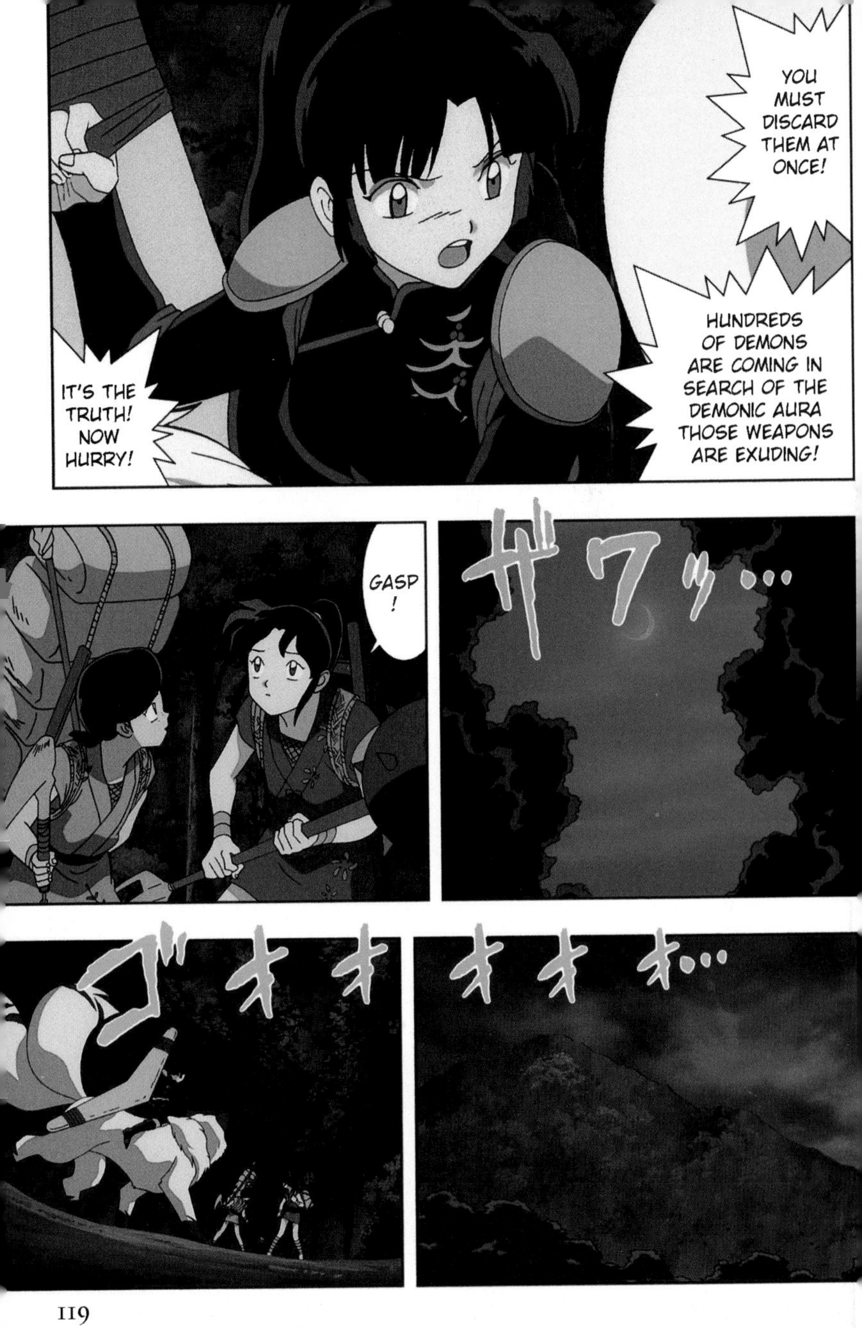
YOU MUST DISCARD THEM AT ONCE!
HUNDREDS OF DEMONS ARE COMING IN SEARCH OF THE DEMONIC AURA THOSE WEAPONS ARE EXUDING!
IT'S THE TRUTH! NOW HURRY!
ザワッ…
GASP!
ゴオオオオオ…

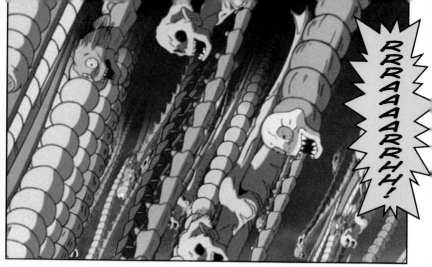

RRRAAAAARRHH!

!!

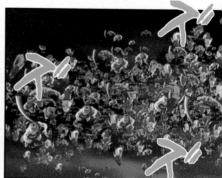

WE'RE TOO LATE!

AH...

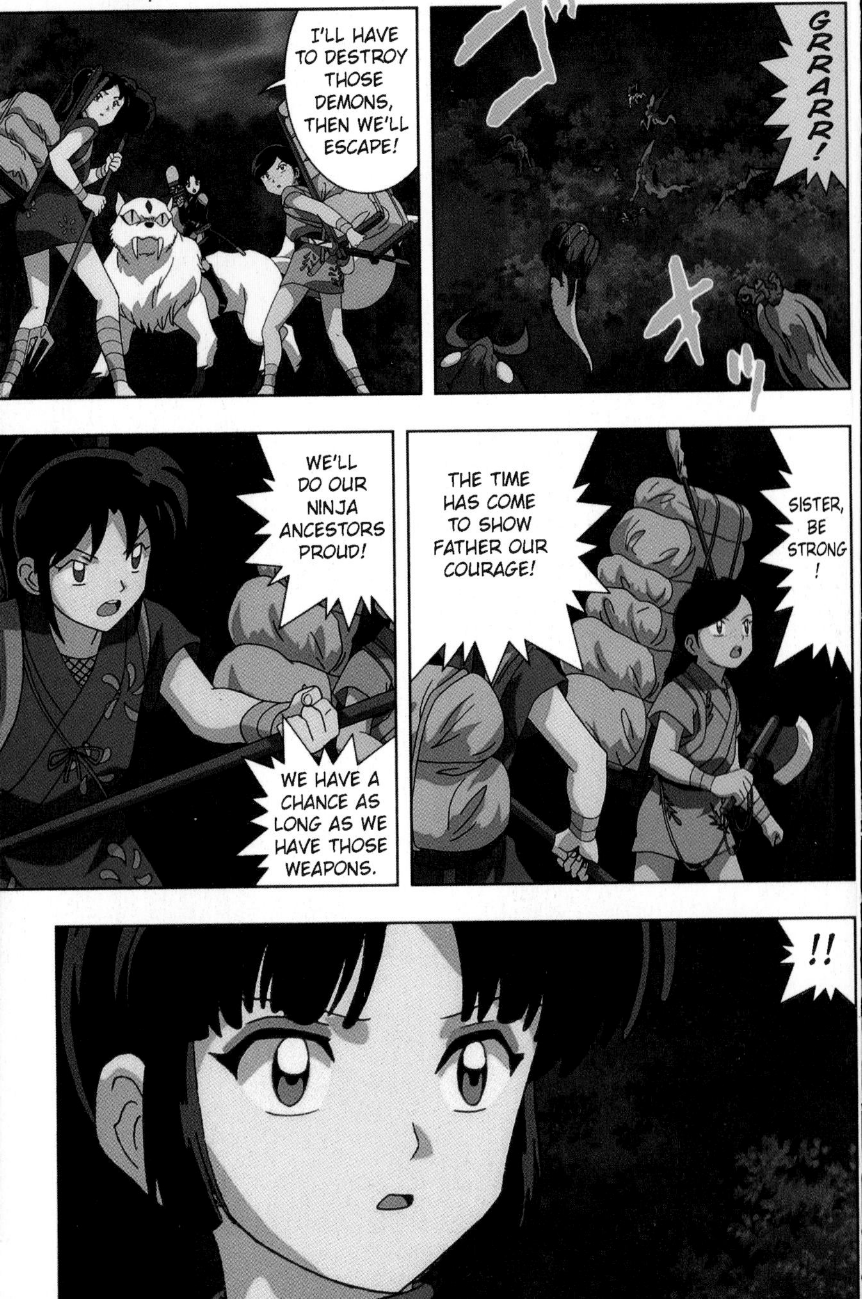
GRRRARR!
ゴォッ
I'LL HAVE TO DESTROY THOSE DEMONS, THEN WE'LL ESCAPE!
SISTER, BE STRONG!
THE TIME HAS COME TO SHOW FATHER OUR COURAGE!
WE'LL DO OUR NINJA ANCESTORS PROUD!
WE HAVE A CHANCE AS LONG AS WE HAVE THOSE WEAPONS.
!!

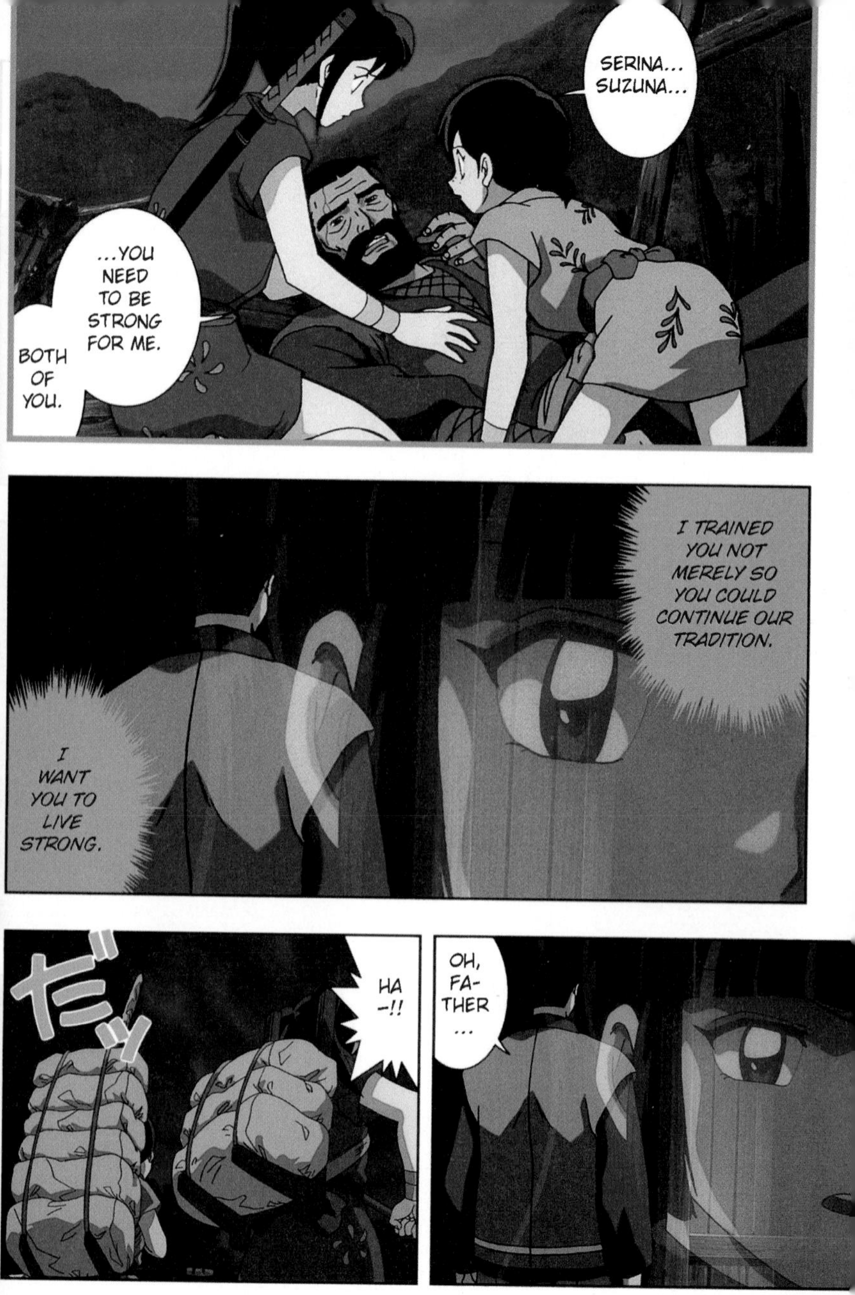
SERINA... SUZUNA...
...YOU NEED TO BE STRONG FOR ME.
BOTH OF YOU.
I TRAINED YOU NOT MERELY SO YOU COULD CONTINUE OUR TRADITION.
I WANT YOU TO LIVE STRONG.
OH, FA-THER ...
HA -!!
ダッ

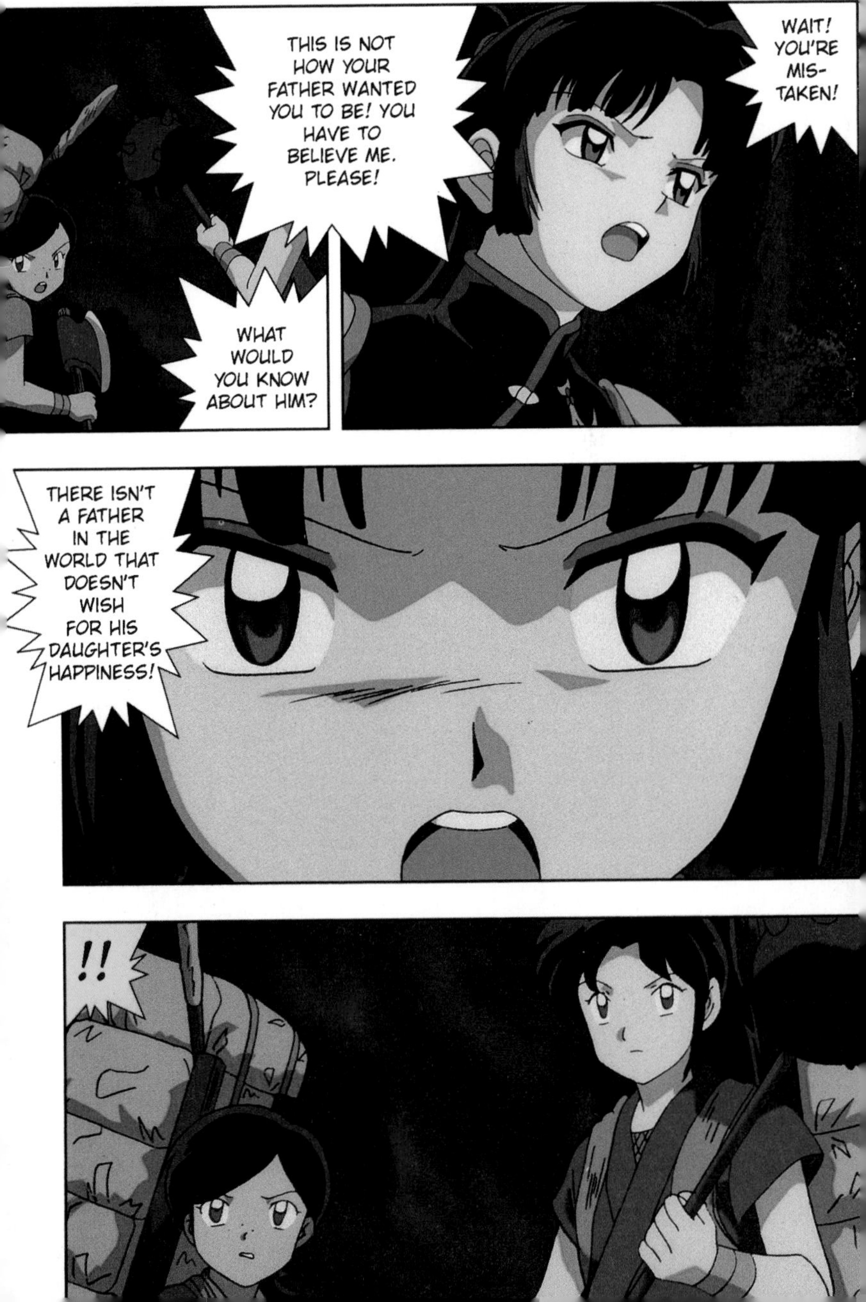
WAIT! YOU'RE MIS-TAKEN!
THIS IS NOT HOW YOUR FATHER WANTED YOU TO BE! YOU HAVE TO BELIEVE ME. PLEASE!
WHAT WOULD YOU KNOW ABOUT HIM?
THERE ISN'T A FATHER IN THE WORLD THAT DOESN'T WISH FOR HIS DAUGHTER'S HAPPINESS!
!!

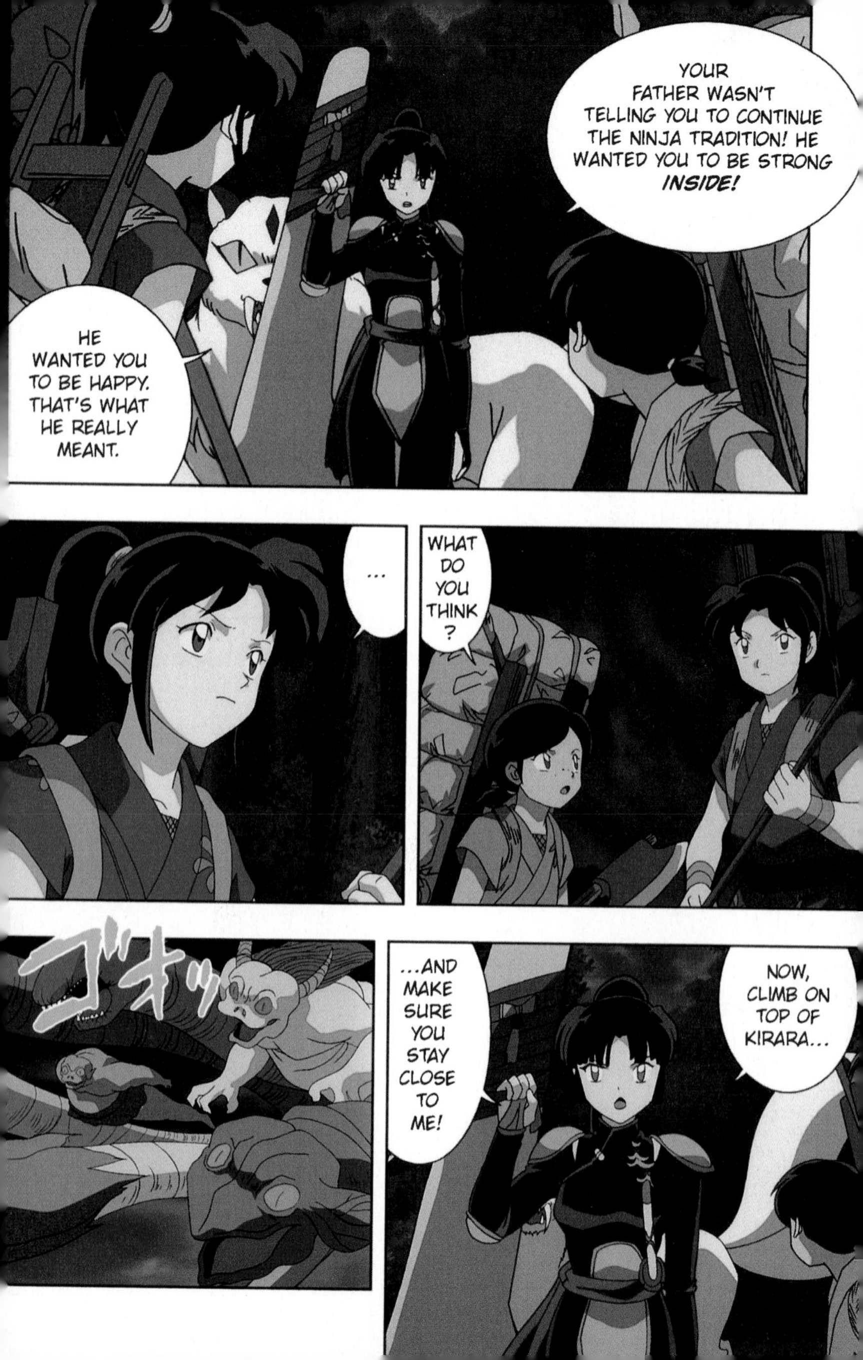
YOUR FATHER WASN'T TELLING YOU TO CONTINUE THE NINJA TRADITION! HE WANTED YOU TO BE STRONG *INSIDE!*
HE WANTED YOU TO BE HAPPY. THAT'S WHAT HE REALLY MEANT.
WHAT DO YOU THINK?
...
NOW, CLIMB ON TOP OF KIRARA...
...AND MAKE SURE YOU STAY CLOSE TO ME!
ゴオッ

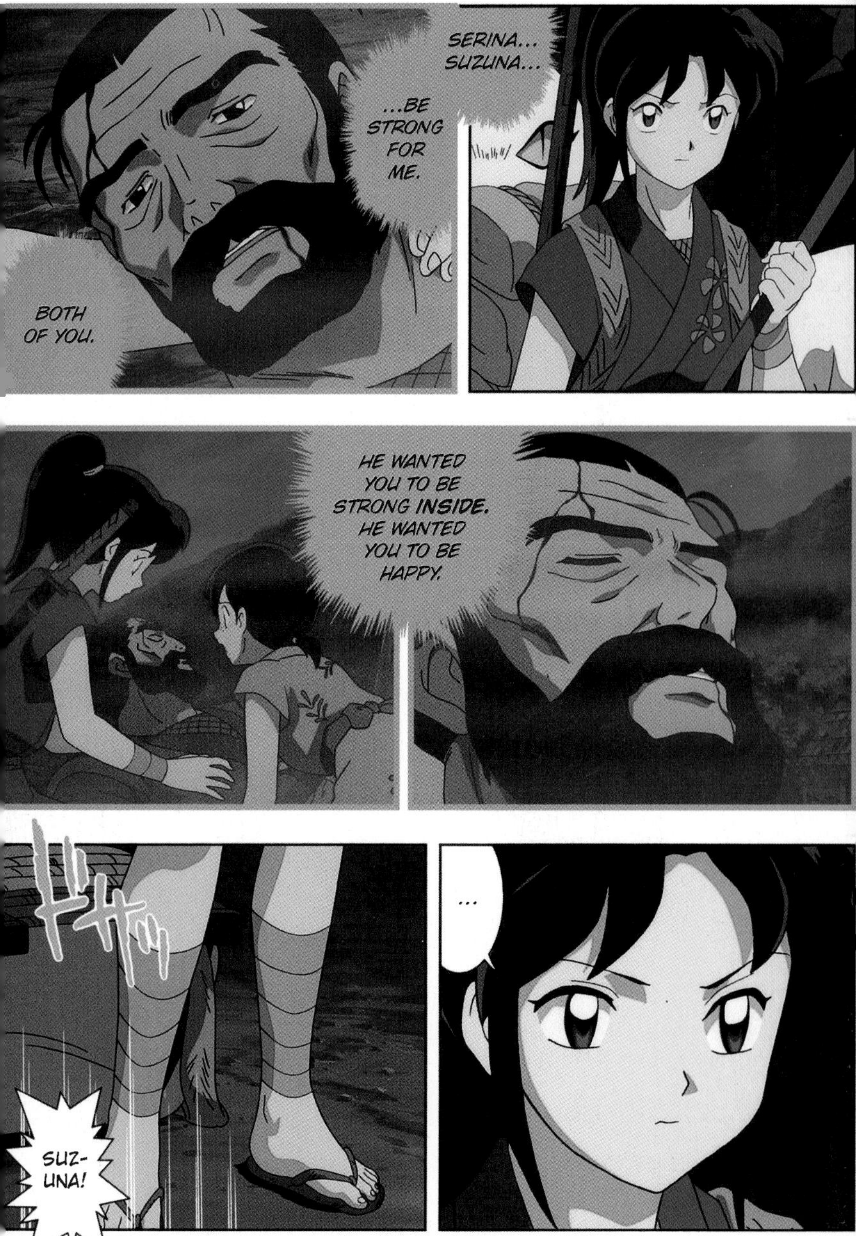
SERINA... SUZUNA...
...BE STRONG FOR ME.
BOTH OF YOU.
HE WANTED YOU TO BE STRONG **INSIDE.** HE WANTED YOU TO BE HAPPY.
...
SUZ-UNA!

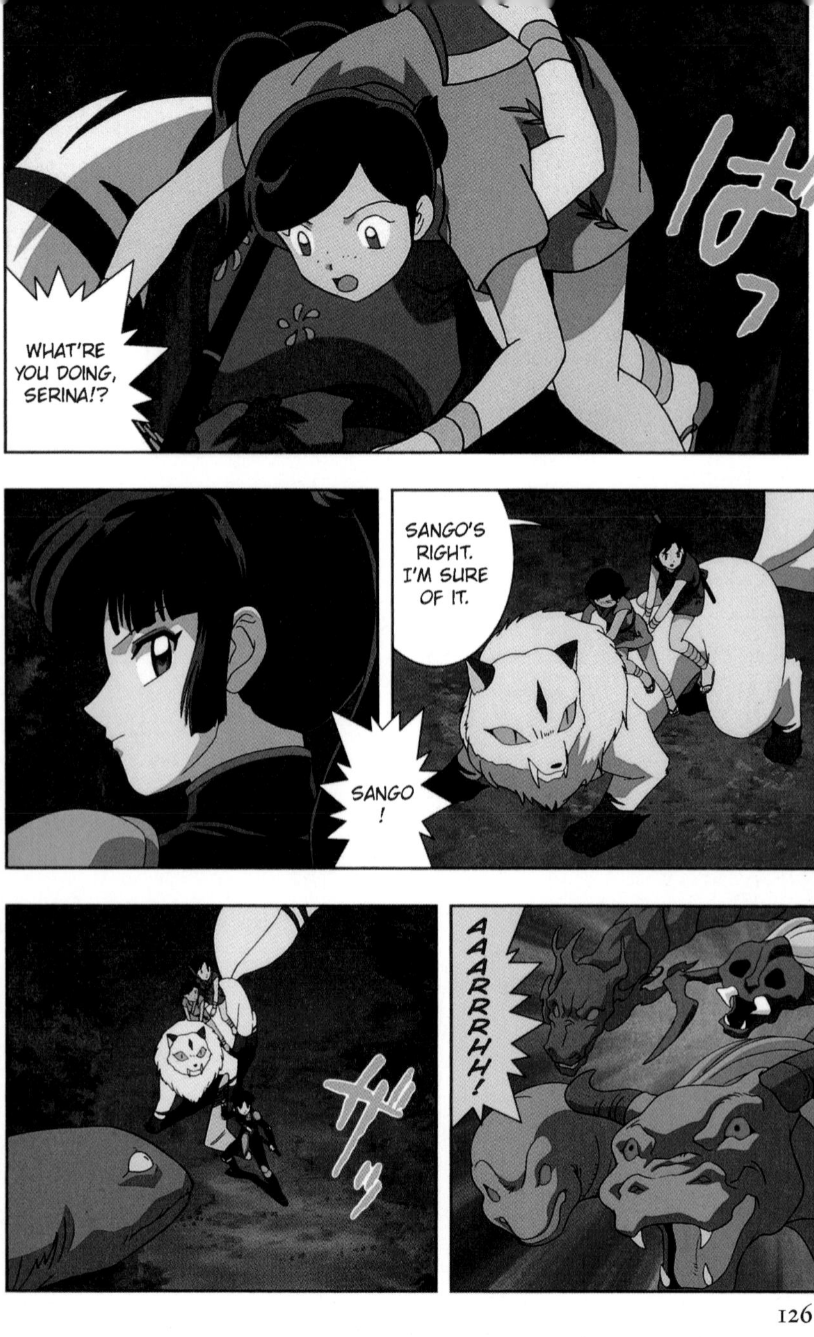
ぱっ
WHAT'RE YOU DOING, SERINA!?
SANGO'S RIGHT. I'M SURE OF IT.
SANGO!
AAAARRRRHH!
ザッ

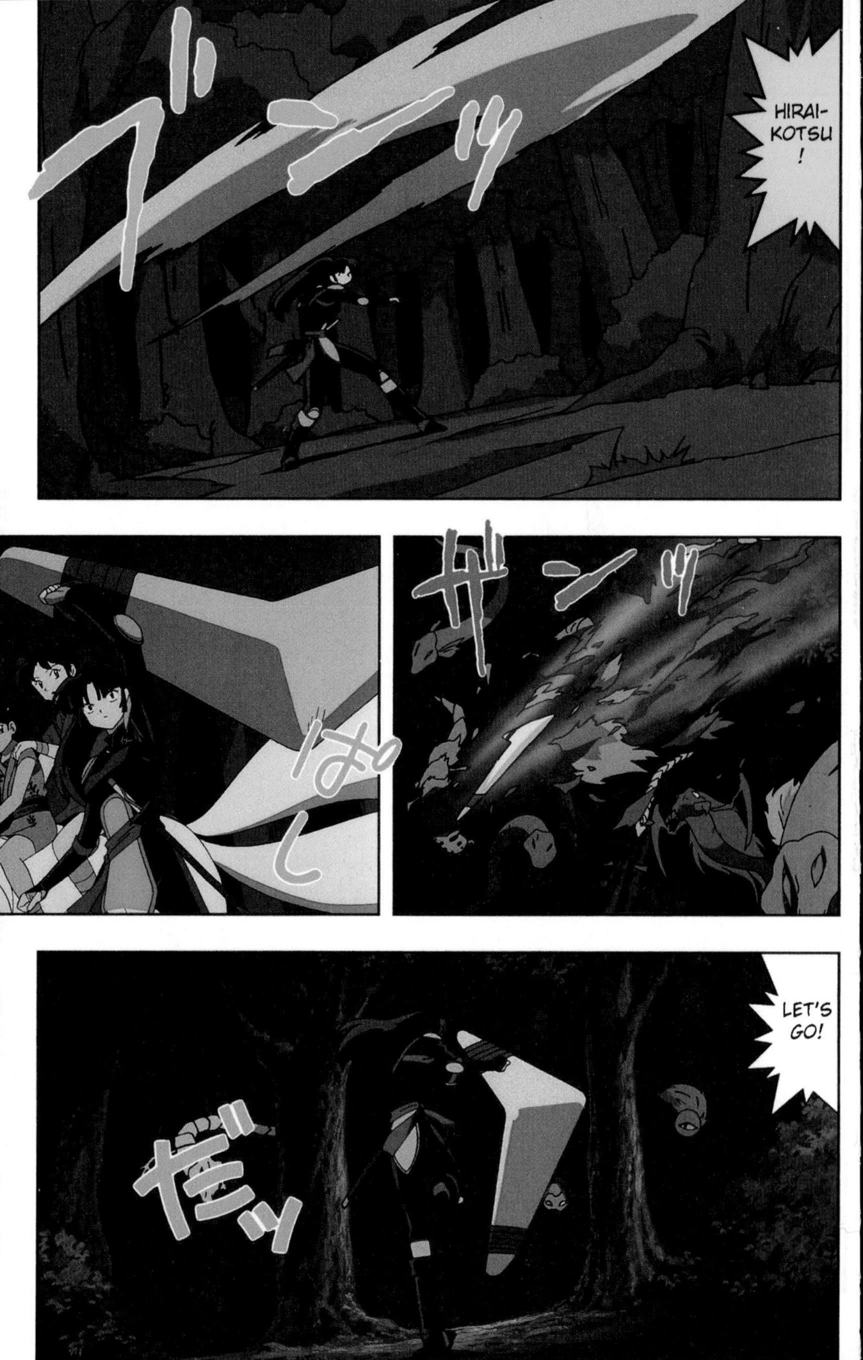
HIRAI-KOTSU!
ブーーッ
ザンッ
ぱし
LET'S GO!
だッ

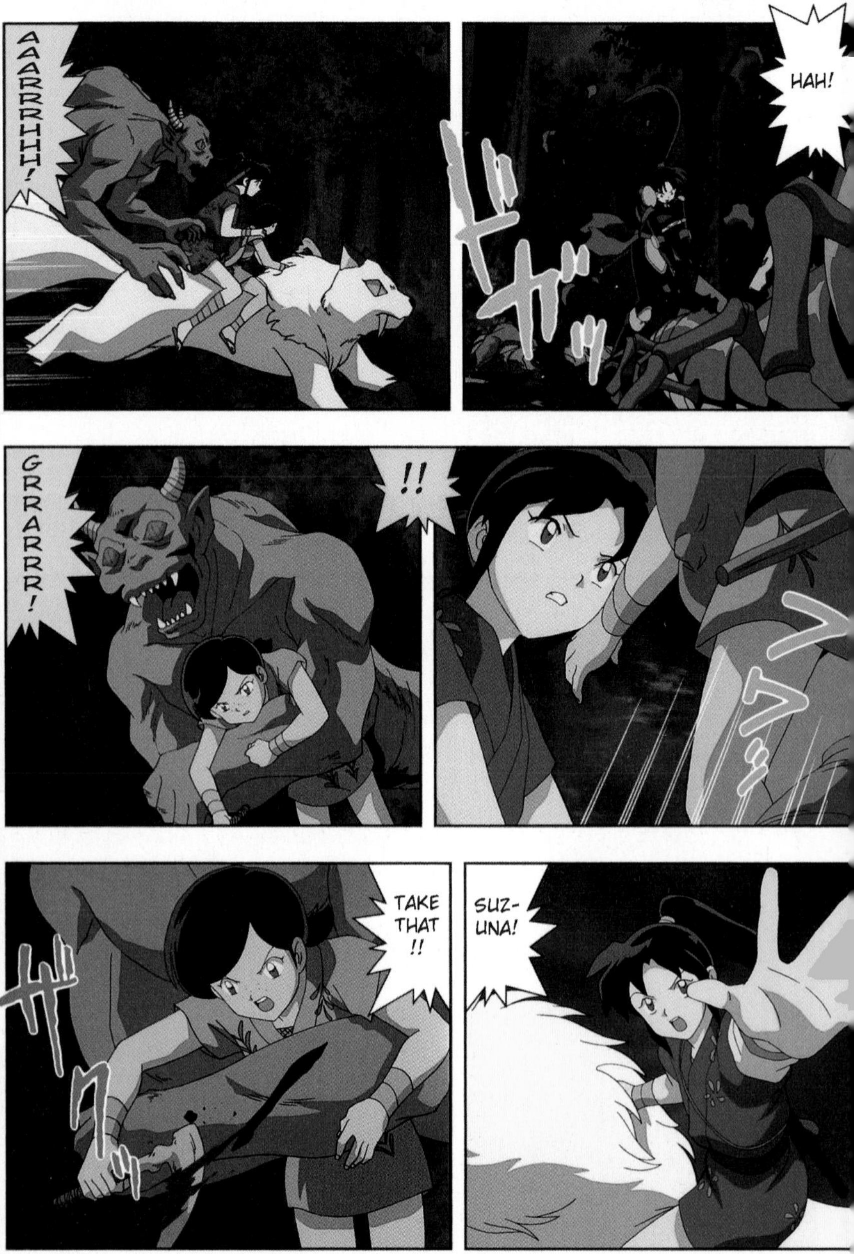
HAH!
ドガッ
AAARRRHHH!
フワッ
!!
GRRARRRR!
SUZ-UNA!
TAKE THAT!!
ザクッ

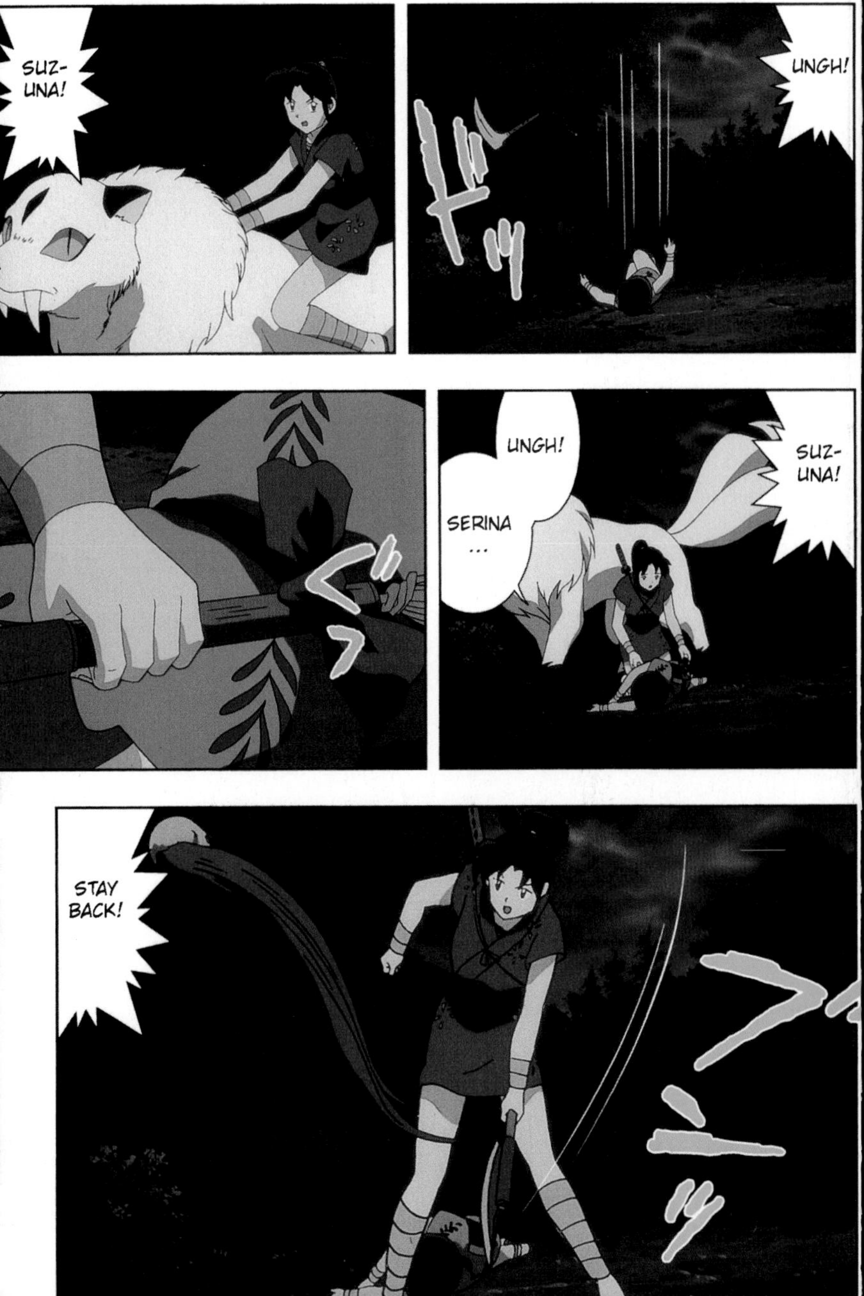
UNGH!
ドッ
SUZ-UNA!
SUZ-UNA!
UNGH!
SERINA ...
STAY BACK!

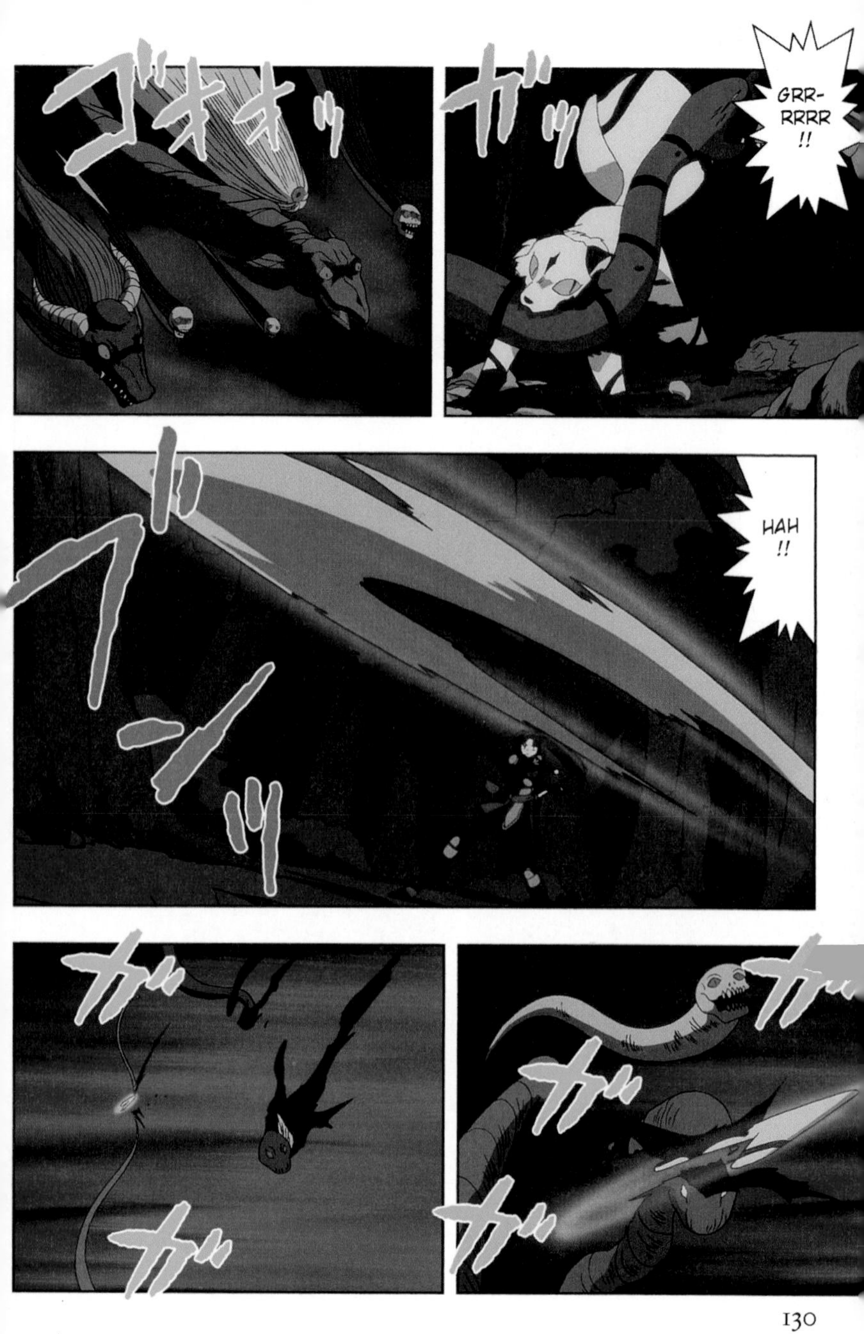
ガッ
GRR-RRRR !!
ゴオオッ
HAH !!
ブンッ
ガッ
ガッ
ガッ
ガッ
ガッ

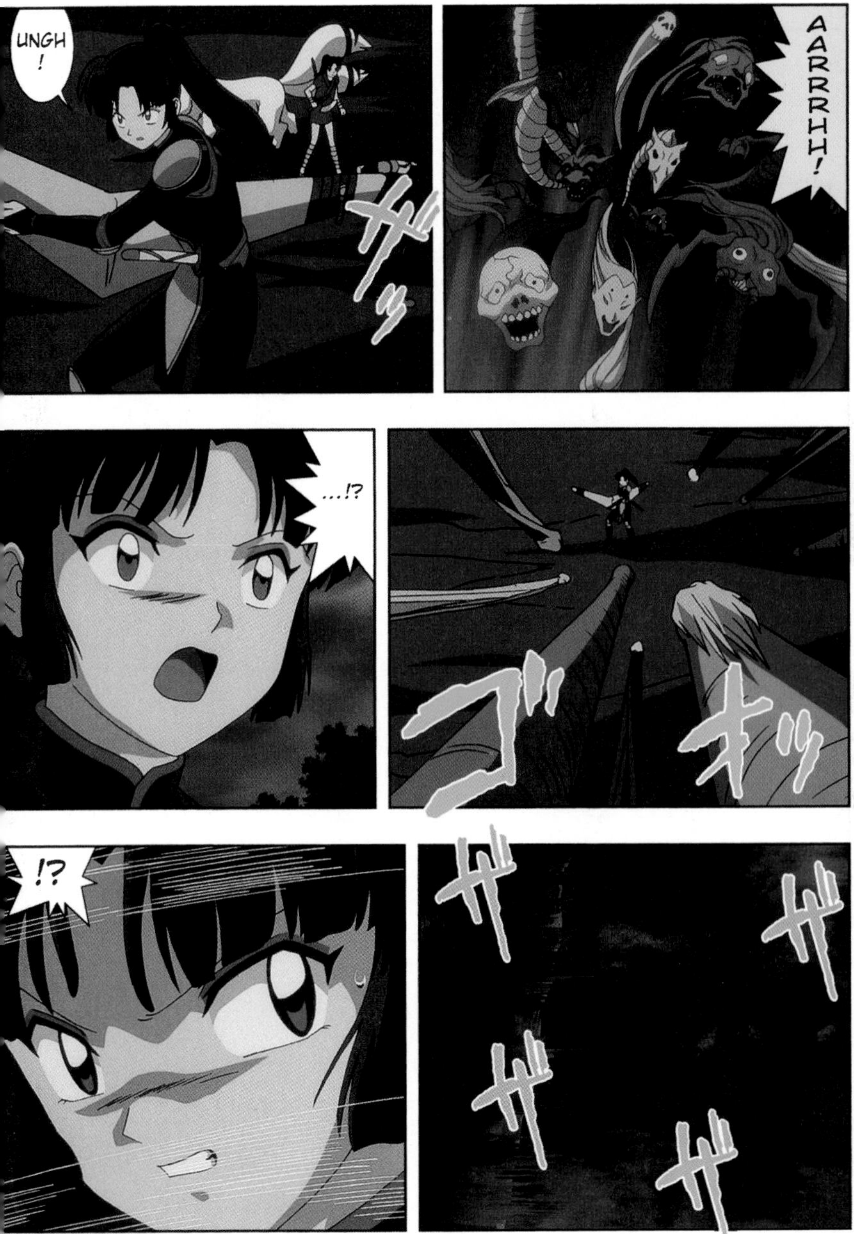
AARRRHH!
UNGH!
ザッ
ゴキッ
...!?
ザ
ザ
ザ
ザ
!?

SANGO!

MIRO-KU!

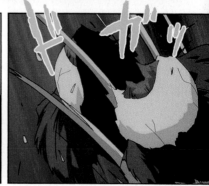

WIND SCAR!

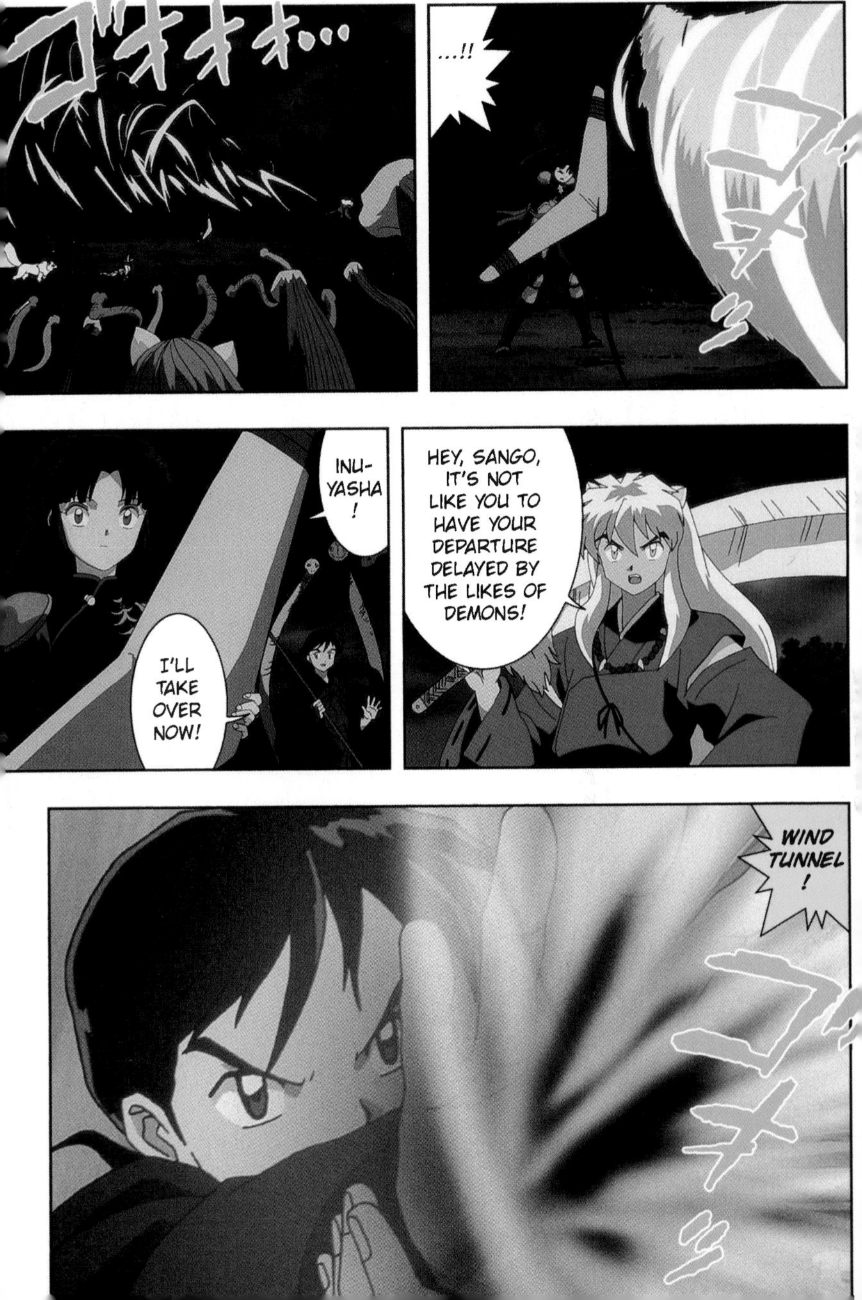
...!!
ゴォォォ…
HEY, SANGO, IT'S NOT LIKE YOU TO HAVE YOUR DEPARTURE DELAYED BY THE LIKES OF DEMONS!
INU-YASHA!
I'LL TAKE OVER NOW!
WIND TUNNEL!

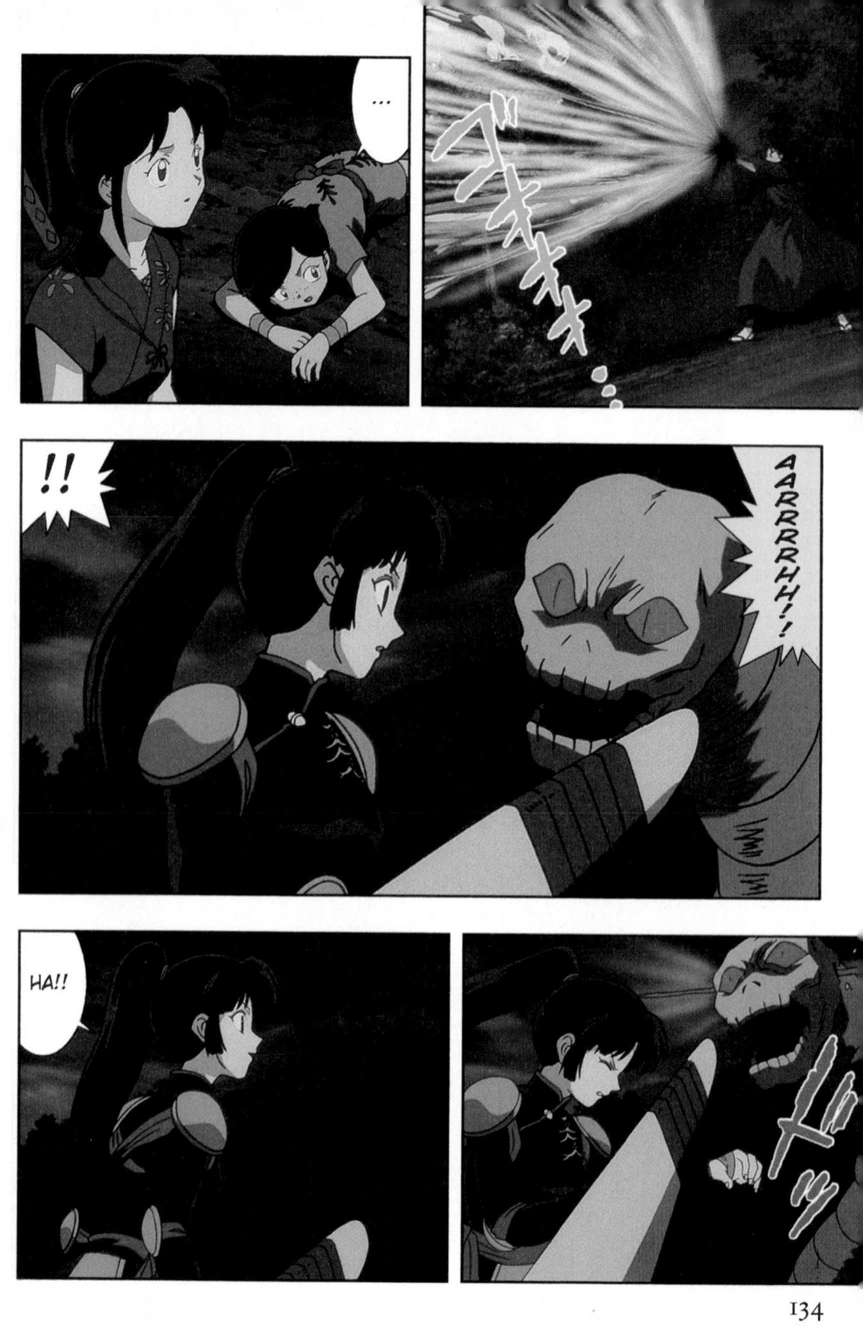
ゴォォォォ…
...
AARRRRHH!!
!!
ドッ
HA!!

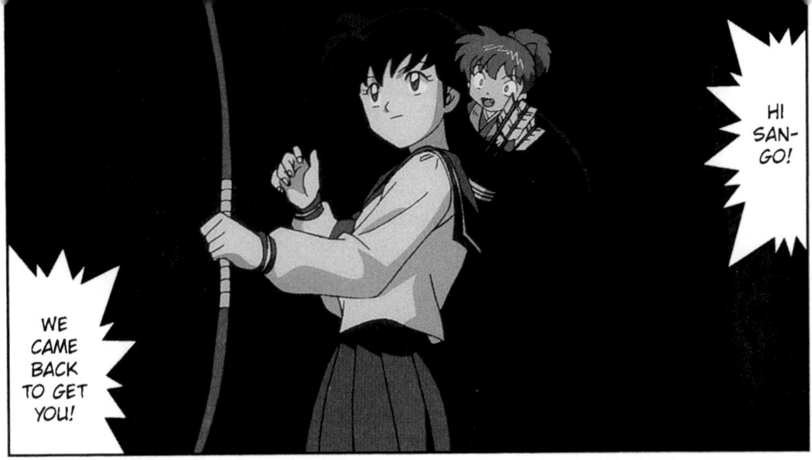
HI SAN-GO!
WE CAME BACK TO GET YOU!

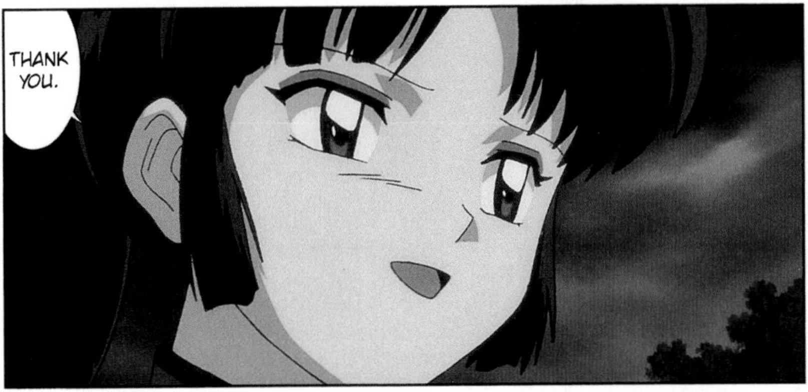
THANK YOU.

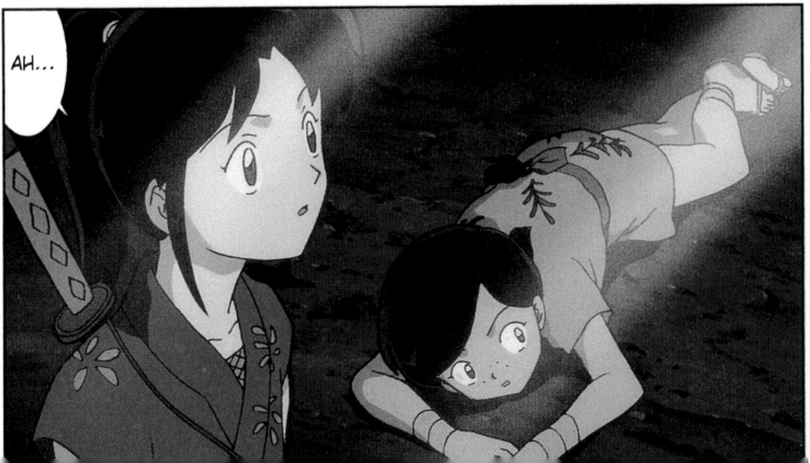
AH...

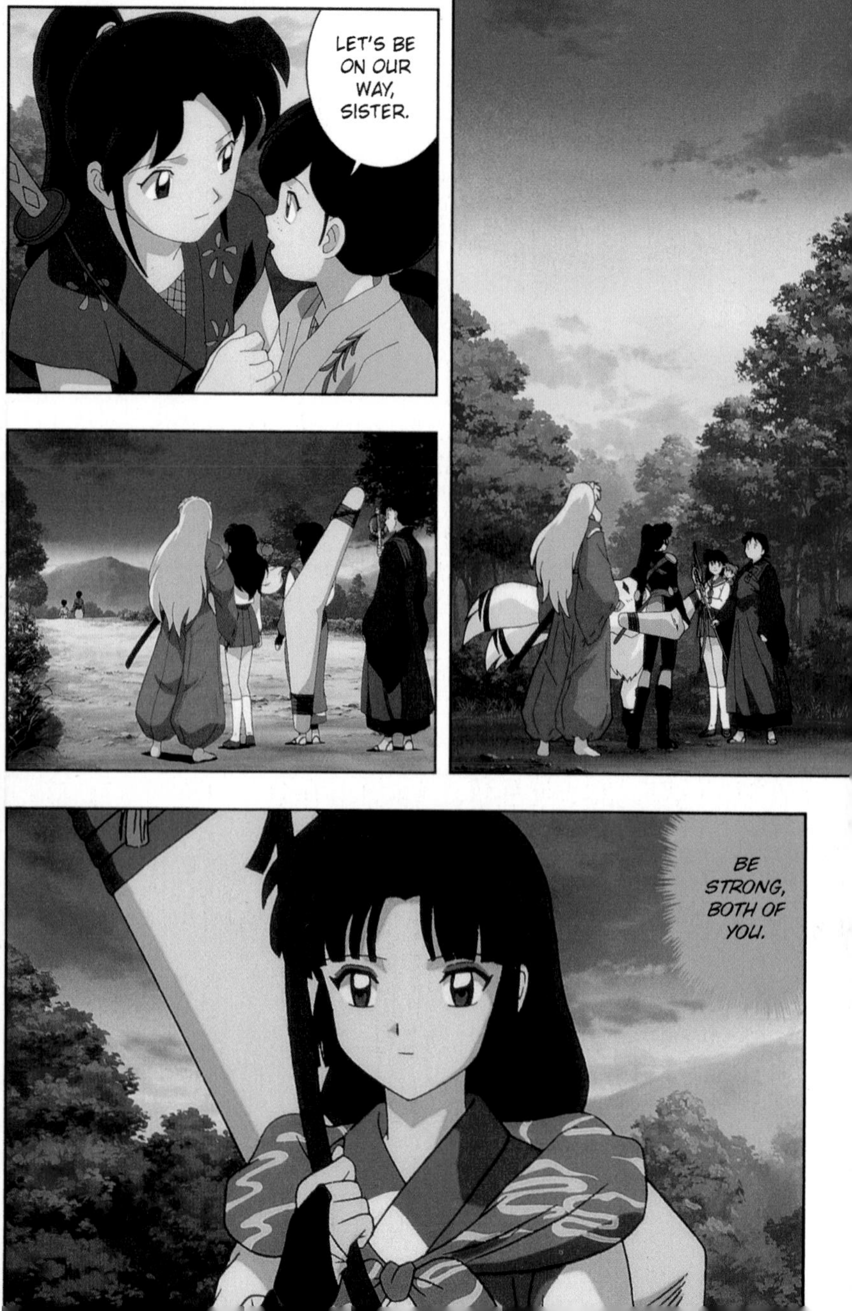
LET'S BE ON OUR WAY, SISTER.
BE STRONG, BOTH OF YOU.

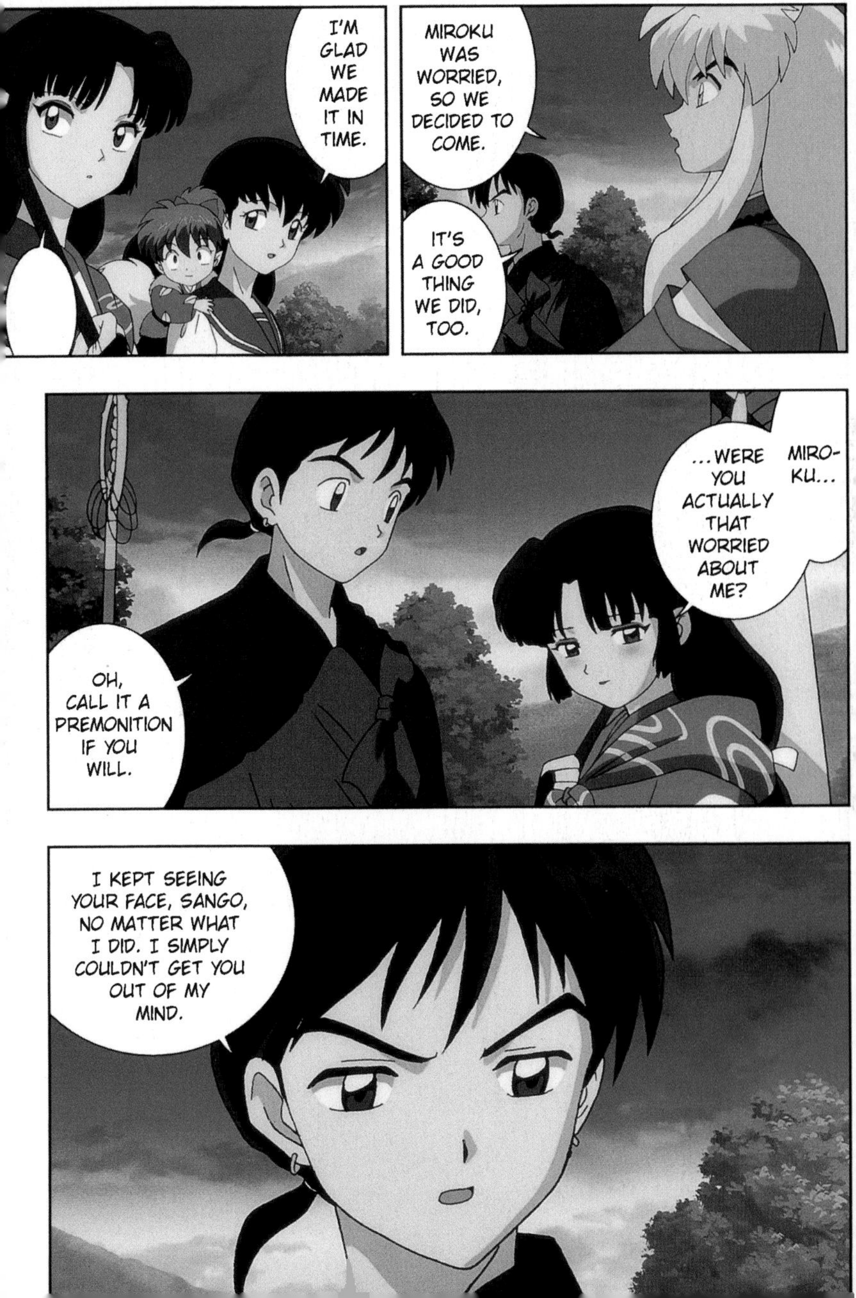
MIROKU WAS WORRIED, SO WE DECIDED TO COME.
IT'S A GOOD THING WE DID, TOO.
I'M GLAD WE MADE IT IN TIME.
MIROKU...
...WERE YOU ACTUALLY THAT WORRIED ABOUT ME?
OH, CALL IT A PREMONITION IF YOU WILL.
I KEPT SEEING YOUR FACE, SANGO, NO MATTER WHAT I DID. I SIMPLY COULDN'T GET YOU OUT OF MY MIND.

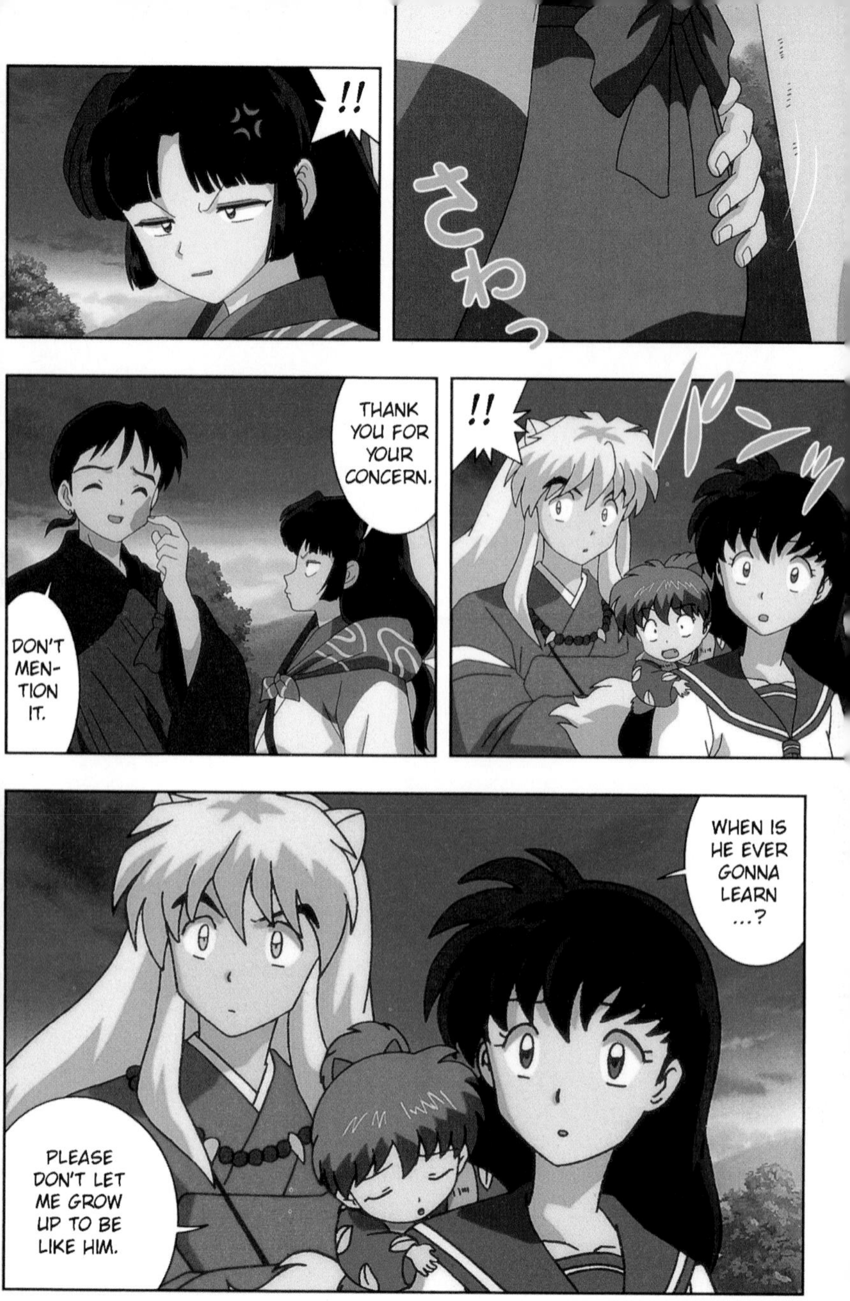
さわっ
!!
!!
パンッ
THANK YOU FOR YOUR CONCERN.
DON'T MEN-TION IT.
WHEN IS HE EVER GONNA LEARN ...?
PLEASE DON'T LET ME GROW UP TO BE LIKE HIM.

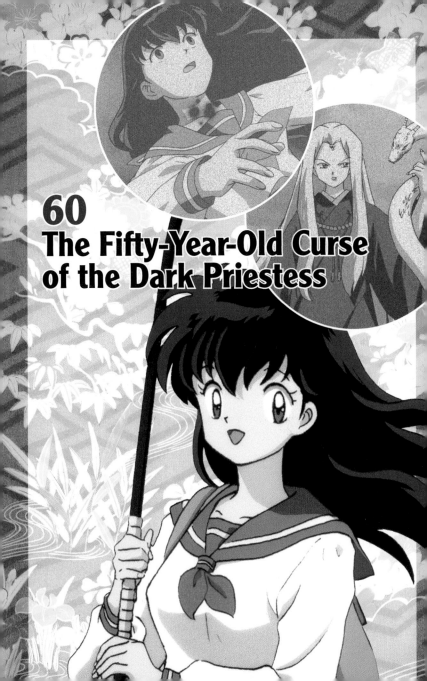

60
The Fifty-Year-Old Curse
of the Dark Priestess

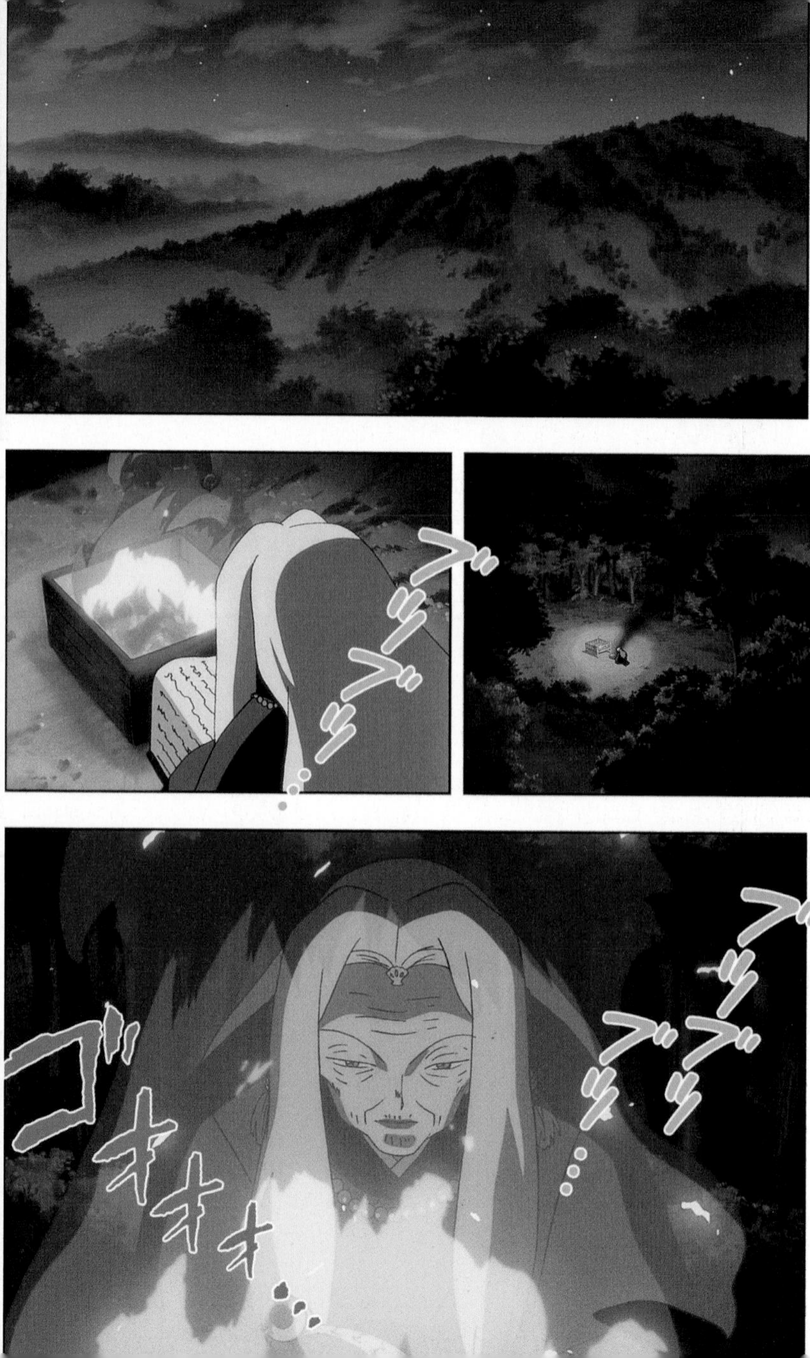
ブツブツ…
ブツブツ
ブツブツ…
ゴォォォ…

AH!!
AAHH!

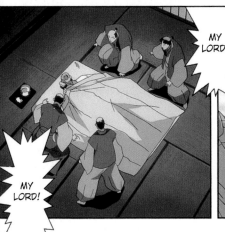

MY
LORD!

MY
LORD!

AH-
AARR-
RGH!

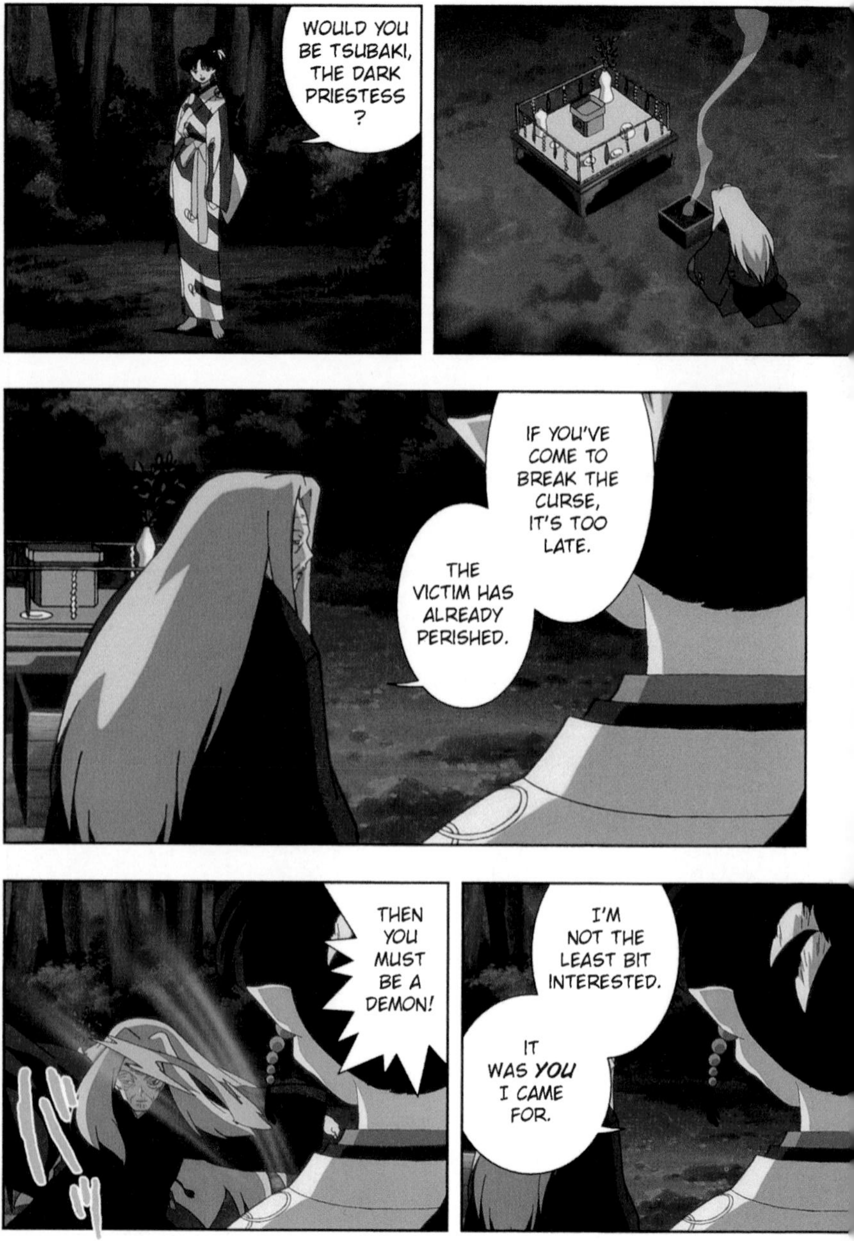
WOULD YOU BE TSUBAKI, THE DARK PRIESTESS ?
IF YOU'VE COME TO BREAK THE CURSE, IT'S TOO LATE.
THE VICTIM HAS ALREADY PERISHED.
I'M NOT THE LEAST BIT INTERESTED.
IT WAS *YOU* I CAME FOR.
THEN YOU MUST BE A DEMON!

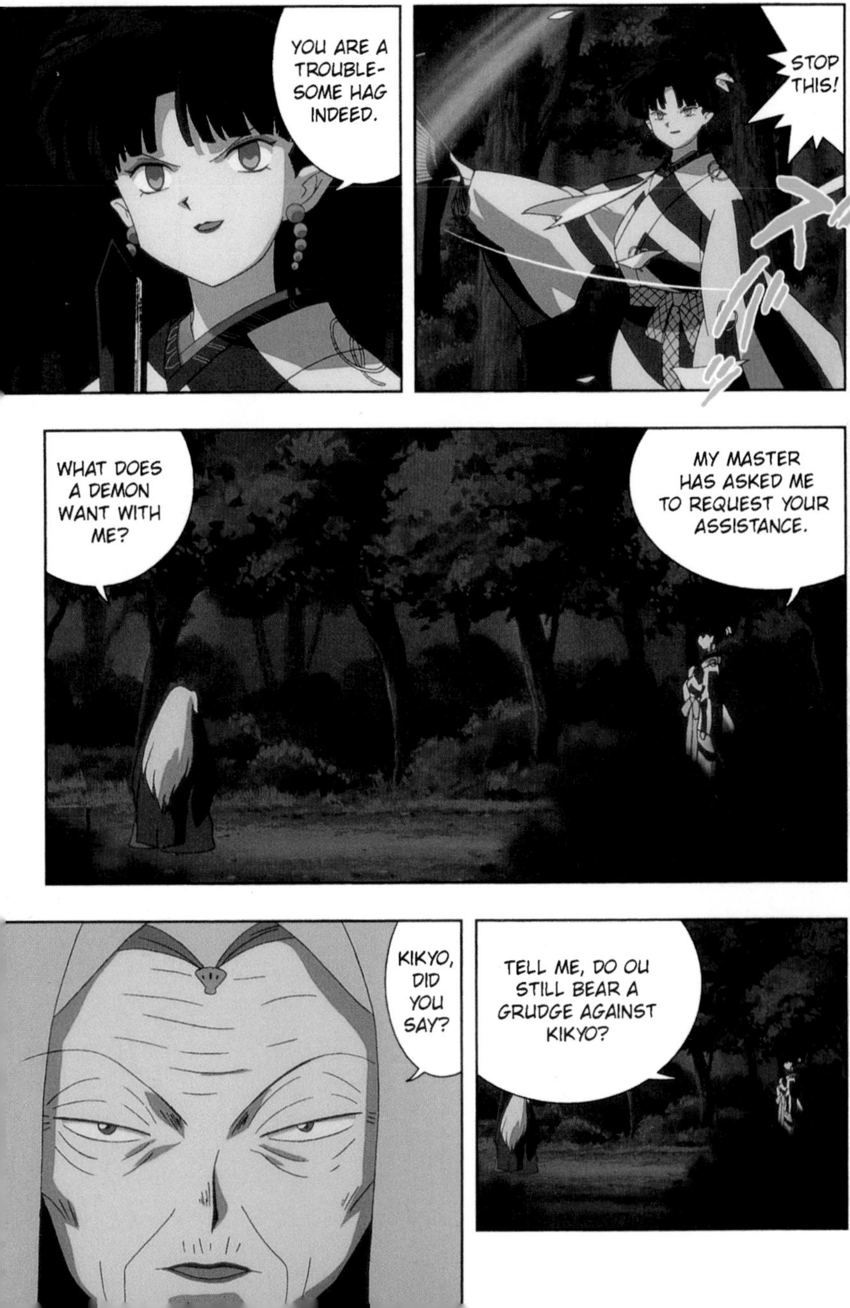
STOP THIS!
YOU ARE A TROUBLE-SOME HAG INDEED.
MY MASTER HAS ASKED ME TO REQUEST YOUR ASSISTANCE.
WHAT DOES A DEMON WANT WITH ME?
TELL ME, DO OU STILL BEAR A GRUDGE AGAINST KIKYO?
KIKYO, DID YOU SAY?

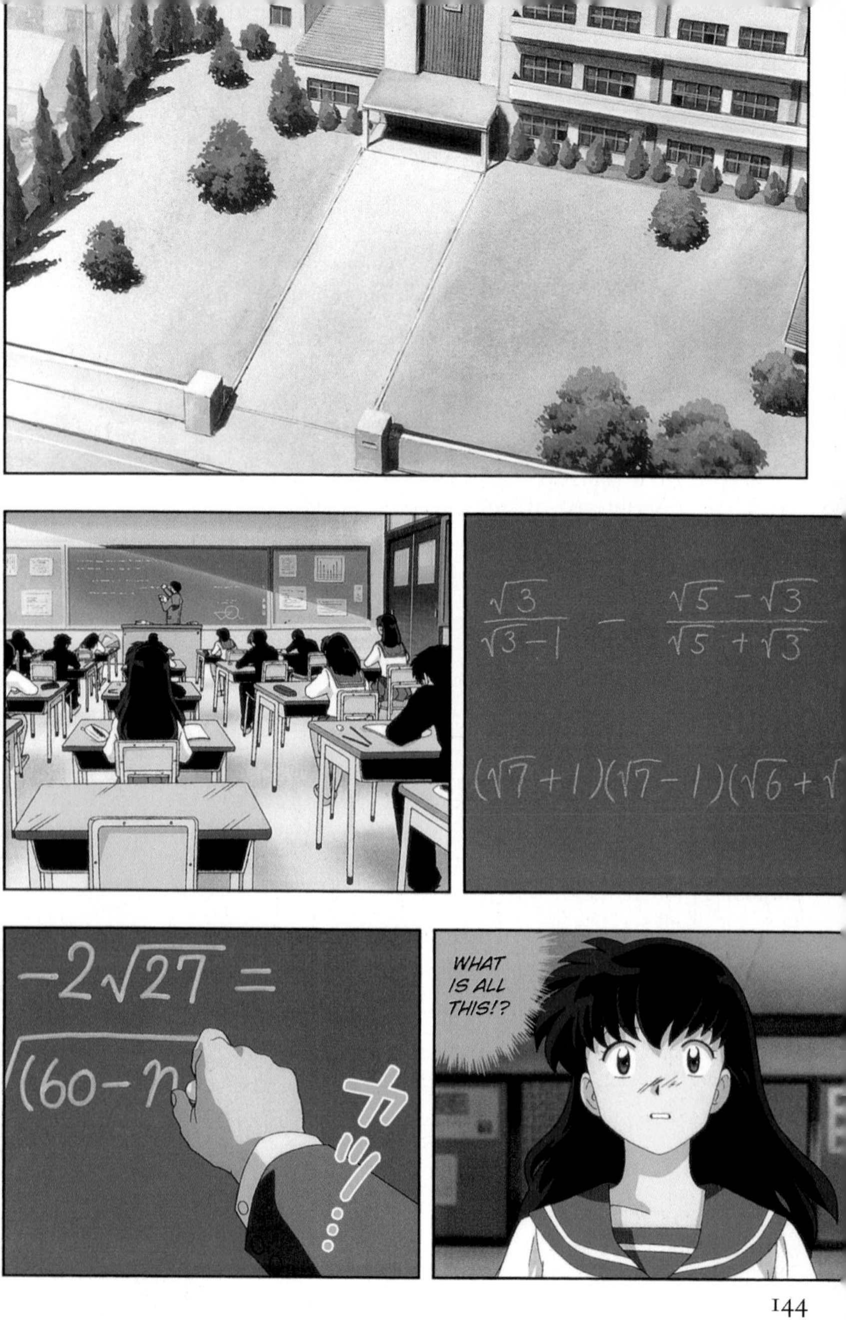
√3 / √3−1 − √5 −√3 / √5 +√3
(√7+1)(√7−1)(√6+√
WHAT IS ALL THIS!?
−2√27 =
√(60−n
カッ…

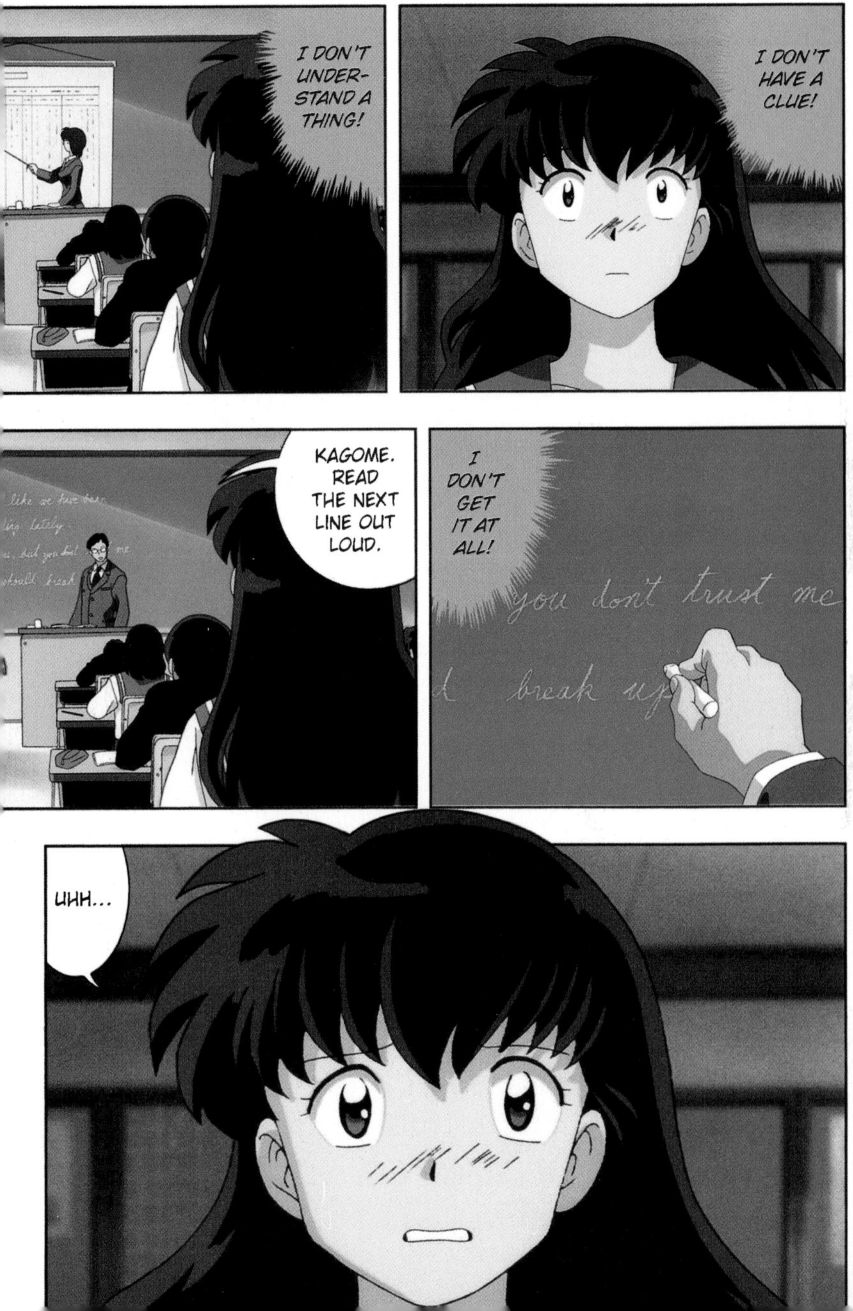
I DON'T HAVE A CLUE!
I DON'T UNDERSTAND A THING!
I DON'T GET IT AT ALL!
you don't trust me
break up
KAGOME. READ THE NEXT LINE OUT LOUD.
UHH...

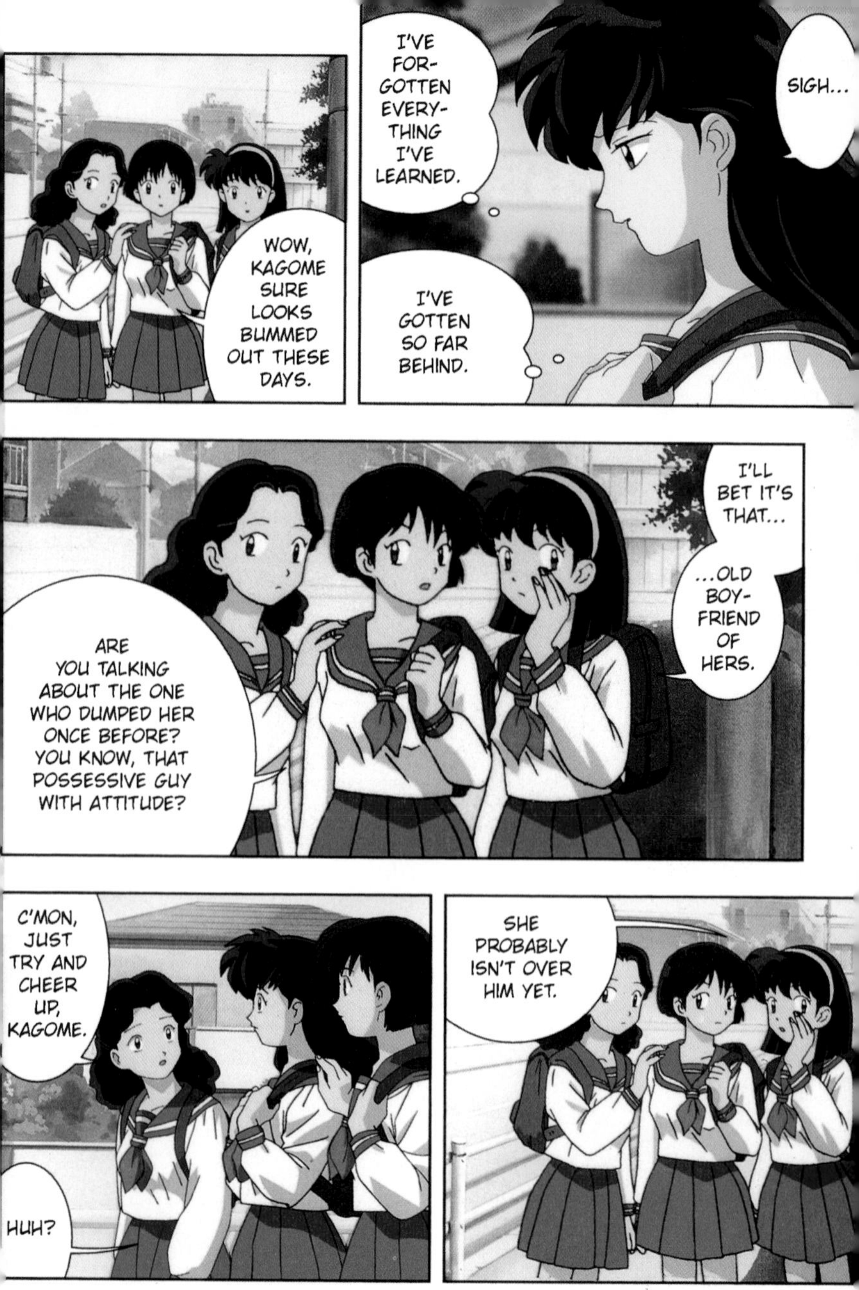
SIGH...
I'VE FOR-GOTTEN EVERY-THING I'VE LEARNED.
I'VE GOTTEN SO FAR BEHIND.
WOW, KAGOME SURE LOOKS BUMMED OUT THESE DAYS.
I'LL BET IT'S THAT...
...OLD BOY-FRIEND OF HERS.
ARE YOU TALKING ABOUT THE ONE WHO DUMPED HER ONCE BEFORE? YOU KNOW, THAT POSSESSIVE GUY WITH ATTITUDE?
SHE PROBABLY ISN'T OVER HIM YET.
C'MON, JUST TRY AND CHEER UP, KAGOME.
HUH?

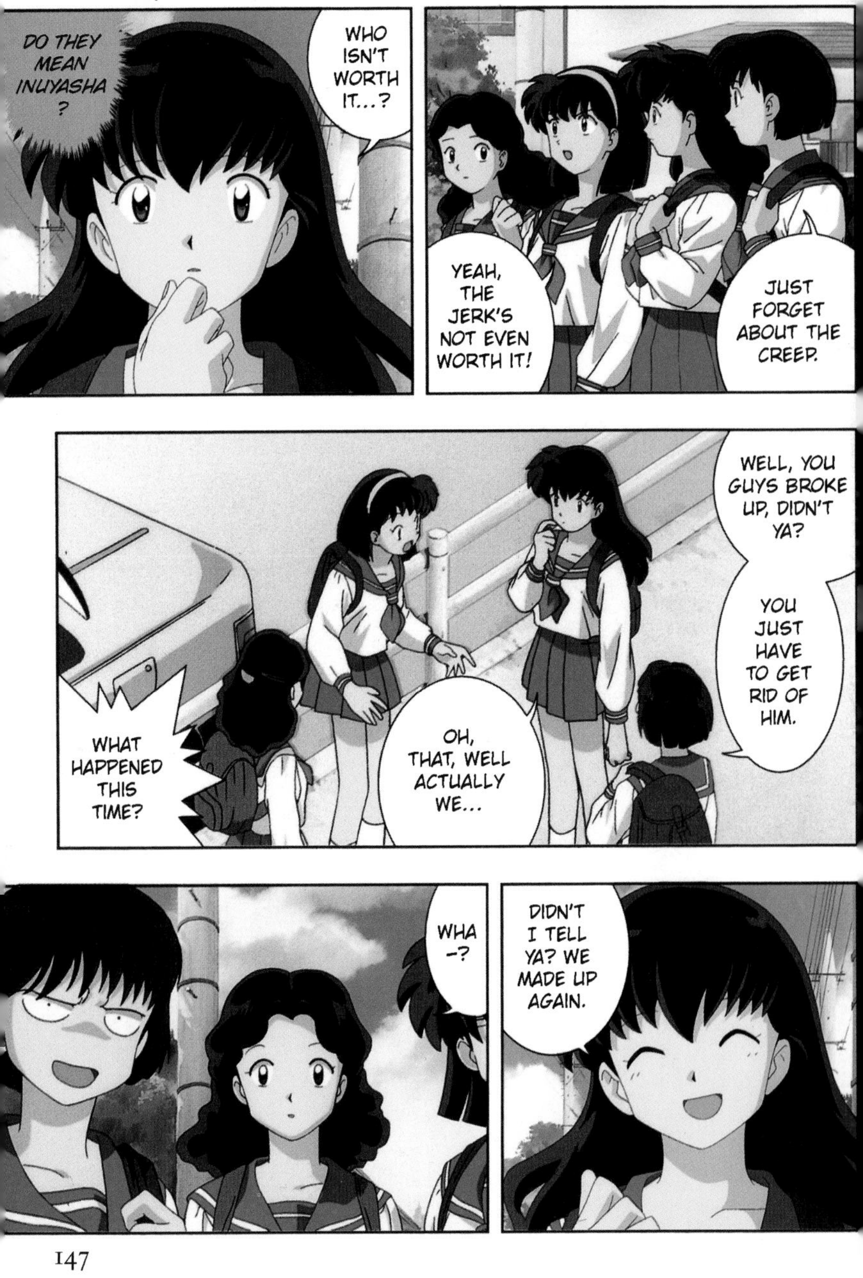
JUST FORGET ABOUT THE CREEP.
YEAH, THE JERK'S NOT EVEN WORTH IT!
WHO ISN'T WORTH IT...?
DO THEY MEAN INUYASHA?
WELL, YOU GUYS BROKE UP, DIDN'T YA?
YOU JUST HAVE TO GET RID OF HIM.
OH, THAT, WELL ACTUALLY WE...
WHAT HAPPENED THIS TIME?
DIDN'T I TELL YA? WE MADE UP AGAIN.
WHA-?

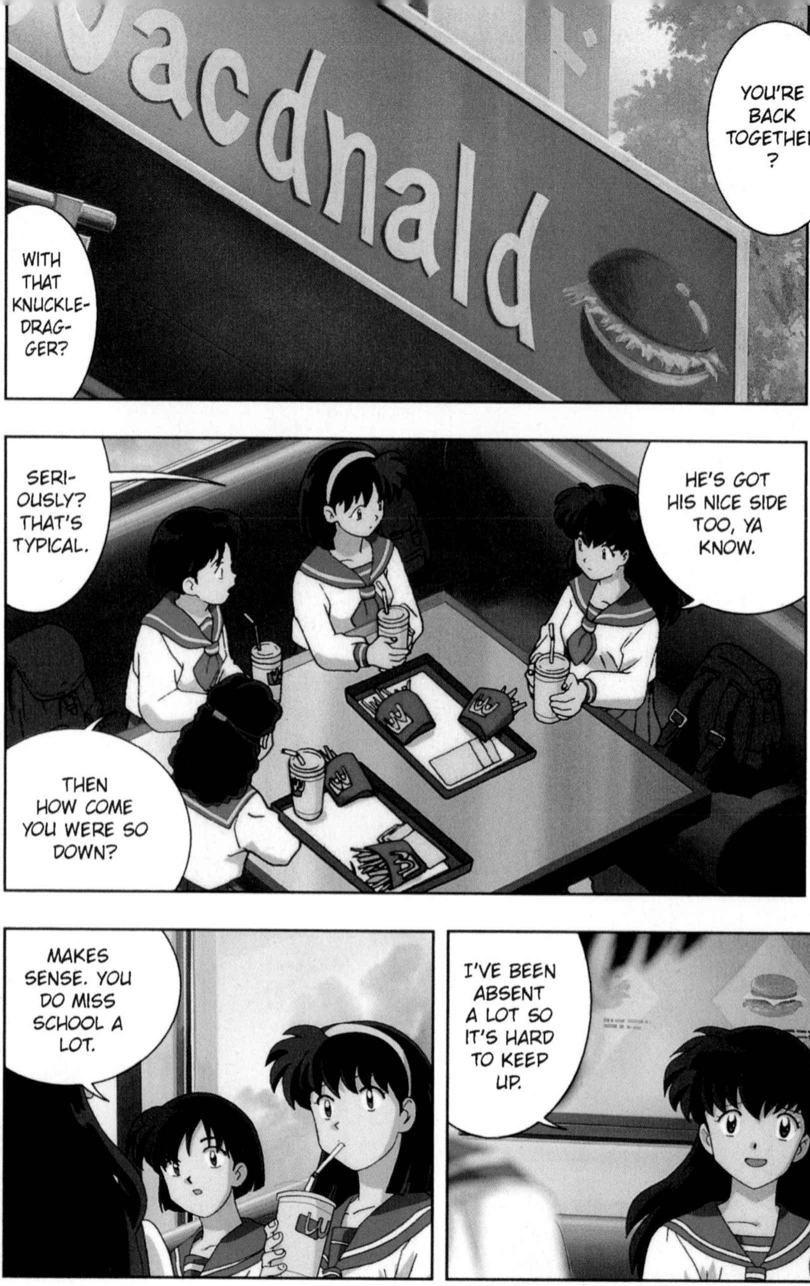
acdnald
YOU'RE BACK TOGETHER?
WITH THAT KNUCKLE-DRAGGER?
HE'S GOT HIS NICE SIDE TOO, YA KNOW.
SERI-OUSLY? THAT'S TYPICAL.
THEN HOW COME YOU WERE SO DOWN?
I'VE BEEN ABSENT A LOT SO IT'S HARD TO KEEP UP.
MAKES SENSE. YOU DO MISS SCHOOL A LOT.

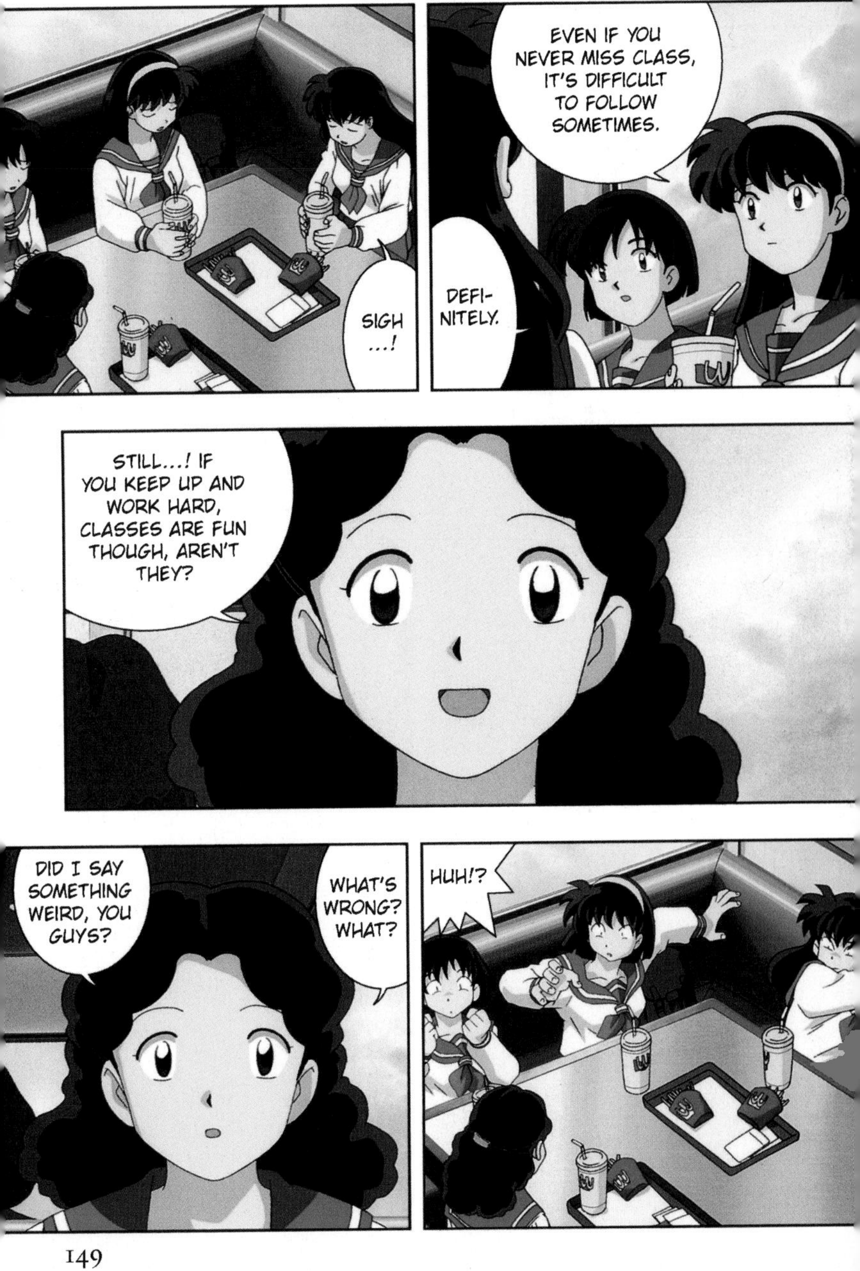
EVEN IF YOU NEVER MISS CLASS, IT'S DIFFICULT TO FOLLOW SOMETIMES.
DEFI-NITELY.
SIGH ...!
STILL...! IF YOU KEEP UP AND WORK HARD, CLASSES ARE FUN THOUGH, AREN'T THEY?
HUH!?
WHAT'S WRONG? WHAT?
DID I SAY SOMETHING WEIRD, YOU GUYS?

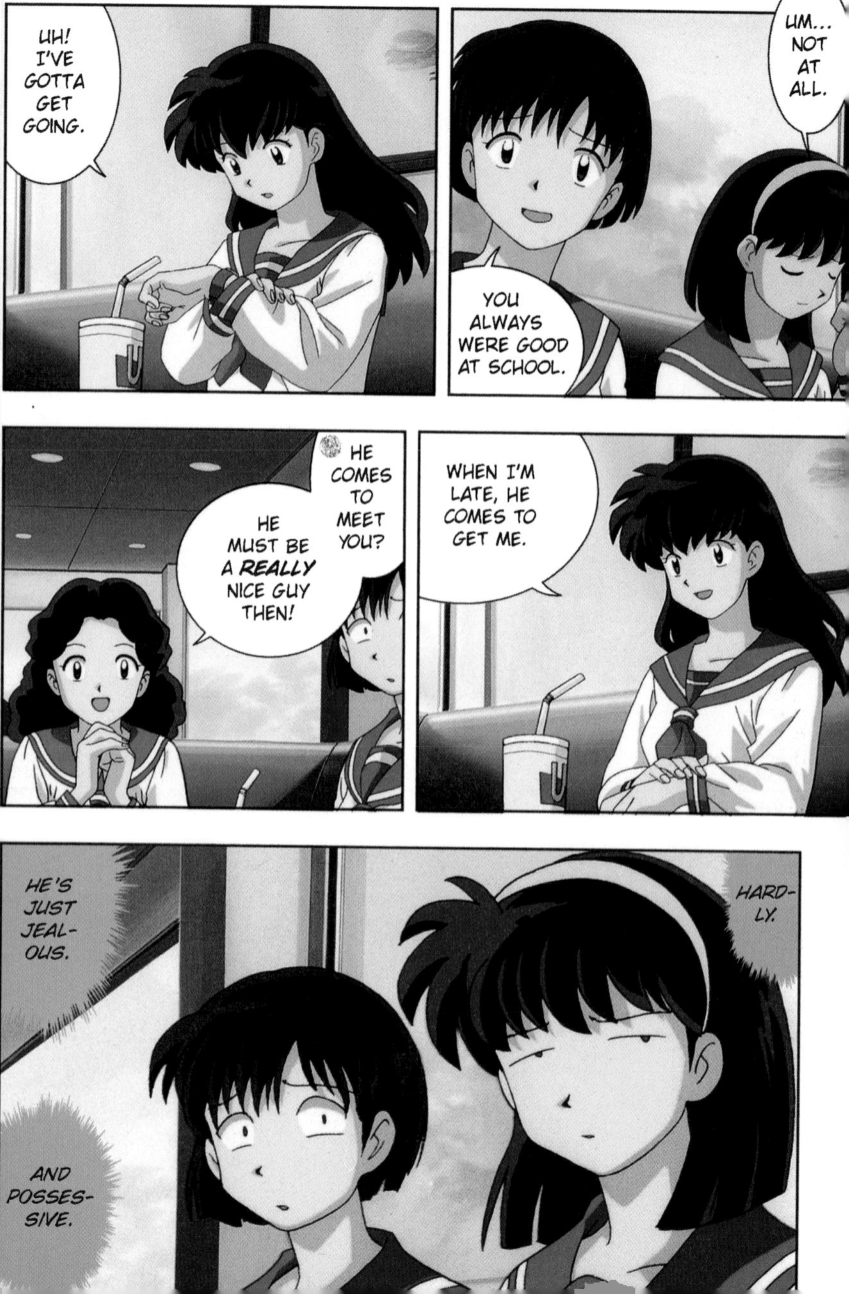
UM... NOT AT ALL.
YOU ALWAYS WERE GOOD AT SCHOOL.
UH! I'VE GOTTA GET GOING.
WHEN I'M LATE, HE COMES TO GET ME.
HE COMES TO MEET YOU?
HE MUST BE A **REALLY** NICE GUY THEN!
HARD-LY.
HE'S JUST JEAL-OUS.
AND POSSES-SIVE.

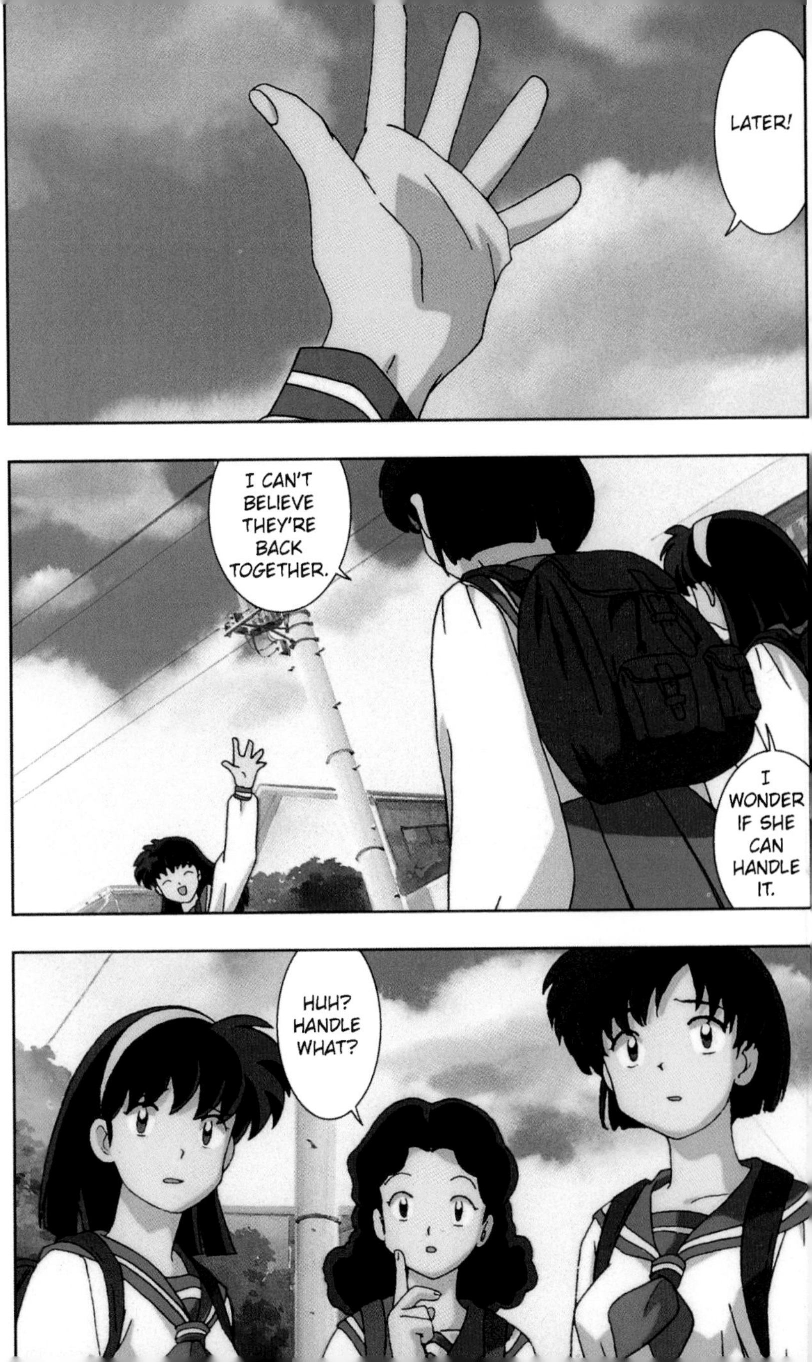
LATER!
I CAN'T BELIEVE THEY'RE BACK TOGETHER.
I WONDER IF SHE CAN HANDLE IT.
HUH? HANDLE WHAT?

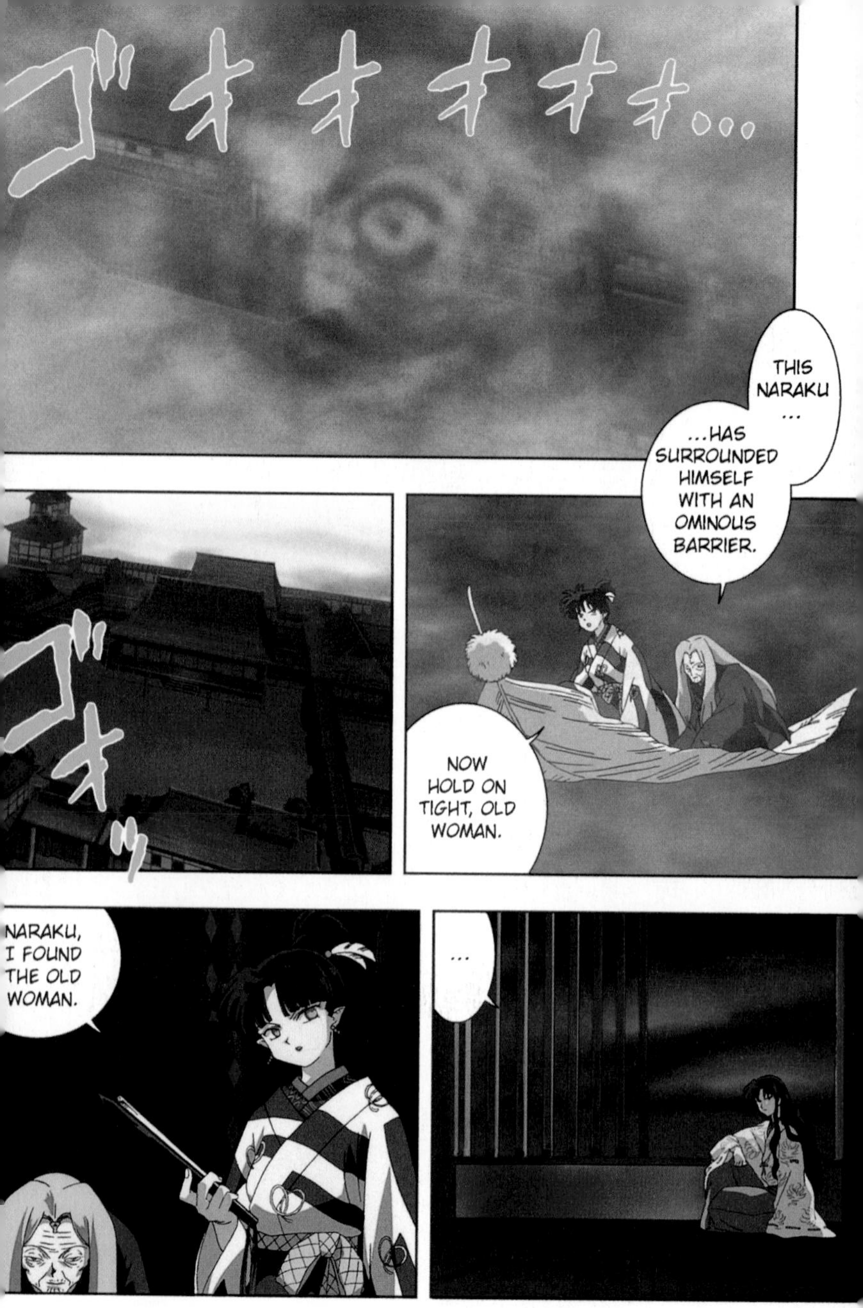
ゴオオオオオ…
THIS NARAKU ...
...HAS SURROUNDED HIMSELF WITH AN OMINOUS BARRIER.
NOW HOLD ON TIGHT, OLD WOMAN.
ゴオッ
...
NARAKU, I FOUND THE OLD WOMAN.

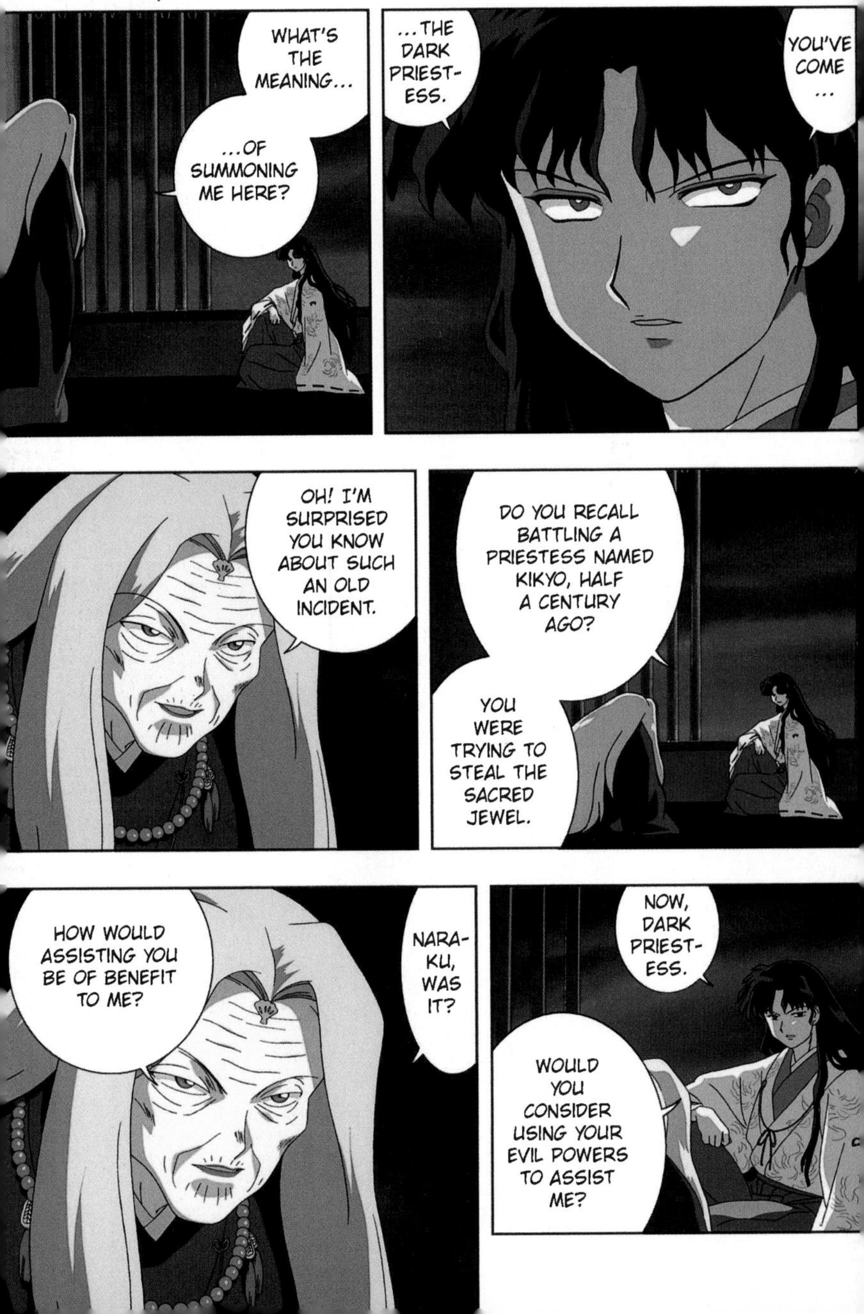
YOU'VE COME ...
...THE DARK PRIEST-ESS.
WHAT'S THE MEANING...
...OF SUMMONING ME HERE?
DO YOU RECALL BATTLING A PRIESTESS NAMED KIKYO, HALF A CENTURY AGO?
YOU WERE TRYING TO STEAL THE SACRED JEWEL.
OH! I'M SURPRISED YOU KNOW ABOUT SUCH AN OLD INCIDENT.
NOW, DARK PRIEST-ESS.
WOULD YOU CONSIDER USING YOUR EVIL POWERS TO ASSIST ME?
NARA-KU, WAS IT?
HOW WOULD ASSISTING YOU BE OF BENEFIT TO ME?

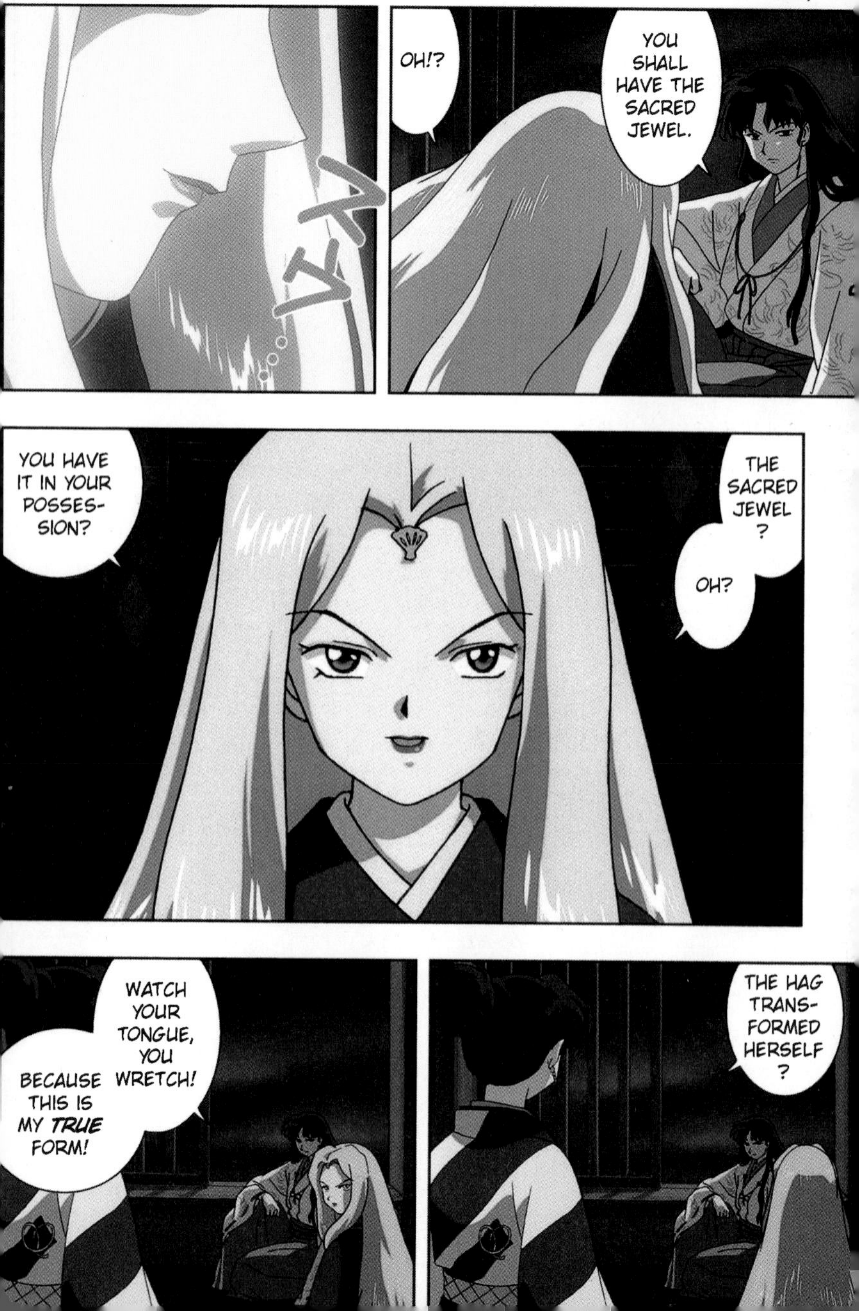
YOU SHALL HAVE THE SACRED JEWEL.
OH!?
THE SACRED JEWEL?
OH?
YOU HAVE IT IN YOUR POSSES-SION?
THE HAG TRANS-FORMED HERSELF?
WATCH YOUR TONGUE, YOU WRETCH!
BECAUSE THIS IS MY *TRUE* FORM!

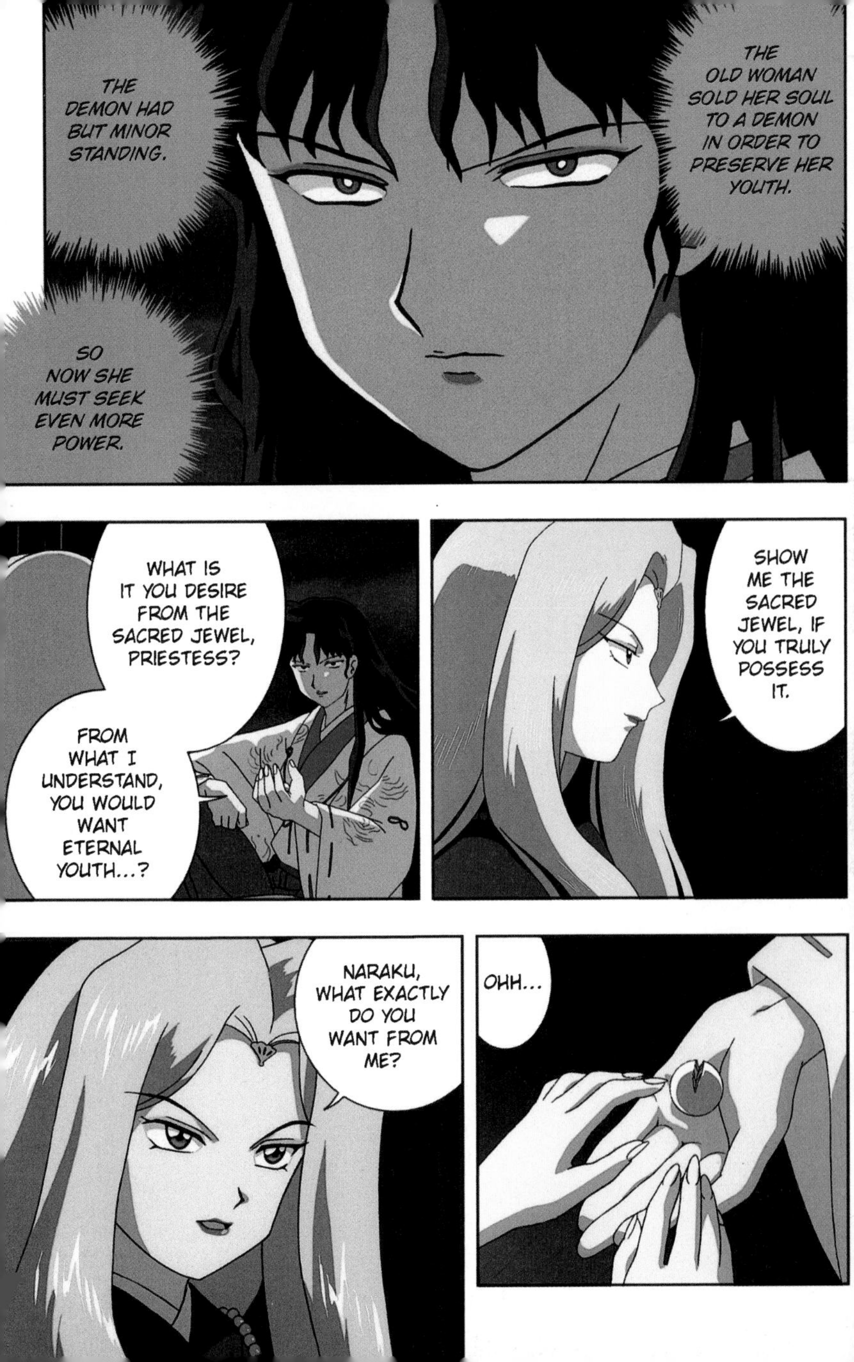
THE OLD WOMAN SOLD HER SOUL TO A DEMON IN ORDER TO PRESERVE HER YOUTH.
THE DEMON HAD BUT MINOR STANDING.
SO NOW SHE MUST SEEK EVEN MORE POWER.
SHOW ME THE SACRED JEWEL, IF YOU TRULY POSSESS IT.
WHAT IS IT YOU DESIRE FROM THE SACRED JEWEL, PRIESTESS?
FROM WHAT I UNDERSTAND, YOU WOULD WANT ETERNAL YOUTH...?
OHH...
NARAKU, WHAT EXACTLY DO YOU WANT FROM ME?

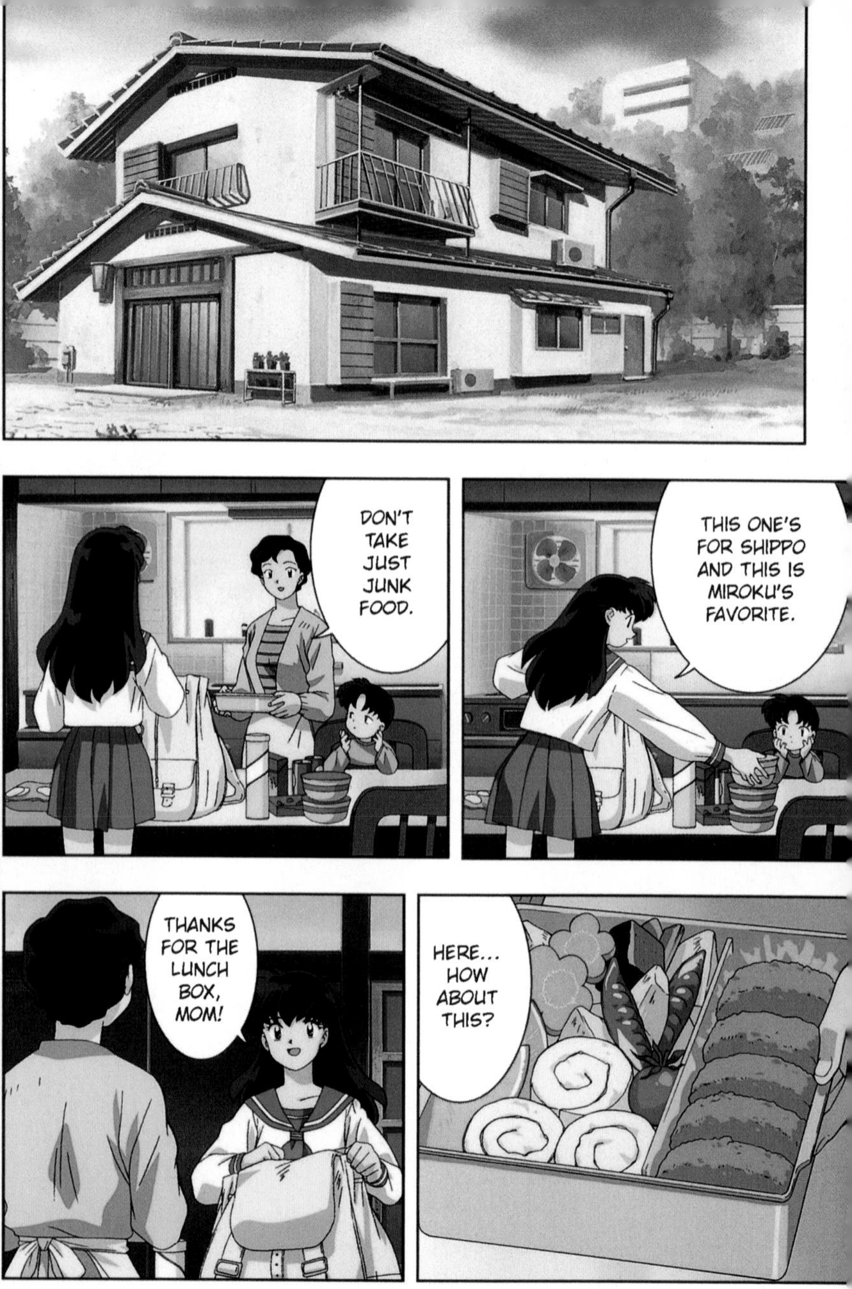
THIS ONE'S FOR SHIPPO AND THIS IS MIROKU'S FAVORITE.
DON'T TAKE JUST JUNK FOOD.
HERE... HOW ABOUT THIS?
THANKS FOR THE LUNCH BOX, MOM!

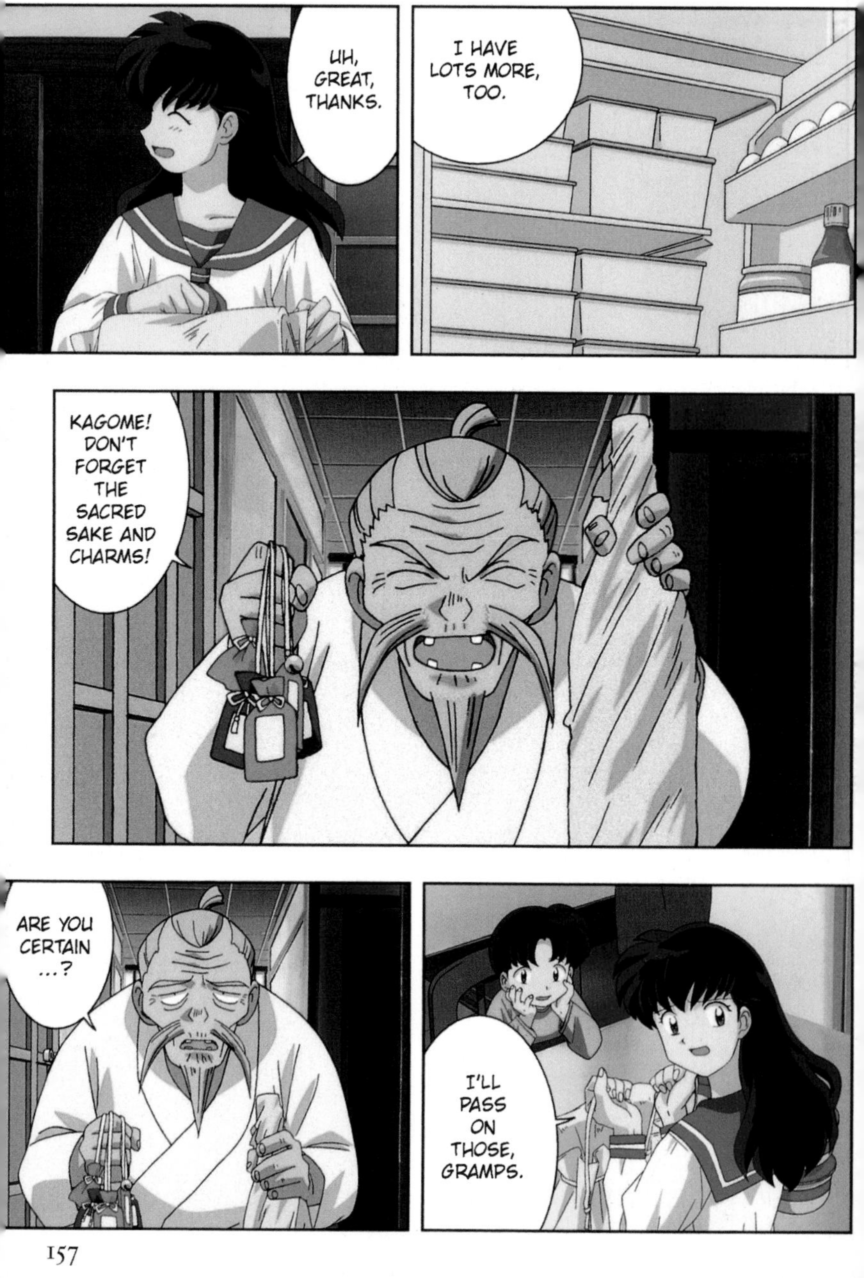
I HAVE LOTS MORE, TOO.
UH, GREAT, THANKS.
KAGOME! DON'T FORGET THE SACRED SAKE AND CHARMS!
I'LL PASS ON THOSE, GRAMPS.
ARE YOU CERTAIN ...?

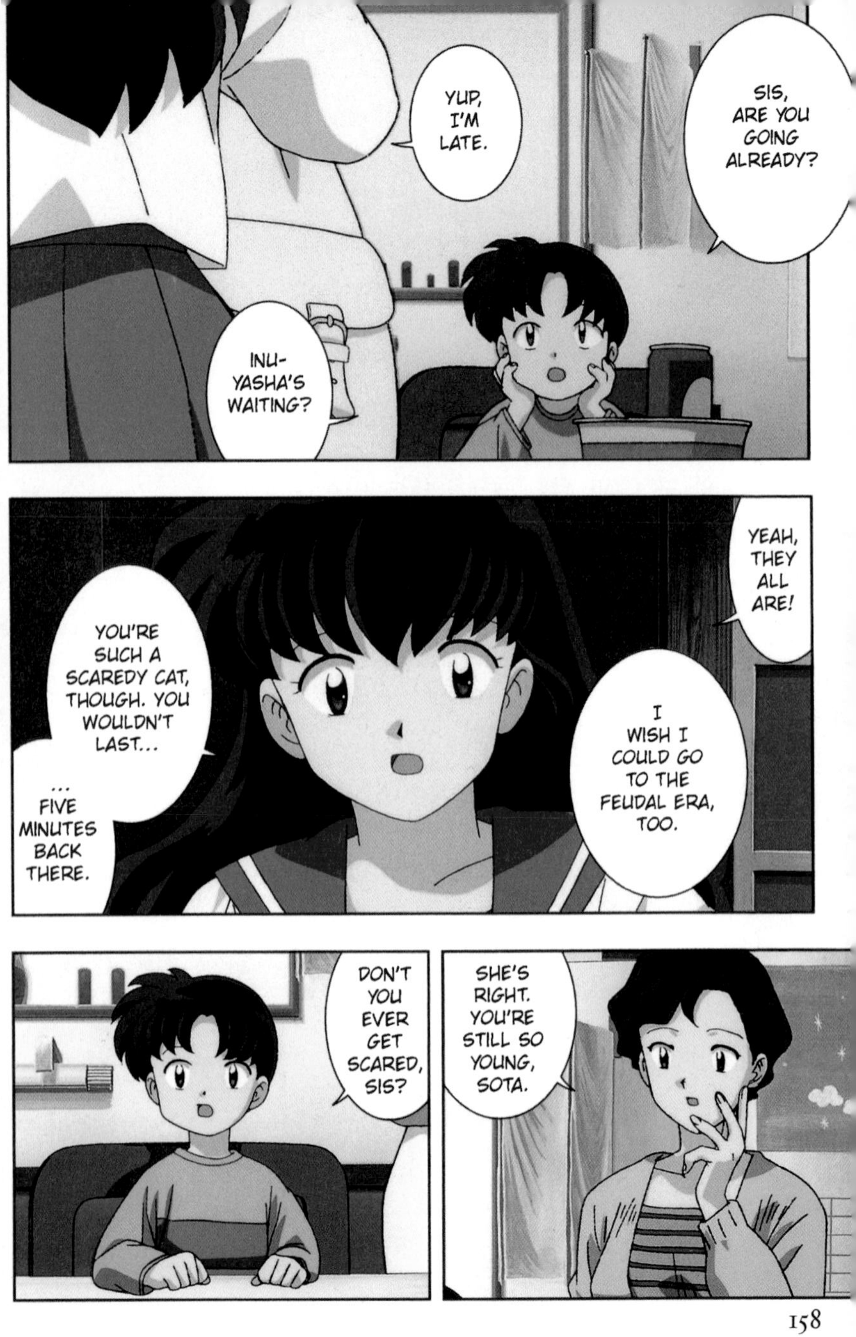
SIS, ARE YOU GOING ALREADY?
YUP, I'M LATE.
INU-YASHA'S WAITING?
YEAH, THEY ALL ARE!
I WISH I COULD GO TO THE FEUDAL ERA, TOO.
YOU'RE SUCH A SCAREDY CAT, THOUGH. YOU WOULDN'T LAST...
... FIVE MINUTES BACK THERE.
SHE'S RIGHT. YOU'RE STILL SO YOUNG, SOTA.
DON'T YOU EVER GET SCARED, SIS?

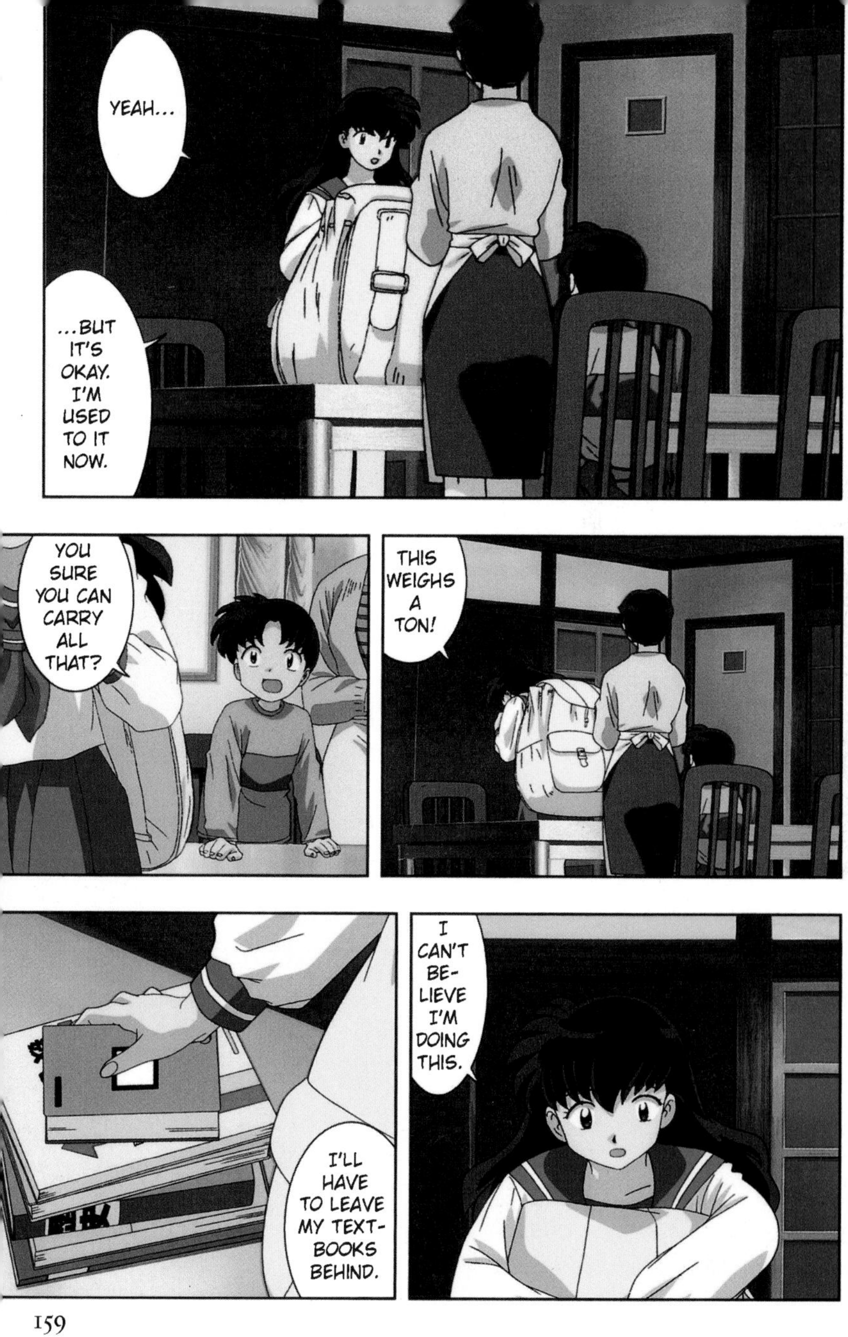
YEAH...
...BUT IT'S OKAY. I'M USED TO IT NOW.
THIS WEIGHS A TON!
YOU SURE YOU CAN CARRY ALL THAT?
I CAN'T BE-LIEVE I'M DOING THIS.
I'LL HAVE TO LEAVE MY TEXT-BOOKS BEHIND.

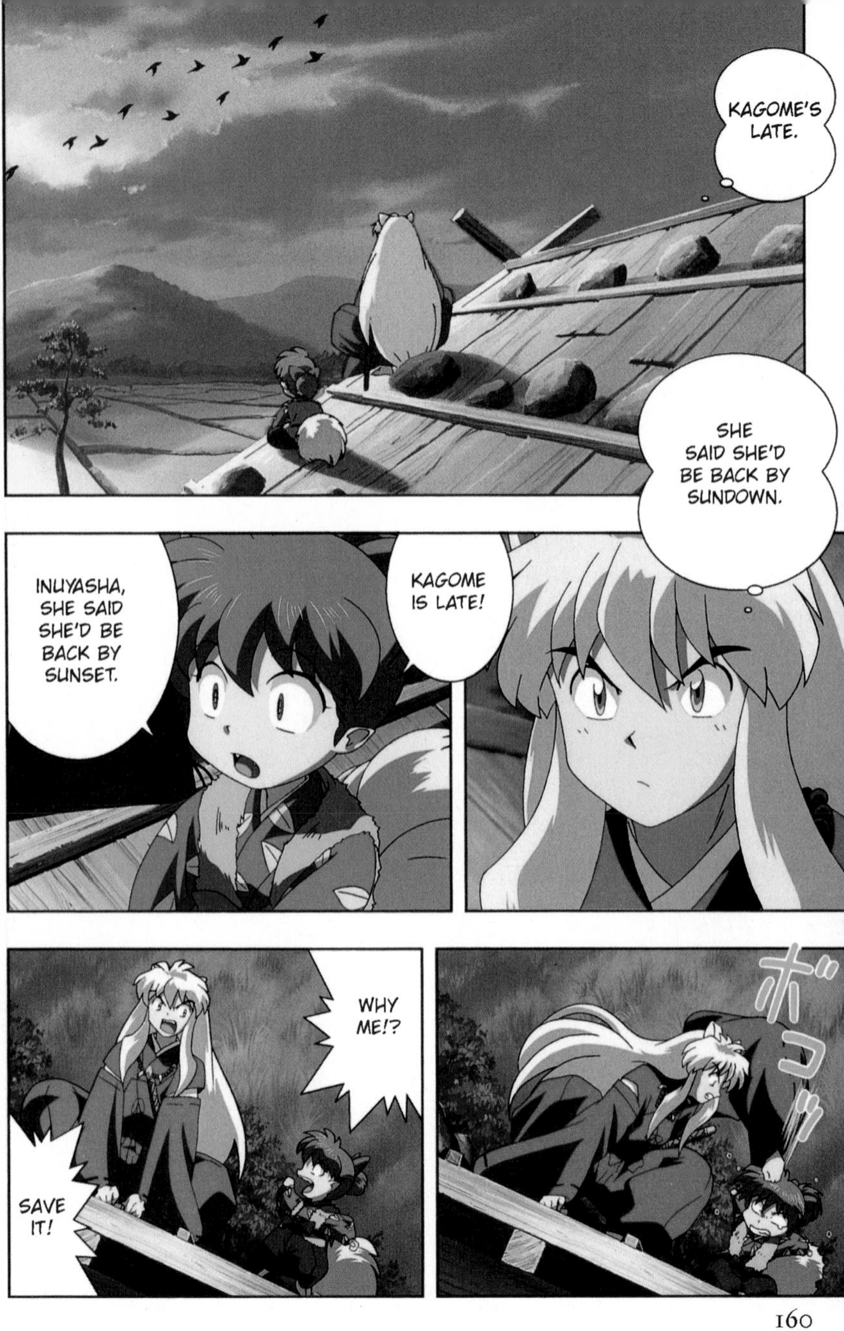
KAGOME'S LATE.
SHE SAID SHE'D BE BACK BY SUNDOWN.
KAGOME IS LATE!
INUYASHA, SHE SAID SHE'D BE BACK BY SUNSET.
ボコッ
WHY ME!?
SAVE IT!

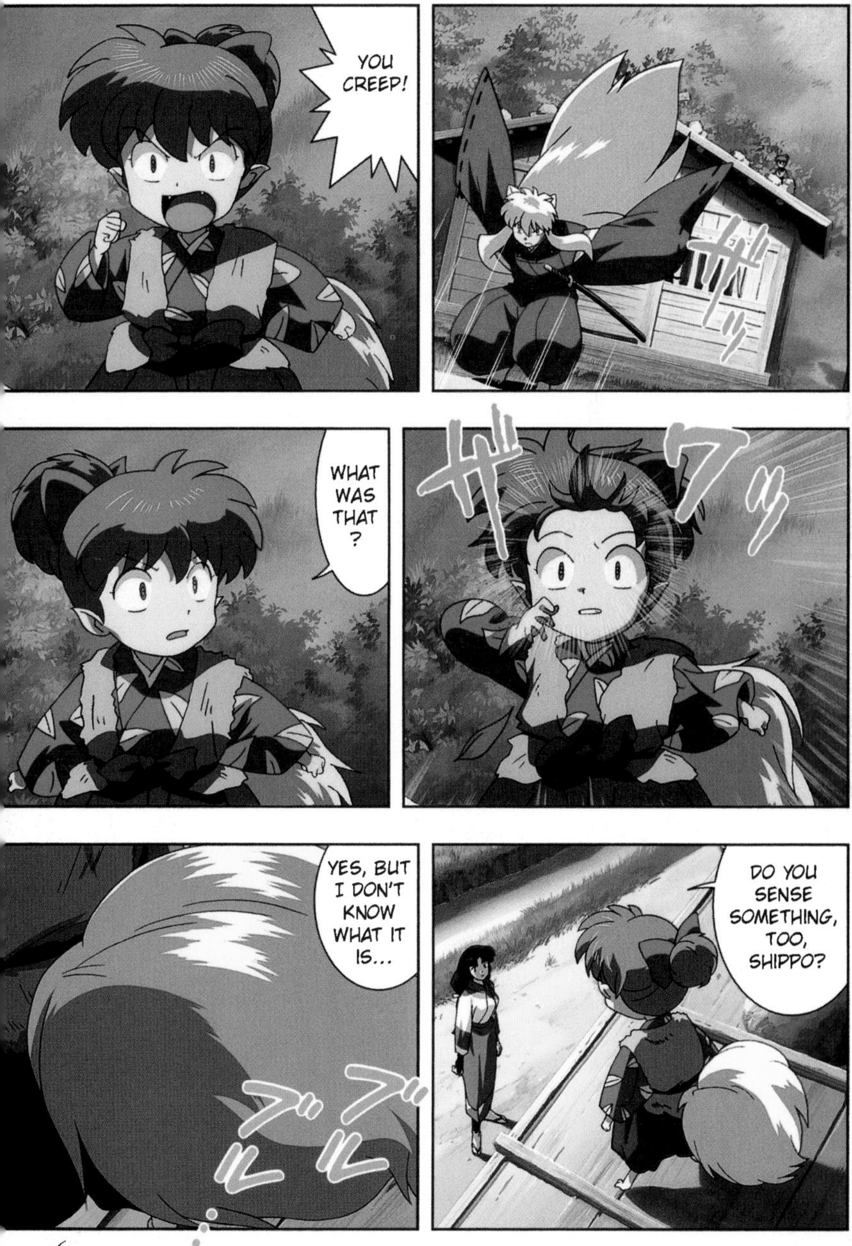
YOU CREEP!
WHAT WAS THAT?
DO YOU SENSE SOMETHING, TOO, SHIPPO?
YES, BUT I DON'T KNOW WHAT IT IS...

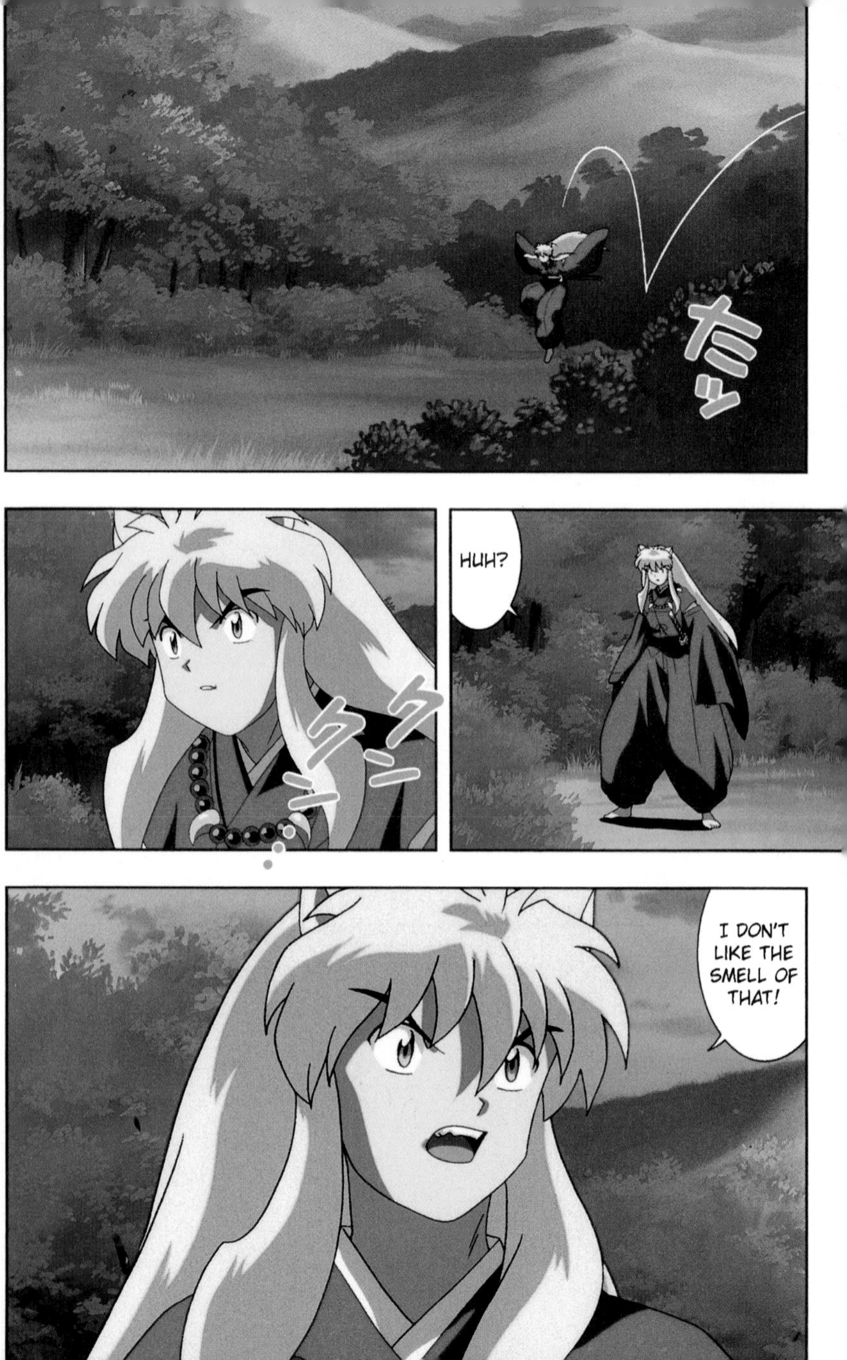
たッ
HUH?
クンクン
I DON'T LIKE THE SMELL OF THAT!

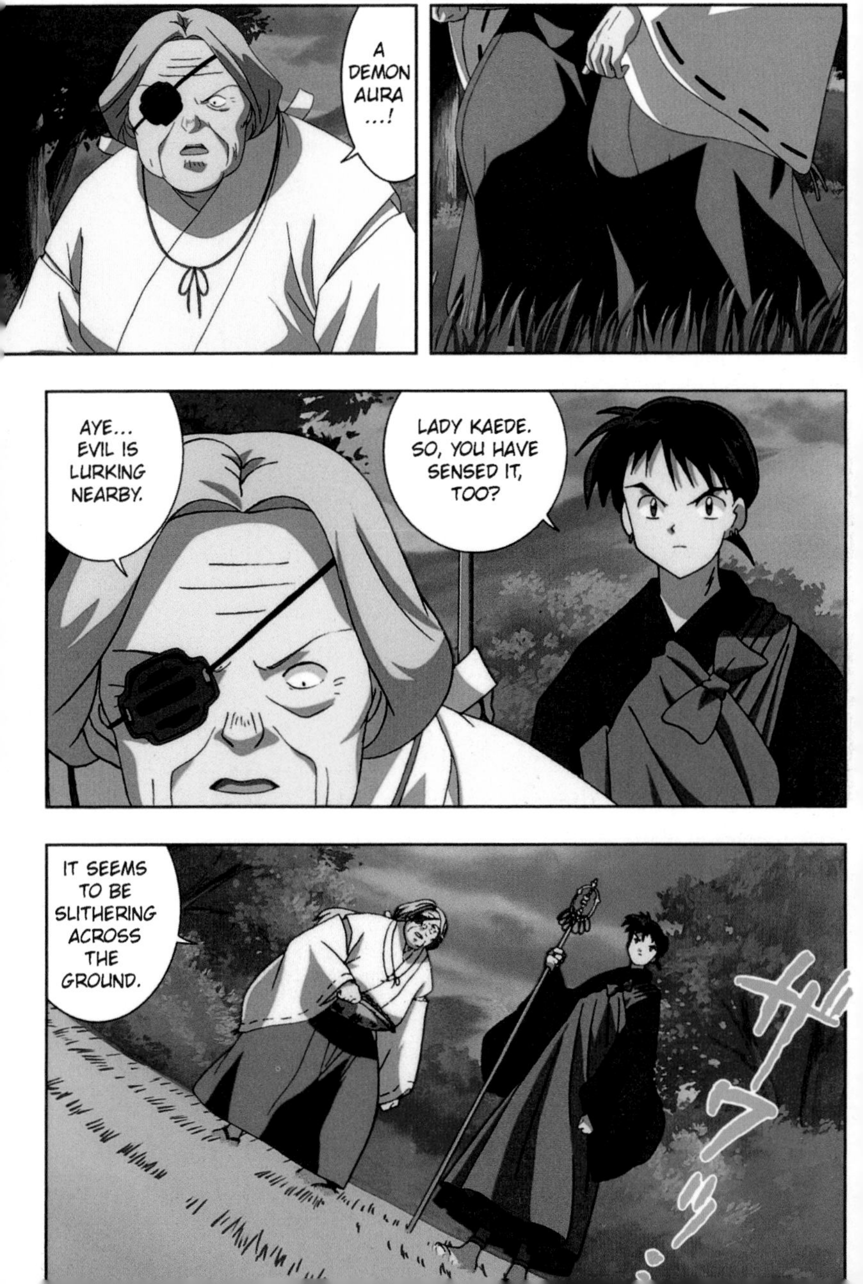
A DEMON AURA ...!
LADY KAEDE. SO, YOU HAVE SENSED IT, TOO?
AYE... EVIL IS LURKING NEARBY.
IT SEEMS TO BE SLITHERING ACROSS THE GROUND.
ザワッ

THAT WAS A WORK-OUT.

UP AND OVER!

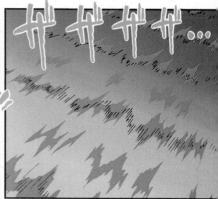

OUCH!

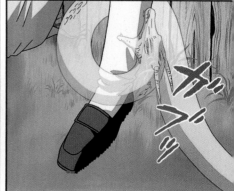

WHAT WAS IT, THOUGH?

SOMETHING BIT ME!

HEY...

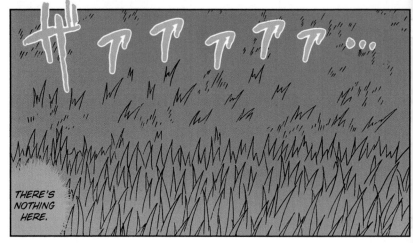

THERE'S NOTHING HERE.

SOMETHING BIT ME! I THINK IT CAME FROM OVER THERE!

WHAT!?

WHAT TOOK YA SO LONG!?

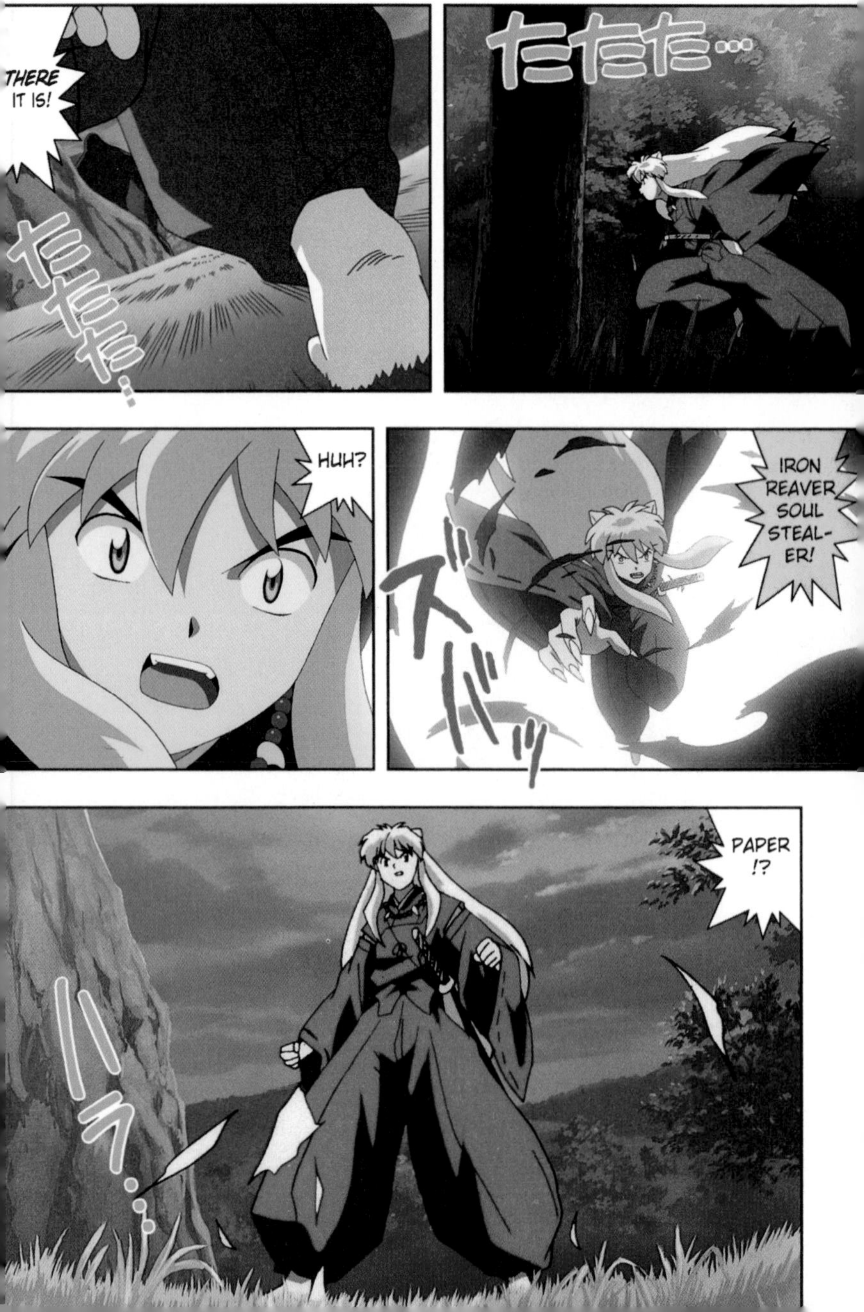

たたた…
THERE IT IS!
たたたた…
IRON REAVER SOUL STEALER!
ズバッ
HUH?
PAPER!?
ハラ…

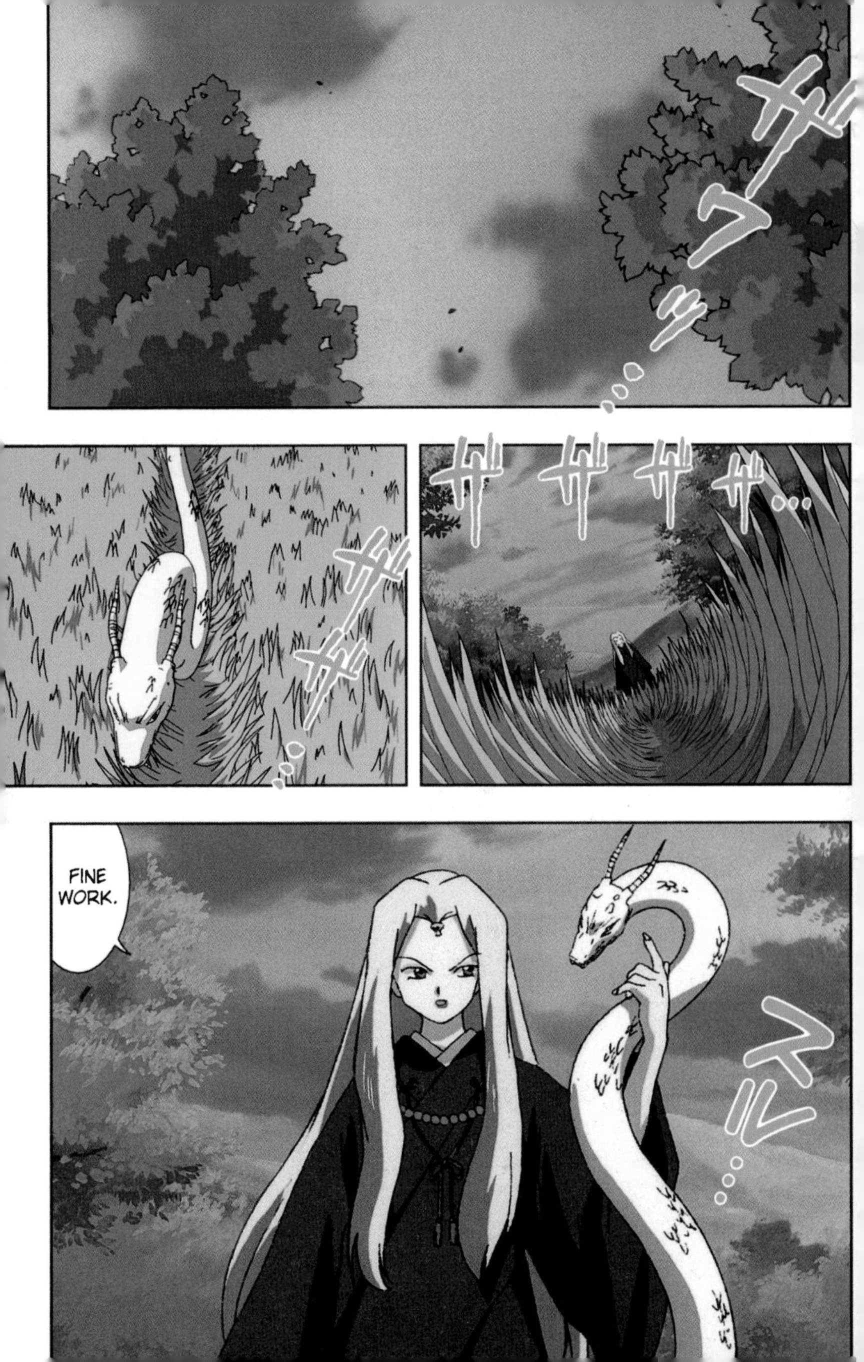
ザワッ…
ザザザザ…
ザザ…
スル…
FINE WORK.

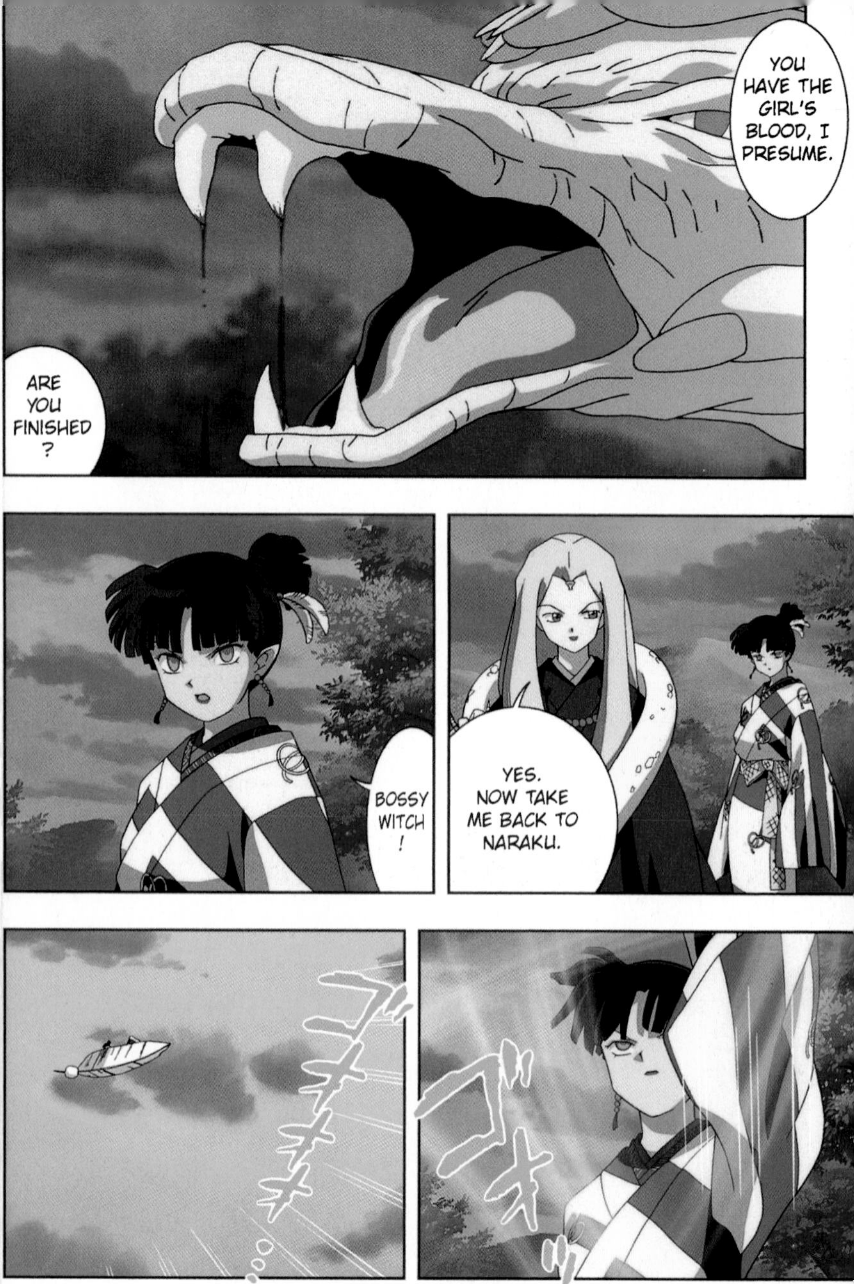
YOU HAVE THE GIRL'S BLOOD, I PRESUME.
ARE YOU FINISHED?
YES. NOW TAKE ME BACK TO NARAKU.
BOSSY WITCH!

THERE WAS SOMETHING STRANGE HERE.

...

I ATTACKED IT, BUT LOOK.

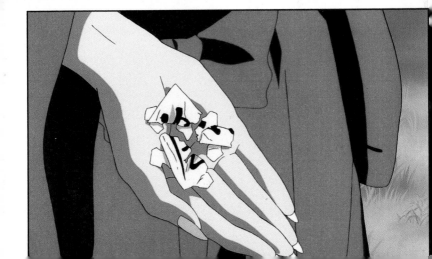

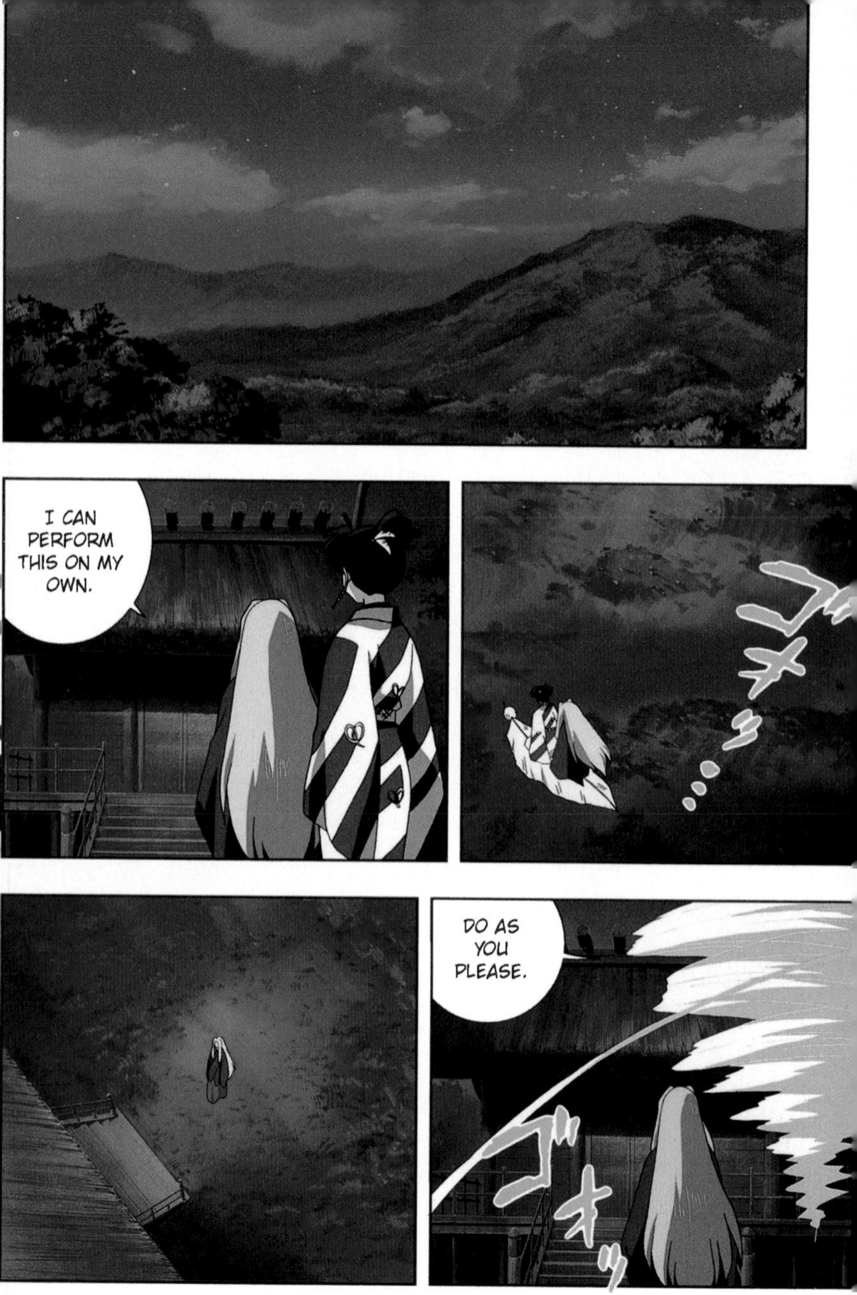
I CAN PERFORM THIS ON MY OWN.
DO AS YOU PLEASE.

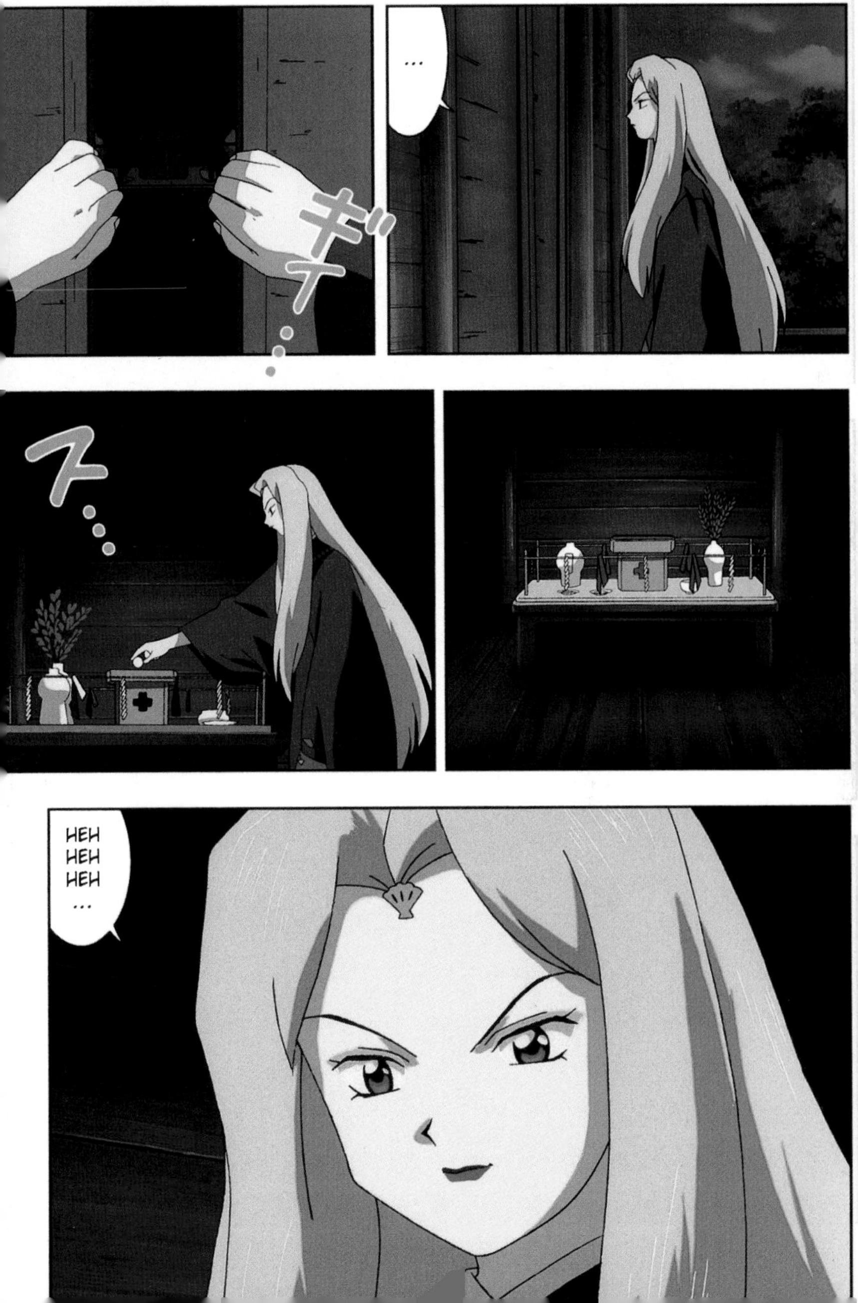
...
ギィ...
ス...
HEH
HEH
HEH
...

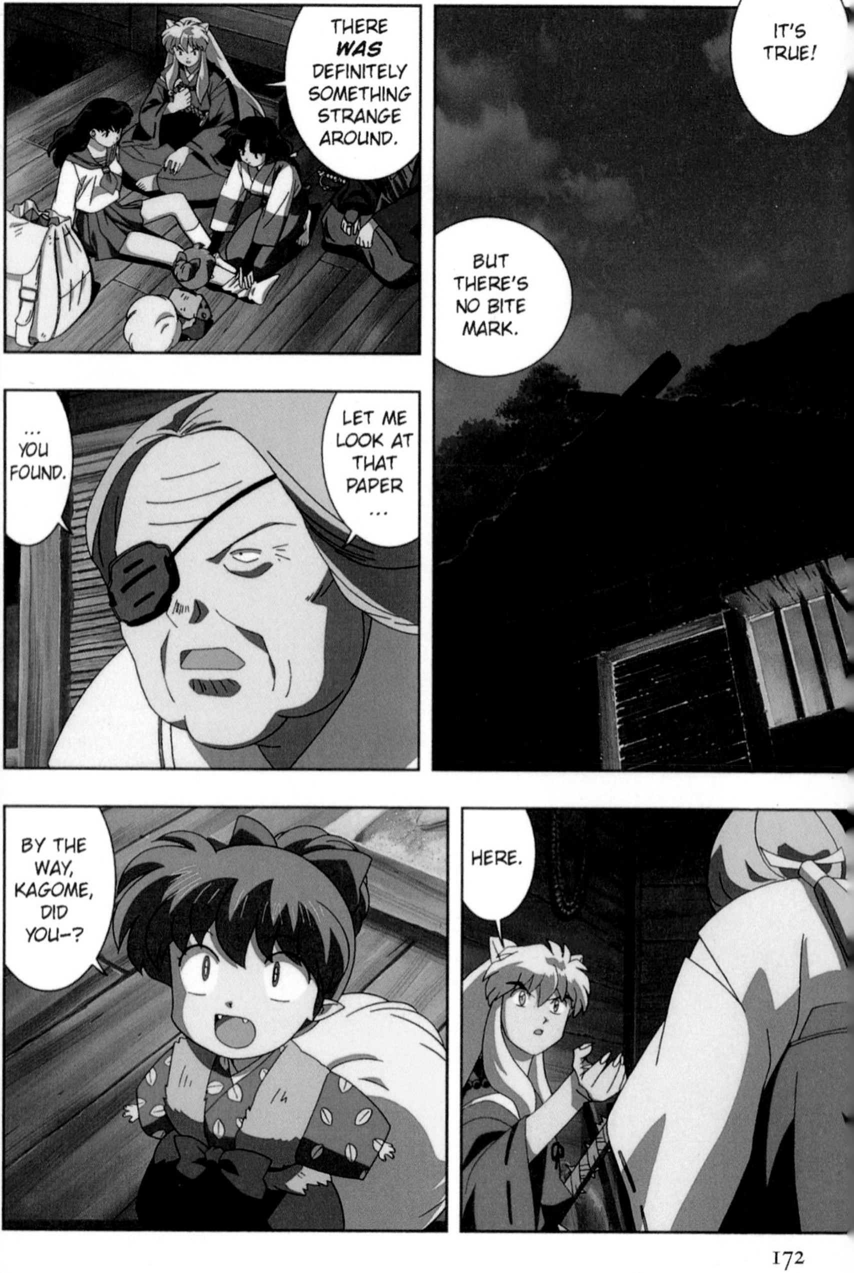
IT'S TRUE!
BUT THERE'S NO BITE MARK.
THERE **WAS** DEFINITELY SOMETHING STRANGE AROUND.
LET ME LOOK AT THAT PAPER ...
... YOU FOUND.
HERE.
BY THE WAY, KAGOME, DID YOU-?

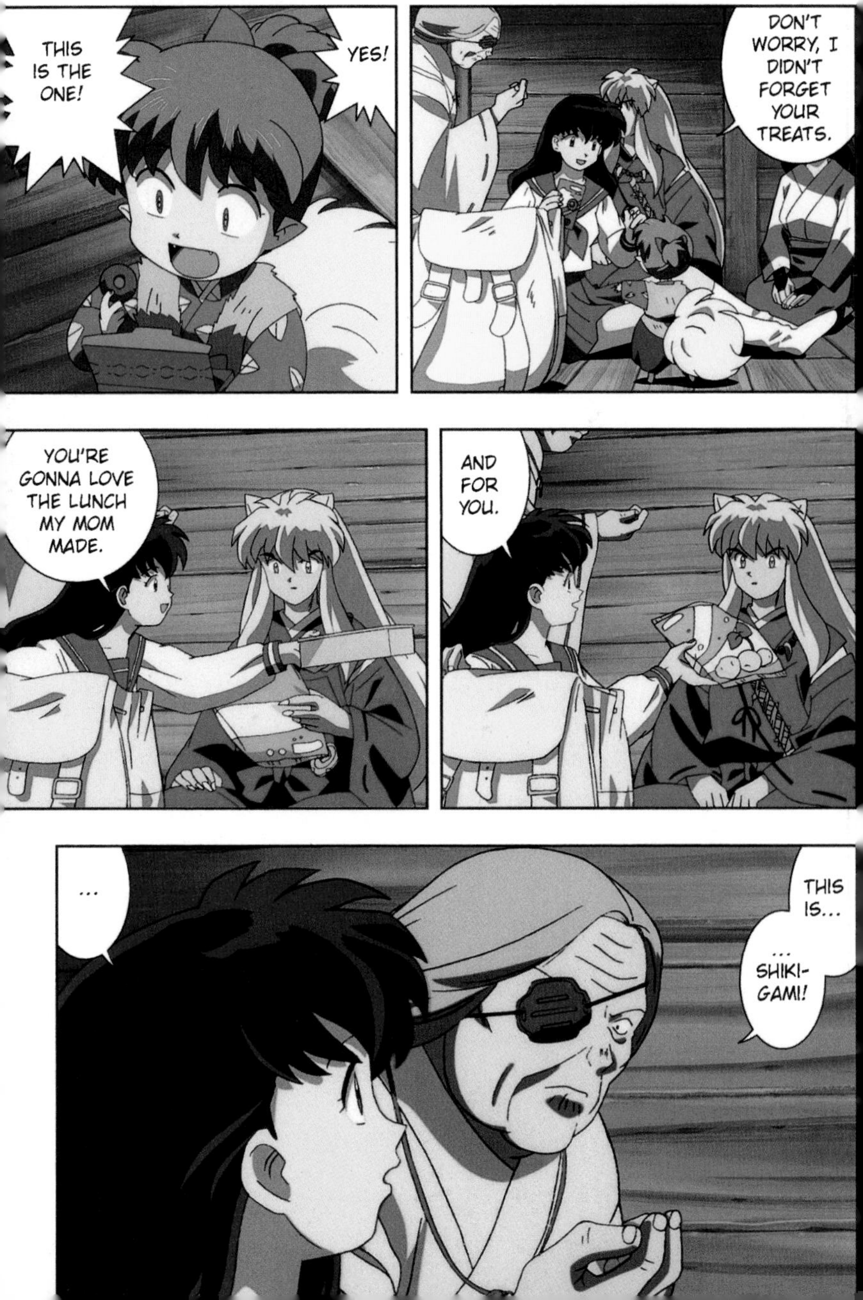
DON'T WORRY, I DIDN'T FORGET YOUR TREATS.
YES!
THIS IS THE ONE!
AND FOR YOU.
YOU'RE GONNA LOVE THE LUNCH MY MOM MADE.
THIS IS...
...SHIKI-GAMI!
...

WHAT WAS THAT? THE SACRED JEWEL SHARDS...!

AH!!

WHAT IS IT, KAGOME?

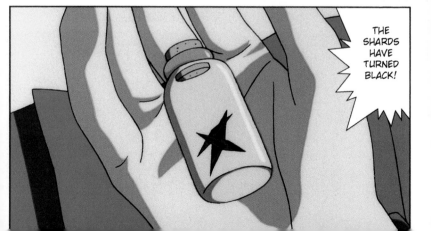

THE SHARDS HAVE TURNED BLACK!

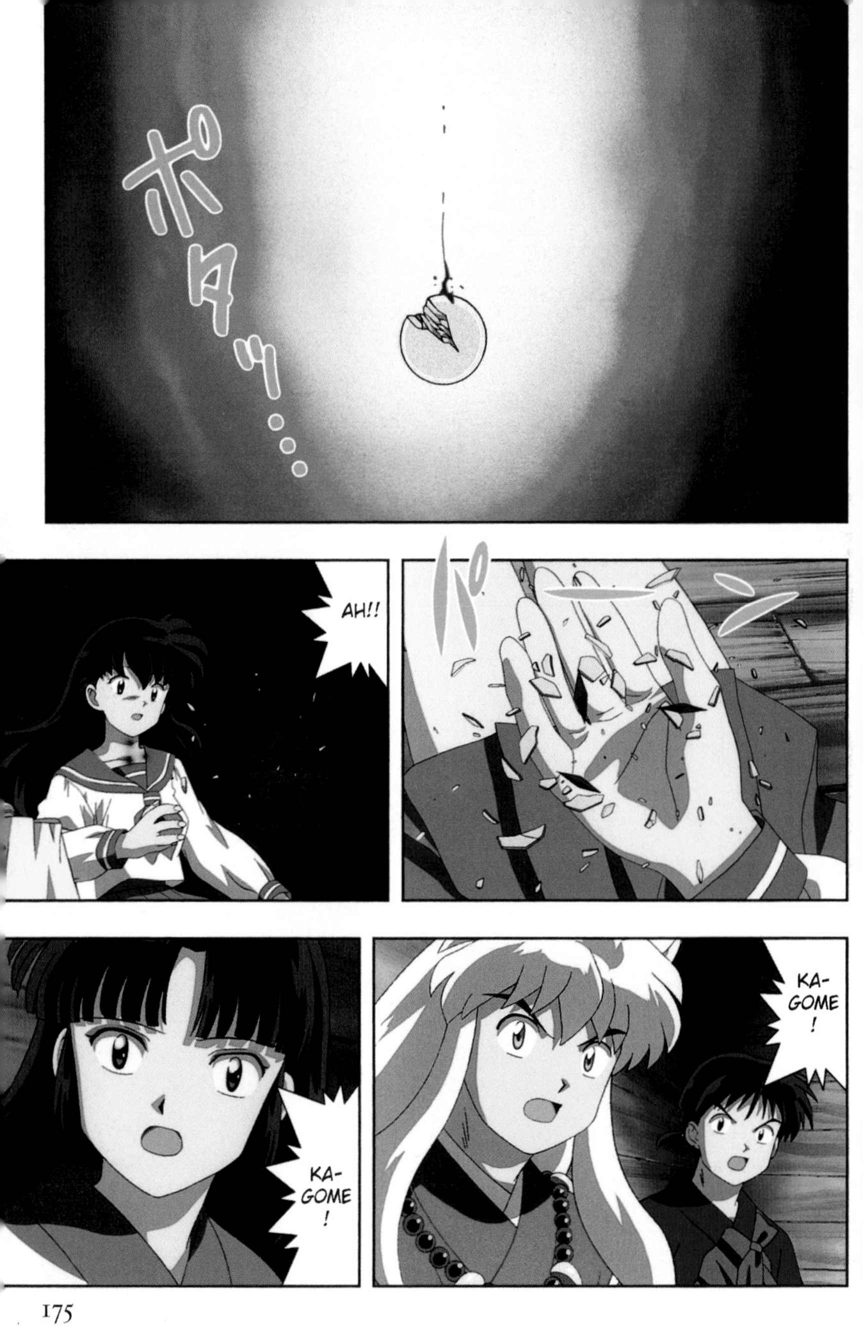
ポタッ...
パ
AH!!
KA-GOME!
KA-GOME!

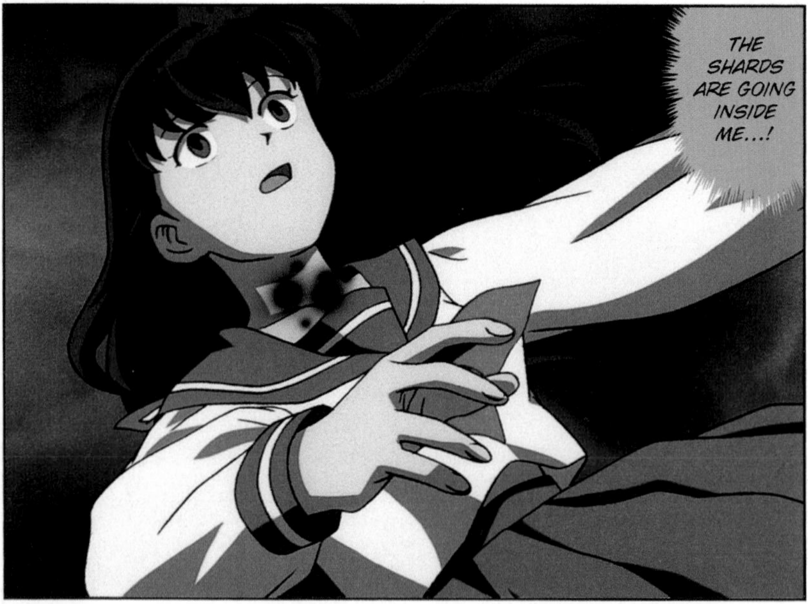
THE SHARDS ARE GOING INSIDE ME...!

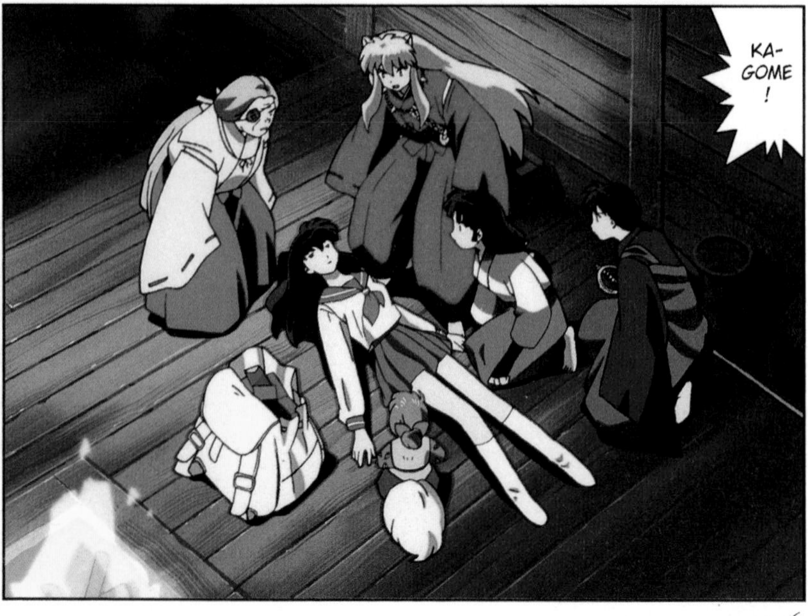
KA-GOME!

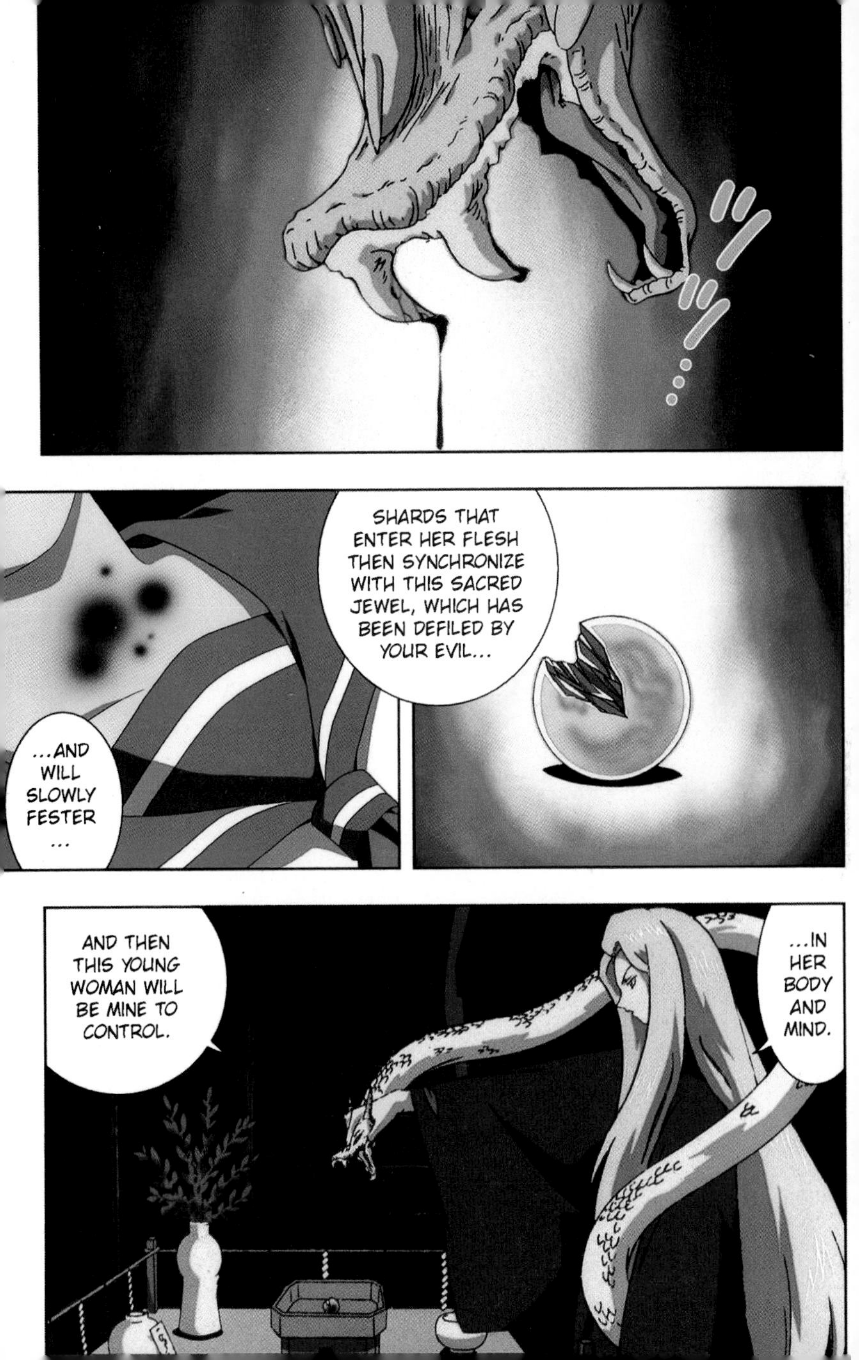
SHARDS THAT ENTER HER FLESH THEN SYNCHRONIZE WITH THIS SACRED JEWEL, WHICH HAS BEEN DEFILED BY YOUR EVIL...
...AND WILL SLOWLY FESTER ...
...IN HER BODY AND MIND.
AND THEN THIS YOUNG WOMAN WILL BE MINE TO CONTROL.

TSUBAKI, DON'T UNDERESTIMATE THIS YOUNG WOMAN, KAGOME.

DON'T MAKE ME LAUGH.

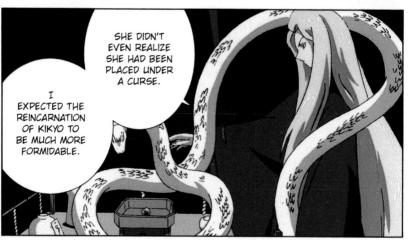

SHE DIDN'T EVEN REALIZE SHE HAD BEEN PLACED UNDER A CURSE.

I EXPECTED THE REINCARNATION OF KIKYO TO BE MUCH MORE FORMIDABLE.

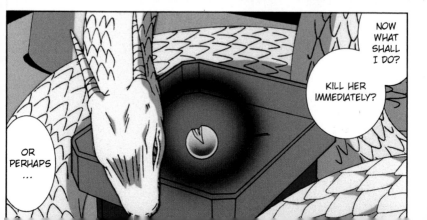

NOW WHAT SHALL I DO?

KILL HER IMMEDIATELY?

OR PERHAPS ...

LET'S MAKE INUYASHA SUFFER THROUGH ANOTHER NIGHTMARE. A NOSTALGIC DREAM ABOUT...

HEH HEH HEH ...

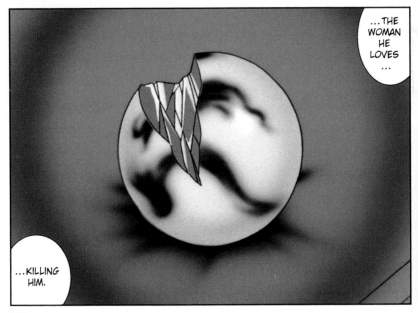

...THE WOMAN HE LOVES ...

...KILLING HIM.

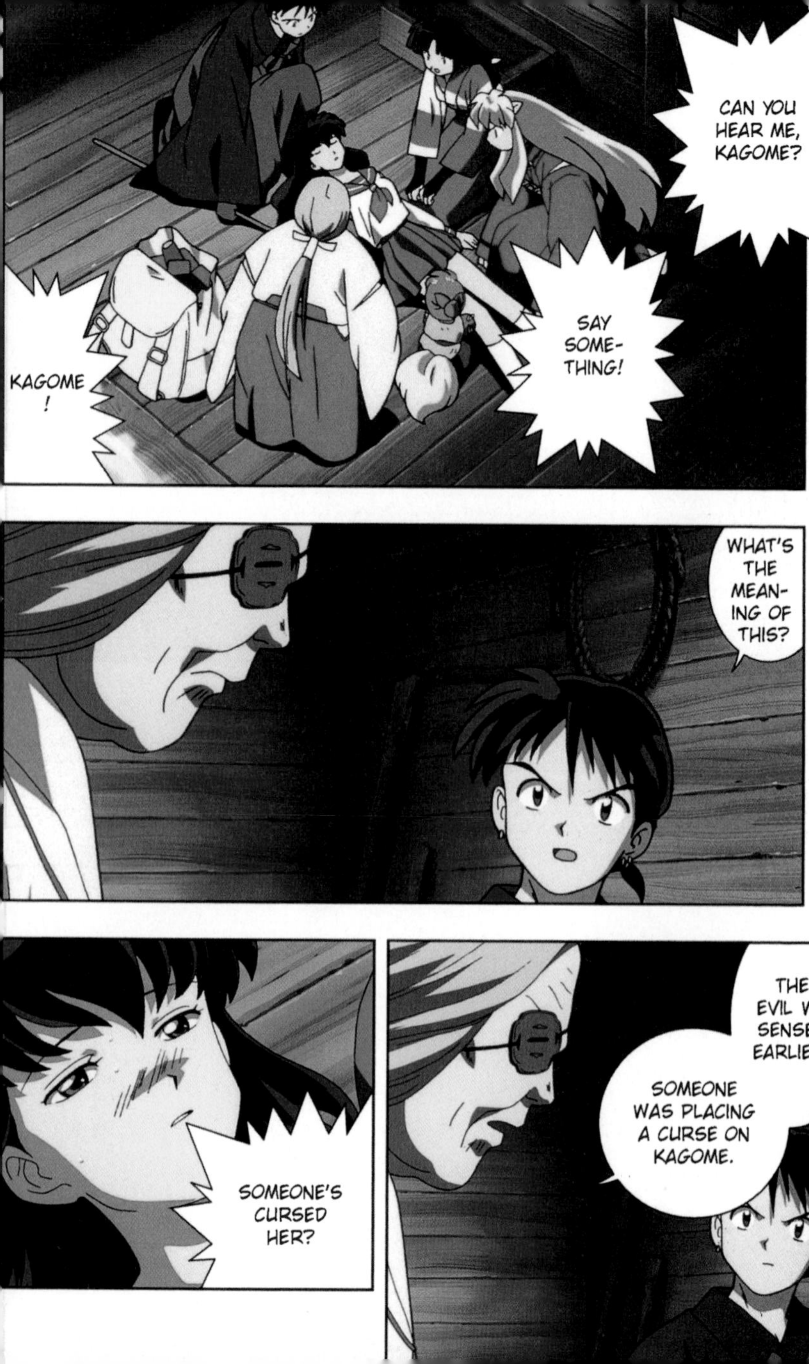
CAN YOU HEAR ME, KAGOME?
SAY SOME-THING!
KAGOME!
WHAT'S THE MEAN-ING OF THIS?
THE EVIL WE SENSED EARLIER.
SOMEONE WAS PLACING A CURSE ON KAGOME.
SOMEONE'S CURSED HER?

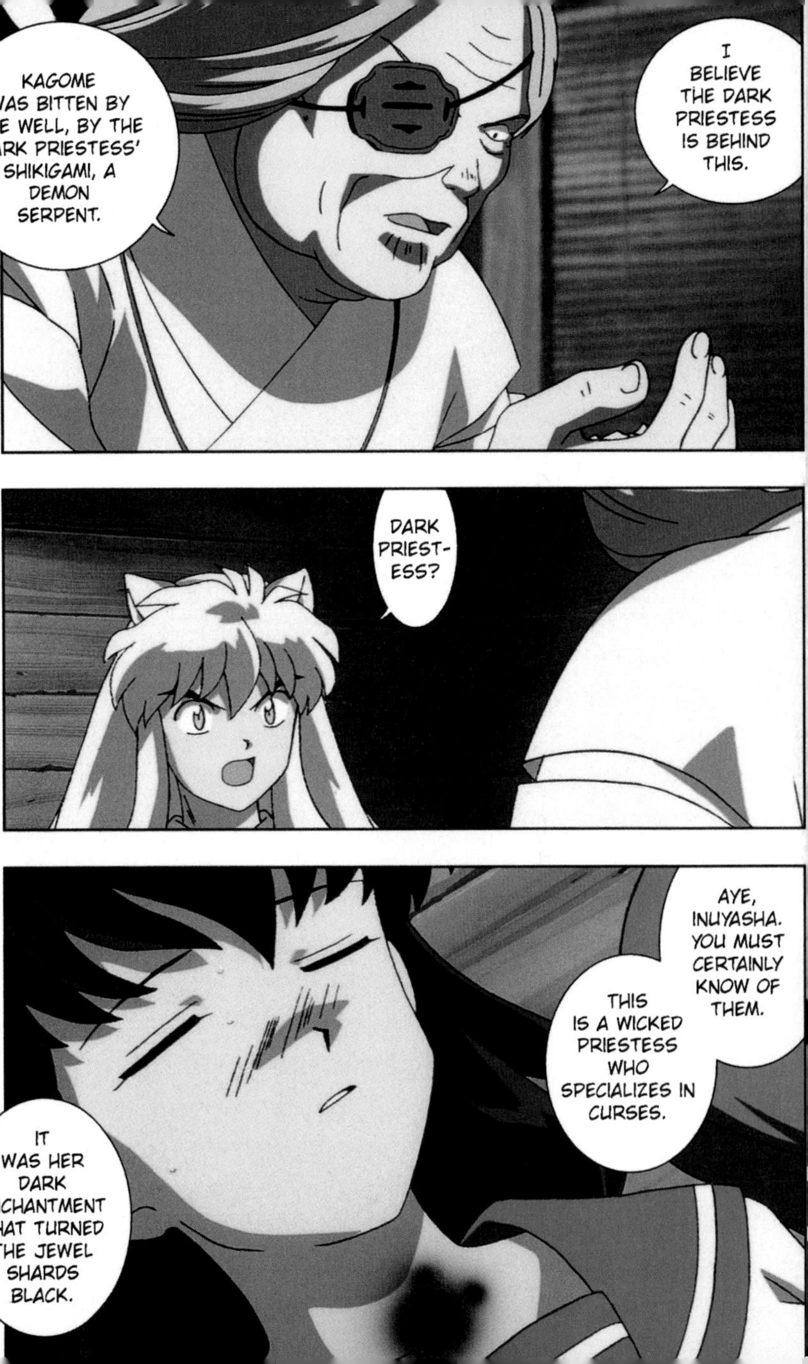
I BELIEVE THE DARK PRIESTESS IS BEHIND THIS.
KAGOME WAS BITTEN BY THE WELL, BY THE DARK PRIESTESS' SHIKIGAMI, A DEMON SERPENT.
DARK PRIEST-ESS?
AYE, INUYASHA. YOU MUST CERTAINLY KNOW OF THEM.
THIS IS A WICKED PRIESTESS WHO SPECIALIZES IN CURSES.
IT WAS HER DARK ENCHANTMENT THAT TURNED THE JEWEL SHARDS BLACK.

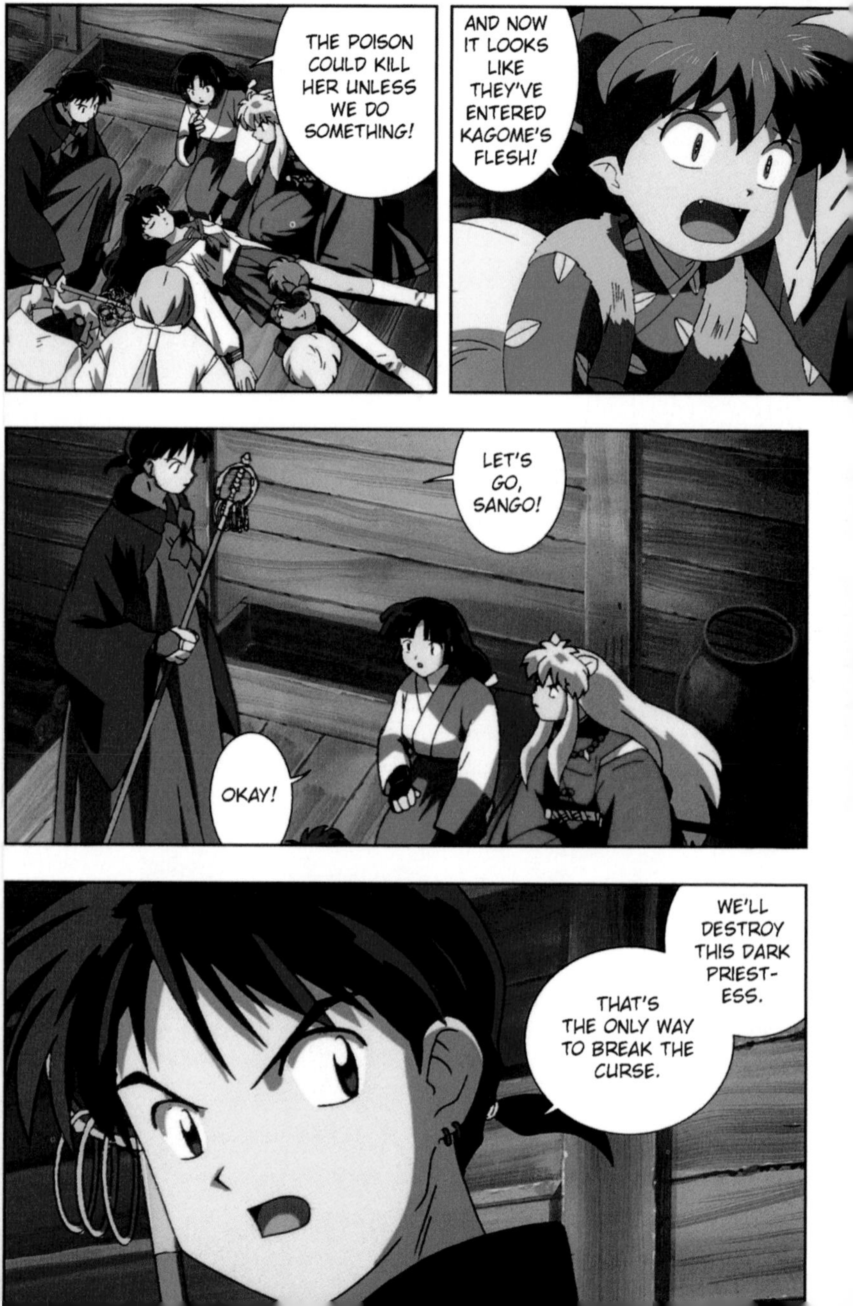
AND NOW IT LOOKS LIKE THEY'VE ENTERED KAGOME'S FLESH!
THE POISON COULD KILL HER UNLESS WE DO SOMETHING!
LET'S GO, SANGO!
OKAY!
WE'LL DESTROY THIS DARK PRIEST-ESS.
THAT'S THE ONLY WAY TO BREAK THE CURSE.

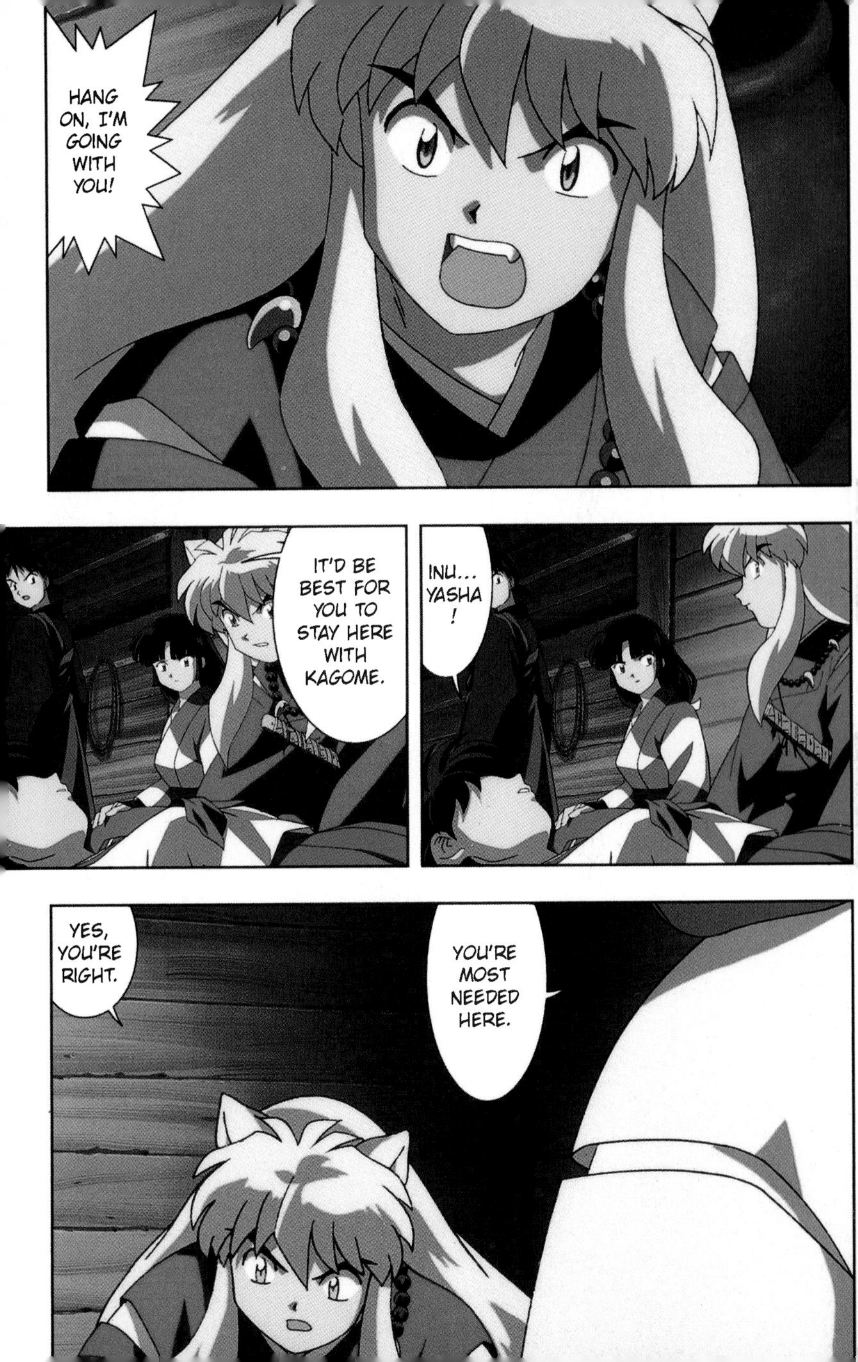
HANG ON, I'M GOING WITH YOU!
INU... YASHA!
IT'D BE BEST FOR YOU TO STAY HERE WITH KAGOME.
YOU'RE MOST NEEDED HERE.
YES, YOU'RE RIGHT.

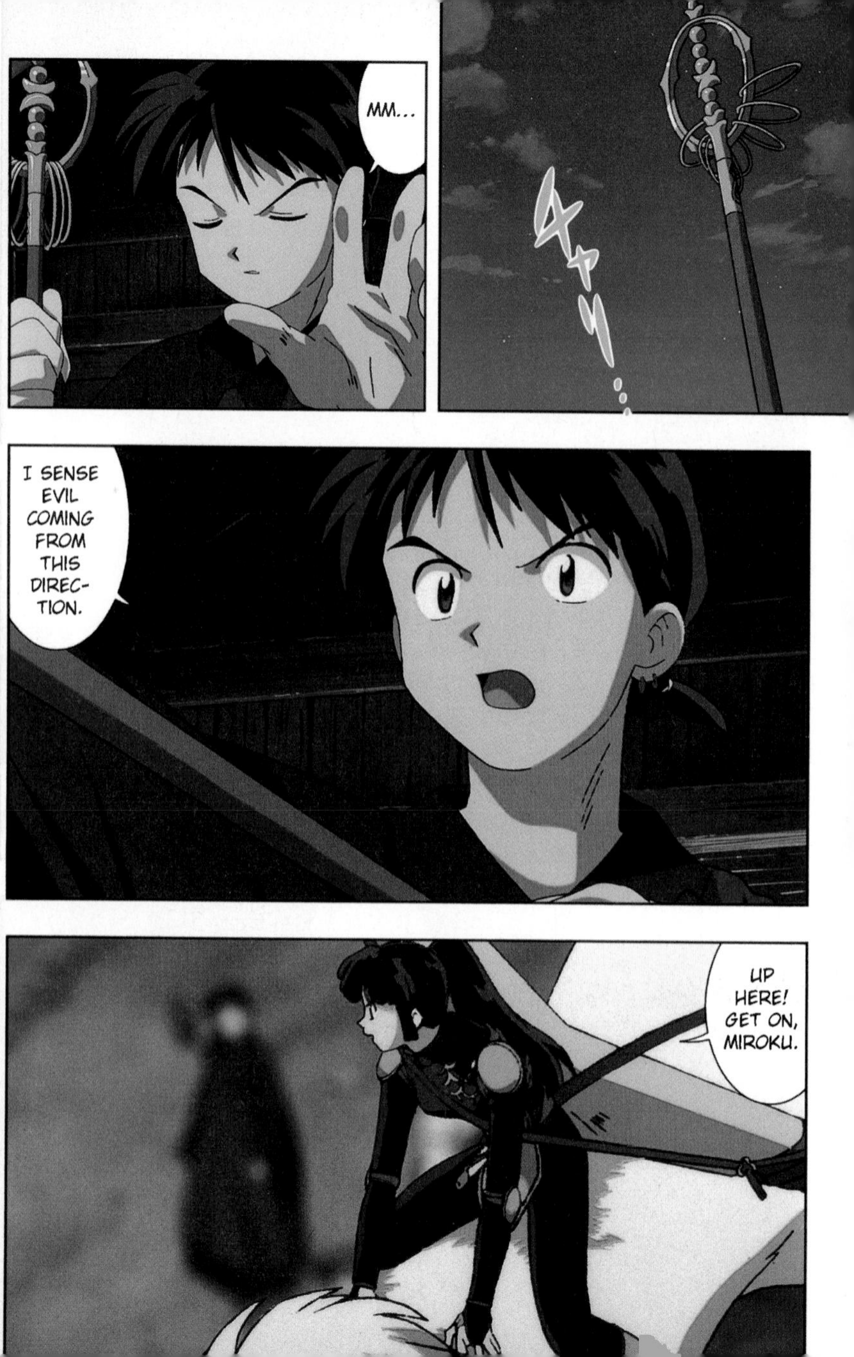
MM...
I SENSE EVIL COMING FROM THIS DIREC-TION.
UP HERE! GET ON, MIROKU.

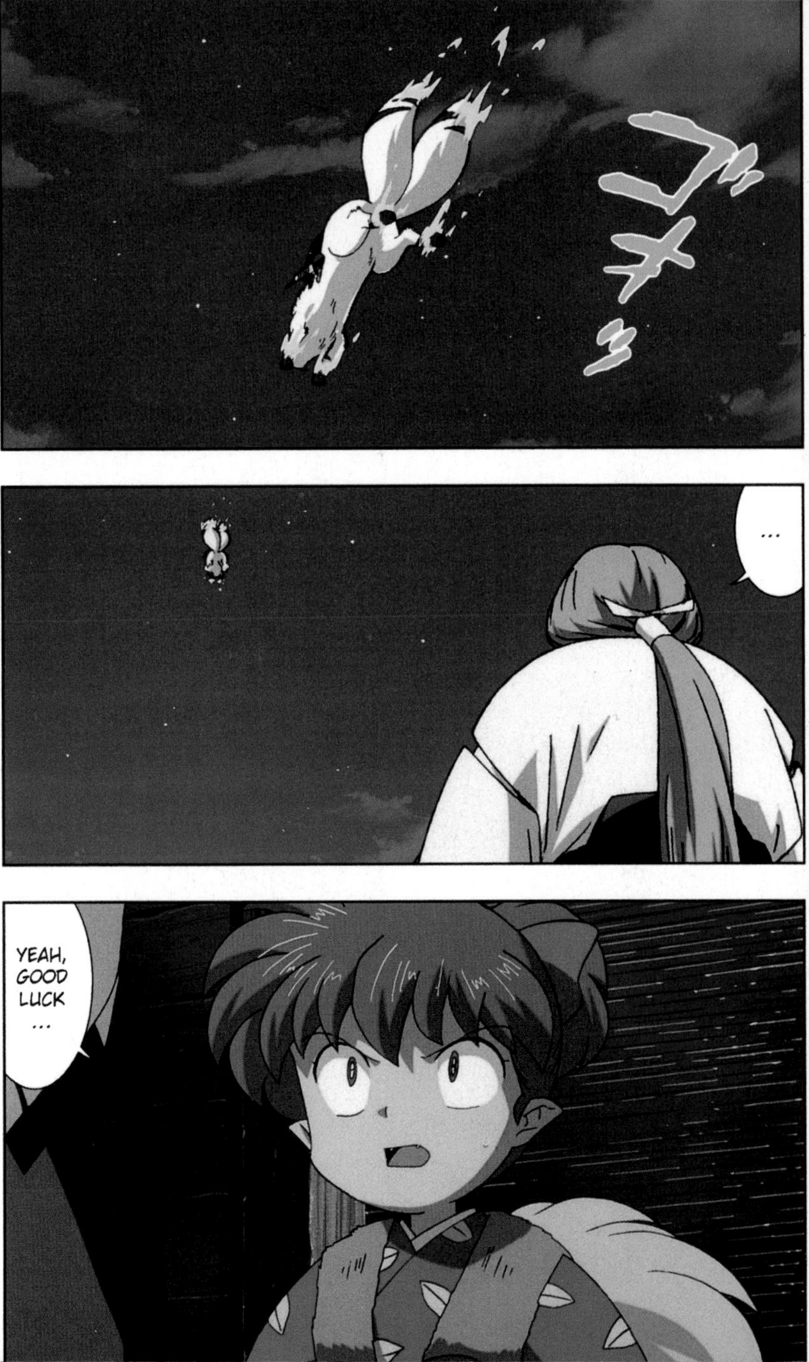
...
YEAH, GOOD LUCK ...

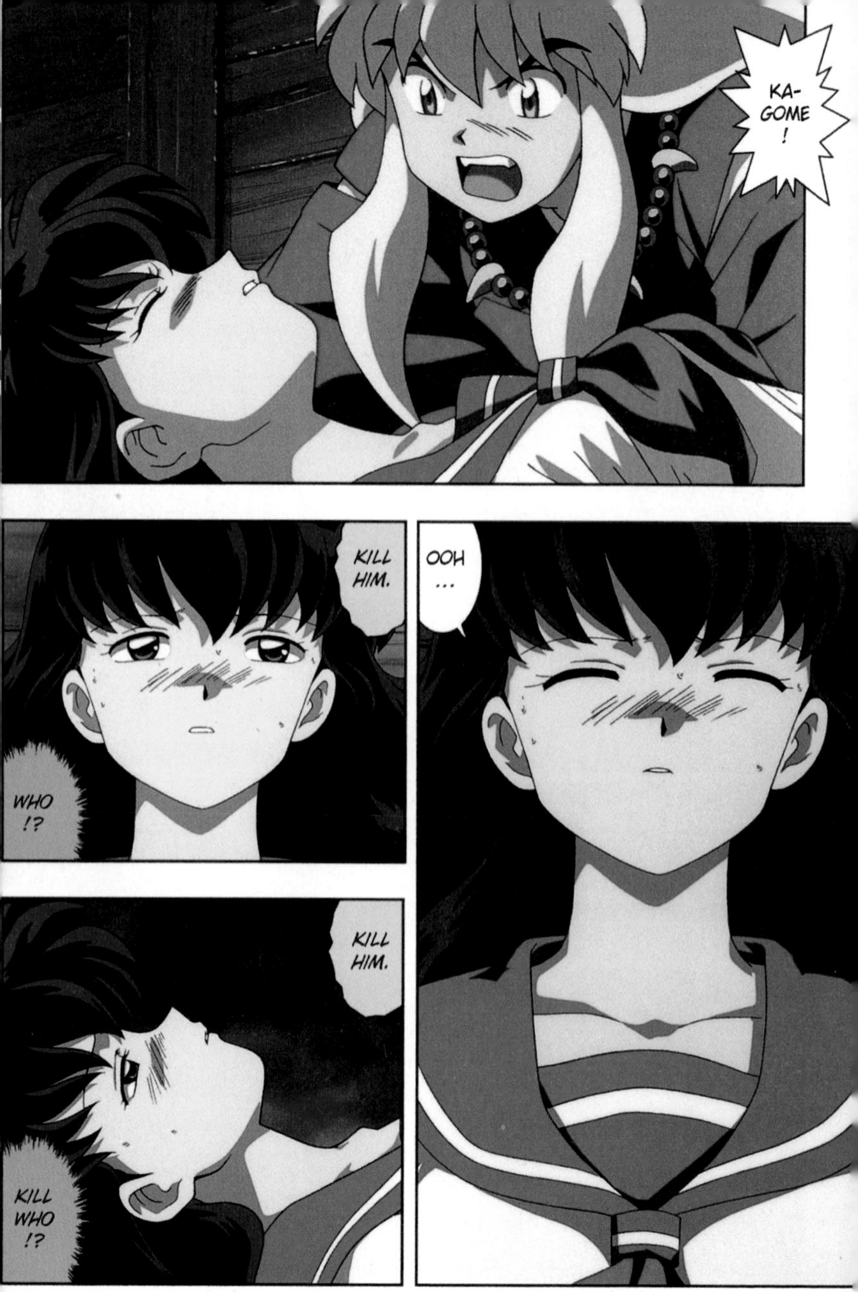
KA-GOME!
OOH ...
KILL HIM.
WHO !?
KILL HIM.
KILL WHO !?

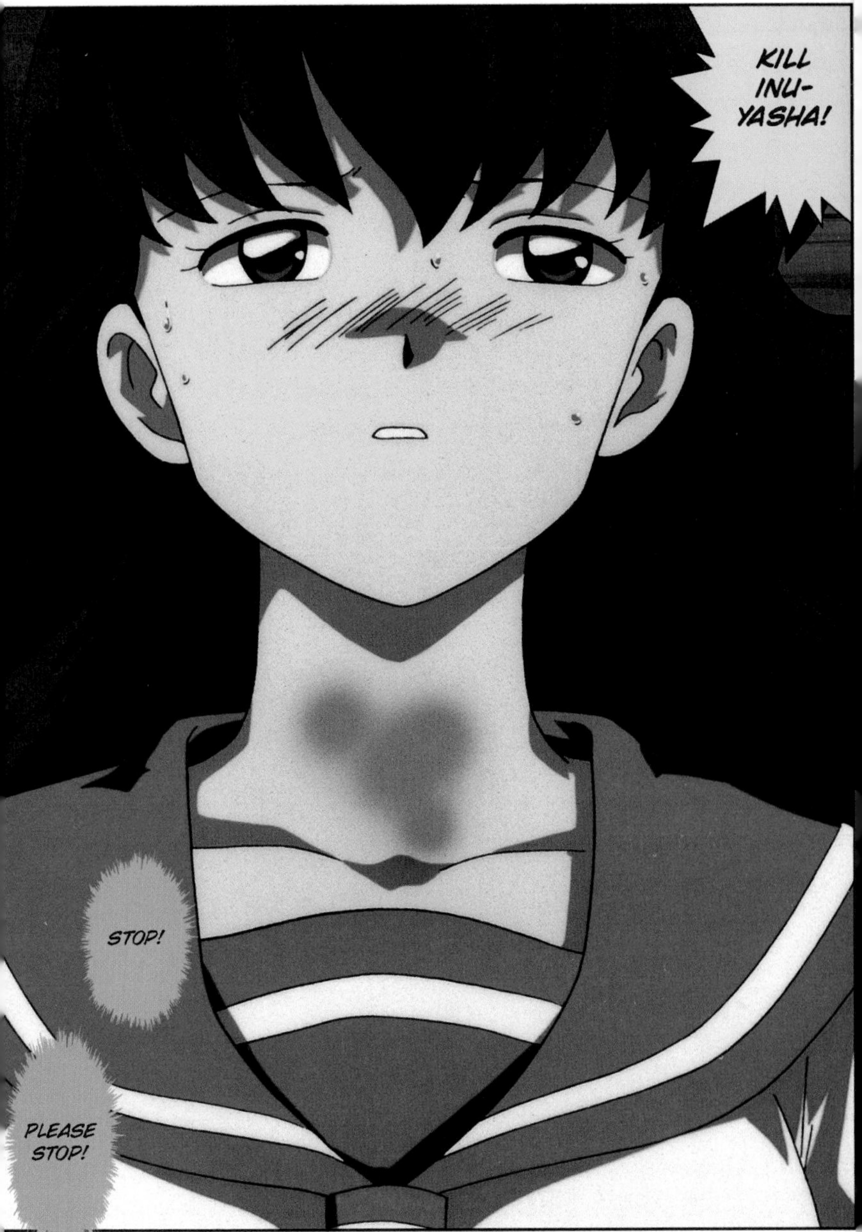
KILL INU-YASHA!
STOP!
PLEASE STOP!

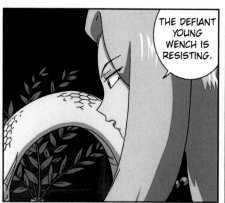

HUH!
THE DEFIANT YOUNG WENCH IS RESISTING.
AS I TOLD YOU...
...THIS KAGOME IS THE REINCAR-NATION...
...OF KIKYO, THE PRIESTESS TAMING HER...
...WILL REQUIRE MORE THAN A LITTLE EFFORT.
KIKYO!
...

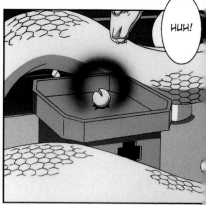

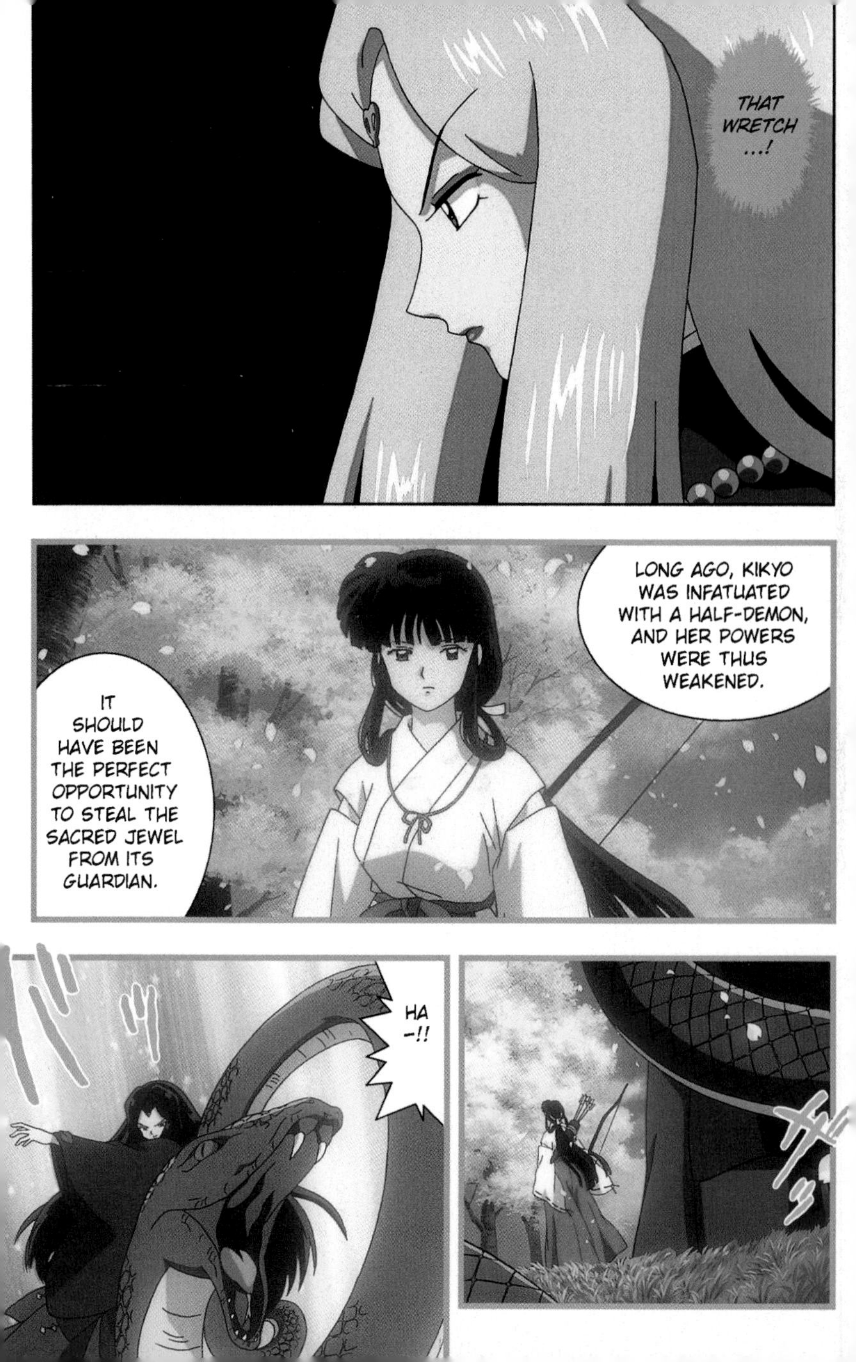
THAT WRETCH ...!
LONG AGO, KIKYO WAS INFATUATED WITH A HALF-DEMON, AND HER POWERS WERE THUS WEAKENED.
IT SHOULD HAVE BEEN THE PERFECT OPPORTUNITY TO STEAL THE SACRED JEWEL FROM ITS GUARDIAN.
HA —!!

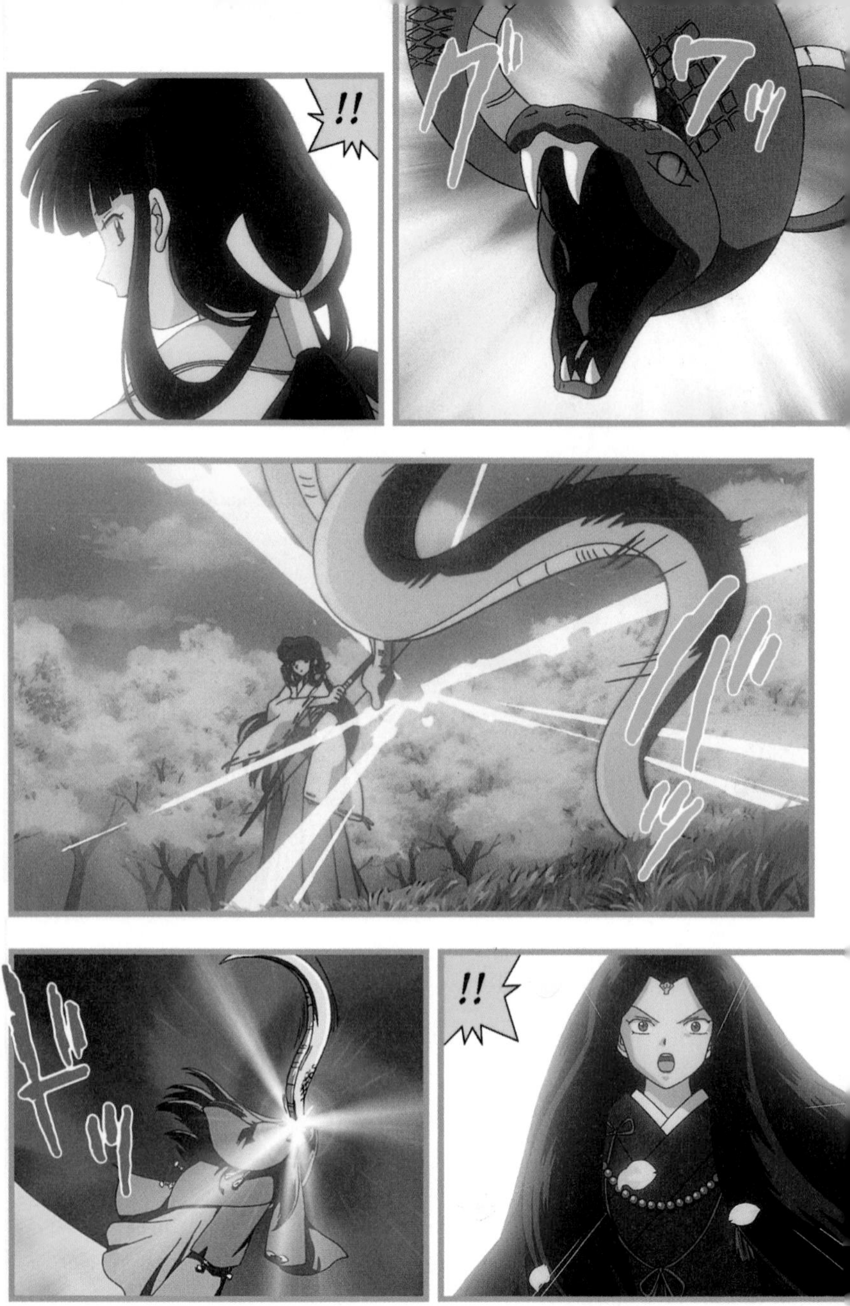
グワッ
!!
グッ
!!
ドッ

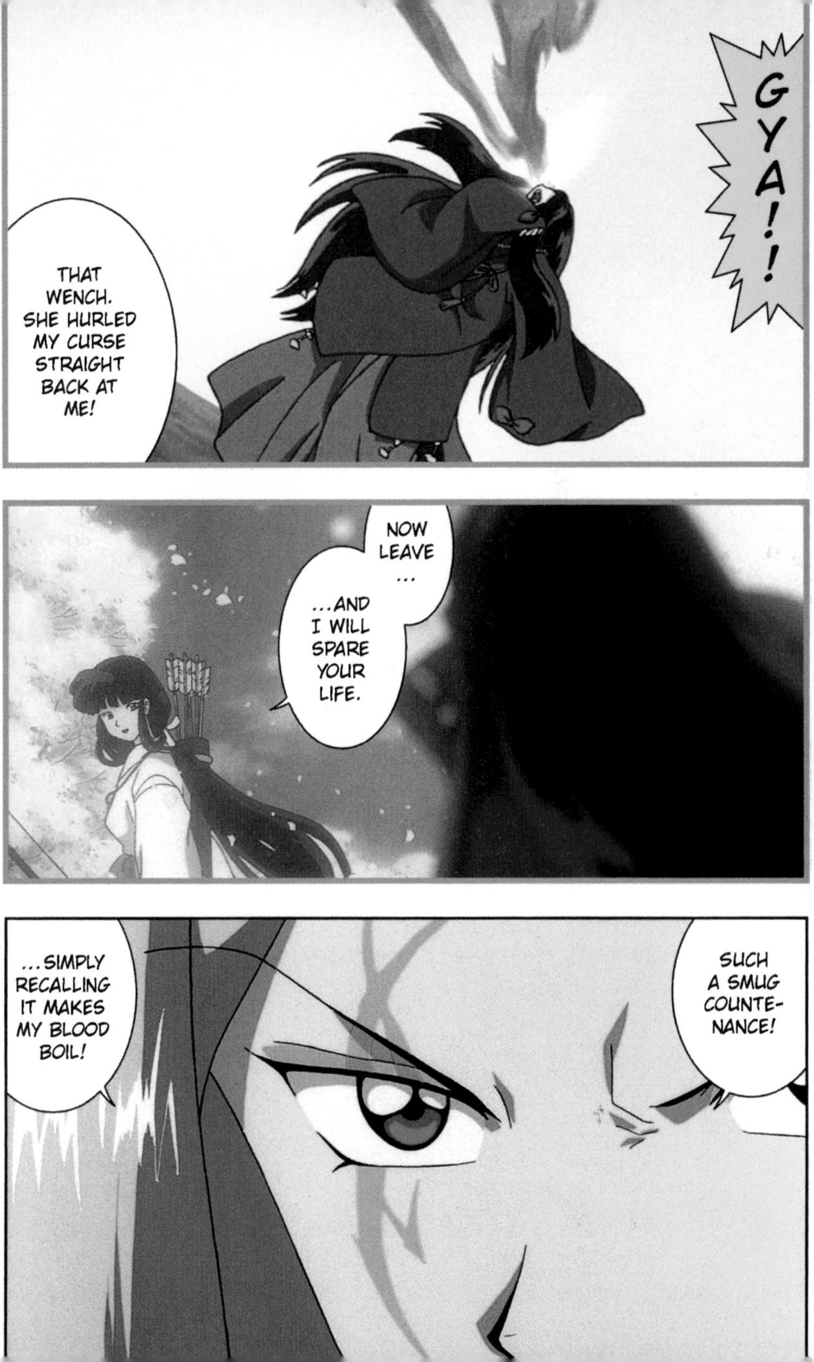
GYA!!
THAT WENCH. SHE HURLED MY CURSE STRAIGHT BACK AT ME!
NOW LEAVE...
...AND I WILL SPARE YOUR LIFE.
SUCH A SMUG COUNTE-NANCE!
...SIMPLY RECALLING IT MAKES MY BLOOD BOIL!

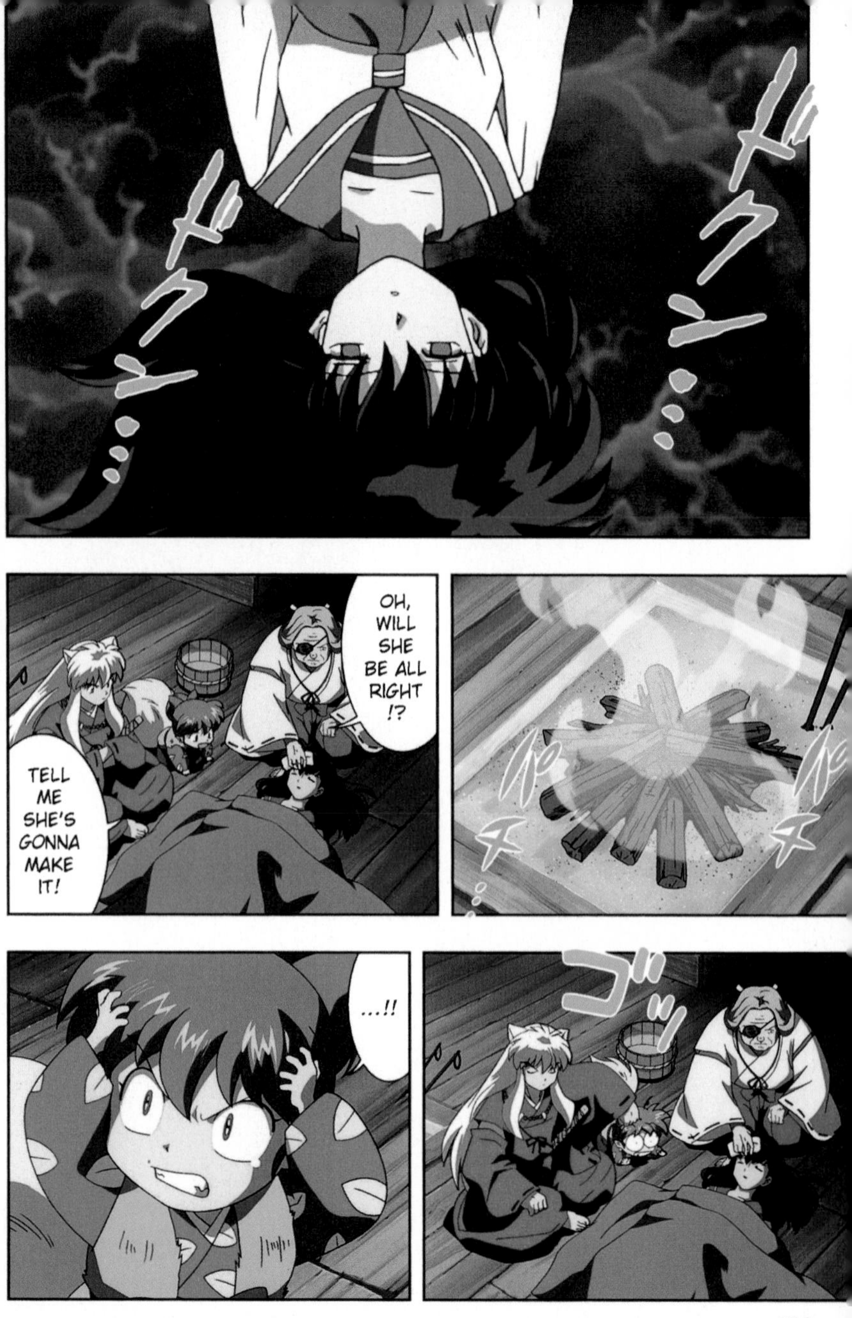
ドクン…
ドクン…
パチ パチ…
OH, WILL SHE BE ALL RIGHT !?
TELL ME SHE'S GONNA MAKE IT!
ゴッ
...!!

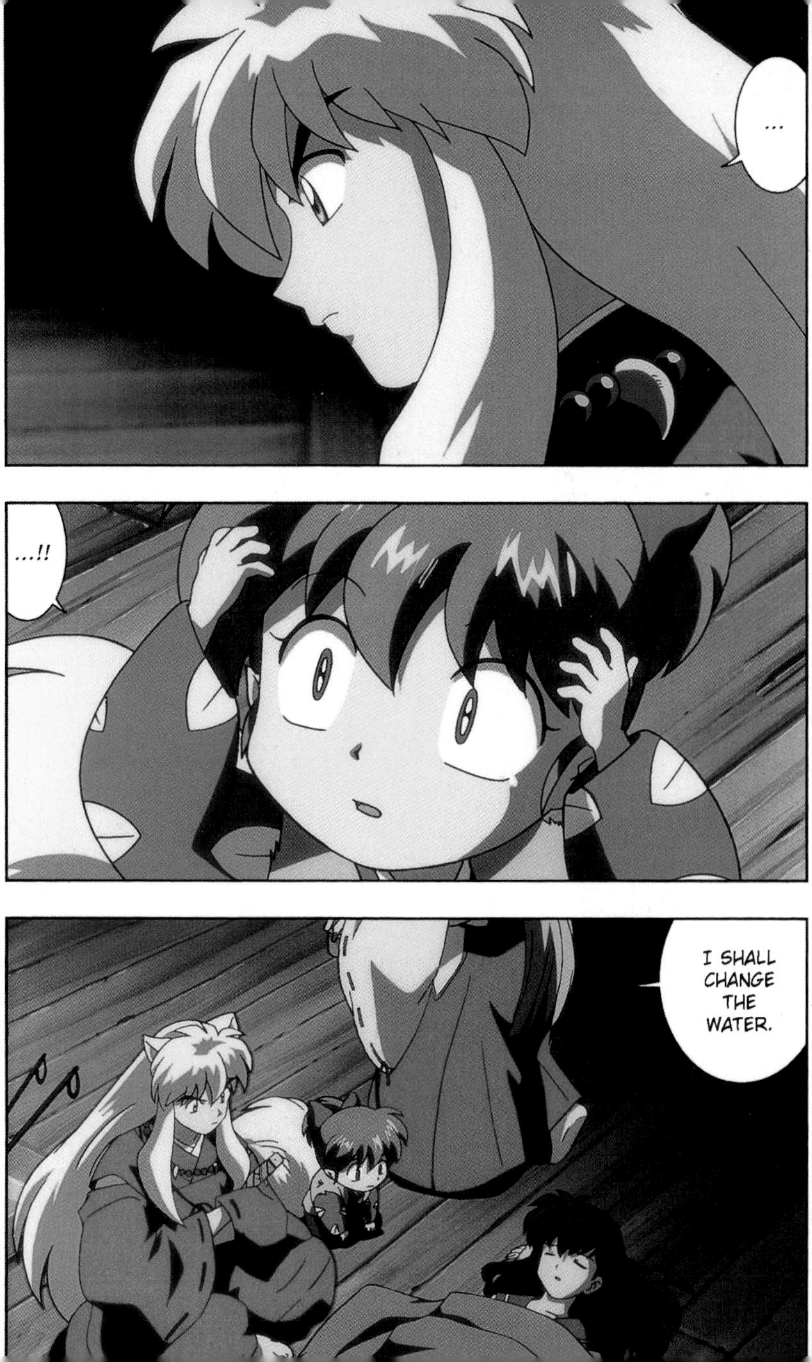
...
...!!
I SHALL CHANGE THE WATER.

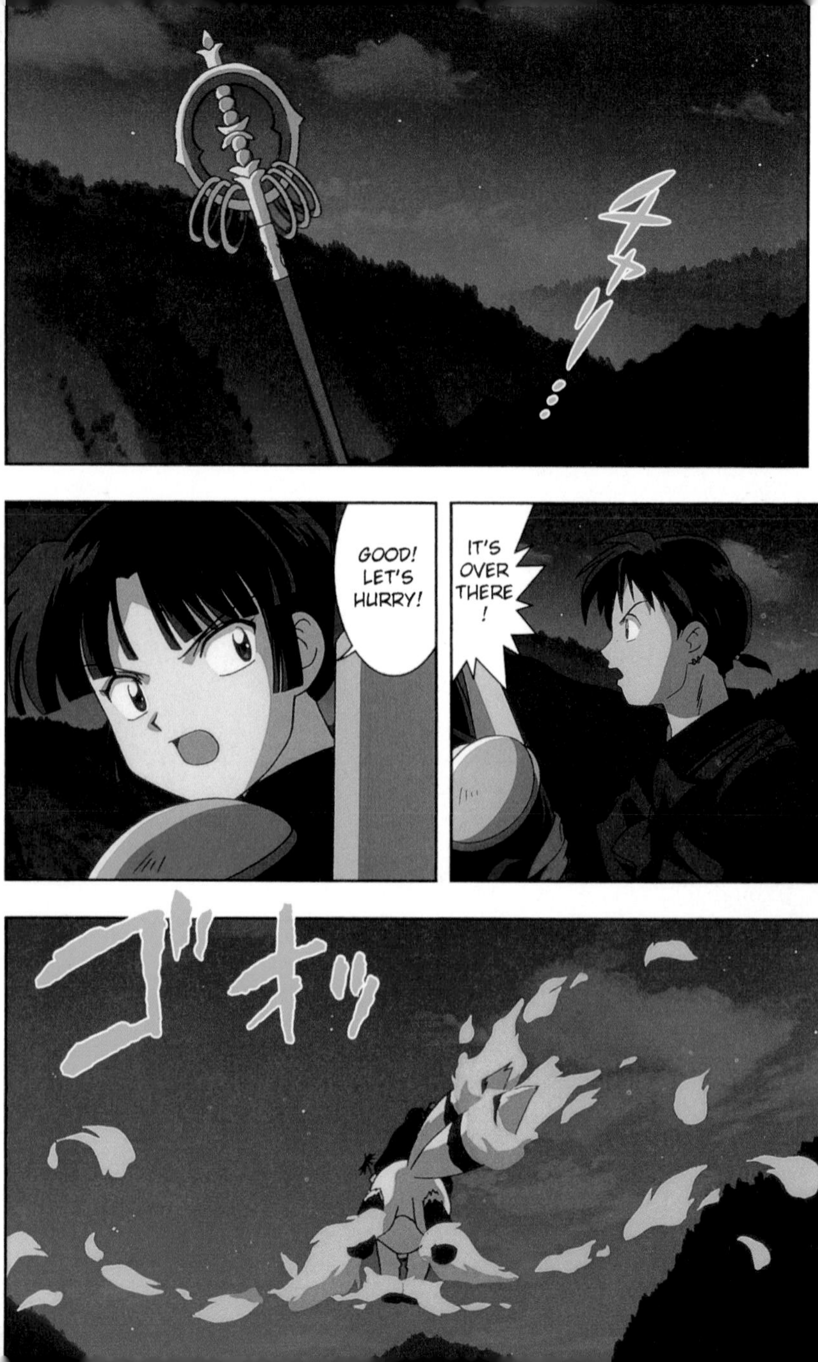
チャリ…
IT'S OVER THERE!
GOOD! LET'S HURRY!
ゴオッ

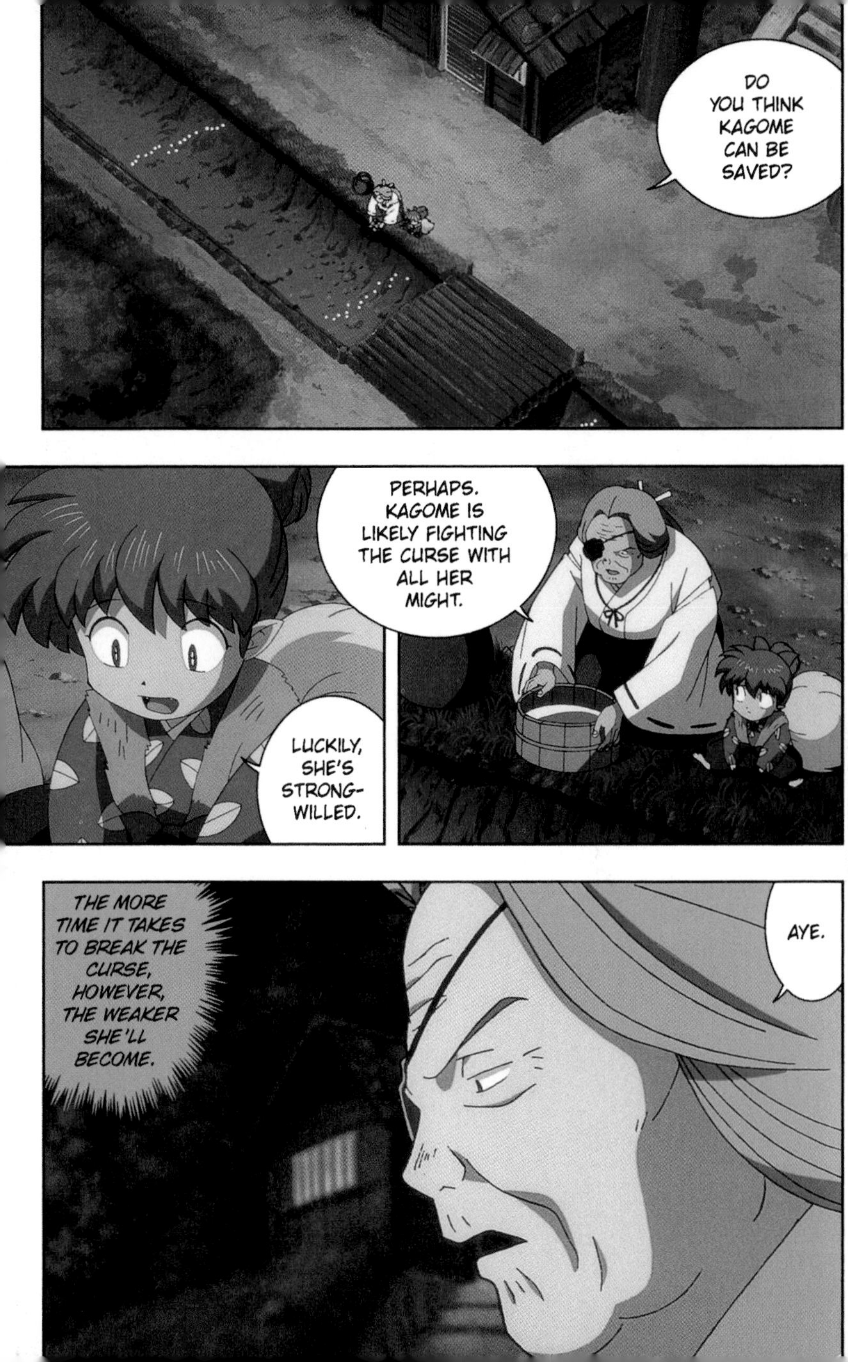
DO YOU THINK KAGOME CAN BE SAVED?
PERHAPS. KAGOME IS LIKELY FIGHTING THE CURSE WITH ALL HER MIGHT.
LUCKILY, SHE'S STRONG-WILLED.
AYE.
THE MORE TIME IT TAKES TO BREAK THE CURSE, HOWEVER, THE WEAKER SHE'LL BECOME.

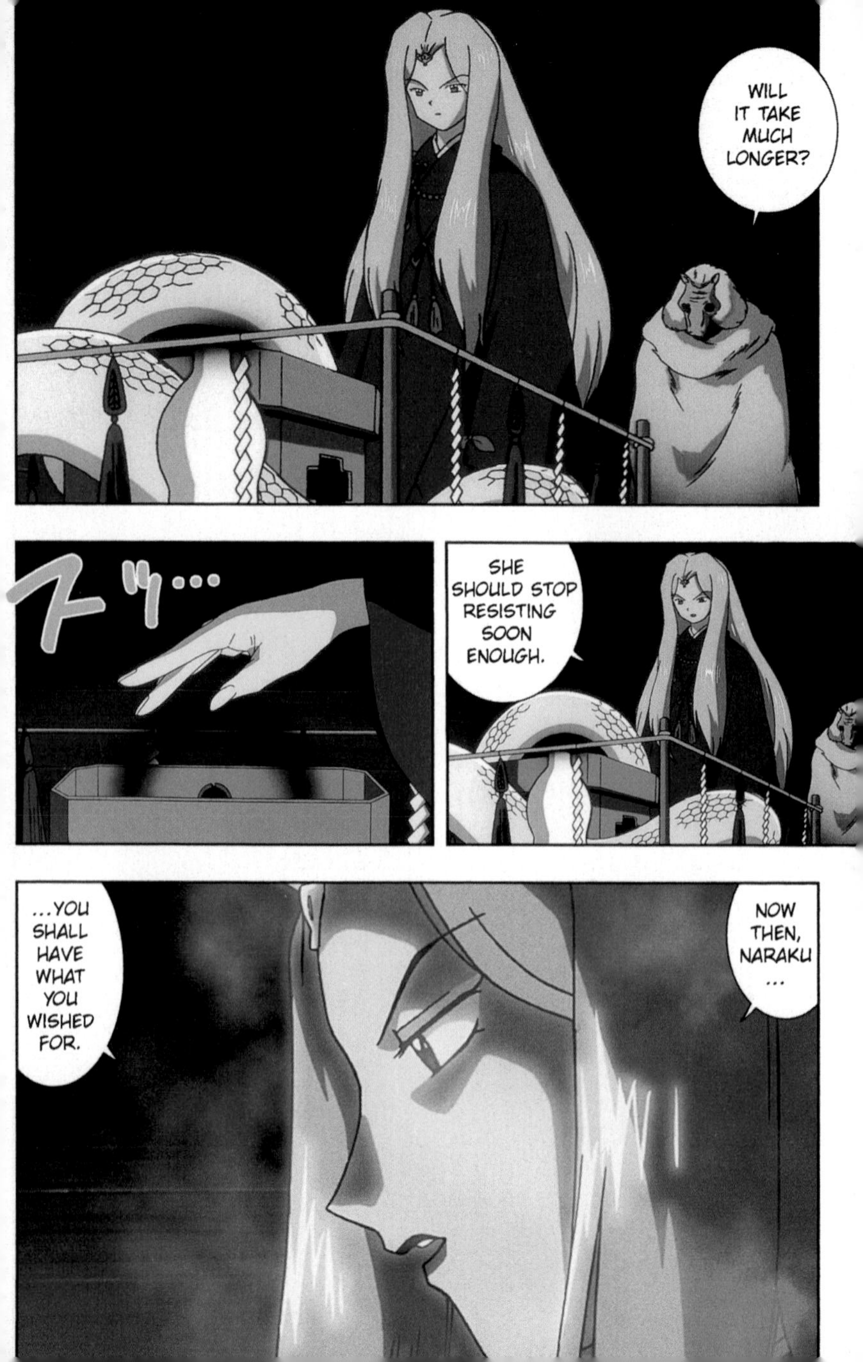
WILL IT TAKE MUCH LONGER?
SHE SHOULD STOP RESISTING SOON ENOUGH.
スッ…
NOW THEN, NARAKU...
...YOU SHALL HAVE WHAT YOU WISHED FOR.

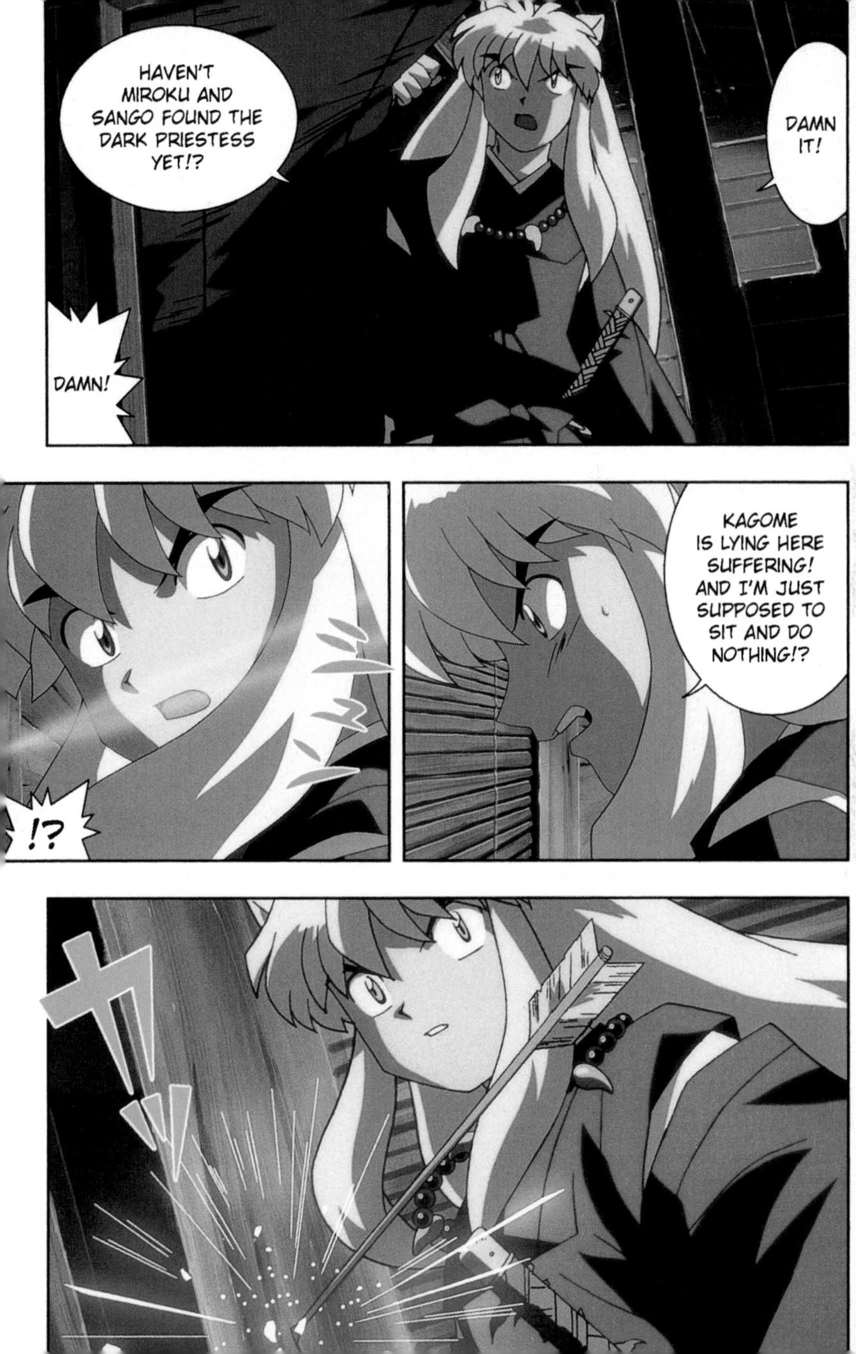
DAMN IT!
HAVEN'T MIROKU AND SANGO FOUND THE DARK PRIESTESS YET!?
DAMN!
KAGOME IS LYING HERE SUFFERING! AND I'M JUST SUPPOSED TO SIT AND DO NOTHING!?
!?

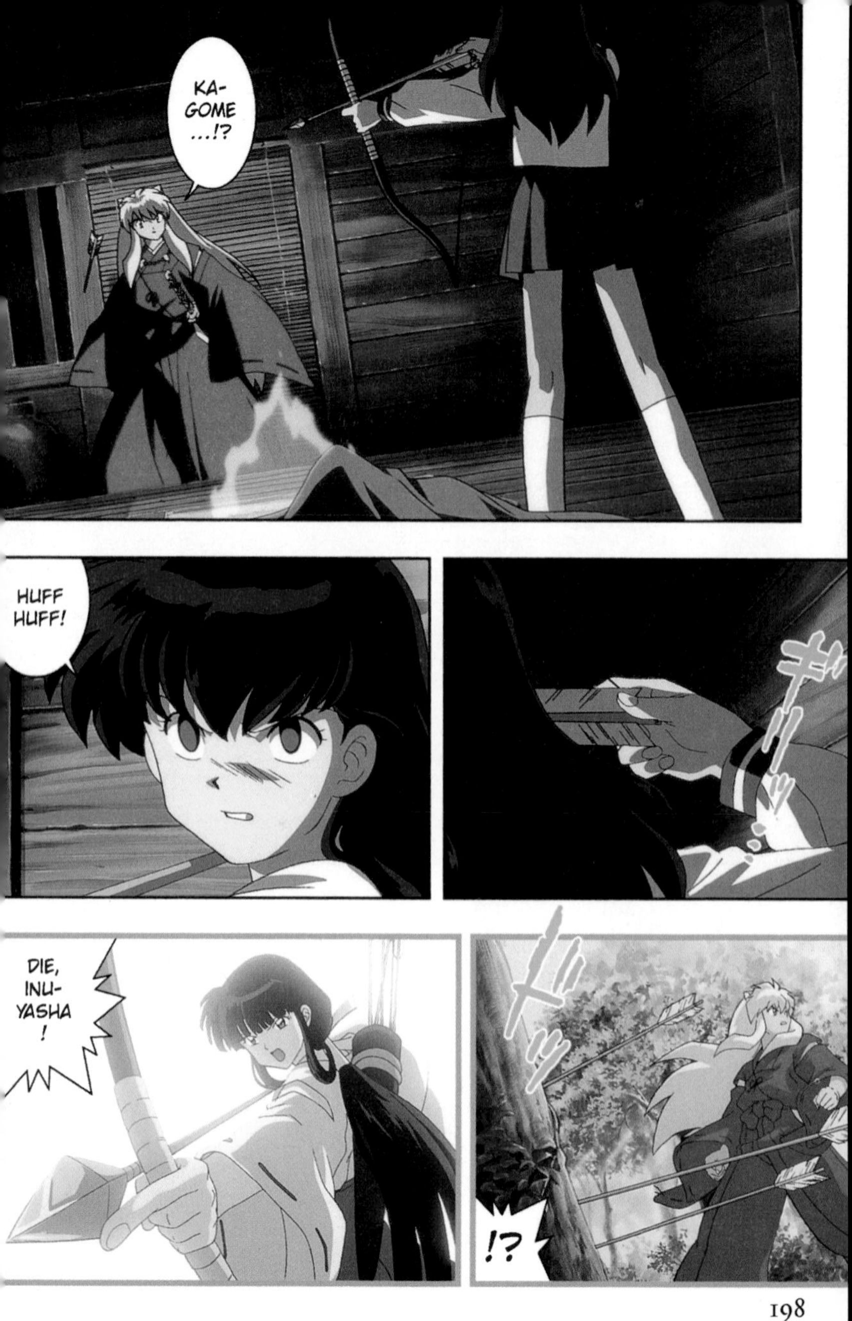
KA-GOME ...!?
HUFF HUFF!
!?
DIE, INU-YASHA!

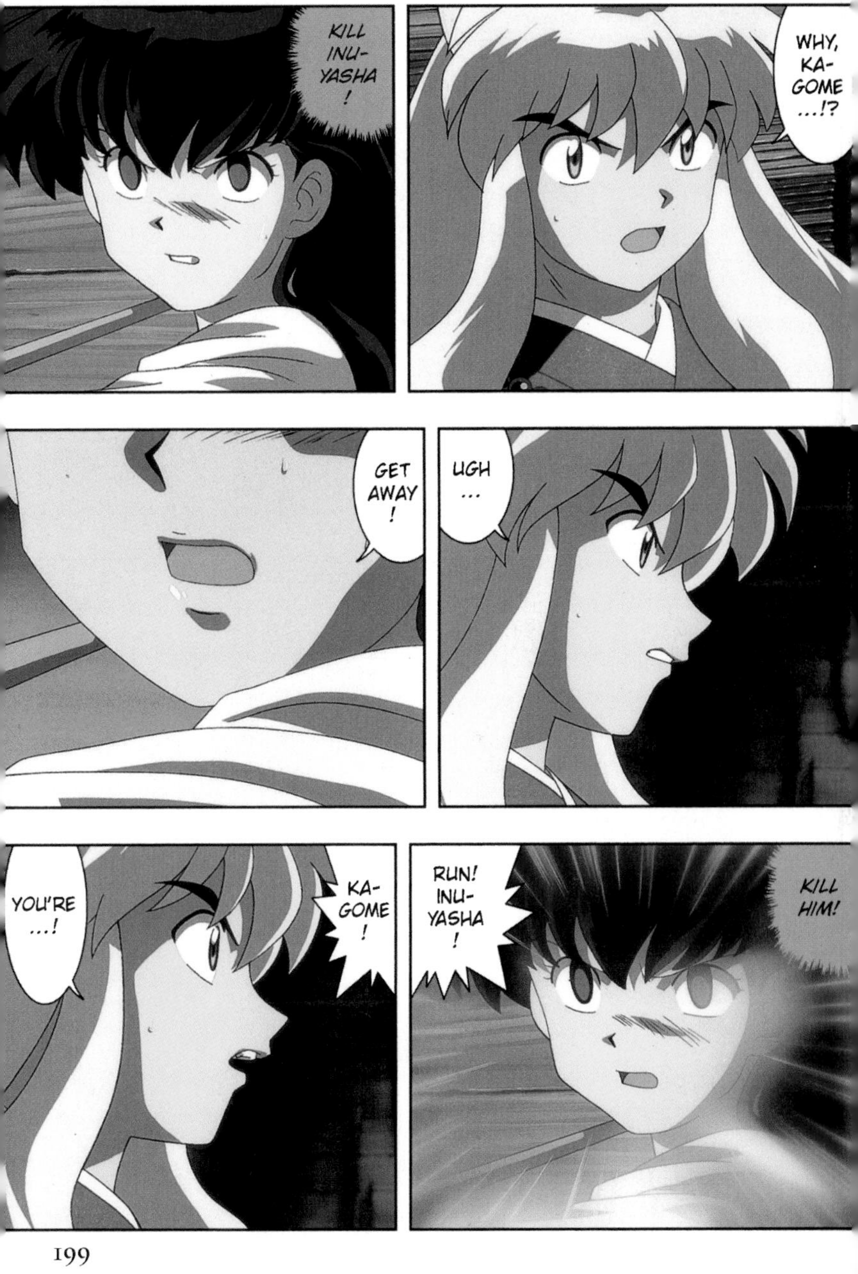
WHY, KA-GOME ...!?
KILL INU-YASHA!
UGH ...
GET AWAY!
KILL HIM!
RUN! INU-YASHA!
KA-GOME!
YOU'RE ...!

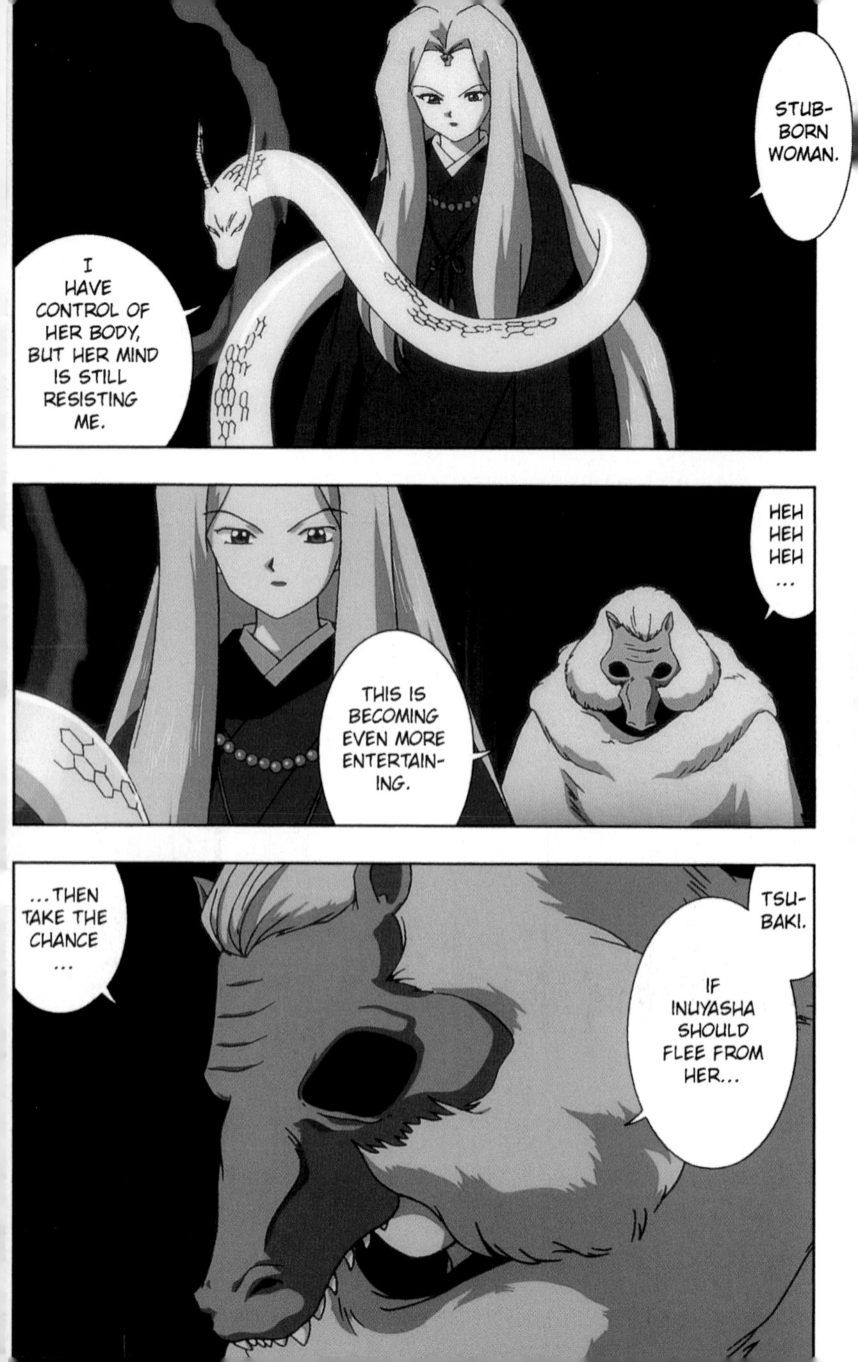
STUB-BORN WOMAN.
I HAVE CONTROL OF HER BODY, BUT HER MIND IS STILL RESISTING ME.
HEH HEH HEH ...
THIS IS BECOMING EVEN MORE ENTERTAIN-ING.
TSU-BAKI.
IF INUYASHA SHOULD FLEE FROM HER...
...THEN TAKE THE CHANCE ...

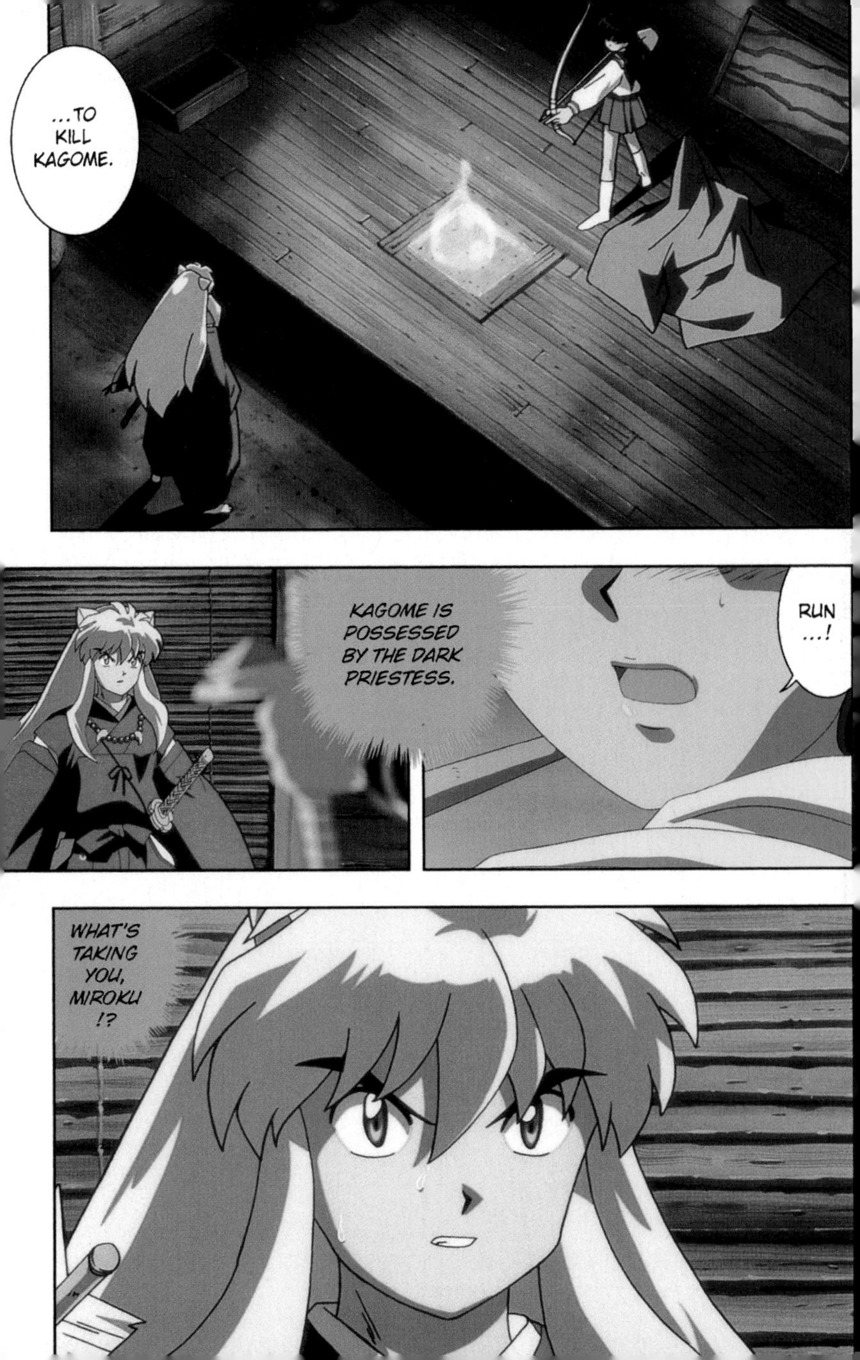
...TO KILL KAGOME.
RUN ...!
KAGOME IS POSSESSED BY THE DARK PRIESTESS.
WHAT'S TAKING YOU, MIROKU !?

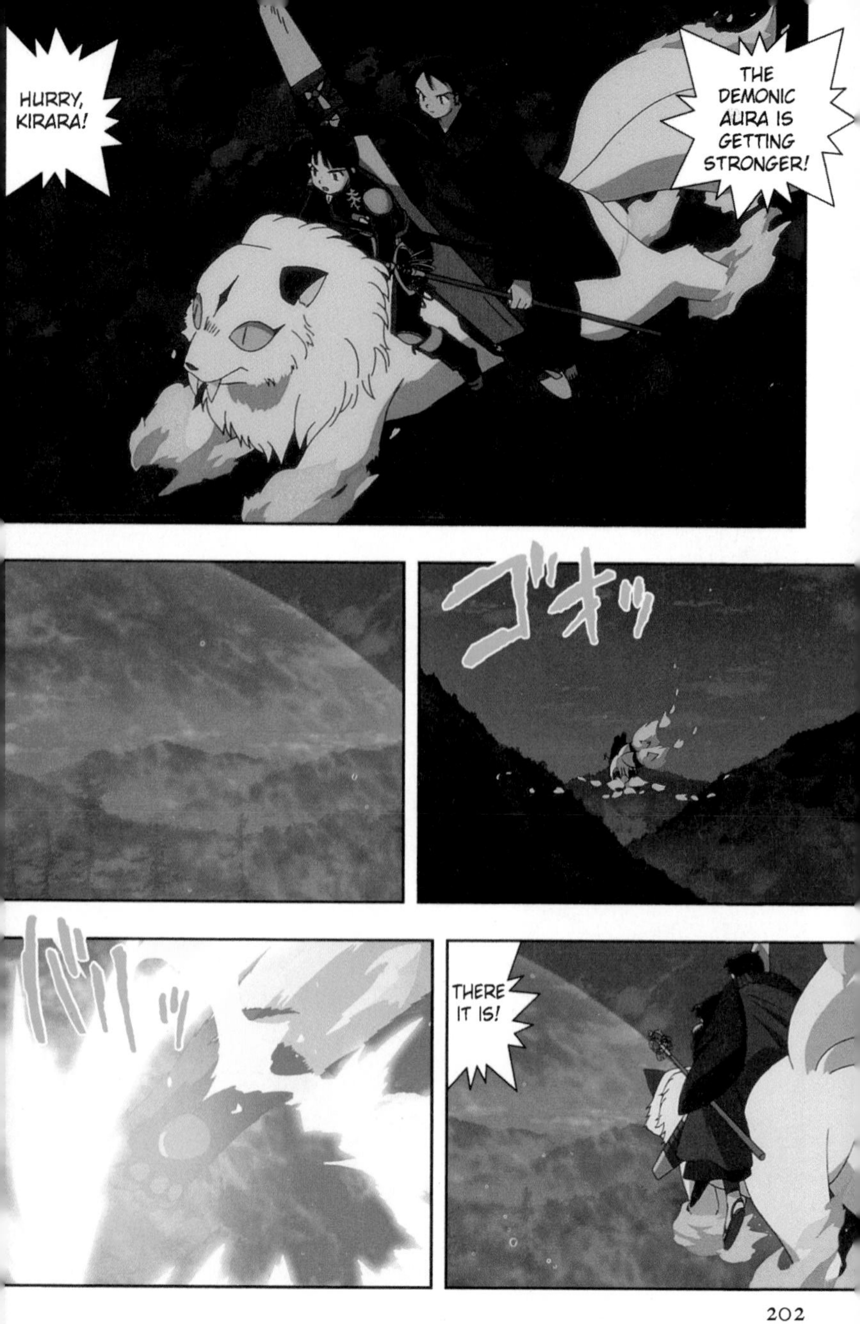
THE DEMONIC AURA IS GETTING STRONGER!
HURRY, KIRARA!
ゴオッ
THERE IT IS!
バリッ

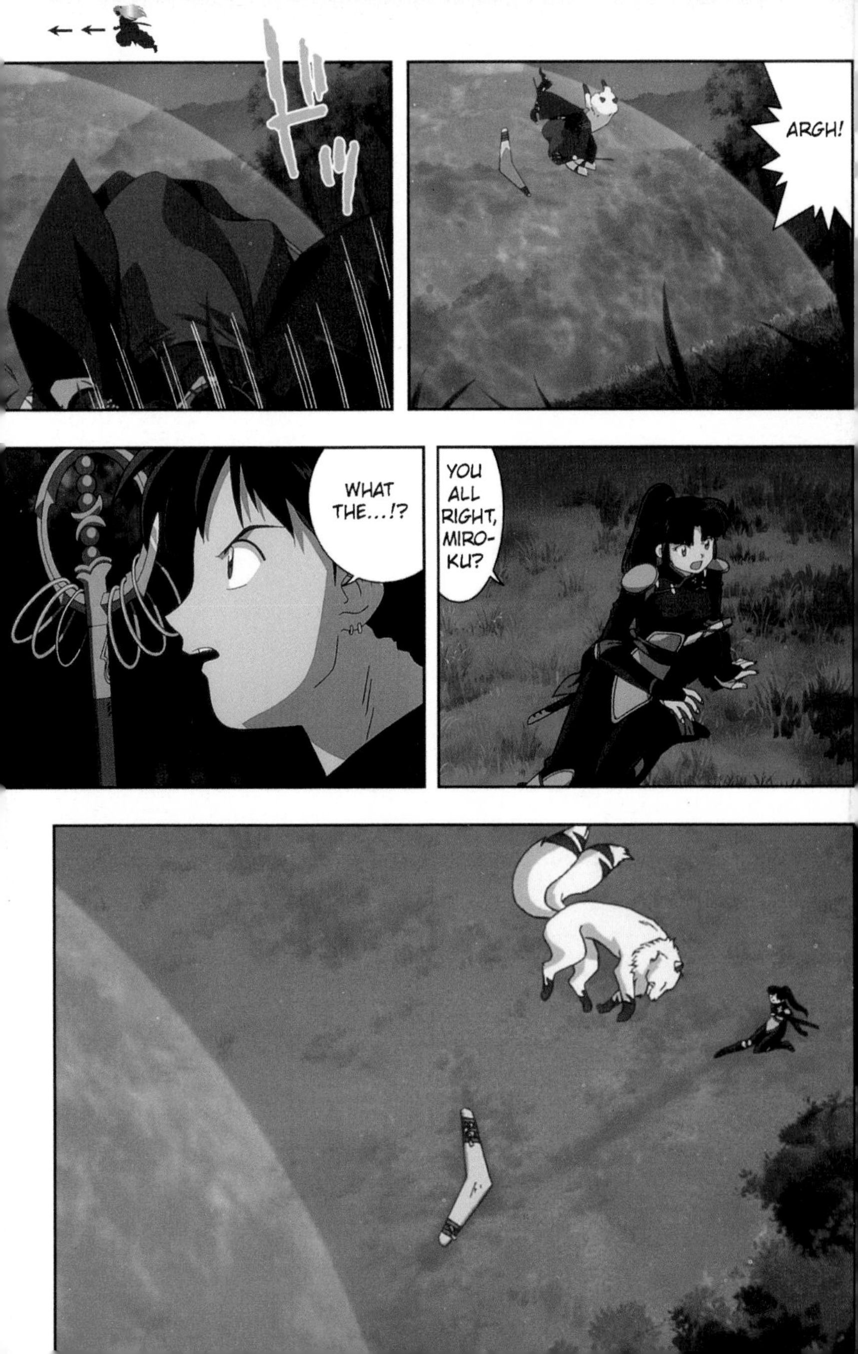
ARGH!
ドッ
YOU ALL RIGHT, MIROKU?
WHAT THE...!?

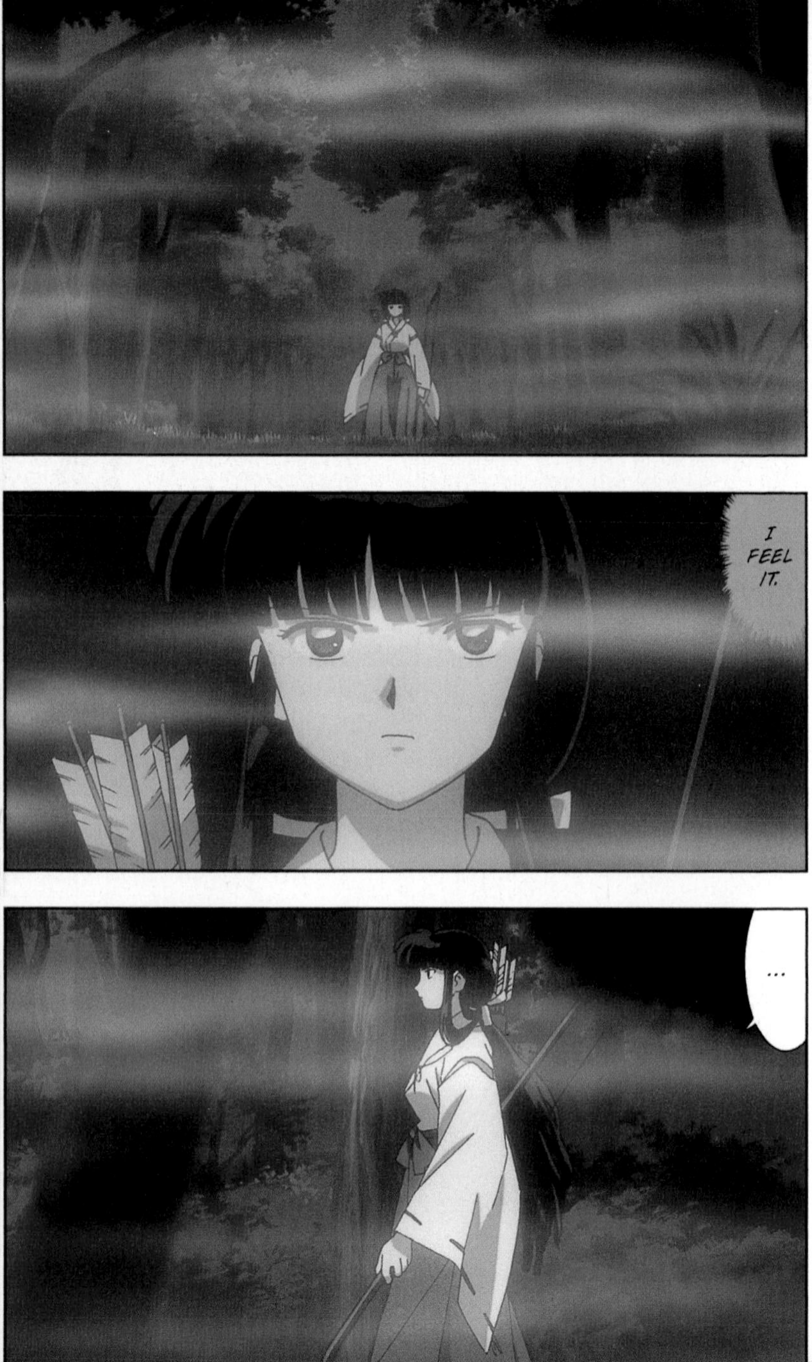
I FEEL IT.
...

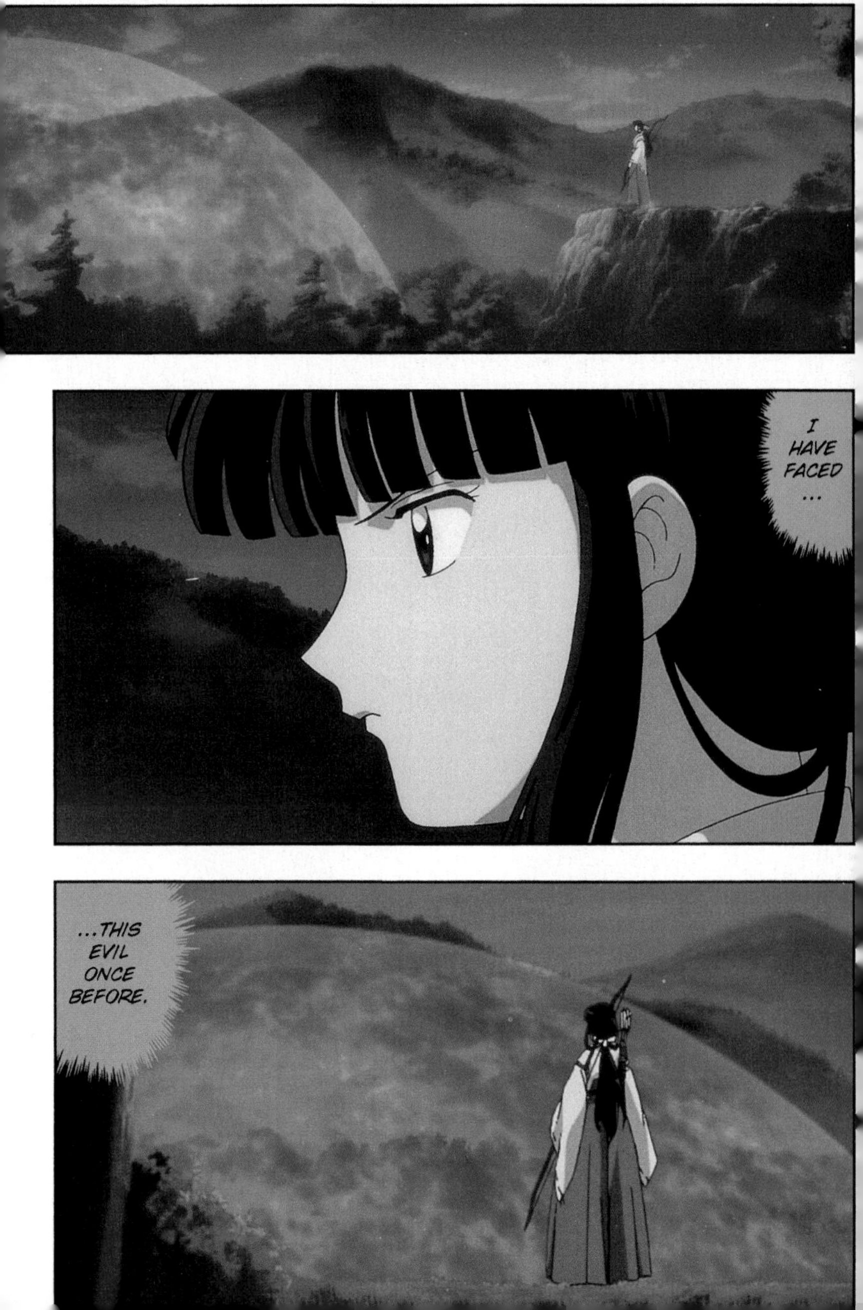
I HAVE FACED ...
...THIS EVIL ONCE BEFORE.

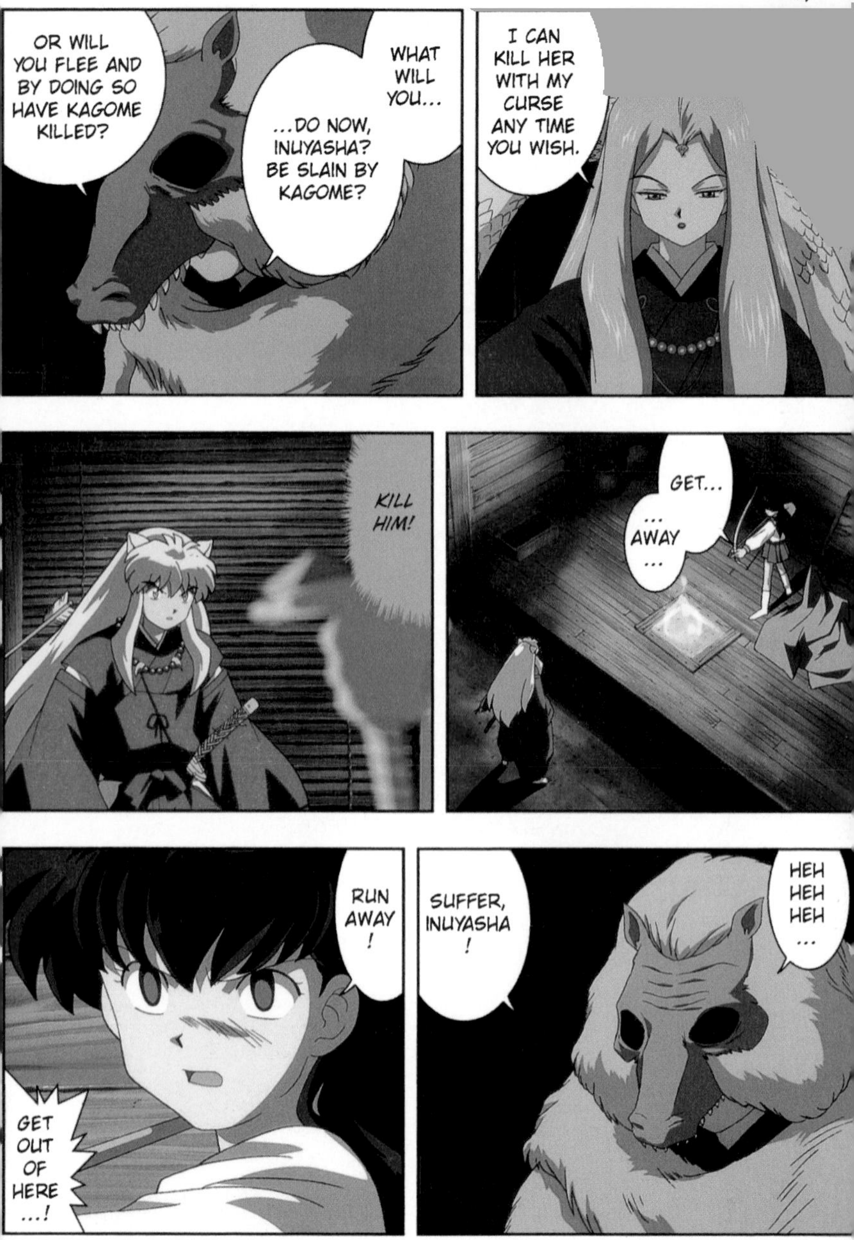
I CAN KILL HER WITH MY CURSE ANY TIME YOU WISH.
WHAT WILL YOU...
...DO NOW, INUYASHA? BE SLAIN BY KAGOME?
OR WILL YOU FLEE AND BY DOING SO HAVE KAGOME KILLED?
GET...
...AWAY...
KILL HIM!
HEH HEH HEH...
SUFFER, INUYASHA!
RUN AWAY!
GET OUT OF HERE...!

TO BE CONTINUED

Glossary of Sound Effects

Each entry includes: the location, indicated by page number and panel number (so 3.1 means page 3, panel number 1); the phonetic romanization of the original Japanese; and our English "translation"—we offer as close an English equivalent as we can.

23.1 FX: Ba (Miroku opens Wind Tunnel)
23.2 FX: Gohhhh… (whooshing)
23.3 FX: Meri meri… (roots start to rip)
23.4 FX: Meri… (roots rip more)

24.2 FX: Gara gara (Inuyasha breaks through roots)
24.3 FX: Doga (knocks over Tokajin)

26.3 FX: Basha (splash)

27.1 FX: Baki (Inuyasha breaks down door)
27.2 FX: Basha (splash)
27.5 FX: Zaba (Kagome dives for cover)

28.2 FX: Za… (Kagome steps out of bath)
28.5 FX: Basa (Inuyasha tosses Kagome his robe)
29.3 FX: Doh (Inuyasha collapses)

30.4 FX: Kaa… (Kagome's blush)

31.2 FX: Zun… zun… (Tokajin's heavy footsteps)
31.3 FX: Zun… (heavy footstep)

34.3 FX: Hyuuuu… (wind blowing through cliffs)

37.4 FX: Poi (flick)

38.4 FX: Gabu (Tokajin takes a bite of fruit)

40.1 FX: Zun… (big footstep)

41.1 FX: Bun (Tokajin swings club)

Chapter 58
Fateful Night in Togenkyo, Part Two

8.2 FX: Goto… (Tokajin moves clay pot)
8.4 FX: Kira (sparkling)

12.1 FX: Gu (Shippo places cans under rock)
12.2 FX: Ta (running)

13.1 FX: Gohh (whoosh)
13.2 FX: Dohn (explosion)
13.3 FX: Zu zu zu zu (boulder rolls down)
13.5 FX: Ba (Miroku opens wind tunnel)

14.1 FX: Gohhhhh… (whooshing)
14.3 FX: Goro goro goro… (boulder rolls)
14.5 FX: Dohn
(Miroku rushes Kagome out of the way)

15.3 FX: Giro (big rolling eye appears)
15.5 FX: Nu… (giant hand reaches down)

18.3 FX: Giri… (squeezing)
18.4 FX: Gaku (Kagome passes out)

19.3 FX: Ta ta ta…
(tiny figures scamper across floor)

20.4 FX: Basa
(Tokajin tosses Kagome's clothes on floor)

22.1 FX: Ba (Inuyasha struggles)
22.2 FX: Gishi (Inuyasha pulls some vines loose)

42.2 FX: Zan (Inuyasha pushes Kagome out of harm's way)
42.3 FX: Doh (Inuyasha and Kagome hit the ground)

44.3 FX: Goh (whoosh of contents in jar)
44.4 FX: Gasha (Tokajin punches away contents of jar)

45.3 FX: Ga (Inuyasha gets hit)
45.4 FX: Baki (Tokajin punches Inuyasha again)
45.5 FX: Doh (Inuyasha slams into jar, breaking it)

48.2 FX: Da (Inuyasha rushes at Tokajin)
48.3 FX: Ba (Tokajin swings club)
48.4 FX: Zuba (Inuyasha struck by vines)
48.5 FX: Ga (Tokajin grabs Inuyasha by throat)

49.3 FX: Giri (Kagome nocks arrow)

50.1 FX: Giri (Kagome aims arrow)
50.3 FX: Baki (bow shatters)

51.2 FX: Buchi (Inuyasha brandishes sharp thorn)
51.3 FX: Doh (Inuyasha stabs Tokajin in eye)
51.5 FX: Da (Inuyasha gets the heck out of Dodge)

52.2 FX: Kaaaa.... (shining)
52.3 FX: Suu... (Tokajin's mentor transforms himself into bow and arrow)

53.1 FX: Doh doh doh... (Tokajin lumbers over to Inuyasha)
53.4 FX: Shu (Kagome lets arrow fly)

54.1 FX: Doh (Tokajin struck by arrow)
54.2 FX: Poro (jewel shards pop out)
54.4 FX: Suuu... (jewel shards fly out of Tokajin)
54.5 FX: Toh (jewel shards fly toward Inuyasha)

55.1 FX: Sara... (bow transforms)
55.2 FX: Doh doh doh (Tokajin lumbers)
55.4 FX: Doh doh doh (Tokajin thunders toward Kagome)

56.1 FX: Da (Inuyasha runs to protect Kagome)
56.2 FX: Doga (smack)
56.6 FX: Goh (whoosh of fall)

58.2 FX: Zubu... (tree takes in shards)
58.3 FX: Pohh... (little light pops out)
58.4 FX: Gohhh... (Inuyasha and Tokajin continue to whoosh down)

59.1 FX: Go go go go (tree tendrils reach down)
59.2 FX: Shururu, ru... (tendril wraps around Tokajin's ankle)
59.3 FX: Shururuu... (tendril wraps around Inuyasha's ankle)

60.1 FX: Giri giri (tree squeezes)
60.2 FX: Giri... (squeezing)

61.2 FX: Giri (squeezing)
61.3 FX: Kaaa... (shining of dawn)
61.5 FX: Gishi (tree covers Inuyasha completely)

62.1 FX: Zuba (Inuyasha busts out of plant cocoon)

63.1 FX: Ba (here comes Ninmenka)
63.2 FX: Da (Inuyasha lands on tendril)
63.4 FX: Goh (whooshing)

64.1 FX: Goh (big whoosh)
64.3 FX: Shuuuu... (Ninmenka explodes)

65.1 FX: Doohn (explosion)
65.2 FX: Kira (glittering)
65.3 FX: Pashi (Inuyasha swipes jewel shards out of mid-air)
65.4 FX: Toh (Inuyasha lands)

66.1 FX: Suu... (Shippo and Miroku grow back to real size)

72.3 FX: Doh (Inuyasha does face plant)

Chapter 59
The Beautiful Sister Apprentices

74. 2 FX: Dosa (sack lands)

76.2 FX: Ji--… (slurp)

78.1 FX: Ka—n ka—n [note: we're not supposed to find out what these are until p. 79.1]
78.2/3 FX: Ka—n
78.3 FX: Ka—n
78.4 FX: Ka—n
78.4/5 FX: Ka—n

79.1 FX: Ka—n (Sango clanging away at the forge)
79.2/4 FX: Ka—n (clang)
79.4 FX: Ka—n (clang)

80.1 FX: Gohhh… (whoosh as Sango uses bellows)
80.2 FX: Gohhh… (whooshing)
80.3 FX: Ka—n ka—n (clang clang)
80.5 FX: Juwa (hissing of steam)

83.3 FX: Gyurururururu… [Hiraikotsu whirls]
83.4 FX: Pashi (Sango catches Hirakotsu neatly)

85.2 FX: Ta ta ta… (running)

86.1 FX: Hyu (rock thrown at Sango)
86.2 FX: Ba (Sango jumps)
86.3 FX: Ta (Kirara lands)
86.4 FX: Goh (whoosh as Kirara transforms)
86.6 FX: Da (Kirara dashes off)

87.1 FX: Ta ta ta… (running)
87.2 FX: Zun (Kirara knocks down girl)
Suzuna: Uh!

88.3 FX: Su (Kirara's fang stops just short of piercing girl's throat)
88.4 FX: Ba (Suzuna throws herself across her sister)

89.1 FX: Doh (Serina collapses)
89.3 FX: Guu… (stomach gurgling)

90.2 FX: Gu gu (stew bubbling)
90.3 FX: Ga ga (voracious eating)

91.1 FX: Sa (sisters thrust bowls out)
91.3 FX: Gaba (Serina bows her head to the floor)

92.2 FX: Go (Serina smacks Suzuna on the head for insolence)

93.1 FX: Sa (Suzuna zips over to massage Sango's shoulders)

98.3 FX: Sa (Sango proffers fan and cloth)

99.3 FX: Bo (Sango adds powder to fire)
99.5 FX: Pata pata (fanning)

100.1 FX: Moh moh (smoke sound)
100.4 FX: Da (animals dash out of burrow)

103.5 FX: Uro uro… (Miroku looks around anxiously)

105.1 FX: Ta ta ta… (running)
105.2 FX: Ta ta ta… (running)
105.4 FX: Gacha (lock breaks)

107.1 FX: Doh (Suzuna smacks her head on her sister's pack)

108.1 FX: Bun (Suzuna's throws something that might be shuriken)
108.2 FX: Ba (Sango dodges)
108.3 FX: Ta ta ta… (running)

109.2 FX: Ba (ninja throws weighted rope)
109.3 FX: Gishi (ropes ensnare demon)
109.4 FX: Bun (ninjas pull of ropes)
109.5 FX: Dohn (demon explodes)

111.4 FX: Gaku… (father's head d-rops as he dies)

112.5 FX: Bohn (smoke screen)

113.1 FX: Moh moh (smoke dissipates)

114.1 FX: Goh (whoosh of fire from Kirara's feet)
114.2 FX: Da (Kirara takes off)
114.4 FX: Gohhh… (whooshing)

115.1 FX: Ta ta ta… (running)

116.2/3 FX: Fu… (ominous clouds block light)
116.4 FX: Gohhh… (ominous whooshing)

117.1 FX: Ta ta ta… (running)
117.4 FX: Goh (more ominous whooshing)

118.2 FX: Za (Kirara alights)
118.4 FX: Cha (weapons are drawn)

119.2 FX: Zawa…
(ominous wind rustles tree leaves)
119.4/5 FX: Gohhhhh… (ominous whooshing)

120.2 FX: Zu zu zu (demons hover)

121.1 FX: Goh (whooshing)

122.4 FX: Da (sister lunges toward demons)

125.5 FX: Goh (demons whoosh in)
125.6 FX: Dosa (Serina drops stolen weapons)

126.1 FX: Ba (Serina picks up Suzuna)
126.5 FX: Za (Sango prepares to fight)

127.1 FX: Bun (Sango throws weapon)
127.2 FX: Zan (demons get diced)
127.3 FX: Pashi (Sango catches weapon)
127.4 FX: Da (Sango runs)

128.1 FX: Doga (Sango fells demon)
128.3 FX: Fuwa (demon snatches Suzuna)
128.6 FX: Zaku (Suzuna slashes at demon)

129.1 FX: Doh (Suzuna falls and lands hard)
129.4 FX: Gu (Serina grabs weapon)
129.5 FX: Bun (Serina swings weapon)

130.1 FX: Ga (Kirara chomps demon)
130.2 FX: Gohh (demons whoosh down)
130.3 FX: Bun (Sango throws boomerang)
130.4 FX: Ga ga ga (HIraikotsu slices through demon)
130.4 FX: Ga ga (more slicing)

131.2 FX: Za (Sango catches Hiraikotsu)
131.3 FX: Goh (demons whoosh toward Sango)
131.5 FX: Za za za za (rustling in underbrush)

132.1 FX: Za (Miroku brandishes staff)
132.2 FX: Doga (demon killed)
132.4 FX: Dohn (Wind Scar strikes)

133.1 FX: Goh (whooshing)
133.2 FX: Gohhh… (demons whooshed away)

133.5 FX: Goh (whoosh)

134.1 FX: Gohhh… (whoosh of Wind Tunnel)

134.4 FX: Doh (demon struck by arrow)

138.1 FX: Sawa (Miroku cops a feel)
138.3 FX: Pan (a slap)

Chapter 60
The Fifty-Year-Old Curse of the Dark Priestess

140.3 FX: Butsu butsu… (muttering)
140.4 FX: Butsu butsu butsu… (chanting in a mutter)
140.4 FX: Gohhhh… (flames whoosh)

141.3 FX: Boh (Tsubaki adds powder to flames)

142.5 FX: Ba (Tsubaki attacks)

143.1 FX: Zuba (Kagura swishes fan, cutting up Tsubaki's attack)

144.5 FX: Katsu… (the clicky sound chalk makes on chalkboard)

151.1 FX: Gohhhhh… (whooshing)

152.3 FX: Goh (whoosh)

154.2 FX: Suu… (Tsubaki becomes young again)

160.4 FX: Boko (smack!)

161.1 FX: Za (Inuyasha lands on grass)
161.3 FX: Zawa (a sudden wind)
161.6 FX: Buru buru… (Shippo's tail twitching frantically)

162.1 FX: Ta (leaping)
162. FX: Kun kun… (sniff sniff)

163.3 FX: Zawa (something slithering through grass)

164.1 FX: Dosa (Kagome drops backpack)
164.3 FX: Za za za za… (mysterious presence races through grass)
164.4 FX: Goh (a whoosh as it finds Kagome)
164.5 FX: Gabu (invisible demon serpent takes a bite)

165.3 FX: Zaaaaaa… (rustling in grass)

166.1 FX: Ta ta ta… (running)
166.2 FX: Ta ta ta… (running)
166.3 FX: Zuba (slash)
166.5 FX: Hara… (paper flutters to ground)

167.1 FX: Zawa… (rustling)
167.2 FX: Za za za za… (rusting as a wake forms through the grass)
167.3 FX: Za za… (serpent races through the grass)
167.4 FX: Suru… (serpent curls around Tsubaki's arm)

168.4 FX: Goh (whoosh)
168.5 FX: Gohhhh… (whooshing)

170.2 FX: Goh… (whooshing)
170.4 FX: Goh (Kagura whooshes off)

171.2 FX: Gii… (squeak as door opens)
171.4 FX: Su… (Tsubaki places the sacred jewel on altar)

174.1 FX: Dokun… (pulsation)

175.1 FX: Pota… (blood drops on the jewel)
175.2 FX: Pa—n (glass shatters)

184.1 FX: Chari (staff jingles)

185.1 FX: Goh (Kirara whooshes off)

189.3 FX: Za (rustling)
189.5 FX: Ba (Tsubaki hurls serpent)

190.1 FX: Guwa (serpent gets ready to bite)
190.3 FX: Ba (Kikyo hurls curse back)
190.5 FX: Doh (serpent curse strikes Tsubaki)

192.1 FX: Dokun… dokun… (pulsing heartbeats)
192.2 FX: Pachi pachi (fire crackles)
192.4 FX: Go (smack on head)

194.1 FX: Chari (jingling)
194.4 FX: Goh (Kirara whooshes off)

196.3 FX: Su… (Tsubaki casts powder into the box)

197.4 FX: Ka (shining as sacred arrow strikes and scatters light)

198.2 FX: Giri… (Kagome pulls arrow string tighter)
198.4 FX: Doh (thunk)

202.2 FX: Goh (whoosh)
202.5 FX: Ba (our heroes smack into Naraku's barrier)

203.2 FX: Doh (impact of Kirara on barrier)